AF899185

Digital Twin Technology for Better Health

At a time when technology and healthcare are colliding to alter lives, *Digital Twin Technology for Better Health: A Healthcare Odyssey* throws open the revolutionary possibilities of digital twins in changing patient care, medical research, and healthcare operations. This book brings together the best of the best from healthcare, AI, and IT domains in providing a holistic and forward- looking study of one of the most innovative technologies of our times.

Digital twin technology generally refers to the development of virtual replicas of physical entities. The functioning of healthcare systems is being transformed using this technology. Its applications lie in personalized treatment plans, predicting diagnostics results, optimized workflows in hospitals, and aid in the drug discovery process. The book examines the principles of digital twin technology in healthcare and their application in the real world and future directions.

Features:

- Foundations and evolution of digital twin technology.
- Applications in clinical care, including diagnosis, treatment, and patient monitoring.
- Insights into how digital twins are changing the face of healthcare operations and management.
- Case studies and practical examples illustrating real-world success stories.
- Critical discussions on data security, ethical considerations, and regulatory frameworks.
- Emerging trends and the integration of AI, IoT, and advanced analytics to enhance digital twin efficacy.

Whether you are a healthcare professional, technologist, researcher, or policymaker, this book is an indispensable guide to the science of how digital twin technology can help deliver better health. It is one of the earliest comprehensive works in the field and not only fills the gap between technology and healthcare but also serves as a visionary roadmap for the future. Let's join in on this transition journey in healthcare toward the future, as digital twins promise to reshape the industry and change lives around the world.

Digital Twin Technology for Better Health

A Healthcare Odyssey

Edited by
Manish Dixit, Kirti Raj Bhatele, and
Devanshu Tiwari

CRC Press
Taylor & Francis Group
Boca Raton London New York

CRC Press is an imprint of the
Taylor & Francis Group, an **informa** business

Designed cover image: Shutterstock Image ID 2531207285

First edition published 2026
by CRC Press
2385 NW Executive Center Drive, Suite 320, Boca Raton FL 33431

and by CRC Press
4 Park Square, Milton Park, Abingdon, Oxon, OX14 4RN

CRC Press is an imprint of Taylor & Francis Group, LLC

© 2026 selection and editorial matter, Manish Dixit, Kirti Raj Bhatele and Devanshu Tiwari; individual chapters, the contributors

Reasonable efforts have been made to publish reliable data and information, but the author and publisher cannot assume responsibility for the validity of all materials or the consequences of their use. The authors and publishers have attempted to trace the copyright holders of all material reproduced in this publication and apologize to copyright holders if permission to publish in this form has not been obtained. If any copyright material has not been acknowledged please write and let us know so we may rectify in any future reprint.

Except as permitted under U.S. Copyright Law, no part of this book may be reprinted, reproduced, transmitted, or utilized in any form by any electronic, mechanical, or other means, now known or hereafter invented, including photocopying, microfilming, and recording, or in any information storage or retrieval system, without written permission from the publishers.

For permission to photocopy or use material electronically from this work, access www.copyright.com or contact the Copyright Clearance Center, Inc. (CCC), 222 Rosewood Drive, Danvers, MA 01923, 978-750-8400. For works that are not available on CCC please contact mpkbookspermissions@tandf.co.uk

Trademark notice: Product or corporate names may be trademarks or registered trademarks and are used only for identification and explanation without intent to infringe.

ISBN: 978-1-032-80234-3 (hbk)
ISBN: 978-1-032-80680-8 (pbk)
ISBN: 978-1-003-49811-7 (ebk)

DOI: 10.1201/9781003498117

Typeset in Sabon
by Newgen Publishing UK

Contents

Preface

In recent years, the healthcare sector has experienced a wonderful revolution through advanced technologies and data-driven solutions. Of these developments, "digital twin technology" has been at the forefront, changing the way one perceives the paradigm for patients, medical research, and operations in the healthcare sector. *Digital Twin Technology for Better Health: A Healthcare Odyssey* discusses this transformative area in detail with the help of a comprehensive exposition on its principles, applications, and future directions.

Already, digital twins have been shown to hold great promise across many sectors, including in the healthcare industry, promising unprecedented opportunities for personalized medicine, predictive diagnostics, surgical simulations, and optimization of operations. However, it is an underexplored field with minimal literature to support the professional, research, and policymaking activities in this domain. This book fills that gap by considering the integration of digital twins into healthcare systems from a 360-degree angle.

The book chapters are a result of fine-tuned work from experts who come from different backgrounds-academicians, artificial intelligence (AI) specialists, IT professionals, and healthcare practitioners. Their insight will provide readers with a well-rounded view of digital twin technology from its fundamentals to real applications and the hurdles of implementation. The book introduces digital twin technology, tracing its historical development and underlying principles, and goes on to discuss its application in clinical care and health operations, personalized medicine, and beyond-questions involving real cases and practical examples.

One special feature of this book is its forward-looking perspective. Although it discusses current trends in digital twin technology, the book examines emerging trends and the potential of integrating complementary technologies, such as AI, the Internet of Things, and advanced data analytics. It also addresses topics critical to adoption, including data security, ethical considerations, and regulatory frameworks for responsible use of the technology.

We would like to consider this book not as a technical guide but more as a roadmap for the future health industry. That is, we are aiming to empower healthcare professionals, technologists, researchers, and decision-makers with the knowledge necessary to take full advantage of the capabilities of the developing technology called "the digital twin", thus inspiring innovation, improved patient outcomes, and enhanced health system efficiency worldwide.

We extend our thanks to the contributing authors for the invaluable expertise and commitment they bring to this project. Their work has made this book an authoritative and comprehensive resource. Finally, we thank the growing community of healthcare innovators whose innovative work continues to push the envelope of what's possible.

We offer readers the opportunity to take on this journey through the changing face of digital twin technology in healthcare. Together, let us look into the opportunities and challenges that lie ahead and envision a future where technology and humanity converge to deliver better health for all.

The healthcare industry finds itself on a journey of unprecedented transformation, and the coming together of technology, data, and innovation at its very core is rewriting how we view care and make it available. Among the many technological strides leading to that transformation, one specific approach is digital twin technology – a revolutionary piece capable of reshaping the future of healthcare. It is my honour to introduce this book, *Digital Twin Technology for Better Health: A Healthcare Odyssey*, as the lead editor, capturing the essence of this transformative journey.

Digital twin technology creates virtual replicas of physical entities and offers unparalleled opportunities to enhance personalized medicine, optimize clinical operations, and revolutionize medical research. From simulating patient-specific conditions to predictive diagnostics and working to improve hospital workflows, digital twins have the potential to address some of the most pressing challenges in modern healthcare. Yet, while the concept has gained momentum in manufacturing and aerospace industries, its application in healthcare is still found in its nascent stages, with immense untapped potential.

It is a multidisciplinary collaboration of experts working together to gather diverse perspectives on healthcare, AI, information technology, and clinical research. The chapters have been carefully crafted to give readers a holistic view of digital twin technology: how it came to be, the principles that drive it, and its applications in real life. It also goes into the exploration of the ethical, regulatory, and technical challenges of using this technology.

This book stands out in that it balances its approach between technicalities and applications of digital twin technology, with the examination of broader issues like data security, patient privacy, and ethical considerations.

Case studies and practical examples have also been included to help readers connect theoretical concepts to tangible outcomes.

I deeply appreciate the contributors, whose expertise and passion have brought so much value to this project. Their collective insight has enriched content, making the book a true resource for the healthcare professional, technologist, policymaker, and academic alike. I wish to thank all readers for whom I hope this book shall be enlightening and inspiring.

Editor biographies

Manish Dixit is a distinguished professional in the field of computer science and engineering, currently holding the position of Senior Professor and Head in the Department of Computer Science and Engineering at the Madhav Institute of Technology & Science, Gwalior, Madhya Pradesh, India, a NAAC-accredited Deemed University with A++ grade. With a career spanning 27 years, he has acquired a wealth of experience and expertise in various domains of computer science. His educational background includes a PhD in computer science and Engineering from Rajiv Gandhi Technological University, Bhopal, ME in communication control and Networking, and BE in computer technology. He has supervised a significant number of research projects and guided nine PhD scholars in the field of computer science and engineering. In addition, he has overseen the progress of 26 ME/MTech scholars and 200 BE/BTech students, demonstrating his commitment to fostering academic growth. A prolific researcher, Dr. Dixit has authored more than a hundred research papers, including 11 published in SCI-indexed journals, showcasing his profound involvement in advancing knowledge in the fields of human–computer interaction, image processing, artificial intelligence, and computer graphics. His remarkable career is further embellished with various accolades, including the IEEE Extreme Programming Award, his election as a Fellow of IETE, and Senior Member status in IEEE, which highlight his substantial contributions to professional organizations. Notably, he is currently serving as the Chairman of the IETE Gwalior Sub-Center and Vice-chair of the IEEE Madhya Pradesh section. In addition to his academic and research achievements, Dr. Dixit has organized and led numerous workshops, including an AICTE-sponsored Short Term Course on “Applications of Image Processing, Computer Vision and Intelligent Technologies in Pandemic”, reflecting his commitment to knowledge dissemination and education.

Kirti Raj Bhatele is working as an assistant professor in the Department of Computer Science and Engineering, Madhav Institute of Technology & Science, a NAAC-accredited Deemed University, Gwalior, Madhya Pradesh,

India, with A++ grade. He has done PhD, MTech, and BE in information technology. He has also done postgraduate diploma in cyber law from the National Law Institute University, Bhopal, India. He has published six SCI/SCIE-indexed publications along with many SCOPUS/ESCI-indexed publications. He has also published more than 12 book chapters in the various edited book titles of the IGI Global publications, USA. He has also done two patents and received research fellowships.

Devanshu Tiwari is working as an assistant professor in the Centre for Computer Science and Business Management at the Madhav Institute of Technology & Science, a NAAC-accredited Deemed University, Gwalior, Madhya Pradesh, India, with A++ grade. She has completed her PhD in the computer science and engineering discipline from the Rajiv Gandhi Technical University, Bhopal, Madhya Pradesh, India. She also did MTech in computer science and engineering and BE in information technology from Rajiv Gandhi Technical University, Bhopal, Madhya Pradesh, India. She has also done postgraduate diploma in cyber law from the National Law Institute University, Bhopal, Madhya Pradesh, India. She has teaching and research experience of more than ten years and published four SCI/SCIE-indexed publications along with many SCOPUS/ESCI-indexed publications. She has also published many book chapters in the various edited books titles of the IGI Global publications, USA. He has also done one patent and received research fellowships.

Contributors

Karm Veer Arya
ABV-Indian Institute of Information Technology and Management, Gwalior, Madhya Pradesh, India

Prajna Parimita Dash
Birla Institute of Technology, Mesra, Jharkhand, India

Manish Dixit
Department of Computer Science and Engineering, MITS, Gwalior, Madhya Pradesh, India

Umashankar Ghugar
Department of Computer Science and Engineering, OP Jindal University, Raigarh, Chhattisgarh, India

Priyanka Gupta
Department of Computer Engineering and Applications, GLA University, Mathura, Uttar Pradesh, India

Vijay Hasanpuri
UIET, Kurukshtera University, Haryana, India

Anand Jawdekar
Parul University, Vadodara, Gujrat, India

Anand Jha
Department of IT, Rustamji Institute of Technology, BSF, Tekanpur, Gwalior, Madhya Pradesh, India

Aurangjeb Khan
CMR University, Bengaluru, India

Ayush Kumawat
Indian Space Research Organization – Space Application Centre (SAC), Ahmedabad, Gujrat, India

Siva Adithya M. J.
Vellore Institute of Technology, Chennai, Tamil Nadu, India

D. Jeya Mala
Vellore Institute of Technology, Chennai, Tamil Nadu, India

Shubham Mishra
Department of Computer Engineering and Applications, GLA University, Mathura, Uttar Pradesh, India

Rakesh Nayak
Department of Computer Science and Engineering, OP Jindal University, Raigarh, Chhattisgarh, India

Ravi Prakash Pandey
Dr. Rammanohar Lohia Avadh University, Ayodhya, Uttar Pradesh, India

Sanjay Patsariya
Department of IT, Rustamji Institute of Technology, BSF, Tekanpur, Gwalior, Madhya Pradesh, India

V. Pietiläinen
University of Lapland, Rovaniemi, Finland

Puja S. Prasad
Associate Professor, Department of Computer Science and Engineering, Geethanjali College of Engineering and Technology, Hyderabad, Telangana, India

Seema Rani
Jaypee University of Information Technology, Himachal Pradesh, India

A. Pradeep Reynold
NSH Corporation, Chennai, Tamil Nadu, India

R. Rusko
University of Lapland, Rovaniemi, Finland

V. V. Saari
Veli-Veli Oy, Tornia, Finland

Manju Sadasivan
CMR University, Bengaluru, India

Raj Shree
Babasaheb Bhimrao Ambedkar University, Lucknow, Uttar Pradesh, India

Ashwani Kant Shukla
Babasaheb Bhimrao Ambedkar University, Lucknow, Uttar Pradesh, India

Vivek Shukla
Babasaheb Bhimrao Ambedkar University, Lucknow, Uttar Pradesh, India

Saurabh Srivastava
K. K. Wagh Institute of Engineering Education and Research, Nashik, Maharashtra, India

M. T. Vasumathi
New Horizon College of Engineering, Bengaluru, India

Chapter 1

Introduction to digital twin technology

Umashankar Ghugar and Rakesh Nayak

1.1 INTRODUCTION

In the era of digital transformation, the principle of digital twin modern technology has actually become a revolutionary force, reshaping the way we perceive and interact with the physical world. This sophisticated modern technology has actually exceeded conventional limits, offering a virtual representation of physical assets, processes, and systems. As we dive right into the midst of this innovative development, it becomes evident that digital twin technology holds the potential to revolutionize industries, drive unprecedented efficiency, and pave the way for a new era of advancement.

At its core, digital twin technology involves creating a digital replica or twin of a physical entity, whether it's a machine, a building, or an entire ecosystem. This virtual counterpart is not merely a static model; rather, it is a dynamic, real-time representation that mirrors the behaviour, performance, and condition of its physical counterpart. By leveraging a wide variety of modern technologies such as Internet of Things (IoT), expert systems, along with advanced analytics, digital Twins make it possible for continuous surveillance, evaluation, and also optimization of physical possessions and procedures.

One of the key attributes of digital twin technology lies in its ability to provide unprecedented insights and foresight into the performance and behaviour of physical assets. By gathering real-time information from sensing units installed in the physical atmosphere, digital twins provide a comprehensive view of the possession's functional condition, architectural stability, and also ecological effect. This invaluable stream of data empowers organizations to make informed decisions, predict maintenance needs, and maximize efficiency consequently driving considerable set you back financial savings plus functional performances.

Furthermore, the application of digital twin technology encompasses specific properties to include whole systems as well as procedures. For example, when it comes to production, digital twins can replicate production line, anticipate possible bottlenecks, and optimize workflows to

DOI: 10.1201/9781003498117-1

enhance productivity and reduce downtime. In the field of healthcare, digital twins of patients can facilitate personalized treatment plans, predictive diagnostics, and positive wellness administration, introducing a brand-new age of accuracy medication. The potential of digital twin technology is not confined to a specific industry; rather, its impact spans across a multitude of sectors, including aerospace, automotive, energy, and urban development. As we welcome this transformative innovation, they are positioned to open brand-new frontiers of advancement, drive lasting methods, and also provide unmatched worth to consumers and stakeholders.

However, as with any kind of turbulent innovation the fostering of digital twin innovation postures it's very own set of challenges. The integration of diverse data sources, ensuring data security and privacy, and developing scalable models are among the hurdles that organizations should browse on the course to using the complete possibility of digital twins.

The concept of digital twin technology represents a paradigm shift in the way we perceive, analyse, and optimize the physical world. By developing a bridge between the physical and electronic worlds, digital twins encourage companies to acquire extraordinary understandings, enhance efficiency, and also drive advancement. As we stand at the cusp of a digital revolution, the potential of digital twin technology to redefine industries and elevate human capabilities is indeed awe-inspiring [1].

1.2 EXPLORING THE FOUNDATIONS OF DIGITAL TWIN TECHNOLOGY

The emergence of digital twin technology marks a pivotal moment in the evolution of digitalization, transforming the way we perceive and interact with the physical world. At its core, digital twin innovation incorporates a myriad of fundamental aspects that jointly create the foundation of this ground-breaking advancement. As we look into the various elements of its structures, it ends up being apparent that digital twin modern technology is not just a principle but an advanced pressure that holds the possibility to change markets together with redefining human abilities.

Data integration and interoperability: One of the vital columns of digital twin modern technology hinges on its capacity to perfectly incorporate information from varied resources coupled with systems. Whether it's sensor data from physical assets, historical performance metrics, or real-time environmental parameters, the digital twin relies on comprehensive data integration to create a holistic representation of the physical entity. This requires interoperability between various information layouts and procedures together with criteria, guaranteeing that the digital twin can efficiently mirror the complexities of its physical equivalent [2].

IoT and sensor technology: At the heart of every digital twin lies a network of sensors and IoT devices that serve as the eyes and ears of the virtual representation. These sensing units record a wide range of real-time information, varying from temperature level plus stress to vibration as well as power intake, allowing the digital twin to mirror the vibrant habits and also problems of the physical property. The seamless integration of IoT as well as sensing unit modern technology creates a crucial structure for the continual tracking, evaluation, and optimization abilities of digital twins [3].

Advanced analytics and artificial intelligence (AI): The ability of digital twins to not only mirror the physical world but also predict and optimize its behaviour is underpinned by the integration of advanced analytics and AI. By leveraging AI formulas and anticipating analytics, cognitive computer digital twins can figure out complicated patterns and spot abnormalities along with projecting future efficiency. This foundation equips organizations to go on from responsive upkeep to positive plus anticipating methods, driving considerable price financial savings and also functional performances [4].

Real-time visualization and simulation: A foundation of digital twin innovation is its ability to give real-time visualization as well as simulation of physical properties coupled with procedures. Through immersive 3D models, interactive dashboards, and simulation environments, digital twins offer a comprehensive view of the operational status, structural integrity, and performance of the physical entity. This fundamental aspect allows investors to get workable understandings, carry out online experiments, and enhance procedures in a risk-free electronic setting [5].

Cybersecurity and data privacy: As organizations welcome the capacity of digital twin modern technology, the structure of cybersecurity as well as information personal privacy ends up being critical. Protecting the integrity and confidentiality of the data that fuels the digital twin is essential to ensure trust and reliability. Robust cybersecurity measures, information security, as well as accessibility controls create the foundation of a safe and secure digital twin environment, protecting delicate details from unapproved accessibility together with cyber risks [6].

The foundations of digital twin technology represent a convergence of diverse elements that collectively form the backbone of this transformative innovation. By entwining information combination, IoT, progressed analytics, visualization, and also cybersecurity, digital twin modern technology blazes a trail for a brand-new period of insight-driven choice making, anticipating upkeep along with unsurpassed functional performances. As organizations continue to unlock the potential of digital twins, the evolution of this foundational technology promises to redefine industries, drive sustainable practices, and elevate human capabilities into uncharted realms of innovation.

1.3 THE EVOLUTION OF DIGITAL TWIN TECHNOLOGY: A COMPREHENSIVE OVERVIEW

Digital twin technology has seen growth and development since its inception. Here are some key points that showcase how it has evolved over time [7].

Conceptualization in the 1960s:

- The roots of technology can be traced back to the 1960s when NASA pioneered its use during space missions. They created replicas of spacecraft on Earth for study and simulation purposes.
- During this era, basic twinning concepts were employed for space programming leading to the creation of replicated systems.

Formal introduction and development:

- The concept of twins was first mentioned in 1991 with the publication of "Mirror Worlds" by David Gelernter.
- Dr. Michael Grieves is recognized as the pioneer who applied twin concepts to manufacturing in 2002 and introduced the idea of digital twin software.
- The recognition of technology grew in 2002 after Dr. Michael Grieves presented it at the University of Michigan, focusing on establishing a product life cycle management centre.

Continuous evolution and adoption:

- Since 2002 digital twin technology has been continuously evolving, with an eye on innovations and technological advancements.
- The integration of AI machine learning and IoT technologies has been consistently utilized across the product life cycle, spanning from design and manufacturing to construction, operation, and maintenance.
- The advancement of the IoT has played a role in enhancing the twin technology by facilitating connectivity between tangible components and their virtual representations.

1.4 DEMYSTIFYING DIGITAL TWIN TECHNOLOGY: A BEGINNER'S GUIDE

In the ever-evolving landscape of technology, the term "digital twin" has been gaining attention as a transformative concept with wide-ranging implications across various industries. Despite its growing prominence, digital twin technology remains a relatively unfamiliar concept for many. This chapter aims to demystify digital twin technology and provide a beginner's guide to understanding its significance and potential applications.

At its core, a digital twin is a virtual representation of a physical object, process, or system. It is an exact digital replica that mirrors the physical entity in real time, capturing its behaviour, characteristics, and performance. This digital counterpart is connected to its physical counterpart through a continuous exchange of data, enabling seamless monitoring, analysis, and simulation of the physical entity's behaviour and performance [8].

A digital twin consists of several key components:

- **Physical entity**: This refers to the tangible object, equipment, or system that is being replicated in the digital world.
- **Sensors and data collection**: Data is collected from the physical entity through sensors, IoT devices, and other sources, providing real-time information about its state and performance.
- **Data integration and processing**: The collected data is integrated and processed to create an accurate digital representation, reflecting the physical entity's behaviour and characteristics.
- **Analytics and visualization**: Advanced analytics and visualization tools are used to interpret and analyse the data, enabling insights into the performance and potential improvements of the physical entity.
- **Feedback loop**: The digital twin continuously receives real-time data from the physical entity, creating a feedback loop that allows for monitoring, analysis, and optimization.

Figure 1.1 depicts the interaction between the physical and digital worlds through the concept of digital twins. It shows three steps in a process: "Physical Twin" in the "Physical World" connected by "IT Data Commands" to "Digital Twin'" in the "Digital World", which is then linked

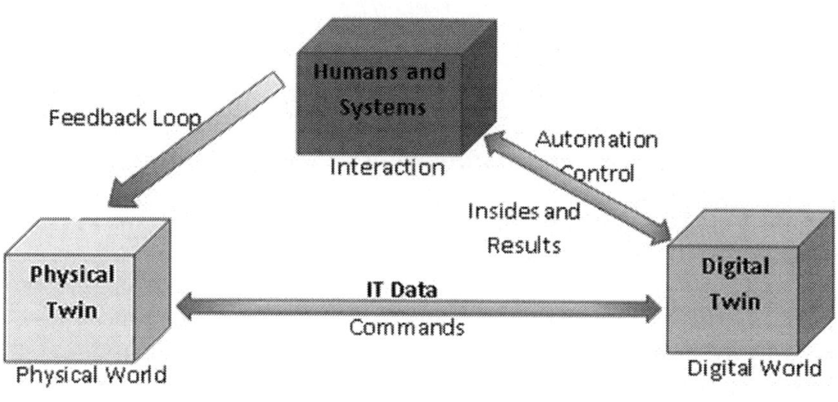

Figure 1.1 Conceptual view of digital twin.

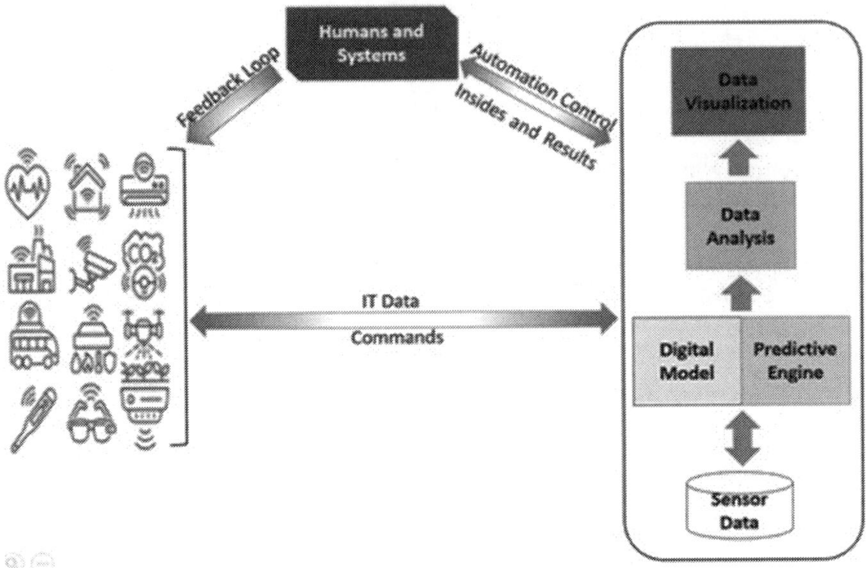

Figure 1.2 Functional view of digital twin.

by "Insides and Results Automation Control' " to "Humans and Systems Interactions". Each step is represented by a 3D block with arrows indicating the flow of information from the physical to the digital and ultimately to human-system interaction.

The below flowchart presented with the aid of Figure 1.2 illustrates the data processing pipeline from sensor data to business applications. On the left side, various sensor-related icons represent different data sources. This data flows into a "Digital Model", represented by a smartphone-like shape. Inside this model, "Sensor Data" feeds into a "Predictive Engine", which then leads to "Data Analysis", and subsequently "Data Visualization". The process culminates in "Humans and Systems", depicted as a rightward arrow pointing away from the digital model. The flowchart emphasizes a structured approach to transforming raw sensor data into actionable business insights.

The use of electronic twin innovation has many different and extensive applications. Electronic twins are used in production to mimic manufacturing processes, increase device efficiency, and help anticipate maintenance, which ultimately improves functional effectiveness and reduces downtime. Electronic twins in the healthcare industry have the ability to create personalized patient profiles, enabling the development of pharmaceutical simulations, tailored therapy plans, and medical interventions based on unique physiological variations. Electronic twins are also employed in smart cities and city planning to manage and update infrastructure, predict website traffic patterns, and optimize energy consumption, all of which contribute to robust and long-lasting urban development.

One of the most important aspects of contemporary electronic twin technology is its potential to create a gap between the real and virtual worlds. The electronic twin is continuously updated with real-world data, which may be used to improve the version and produce even more accurate projections. On the other hand, insights from the digital representation may inform decisions and treatments in the real world, creating a mutually beneficial relationship that promotes ongoing improvement and progress.

Moreover, electronic twins are not limited to static representations; rather, they may grow into dynamic, multi-physics simulations that comprise complex connections amongst different components of a system. This capability allows the modelling of sophisticated behaviours, such the interaction of organic processes in an online microbe or the liquid properties in a nuclear power plant's architectural integrity of a building. Electronic twins are crucial components for autonomous systems and also intelligent automation since they may independently adapt and improve their behaviours based on the information they receive, thanks to advancements in expert systems and AI.

It is impossible to overstate the potential impact of electronic twin contemporary technology on performance and technology as long as businesses and industries continue to embrace it. Through the utilization of insights derived from electronic twins, services are able to make data-driven decisions that proactively address functional roadblocks and create new opportunities for growth and efficiency. Furthermore, the fusion of emerging modern technologies like block chain and enhanced truth with electronic pairs is poised to further enhance their capabilities and open up new avenues for safe and immersive electronic representations of the real world.

The features of contemporary electronic twin technology range widely, from lively simulations and autonomous adjustment to real-time monitoring and predictive analytics. As this revolutionary innovation develops and combines with other emerging trends, it will undoubtedly shape different markets' futures and help us get ready for a connected and intelligent world. It can also drive progress, improve processes, and facilitate better decision-making. Acknowledging and using the potential of electronic twin innovation is not only a technical endeavour but also a strategic requirement for businesses hoping to thrive in the electronic era.

1.5 TYPES OF DIGITAL TWIN

Digital twins manifest in various forms contingent upon the degree of product magnification, with the primary distinguishing factor being the application domain. It is not uncommon for disparate types of digital twins to concurrently subsist within a given system or process. This avant-garde technology possesses the potential to effectuate paradigm shifts across an array of industries, including but not limited to manufacturing, healthcare, and urban planning. This discourse will delineate the sundry types of digital twins and their respective applications across diverse sectors:

1. **Product digital twin**: Predominantly, the product digital twin constitutes a digital representation of a tangible product or asset. This genre of digital twin is prevalently employed within the manufacturing sector, wherein it facilitates the emulation of the behaviour and performance of products across their entire life cycle. The employment of product digital twins empowers manufacturers to enhance design, prognosticate maintenance requisites, and ameliorate overall product quality.
2. **Process digital twin**: Process digital twins are implicated in the modelling and simulation of intricate industrial processes, encompassing manufacturing operations, supply chain logistics, and energy production. Through the construction of a digital facsimile of a physical process, entities can scrutinize, optimize, and anticipate the comportment of said processes in real time. The deployment of process digital twins is pivotal in augmenting operational efficiency, curtailing downtime, and abating costs.
3. **System digital twin**: An entire system or environment, not just an individual product or process. For instance, in a smart city, a system digital twin will replicate the interaction among the many different parts of an urban infrastructure: transportation networks, energy grids, public services, etc. This thus aids city planners and policymakers in making educated decisions towards sustainable urban development.
4. **Performance digital twin**: Performance digital twins observe and analyse, in real time, the performance of the physical asset or system. Performance digital twins are driven by data from sensors and IoT devices related to the operational status, health, and efficiency of assets. These are the most common types of digital twins used in predictive maintenance, which allows for proactive measures to be taken against equipment failures and downtime.
5. **Enterprise digital twin**: Holistic modelling of an organization involving assets, processes, and resources. It is an integration of the various departmental and business-function data repositories to afford a view of the total operation of the organization. It is applicable in a wide range of industries for strategic decision-making, process optimization, and scenario planning.
6. **Healthcare digital twin**: In healthcare, digital twins present a new opportunity to personalize medical treatment and patient care.

Health digital twins may simulate the physiological character of a patient, which helps to have an individualized treatment plan and predictive diagnostics. More so, the digital twin for medical equipment improves the performance of such medical equipment for patient safety.

In recognizing the potential of digital twin technology, evolution continues to inspire innovation and bring about the required transformation in industries. It empowers organizations to effectively tap the potential of digital twins in finding new ways to be efficient, sustainable, and innovative. From manufacturing and urban planning to healthcare, digital twins are changing how humanity understands and interacts with the physical world to a data-driven future through virtual representations.

1.6 HARNESSING THE POWER OF DIGITAL TWIN TECHNOLOGY IN INDUSTRY

Digital twin technology has become a game changer in industries, transforming how businesses create, monitor, and upkeep systems. By crafting copies of assets and processes, digital twins bring about a range of advantages that are reshaping industry norms.

Advantages of digital twin technology

1. **Improvements in product quality**: Digital twins can lead to enhancements in product quality. By simulating the product across the manufacturing journey, it becomes possible to detect design flaws. This capability allows for adjustments or redesigns ultimately resulting in product quality and performance.
2. **Predictive maintenance and optimization**: Proactive Maintenance and Optimization; Businesses are utilizing twins to facilitate maintenance and optimization efforts. Through the creation of replicas of physical assets, real-time data continuously feeds into the digital twin. This enables testing configurations to optimize production output, minimize errors, and enhance efficiency within machinery and systems.
3. **Cost savings and efficiency**: Digital twins play a role in cost savings during production and maintenance processes. Acting as prototypes of objects, they assimilate insights from individuals, machines, and the environment. Enabling necessary adaptations, for creating more efficient designs.

   Digital twins play a role in cutting down production expenses, speeding up product launches, and enhancing the quality of products. Moreover, digital twins enable organizations to make decisions based on data-driven insights. By mimicking and simulating the actions of objects in time, digital twins offer valuable information that guides decision-making processes.

4. **Enhanced decision-making**: The insights derived from digital twins empower organizations to make data-driven decisions. By modelling and simulating the behaviour of physical objects in real time, digital twins provide valuable insights that inform decision-making, predict future behaviours, and optimize outcomes
5. **Security and information integrity**: While leveraging the large quantity amount of data collected from various endpoints, companies should assess and update their security protocols before adopting digital twin technology. Despite the potential security vulnerabilities, digital twins offer a secure and accurate representation of physical assets, processes, and systems, providing an accurate view of current and future scenarios.
6. **Insights into production and manufacturing processes**: Digital twins supply understandings right into all elements of assembly lines and also production procedures. By developing digital designs of procedures, systems, solutions, and items as well as various other physical items, electronic doubles provide designers the capacity to properly assess physical properties as well as gain understandings right into present, coupled with future circumstances.
7. **Training and predictive modelling**: With digital twins, people can be educated without requiring to literally existing in possibly active or risky circumstances. Better anticipatory modelling utilizing electronic doubles can drastically change the method centre supervisors regulate structures, causing lowered expenses along with enhanced customer contentment.
8. **Remote monitoring and assistance**: Digital twins allow offsite experts to observe active equipment through systems that utilize digital twin technology. This enables remote monitoring and assistance, where problems can be detected, and onsite employees can be guided through maintenance procedures with the help of augmented reality. This capacity not just improves functional performance but additionally mitigates difficulties associated with worker turn over plus retention by maintaining expertise as well as experience within the organization.

The advantages of using electronic doubles include remote monitoring, predictive maintenance, cost savings, improved decision-making, enhanced safety, better insights into manufacturing processes, and more effective training. As companies remain to incorporate electronic double innovation right into their procedures, the possibility for technology, effectiveness, as well as tactical decision-making will certainly drive considerable developments throughout varied markets.

1.7 CHALLENGES AND CONSIDERATIONS

While digital twin technology holds great promise, there are challenges and considerations to be mindful of:

- **Data security**: The sensitive nature of the data collected and shared between the physical and digital twins requires robust security measures to safeguard against unauthorized access and cyber threats.
- **Interoperability**: Ensuring compatibility and seamless integration of digital twin systems with existing infrastructure and technologies is essential for their successful implementation.
- **Ethical and legal implications**: The use of digital twins raises ethical considerations regarding data privacy, consent, and ownership, necessitating clear guidelines and regulations [9].

1.8 NOTABLE SUCCESS STORIES WITH DIGITAL TWINS

Several companies have successfully harnessed the power of digital twin technology to drive innovation and achieve significant milestones:

1. **Bayer's manufacturing operations**: Bayer leveraged digital twins to optimize its manufacturing operations, utilizing software simulations to improve capacity, process controls, and machine uptime through predictive maintenance. This initiative resulted in reduced waste associated with packaging inconsistent product quantities.
2. **Mars' virtual app store**: Mars utilized digital twin technology to create a virtual app store of use cases that could be reused across its business lines. Additionally, the company plans to use digital twin data to account for climate and other situational considerations that affect its products, establishing greater versatility.
3. **Change2Twin project for SMEs**: The Change2Twin project made digital twins more accessible and crucial for small- and medium-sized enterprises (SMEs) to join the Industry 4.0 revolution. This initiative has enabled SMEs to enhance efficiency, reduce costs, and improve competitiveness through digital twin technology.

These success stories exemplify the diverse applications and benefits of digital twin technology across different industries, showcasing its potential to drive efficiency, innovation, and strategic decision-making.

1.9 CONCLUSION

The widespread adoption of digital twin technology is poised to reshape the future of organizations, industries, and cities. As technology continues to advance, digital twins will play a critical role in shaping virtual experiences, enhancing collaboration, and revolutionizing various sectors. Embracing digital twins presents an array of opportunities, from optimizing operations to driving innovation and sustainability. With its potential to bridge the physical and digital realms, digital twin technology is set to play a pivotal role in the ongoing digital transformation.

As we continue to explore the potential of digital twins, it is essential to address challenges such as data security, privacy, and interoperability to ensure the seamless integration of this transformative technology into our digital ecosystem.

The future of digital twins is indeed promising, offering a glimpse into a world where every entity, from individuals to entire cities, could have its digital twin. This trend is set to evolve and grow, presenting new opportunities for organizations to leverage digital twin capabilities and drive disruptive transformations in the years to come.

REFERENCES

1. Golovina, T., Polyanin, A., Adamenko, A., Khegay, E., & Schepinin, V. (2020). Digital twins as a new paradigm of an industrial enterprise. *International Journal of Technology*, 11(6), 1115–1124.
2. Jeddoub, I., Nys, G. A., Hajji, R., & Billen, R. (2023). Digital twins for cities: Analyzing the gap between concepts and current implementations with a specific focus on data integration. *International Journal of Applied Earth Observation and Geoinformation*, 122, 103440.
3. Murthy, A., Irshad, M., Noman, S. M., Tang, X., Hu, B., Chen, S., & Khader, G. (2022). Internet of Things, a vision of digital twins and case studies. In *IoT and Spacecraft Informatics* (pp. 101–127). Elsevier.
4. Lv, Z., & Xie, S. (2022). Artificial intelligence in the digital twins: State of the art, challenges, and future research topics. *Digital Twin*, 1, 12.
5. Korth, B., Schwede, C., & Zajac, M. (2018, December). Simulation-ready digital twin for realtime management of logistics systems. In *2018 IEEE International Conference on Big Data (Big Data)* (pp. 4194–4201). IEEE.
6. Alshammari, K., Beach, T., & Rezgui, Y. (2021). Cybersecurity for digital twins in the built environment: Current research and future directions. *Journal of Information Technology in Construction*, 26, 159–173.
7. Jeong, D. Y., Baek, M. S., Lim, T. B., Kim, Y. W., Kim, S. H., Lee, Y. T., ... & Lee, I. B. (2022). Digital twin: Technology evolution stages and implementation layers with technology elements. *IEEE Access*, 10, 52609–52620.
8. Li, Q., & He, Y. (2021). An overview of digital twin concept for key components of renewable energy systems. *International Journal of Robotics and Automation Technology*, 8, 29–47.
9. Botín-Sanabria, D. M., Mihaita, A. S., Peimbert-García, R. E., Ramírez-Moreno, M. A., Ramírez-Mendoza, R. A., & Lozoya-Santos, J. D. J. (2022). Digital twin technology challenges and applications: A comprehensive review. *Remote Sensing*, 14(6), 1335.

Chapter 2

Digital twin technology fundamentals

Priyanka Gupta, Shubham Mishra, and Manish Dixit

2.1 THE DEFINITION OF DIGITAL TWIN TECHNOLOGY

As humans, we are always known for our creativity and innovation. But we had a lot of difficulties in knowing about the shortcomings of our innovations, their working, and their assembling due to lack of information. That's why we always want a technology that can help us in visualizing our product or machine performance in different circumstances. Now imagine having a system that can help us in visualizing the overall manufacturing of our product. This problem can be solved by the new technology, which is known as digital twin [1, 2]. Figure 2.1 illustrates an example of digital twin.

Before explaining digital twin in depth, two other closely related concepts are digital model and digital shadow. So here is a little bit of description about these two terms for better understanding [3].

2.1.1 Digital model

A digital model is a simulated version of an actual thing, system, or process. It can take different forms, including 3D models, computer-aided design (CAD) files, simulations, and mathematical algorithms. Digital models allow you to visualize, analyze, and manipulate things or systems in a digital environment, which helps with design, optimization, and testing. A model is typically a forecast or guess about how a physical thing, system, or process will function in the future or in a certain setting. Digital models have applications in a variety of businesses and professions. They are commonly used in architecture, engineering, manufacturing, and entertainment for design, prototyping, and visualization. In scientific study, digital models are valuable for simulations, data analysis, and hypothesis testing.

Let's take an example: an architectural firm may utilize a digital model to produce a virtual walkthrough of a building design, allowing clients to visualize and modify the plan and aesthetics before construction begins. Figure 2.2 illustrates the level of integration.

DOI: 10.1201/9781003498117-2

Figure 2.1 An example of digital twin.

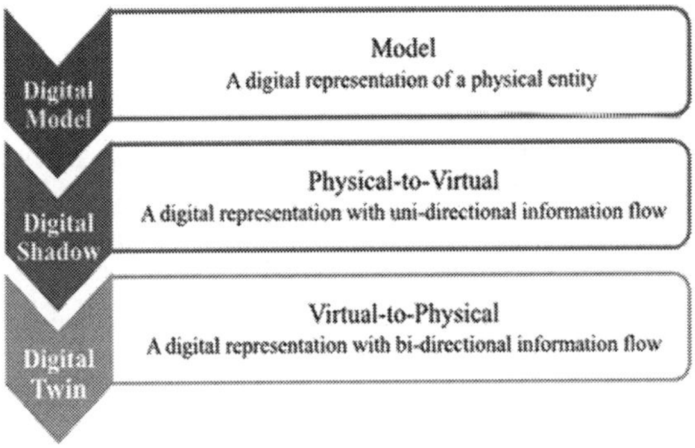

Figure 2.2 Levels of integration.

2.1.2 Digital shadow

A digital shadow is a constantly changing digital representation that reflects the current state and behavior of a real entity or system. It collects data from the asset, which may be a database, a train system, or a banking platform, via sensors, Internet of Things (IoT) devices, or other sources, and then feeds that data into the model. This signifies that the digital shadow is in sync with the physical entity. It displays the asset in adequate depth, making it valuable for gaining a thorough knowledge. They are usually mathematical models, but they can also be 3D representations that focus on specific features, such as performance indicators, operational conditions, or environmental concerns. They facilitate monitoring, predictive analysis, and decision-making. They are useful in situations where monitoring and analysis are crucial. They are widely used in areas, including logistics, supply

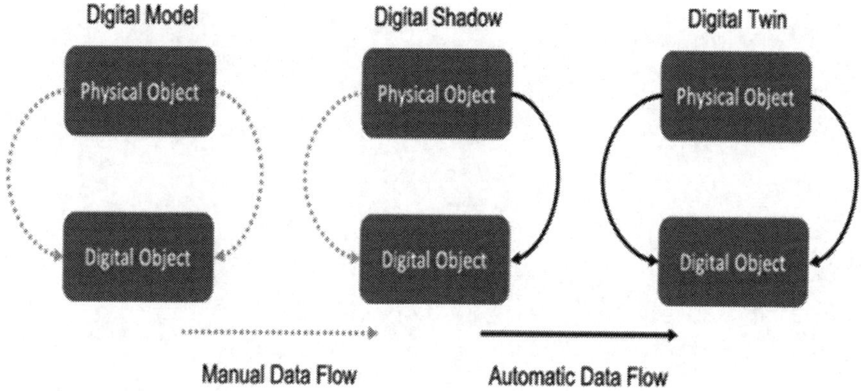

Figure 2.3 Digital model, shadow, and twin [3].

chain management, energy, and transportation. By collecting and analyzing data from sensors and IoT devices, digital shadows assist predictive maintenance, anomaly detection, and process and operation optimization.

Let's look at another example to further grasp how digital shadows are used. A manufacturing company may build a digital shadow of its production line. The digital shadow enables the organization to monitor and analyze production processes, identify bottlenecks, and make data-driven decisions to optimize processes and increase quality. In the event of an unanticipated disruption or data loss, the digital shadow can be employed to restore the most recent operating state, reducing downtime. Figure 2.3 illustrates the digital model, shadow, and twin.

2.1.3 Digital twins

Digital twins bring the virtual and physical worlds together by establishing a real-time connection between the physical thing and its digital copy, in which the physical object provides information to the digital replica and vice versa. Digital twins simulate, monitor, and control physical items or systems, allowing for more efficient analysis, optimization, and predictive maintenance. They offer live feedback loops and promote insights for boosting performance, efficiency, and dependability [4]. To put it another way, there is a two-way interaction between the physical and digital environments, with the digital duplicate able to influence how the real entity functions. For example, this is necessary when dealing with a critical asset that adds value in areas of national concern, such as safety or competitive advantage. In these instances, it is critical to ensure that the asset is resilient in terms of how it responds to possible deviations [5].

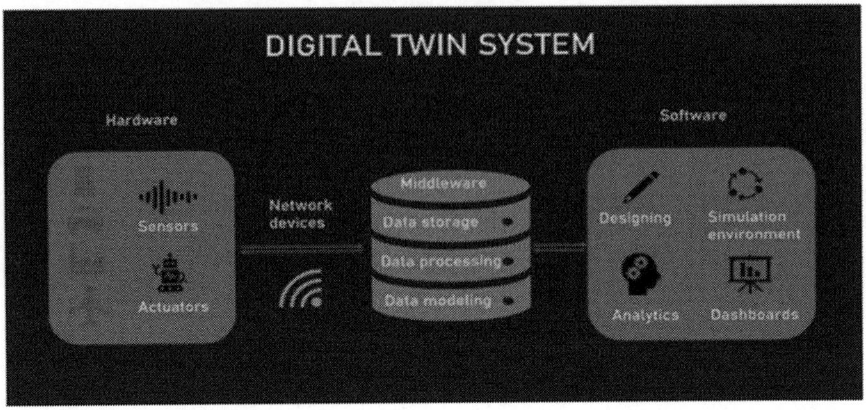

Figure 2.4 Components of digital twin system.

So, let us understand digital twin in detail by understanding it's components and process of creating any virtual object.

2.2 COMPONENTS OF DIGITAL TWIN SYSTEM

A digital twin is essentially a multidimensional concept that involves the many components that, when put together, play an important role in producing a dynamic and realistic copy of a person. Having understanding of those components is important in the effective and efficient use of digital twin technology. Figure 2.4 illustrates the components of digital twin system.

2.2.1 Physical entity

It is an entity in real life or an object of which the digital twin is used. It can be an artifact used in manufacturing a structure part, vehicle, or a complex structure [6].

2.2.2 Virtual representation

The representation that includes the virtual model of any physical entity [7]. It shows all the characters, behaviors, algorithms, and geometry of the physical entity (object) [8].

2.2.3 Sensors and data sources

These are attached to the object in order to have real-time information about its performance, surrounding and circumstances. This information helps the digital twin for analysis, simulation, and optimization [7].

2.2.4 Data integration and analytics

The data gathered undergoes analysis by different mechanisms, for example, machine learning and artificial intelligence (AI), and is processed in order to predict the behavior, patterns, and potential problems that can occur in the object [9].

2.2.5 Visualization and simulation tools

Users interact with the digital twin through many visualization and simulation tools, giving a dynamic illustration of the real item's condition and its response [10].

2.2.6 Connectivity and IoT

Data that continuously transmogrify from the physical object to its virtual counterpart use this digital twin for seamless exchange between the two. This is enabled by connectivity with the IoT through which data is sent, received, and evaluated [11].

2.3 WORKING OF DIGITAL TWIN SYSTEMS

The detailed working of digital twin technology involves several interconnected components and processes. Here's a breakdown of how digital twin technology operates.

2.3.1 Model planning

The process initiates with a mathematics or data science expert who can develop a mathematical model capable of replicating the functions performed by the original object [12].

2.3.2 Data acquisition

After the planning process, this step proceeds by gathering data from a range of sources: sensors, devices, databases, and historic records. These real-time and historical data show an integrative insight of the entity's characteristics and behavior (Figure 2.5).

2.3.3 Modeling and simulation

Once obtained, it is modeled and simulated using several advanced level mathematics and machine learning algorithms to produce a digital representation of the real-world object. This set of digital twins would simulate the object's physical appearance and dynamic behavior through these developed algorithms and data.

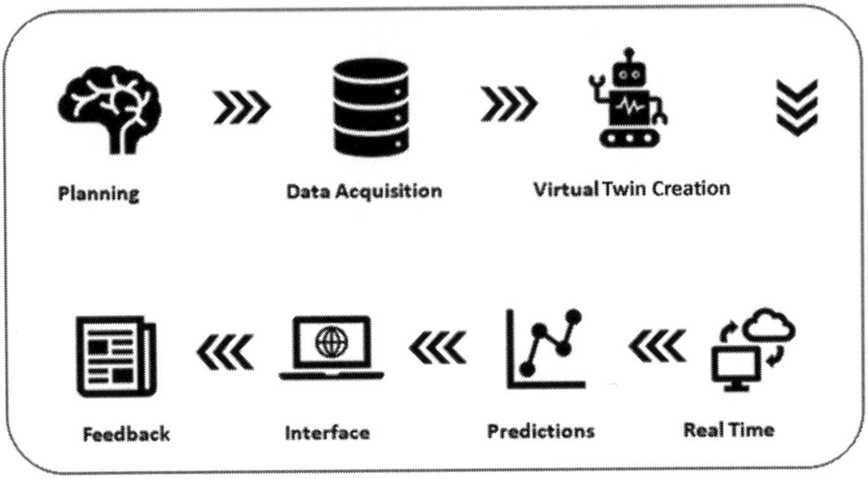

Figure 2.5 The detailed working of digital twin technology involves several interconnected components and processes.

2.3.4 Real-time monitoring and feedback

Data is considered a very critical part of the entire digital twin system; hence, there is a need for continuous data transaction between the sensors installed in the object and the model. It assists in analyzing and understanding the real-time status of some physical entity. The deflection or abnormality detected in the data triggers the alert to the system and further generates the corrective actions through this process [13].

2.3.5 Predictive analytics and optimization

It crunches up past and present data to predict future behavior, trends, or outcomes. Predictive algorithms can give support in proactive, visionary decision-making, preventive measures, and optimization processes. The strategies improve the efficiency and effectiveness of the system, and the downtime and bugs are reduced.

2.3.6 Visualization and interface

A digital twin has many in-built visualization tools that make it interactive for a user. Many graphic representations, dashboards, and analytical tools offer so much in one way to be used for exploring and understanding data and gaining insights from the same [14].

2.3.7 Feedback loop and iterative improvement

Digital twin technology operates within a feedback loop, where insights and lessons learned from the virtual model inform improvements in the physical system [15]. Continuous monitoring, analysis, and optimization foster iterative refinement of both the digital twin and its physical counterpart, driving ongoing improvements in performance and efficiency [16].

2.4 TYPES OF DIGITAL TWINS

Digital twins can be categorized into several types based on their specific applications, the complexity of their models, and the level of detail they encompass [12, 17]. Understanding these different types [18] helps to select the appropriate digital twin for a given task and optimize the benefits they can provide.

2.4.1 System/unit digital twin

System twins are asset replicas that demonstrate how numerous components interact to generate functional components at the system level. They provide a comprehensive overview of the plant or industrial facility. This allows for the evaluation of various system settings for maximum efficacy or the identification of new opportunities for the creation of additional revenue streams.

The scope of the system twin encompasses a set of assets employed in a certain function. These include the manufacture of a primary product within the facility and the transmission of energy. At this level, continuous tracking and digital twin modeling outperform the primary digital twins' ability to detect faults and breakdown. It is a path to getting knowledge required for making tactical decisions and attaining entire process transparency.

2.4.2 Process twin

Process twins, the most advanced sort of digital twin, merge system twins into a single entity to study system synchronization and collaboration. This system provides the most complete image of what happens within the factory or facility. As a result, it allows for a far more detailed and flexible output examination [19].

Process twinning gives data on results and enables for adjustments to inputs such as raw material feeding rate and manufacturing climate without interfering with the manufacturing technique or reducing output standards.

Instead of relying on gut reactions or theories, executives may now test numerous business predictions swiftly and risk-free. It also aids in the effective monitoring of critical business key performance indicators (KPIs) and data-driven decision-making.

2.4.3 Component or parts twins

These digital twins represent individual components or parts of a larger system. They are the most basic digital twins, focusing on a single part's performance, condition, and life cycle. Component twins are particularly useful for monitoring critical parts of machinery or equipment, where the failure of a single component can lead to significant issues. By tracking the health and performance of these parts, maintenance can be predicted and planned, reducing downtime and extending the component's lifespan [20].

2.4.4 Asset/product digital twin

A product or asset digital twin is a digital representation of a physical object, such as machinery, buildings, or automobiles. It provides current information on an asset's environment, performance indicators, and functional health.

Typically, they are composed of numerous component twins or use the information generated by component twins to represent a complex asset, such as an engine, pump, or structure. An asset twin investigates how well diverse components interact and function as a single entity.

Engineers can use asset/product digital twins to identify potential development opportunities and obtain insights into how their equipment operates. This reduces downtime for organizations and increases operational effectiveness.

2.4.5 Organization twins

These are the most complex type of digital twin, as they simulate an organization in its entirety with all its processes, systems, assets, and interactions. From the standpoint of organization twins, an overview of the operations is obtained at the highest level in the firm and how to undertake strategic planning, performance optimization, and decision-making. Large enterprises make use of organization twins to align business strategy with operation realities so that various parts of the organization function harmoniously and in a coordinated way to achieve set goals.

An organization twin could integrate data from all departments of a multinational corporation: production, logistics, sales, and human resources. This would give a single, full model that would digitally help business executives in decision-making, seeing the holistic view of the company's performance and the possibility of improvement in the whole organization.

2.4.6 Simulation twins

These are specialized digital twins used primarily for simulating various scenarios with the view to predicting outcomes. Simulation twins find broad applications in research and development, product design, and training. They let users test various conditions, variables, and configurations in a virtual space while reducing the risks and costs associated with physical trials to a minimum. In this respect, simulation twins turn out to be very useful in the scenario of "what-ifs," thus helping optimize designs and train for unexpected situations [21].

This twin could possibly be used in simulating a new car design with various driving conditions during the production of automotive. The types of road surfaces, weather, and driving styles could be simulated by engineers, aiming for the car to do well under any scenario, reducing the need for copious tests and prototypes.

2.4.7 Hybrid twins

Hybrid twins are capable of combining various aspects of the aforementioned types of digital twin, hence allowing a more flexible and integrated approach. These can be tailored for need and bring together component, asset, system, and process information to provide a holistic view of the entity being modeled. In complex environments, where multiple layers of detail and interaction are to be considered at one time, hybrid twins come in extremely handy. They offer a means of flexibility and accommodation with the changing requirements and can provide a holistic insight. For instance, the hybrid twin in a smart city project will combine data coming from independent urban systems—that is, transportation, utilities, and public services—into a consolidated model, which will help the urban city planners optimize the running of traffic, the utilization of energy, and the enhancement of public safety to build a smart and more productive, livable urban setup.

2.4.8 Application-specific twins

2.4.8.1 Product twins

In manufacturing and product development, product twins are widely applied, following the entire life cycle of a product, from design and into production until its end of life. They help optimize product designs, ensure quality at every stage of a product's making, and manage performance in the field. A continuous stream of data throughout the life cycle of the product means manufacturers and designers can continually work on improving products and processes.

For example, a product twin for a smartphone could trace that device's performance from the initial design phase to the production phase and finally to actual customer use. Such a twin would close the loop on design changes, manufacturing processes, and real-world usage, allowing manufacturers to make data-driven improvements to the delivery of high-quality products.

2.4.8.2 *Building twins*

Building twins acts as a digital replica in buildings or infrastructure projects relating to the construction and real estate sectors. Such twins help in designing, constructing, operating, or even completing construction within the time frame and budget set up for the completion of the project. Building twins also find applications in facility management, which aids in the optimization of energy use, enhances security, and efficiently maintains building systems.

It can be used to monitor HVAC systems, lighting, elevators, and security systems for a large commercial building. Using such a digital model, a facility manager will be able to optimize energy consumption, comfort to occupants, and building security, all working in tandem to bring down operational costs and improve the building's performance.

2.4.8.3 *Infrastructure twins*

Large-scale infrastructure projects, such as bridges, roads, and utilities, use infrastructure twins for health and structural surveillance, scheduling maintenance, and appealing for safe and efficient structural features. The data from these form essential aspects of planning and decision-making for the effectiveness of infrastructure systems in ensuring that it meets the needs of the community.

For instance, an infrastructure twin of a city's water supply would monitor pipe, pump, and treatment facility conditions. It aids city planners and engineers in predicting leaks and mitigating them, in the optimization of water flows, and in being sure the system will meet increasing demands into the future.

2.5 APPLICATIONS OF DIGITAL TWIN TECHNOLOGY

Initially developed for industrial applications, digital twin technology rapidly grew into a number of varied industries due to the form it creates for an accurate, dynamic model of physical objects, systems, or processes. Such virtual replicas provide insight and valuable predictions, transforming operations across several industries [22, 23]. Figure 2.6 illustrates the various areas of digital twin technology application. The following areas are where digital twin technology is creating a large impact.

2.5.1 Aerospace

Aerospace tasks are intrinsically complex. End products like aircraft and spacecraft are massively expensive to design and build, making it all the more imperative to get work done right the first time in order to avoid costly delays.

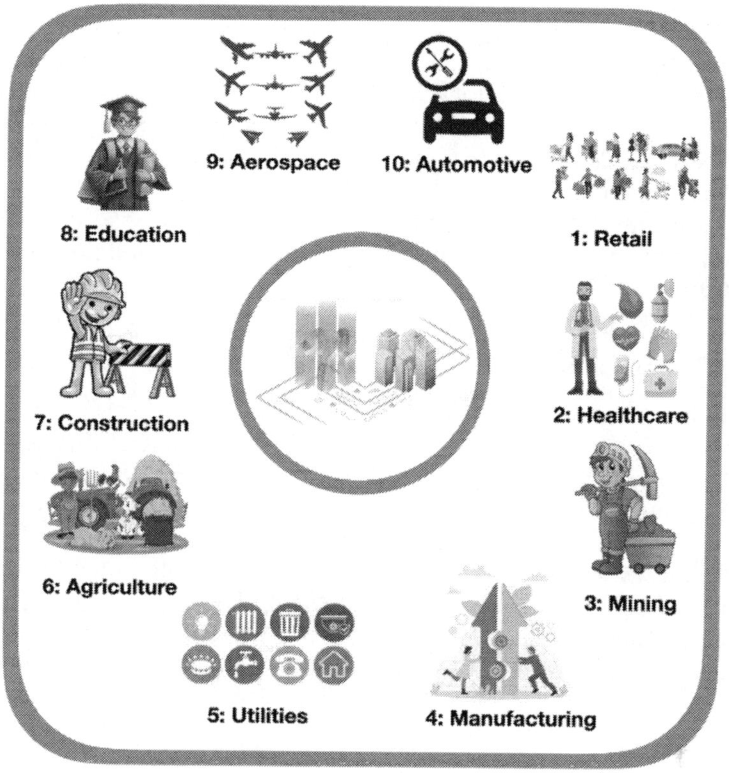

Figure 2.6 The various areas of applications for the digital twin technology.

From design and engineering all the way through to assembly and maintenance, digital twins improve decision-making by allowing teams to visualize and interact with CAD models and other datasets in real-time 3D.

2.5.2 Architecture

At the start of a project, architects produce design materials, including renderings and models, to allow clients to evaluate and approve the design. The problem is there's no shared, collaborative environment with stakeholders to make decisions in real time. Communicating design intent during traditional reviews is a difficult process. Static 2D and 3D models cause details to be lost in translation, renderings aren't flexible enough, and not everyone is on the same page. Digital twins solve these problems so there's no more costly mistakes.

2.5.3 Automotive

In the automotive industry, digital twins are used to simulate and test new design concepts before they are built, optimize production processes, and even predict how a vehicle will perform in different conditions. The top benefit of using digital twins for automotive original equipment manufacturers (OEMs) is the ability to save time and money by identifying and addressing potential issues before they occur. As the industry continues to embrace this technology, it plays an increasingly important role across every workflow in the automotive life cycle, from design and manufacturing to marketing and maintenance.

2.5.4 Construction

Faced with rampant supply chain delays, labor shortages, and inflated material costs, the stakes for builders are at an all-time high. Bad data and poor decision-making can lead to expensive delays and rework. Digital twin and augmented reality (AR) technology allow the construction industry to optimize project data, streamline collaboration, and better visualize projects from design through to operations and maintenance. By using AR to bring valuable building information modelling (BIM) data to the field, contractors are able to capture and communicate design errors in just a few clicks, allowing stakeholders to resolve issues quickly and avoid costly rework.

2.5.5 Energy

Energy companies generate a wealth of data, especially as operations are increasingly outfitted with IoT sensors, high-definition cameras with AI capabilities, and more. Digital technologies like real-time 3D can visualize this data to provide right-time insights, better-informing decisions around production, maintenance, safety and security, and optimization.

2.5.6 Infrastructure

Digital twin technology helps builders, planners, and operators across cities worldwide better understand and optimize these spaces for public use. By using advanced, interactive models and live IoT data, stakeholders are able to simulate traffic flow, mobility patterns, and even the effects of climate change and shifting landscapes surrounding key infrastructure like airports, roads, and transportation hubs. From individual facilities to smart cities, digital twins are helping owners, operators, and policymakers manage large volumes of valuable data that will allow them to better equip our infrastructure for future demands.

2.5.7 Government

The use of real-time 3D, extended reality (XR), and AI technologies are accelerating at a rapid pace in civilian, defense, and intelligence applications. New technologies are being deployed rapidly and putting challenges on government agencies and contractors that need to stay at the forefront of cutting-edge development. Digital twins help reduce the risk, time, and cost of designing, developing, deploying, and supporting cutting-edge applications in simulation and training and beyond.

2.5.8 Luxury goods

Luxury interactive shopping is on the rise, complementing premium in-store experiences. Many luxury brands have been preparing for the future of retail for many years by creating 3D marketing experiences. Investing in this new way of selling can reduce costs and increase revenue.

2.5.9 Manufacturing

As emerging trends such as the fourth industrial revolution (4IR) continue to gain traction, manufacturers are using digital twin technology to transform their product life cycle. From faster time-to-market in product development to increased productivity among frontline workers, many manufacturers are already reaping the benefits. Over 80% of companies that implemented immersive technologies identified improvements in their ability to innovate and collaborate in their production, manufacturing, and operations work phases, according to a Forrester Consulting study commissioned by Unity.

2.5.10 Retail

Spurred on by the pandemic, the need for retailers to leverage digital twins for design, planning, operations, and more has increased exponentially. The importance of engaging customers online likewise increased overnight, and retailers looked to this technology to create immersive virtual experiences to continue connecting with shoppers. Savvy retailers are embracing digital twins to enhance processes, connect with their customers in new and profound ways, and deliver compelling digital and in-store user experiences. Digital twins have several other applications:

1. Healthcare—Digital twin can help make more reliable and efficient healthcare products. It can also be used in the creation of personalized treatments for patients.

2. Smart cities—This technology can help make efficient city infrastructure sustainable and reliant. Real-time data can help understand traffic patterns and environmental challenges.
3. Transportation and vehicles—Automotive vehicles can be manufactured easily by using this technology. It can also help in predicting critical components of life. This system allows to have controlled monitoring of every item and vehicle.
4. Research and development—Digital twins can help in deeply researching the process or working of products. It can help make things more sustainable, reliant, and efficient.
5. Logistics—It can help create and optimize the logistics and warehouse networks and provide effective working. This will help reduce the time and storage overhead and allow tasks to be completed on time.

2.6 ADVANTAGES OF DIGITAL TWINS

Digital twins offer numerous benefits throughout the life cycle of a product or facility, resulting in higher investment returns, more sustainable assets, and increased customer and end-user happiness [24, 25]. Some of the perks are listed in the following.

2.6.1 Project coordination

Digital twins provide a centralized source of reliable information, allowing thousands of documents, high-fidelity models, and product assets from teams across disciplines to be shared and accessed in real time, improving collaboration, reducing design errors and omissions, and avoiding costly system clashes and construction delays.

2.6.2 Design optimization

Designers can use digital twin simulations to explore and test various design scenarios, such as the seismic tolerance of a bridge or railway, the crash resiliency of a car or e-bike, or the accessibility of medical devices in a patient care room, all without the need for manual iterations or multiple physical prototypes. The ultimate effect is speedier innovation and more sustainable, user-friendly products.

2.6.3 Operational efficiency

Owners and asset managers in occupied buildings and metered energy grids can use digital twins to receive scheduled maintenance alerts and optimize asset performance by automating intelligent occupancy detection,

HVAC, lighting, battery charging, demand response, and water systems via the cloud.

2.6.4 Time and cost savings

According to the Center for Integrating Facility Engineering at Stanford University, adopting digital twins can result in a 40% reduction in non-budgeted change orders, a 9% reduction in life cycle operational costs, a 7% faster project completion time, and a 3.5% increase in facility occupancy.

2.6.5 Future-proofing and sustainability

Digital twins are used to forecast the future behavior and performance of built systems, which are frequently outfitted with connected sensors that can collect environmental data, test whether devices are operating within acceptable limits, and automatically adjust output to reduce project energy consumption and carbon footprint.

2.7 DRAWBACKS OF DIGITAL MANUFACTURING

No doubt, digital twin provides many advantages but this new technology has several drawbacks. Some of them are as follows.

2.7.1 Implementation cost

It is a very expensive investment and requires good money for its implementation; small enterprises can't afford it easily. Moreover, it can reduce their competition in the market. The digital twin system also requires continuous updates and technical support, due to which the cost of its maintenance increases.

It is, therefore, due to such costs that SMEs can rarely afford the technology, hence reducing their competitiveness in the market. Large companies could easily absorb these costs because of huge budgets and resources. The financial barrier to SMEs may hinder innovation and growth, leading to a market dominated by larger players who can afford to implement and leverage digital twin technology. Figure 2.7 illustrates the major drawbacks associated with the digital twin technology.

2.7.2 Lack of skilled workers

Since it is a new technology, the market contains very few experienced workers. And it requires the continuity of trained workers working on the working of the twin. This shortage of workers leads to high wages and sometimes makes it less efficient. Competent workforces are in short supply,

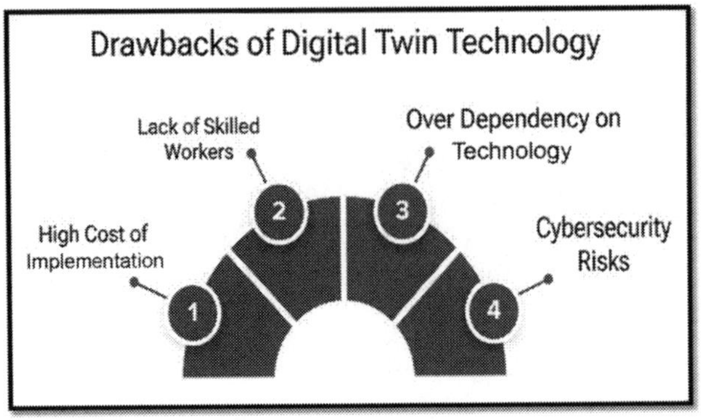

Figure 2.7 The major drawbacks associated with the digital twin technology.

and because of this, companies often have to pay high salaries just to recruit and retain relevantly skilled people, thereby raising operational costs. More importantly, inefficiency and delay in a project on digital twin might be caused by the scarcity. Available workforce may not meet demand. The companies might have to invest heavily in training programs for upskilling their current employees since it is time-consuming and very expensive.

2.7.3 Too much dependency on the technology

This technology fails to successfully do the task whenever any break down, damage, or mishappening happens even if there is a negligible or very small problem in the device. This may lead to delays in the work. For example, if a very small transistor gets damaged due to certain reasons, the whole process of fetching and transferring the data fails. This small problem leads to many problems and consumes time to resolve since the system contains real-time data fetching as one of its important modules.

2.7.4 Cybersecurity threats

Digital twin systems can be subjected to cybersecurity malware and other threats.

This security glitch leads to leakage of confidential information, loss of data, and many more. Also, it loses stakeholder's trust in the company. The complexities and the interconnectedness of digital twins are aspects that cybercriminals easily get attracted to. Ensuring the security of these systems requires the extensive development of cybersecurity measures, upgrading them regularly, and constant monitoring. In any case, even with these measures in place, the risk associated with cyberattacks will be too high.

Successful breaches work to erode stakeholder trust and hurt company reputation, which might lead to financial losses and legal liability.

2.8 CASE STUDY: HOW DIGITAL TWIN TECHNOLOGY CAN HELP IN HEALTHCARE

It is a noteworthy technology, in general, with a lot of impact in many industries, including healthcare. In this case study, a real example will also be given on how such technology is dedicated to helping them boost efficiency and give good impact to the health of their patients. The technology creates virtual replicas of each patient's condition of health, equipped with suitable tools to monitor in real-time and predict results, run a few simulations to fine-tune the treatment plans, spot problems, and make sure everything works as it should [26–29].

Scenario

Let us take the case of a reputed hospital, replete with reputability, handling various types of patients, managing resources, and trying to provide personalized care to every patient. Using digital twin technology, a hospital could create virtual copies in which the health condition of every patient is duplicated. These twin models can be updated in real time by data from electronic health records, medical devices, and patient feedback. The aim is to improve treatments, keep patients safer, and use resources as best as possible.

Working mechanism of the digital twin

The digital twin system will make a digital twin of each patient based upon the patient's medical history, test results, vital signs, and other key data. This model gets constant updates with real-time data from various sources, such as:

1. **Electronic health records:** Detailed case histories can be provided by it with continuous treatment records.
2. **Medical devices:** It will help in the continuous monitoring of vital signs like pulse, blood pressure, and oxygen levels.
3. **Patient feedback:** Directly from the patients through mobile applications or in consultation chambers.

This real-time data is fed to the digital twin, enabling it to present an accurate and dynamic view of the health status of a patient. Medical knowledge combined with historical data and AI/data science empowers the system to make very granulated treatment recommendations at a personalized level. This process will reduce the likelihood that minor issues might escalate into major problems and that treatments are safe and more reliable.

For example, a digital twin tracks a patient with a prior history of cardiac issues in real time. Thus, the system will analyze data from electronic health records (EHRs), wearable devices, and patient feedback in order to try to predict possible cardiac events. In case of picking up some abnormal patterns, an alert will be provided to the medical personnel and the families of patients with preventive actions to avoid a crisis.

Benefits and future prospects

These digital twin technologies bring several benefits to the healthcare setting:

1. **Efficiency in treatment:** By generating treatment recommendations based on real-time data, the digital twin helps health providers make prompt, informed decisions that can significantly improve treatment outcomes.
2. **Better patient safety:** Continuous monitoring and predictive analytics for early identification of potential health problems with timely interventions prevent complications and enhance patient safety.
3. **Resource optimization:** The digital twin system allows for managing resources efficiently, as it can predict the needs of the patient and optimize medical staff, equipment, and other facilities accordingly.
4. **Advanced patient trust:** Timely, personalized, and effective treatment instills patient satisfaction and enhanced trust in the healthcare organization.
5. **Economic Benefits:** This improvement in operational efficiency with better patient outcomes brings cost savings and increased revenues for the health organization.

Such is the immeasurable potentials of digital twin technology in healthcare and other industries. Future development may be involved in more sophisticated AI algorithms, increased health network integrations, and better remote monitoring and telehealth capabilities. All these will get better in terms of healthcare delivery, making it more efficient, personalized, and responsive to patient needs.

2.9 CONCLUSION

Digital twin technology was first used in astronautics and space by NASA for the Apollo 13 lunar exploration mission and the Curiosity Mars rover. The literature review shows that the scale and impact of digital twins continues to expand, making it a rapidly growing IT solution in various industries. As presented in this chapter, most of the manuscripts published in academic journals discuss the application of digital twin solutions in manufacturing, especially in the context of Industry 4.0. Research related to digital twin solutions in manufacturing focuses on production planning and control, which plays a central role in the integration of all data in a production system. Supply chain management is another area where digital dual use cases are examined in the literature. Use cases in construction and healthcare are also on the rise. In the construction industry, the concept of digital twins and mobile equipment and connected objects on a construction site can help to better represent the built project versus the designed project at any given time. Also, it helps reduce errors and rework by allowing updated information to be returned to the field. Digital twin solutions help the healthcare industry to detect undeveloped diseases, experiment with treatments, and improve surgical preparation. Capturing a complete and accurate model of the human body will help doctors detect undeveloped diseases, experiment with treatments, and improve surgical preparation. Researchers are working to develop digital twins to analyze the human body, and significant progress has been made. The Living Heart Project is a mainstream technology for clinical diagnosis, testing, medical device design, and education and training. Digital twin solutions have created the first realistic virtual model of a human organ taking into account blood flow, mechanics, and electricity. Advances in AI, IoT, and cloud computing and the relative power of these technologies have created the basis for digital twin solutions to scale and quickly find applications in manufacturing, supply chain, life sciences, agriculture, energy, and more. AI has enabled digital twins to simulate a complex real-world system. It uses data collected from IoT devices to learn and operate alongside real-world manufacturing systems, continuously identifying areas for improvement and supporting tactical decision-making. It also helps optimize system design to increase efficiency and avoid costly redesign during implementation. Growing demand for automation in various sectors is the factor expected to drive the high demand for digital twin platform during the forecast period. As we recover from the pandemic, digital twin solutions are poised to play an increasingly important role in various industries. The benefits of creating a digital twin solution are huge and have not yet been fully explored. Although there are challenges related to data quality and security, the growing demand for energy and storage, and integration with existing infrastructure, digital twin solutions strive to provide a highly advanced digital revolution to make the world a better place for humanity. In the future, digital twins will expand to more use cases and industries. The solutions will be combined with other technologies, such as AR, for an immersive experience and AI capabilities for better connectivity, insights, and analysis. In addition, more technology allows us to use digital twin solutions, removing the need to check the “real” thing. This exponentially greater insight and analysis, in turn, leads to more opportunities to apply digital twin solutions to complex operations.

REFERENCES

1. Grieves, M. (2014). Digital twin: Manufacturing excellence through virtual factory replication. *White Paper*, 1(2014), 1–7.
2. Boschert, S., & Rosen, R. (2016). Digital twin—The simulation aspect. In P. Hehenberger & D. Bradley (Eds.), *Mechatronic futures* (pp. 59–74). Springer. https://doi.org/10.1007/978-3-319-32156-1_5
3. Fuller, A., Fan, Z., Day, C., & Barlow, C. (2020). Digital twin: Enabling technologies, challenges and open research. *IEEE Access*, 8, 108952–108971.
4. Olsson, T., & Axelsson, J. (2023, June). Systems-of-systems and digital twins: A survey and analysis of the current knowledge. In *2023 18th Annual System of Systems Engineering Conference (SoSe)* (pp. 1–6). IEEE.
5. Schleich, B., Anwer, N., Mathieu, L., & Wartzack, S. (2017). Shaping the digital twin for design and production engineering. *CIRP Annals*, 66(1), 141–144.
6. Mousavi, Y., Gharineiat, Z., Karimi, A. A., McDougall, K., Rossi, A., & Gonizzi Barsanti, S. (2024). Digital twin technology in built environment: A review of applications, capabilities and challenges. *Smart Cities*, 7(5), 2594–2615.
7. El Saddik, A. (2018). Digital twins: The convergence of multimedia technologies. *IEEE Multimedia*, 25(2), 87–92.
8. Tao, F., Qi, Q., Wang, L., & Nee, A. Y. C. (2019). Digital twins and cyber–physical systems toward smart manufacturing and industry 4.0: Correlation and comparison. *Engineering*, 5(4), 653–661.
9. Boje, C., Guerriero, A., Kubicki, S., & Rezgui, Y. (2020). Towards a semantic construction digital twin: Directions for future research. *Automation in Construction*, 114, 103179.
10. W. C. Regli (2021). Cyber-physical systems and digital twins: Key aspects, research requirements, and future directions. *IEEE Internet Computing*, 25(2), 44–52.
11. Leng, J., Wang, D., Shen, W., Li, X., Liu, Q., & Chen, X. (2021). Digital twins-based smart manufacturing system design in Industry 4.0: A review. *Journal of Manufacturing Systems*, 60, 119–137.
12. Programace. (n.d.). 4 main types of digital twins and their characteristics. https://program-ace.com/blog/types-of-digital-twins/
13. altexsoft. (n.d.). Digital twins: Technology, use cases, and implementation tips. www.altexsoft.com/blog/digital-twins/
14. Attaran, M., & Celik, B. G. (2023). Digital twin: Benefits, use cases, challenges, and opportunities. *Decision Analytics Journal*, 6, 100165.
15. Researchandmarkets.com. (2022). Digital twins market by technology, twinning type, cyber- to-physical solutions, use cases and applications in industry verticals 2022–2027, Online: www.researchandmarkets.com/reports/5308850/digital-twins-market-by-technology-twinning?utm_source=dynamic&utm_medium=CI&utm_code=6q68tb&utm_campaign=1366076+The+Future+of+the+Digital+Twins+Industry+to+2025+in+Manufacturing%2c+Smart+Cities%2c+Automotive%2c+Healthcare+and+Transport&utm_exec=joca220cid

16. Technavio. (2022). Digital twin market by end-user, deployment, and geography – Forecast and analysis 2021–2025, Online: https://finance.yahoo.com/news/digital-twin-market-size-share-120000739.html?guccounter=1&guce_referrer=aHR0cHM6Ly93d3cuZ29vZ2xlLmNvbS8&guce_referrer_sig=AQAAANw30cE0o4ot3uSikYsCTMZKDlwV8qPgPuDcskgiBsyv9hr8eEUrRfmyhZU8rR4nm_tkKSAy8vQMlARm-1OtUtHV4hY1Q-qkgDexWDB69KttQZ2_QObuRN-U4lAH5-aYSP6tN9q73O9bcDe_jrB39ImBpLS5XIb-N-DeLPTZX-rY
17. Agrawal, A., Thiel, R., Jain, P., Singh, V., & Fischer, M. (2023). Digital twin: Where do humans fit in?. *Automation in Construction*, 148, 104749.
18. Coursera. (n.d.). What is a digital twin? Definition, types, and uses. www.coursera.org/articles/digital-twin
19. Eckhart, M., & Ekelhart, A. (2019). Digital twins for cyber-physical systems security: State of the art and outlook. In S. Biffl, M. Eckhart, A. Lüder, & E. Weippl (Eds.), *Security and Quality in Cyber-Physical Systems Engineering* (pp. 383–412). Springer. https://doi.org/10.1007/978-3-030-25312-7_14
20. Shao, G., Jain, S., Laroque, C., Lee, L. H., Lendermann, P., & Rose, O. (2019, December). Digital twin for smart manufacturing: The simulation aspect. In *2019 Winter Simulation Conference (WSC)* (pp. 2085–2098). IEEE.
21. Bruynseels, M., Santoni de Sio, F., & Van den Hoven, J. (2018). Digital twins in healthcare: Ethical implications of an emerging engineering paradigm. *Frontiers in Genetics*, 9, 31.
22. Toobler. (n.d.). What are the 4 types of digital twins? www.toobler.com/blog/types-of-digital-twins
23. Grübel, J., Thrash, T., Aguilar, L., Gath-Morad, M., Chatain, J., Sumner, R. W., ... & Schinazi, V. R. (2022). The hitchhiker's guide to fused twins: A review of access to digital twins in situ in smart cities. *Remote Sensing*, 14(13), 3095.
24. Minerva, R., Biru, A., & Rotondi, D. (2015). Towards a definition of the Internet of Things (IoT). *IEEE Internet Initiative*, 1(1), 1–86.
25. DeMarchi, M., Bonello, A., Francalanza, E., & Rauch, E. (2024). A digital twin for SMEs in the context of Industry 5.0. *Procedia CIRP*, 126, 242–247.
26. Chen, C. M., Miao, Q., Kumar, S., & Wu, T. Y. (2023). Privacy-preserving authentication scheme for digital twin-enabled autonomous vehicle environments. *Transactions on Emerging Telecommunications Technologies*, 34(11), e4751.
27. Hadraoui, H. E., Ouahabi, N., Bazi, N. E., Laayati, O., Zegrari, M., & Chebak, A. (2024). Toward an intelligent diagnosis and prognostic health management system for autonomous electric vehicle powertrains: A novel distributed intelligent digital twin-based architecture. *IEEE Access*, 12, 110729–110761.
28. Kuchuk, H., & Malokhvii, E. (2024). Integration of IOT with cloud, fog, and edge computing: A review. *Advanced Information Systems*, 8(2), 65–78.
29. Ullah, H., Nair, N. G., Moore, A., Nugent, C., Muschamp, P., & Cuevas, M. (2019). 5G communication: An overview of vehicle-to-everything, drones, and healthcare use-cases. *IEEE Access*, 7, 37251–37268.

Chapter 3

Digital twin technology for better health

Puja S. Prasad

3.1 INTRODUCTION

A digital twin is a virtual representation of a physical entity or system that mirrors its real-world counterpart in real time. In healthcare, digital twins replicate individual patients, organs, or even entire healthcare systems. These digital replicas are created using a combination of data from medical records, imaging technologies such as MRI (magnetic resonance imaging) and CT (computed tomography) scans, genetic information, and real-time patient monitoring devices.

Digital twin technology is revolutionizing healthcare systems by leveraging real-time data integration, advanced analytics, and virtual simulations to enhance patient care, enable predictive analytics, optimize clinical operations, and facilitate training and simulation. With the ability to gather and analyze a wealth of patient data from various sources, digital twins can offer personalized treatment plans based on individual characteristics, medical history, and real-time physiological data [1]. Predictive analytics and preventive interventions are made possible by machine learning algorithms, allowing for early detection of health risks and proactive interventions. Figure 3.1 simply illustrates the application areas of digital twin in healthcare.

Through workflow analysis and resource allocation, digital twins can optimize clinical operations, resulting in more efficient workflows and better patient care. Furthermore, digital twins can give medical practitioners a secure and authentic setting in which to practice difficult procedures and improve their skills. Digital twin adoption in healthcare might lead to major improvements in patient outcomes, increased patient safety, and stimulate innovation in the sector. Using digital twin technology; real-world systems or items can be virtually replicated. Digital twins are used in healthcare to simulate specific individuals, medical devices, or entire hospitals.

Key components of a digital twin

1. Physical entity: The digital twin's representation of the real, tangible system, process, or thing.

DOI: 10.1201/9781003498117-3

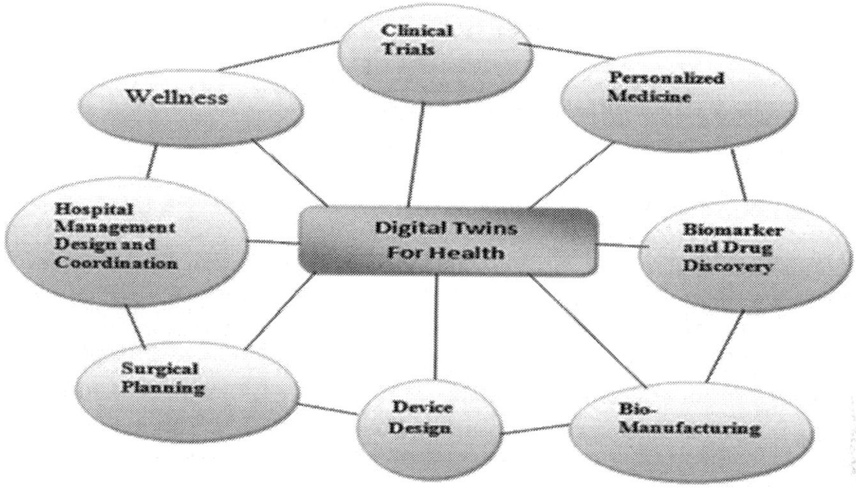

Figure 3.1 Digital twins for healthcare.

2. Digital model: The digital depiction, which comprises data, simulations, and 3D models.
3. Data connectivity: The digital twin receives real-time data from sensors and Internet of Things devices on the physical entity.
4. Analytics and algorithms: Data is processed by artificial intelligence (AI), machine learning, and analytics tools to produce insights and predictive powers.

The digital twin can be analyzed and interacted with by users through dashboards and visualization tools [2].

Benefits:

- Enhanced performance: Digital twins aid in operational optimization by simulating various scenarios.
- Predictive maintenance: Recognize and stop equipment malfunctions before they happen.
- Improved decision-making: Offer data-driven perspectives for more effective strategic planning.
- Cost savings: Streamline procedures, increase productivity, and decrease downtime.
- Innovation: Provide fast virtual environment prototyping and testing for new designs or procedures.

3.2 UNDERSTANDING DIGITAL TWIN TECHNOLOGY

3.2.1 Digital twin technology relies on data

Digital twin data (DTD) gathering refers to the gathering of physical entity-related data, virtual model-related data, service-related data, and domain knowledge. These four kinds of data constitute the foundation of DTD, upon which the fusion data and connection data can be derived. In relation to the physical entity-related data, the following types of data can be obtained: static data (such as entity attributes, identification, and characteristics) can be obtained through off-line measurement and sampling inspection; dynamic data (such as entity state, environment parameters, and abrupt disturbances) can be collected in real time using sensors, embedded systems, radio frequency identification (RFID), and other methods. Usually, modeling, simulating, and testing those geometric, physical, behavioral, and rule models produce the virtual model-related data. Real-time simulation outputs, simulation logs, and manual manuals can all be used to collect data. Specifically, because physical model-based simulations, such computational fluid dynamics (CFD) simulations, can be laborious and even imprecise, a hybrid strategy that blends data-driven methodologies with physical models can be utilized to enhance. In addition, the DTD would also extract essential information from the existing IT systems, such as product life cycle management (PLM) system, product data management (PDM) system, manufacturing execution system (MES), and supervisory control and data acquisition (SCADA) system, which store large amounts of data across the life cycle of the physical entity [3].

3.2.2 Digital twin data interaction

Connection data between any two parts of DTD supports the real-time interactions. First, it is necessary to select the suitable data to support the message transmission between any pair of two parts. In the interest of data transmission, the data is further processed by filtering algorithms, dimensionality reduction algorithms, and relevance analysis algorithms, which are intended to remove data noise and redundancy. Then the data can be transferred between the DTD parts through some types of data transmission protocols and formats suggested by the ISO 23247-4 (Digital twin manufacturing framework—Part 4: Information exchange). During the transmission, the consistency of connection data can be evaluated by calculating the data distances. To better illustrate the interaction, take an autoclave (a key equipment for composites curing) as an example. During curing, temperature distribution of the mold within the autoclave is an important quality indicator, since it largely affects the deformation degree of the composite components. To monitor the component quality, the real mold temperatures are collected by thermocouples. However, the CFD simulation can also be used to create a virtual model that mimics the anticipated mold temperature distribution. To guarantee that the actual cure is carried out as simulated, data interaction between the virtual model and the physical equipment is utilized. In this case, the difference between the maximum and minimum temperatures on the mold upper surface—a major feature reflecting the mold temperature distribution—can be chosen as the connection data, omitting other unnecessary or duplicate facts. The temperature discrepancies between the simulated and collected mold can then be exchanged and compared. The desired composite quality would be attained if their variance is consistently contained within a predetermined threshold. If not, it is necessary to identify the perturbing factors creating the inconsistency, such as unequal airflow field in the autoclave, deteriorating insulation of the autoclave wall, and abrupt changes of curing conditions. These factors should be eliminated by adjusting parameters of the physical autoclave (e.g., heating speed, air speed, pressure) or by maintaining the equipment, which aims at reducing negative effects caused by the disturbances, to keep the collected data close with the simulated ones [4].

3.3 DIGITAL TWIN DATA STORAGE

Data pertaining to physical entities, virtual models, and services that are gathered from various application objects and situations ought to be converted into a single sharing method. In order to achieve this, data must first be standardized in their representation, which entails describing its various attributes, including their content, format, sampling frequency, historical data accumulation, interface, and communication protocol. The properties should then be enclosed with the relevant constraints. Limitations on the accumulation of historical data, for instance, can aid in the filtering of those unqualified application conditions in which digital twin (DT) is not applicable because there is insufficient data. When restrictions are unsatisfactorily met, it means that the related application requirements are not met. For the qualified ones, on the one hand, data with various formats can be converted into a standardized format, for example, eXtensible markup language (XML), for the sake of easier data sharing. On the other hand, since data from different objects would be transmitted by different interfaces and communication protocols, a middleware is needed to support the unified data access to the database, shielding the heterogeneity.

Mining association links among DTD facilitates knowledge discovery. First, preprocessing techniques such as data filtering, data reduction, and feature extraction are used to eliminate unnecessary and irrelevant data from data gathered from the physical entity, virtual model, and service. Second, alignments in both space and time are carried out. For instance, data can be transformed into the same coordinate system in space and time using the least squares method. Next, using techniques like K-means, Apriori algorithm, Pearson correlation analysis38, and others, the relationships (such complementarity, similarity, and causation) between the data are mined. Based on this, further knowledge (e.g., behavioral patterns of the physical entity, simulation mechanisms of virtual models, and behavior-performance mappings between different parts of DT) can be deduced through knowledge reasoning based on logic rules, distributed representations, and neural network, etc., and the deduced knowledge can be expressed in the form of knowledge graph. To support the subsequent data fusion, two kinds of data associations are especially important, that is, the similar relation and complementary relation. The former refers to the relation between data with similar attributes, values, and changing trends, whereas the latter refers to the relation between multimodal data from multiple sources, which can describe the same attribute or behavior from different perspectives [5].

3.4 DIGITAL TWIN DATA FUSION

Existing work on data fusion focuses primarily on the merging of data from the physical world (e.g., fusing sensor data with manual data), while few efforts have been devoted to fusing data from both the physical and virtual worlds. In contrast, DTD fusion involves a holistic merging of physical entity-related data, virtual model-related data, service-related data, and domain knowledge. DTD fusion includes the following aspects. Methods like the weighted average method, Dempster–Shafer theory, and Kalman filter can be used to fuse physical entity-related data with similar virtual model-related data and service-related data to reduce the information entropy in the event that the physical entity-related data is disturbed by environment perturbations, sensor failures, and human interferences. This can help to lessen the fuzziness, unpredictability, and uncertainty of the data. Similarly, techniques like neural networks and the Bayesian approach can be used to combine data with comparable physical entity-related data in order to increase accuracy and dependability in the event that the data connected to virtual models and services differ from reality. Techniques like the weighted average approach can be used for the complimentary multimodal data from various DTD sections [6].

3.5 DIGITAL TWIN DATA EVOLUTION

A dynamic process that continuously adds, processes, and then fuses new data with old data is what defines DTD evolution. The data relation network that was constructed based on the complicated network can be used to explain this process. As new data is added to the network, new association relations are created between it and the historical data by preprocessing the new data, aligning it with the historical data, and then using data mining algorithms to extract association relations from the aligned data. Finally, the new data is fused with related or complementary relations for data supplementation and correction. To lessen the reliance on manual labor, an automatic fusion mechanism can direct this process. Information entropy is used to assess how well data evolution works. In turn, such rules can be used to guide the subsequent data fusions with respect to the selection of fusion data, and methods, to ensure iterative optimization and information growth [7].

3.6 DIGITAL TWIN DATA SERVITIZATION

DTD servitization aims to enable users to access data through on-demand services, including multiple aspects as follows.

The first step is to group different digital resources into services. These services have different functions, like searching, processing, and virtualization of data, as well as inputs, like volume, type, and feature; outputs, like processed data and visual diagrams; quality, like time, cost, and reliability; and states, like working and idle. Relevant services for data extraction, processing, and visualization can be prescribed based on a user demand (e.g., the query of equipment status data, part remaining life data, and maintenance advisory data), respectively. The individual services can then be joined to create an integrated service solution while adhering to pertinent constraints (such time and cost). Such techniques as multi-objective optimization, demand decomposition, and similarity matching are examples of related techniques. Regarding the DTD visualization (i.e., a specific type of DTD service), the creation of a digital twin requires data, whether from sensors, scans, medical records, insurance records or other statistically relevant datasets [8]. It may also rely on high-quality 3D images and animations to accurately represent physical systems. Figure 3.2 illustrates the high level of personal digital twin from a personalized healthcare perspective [9].

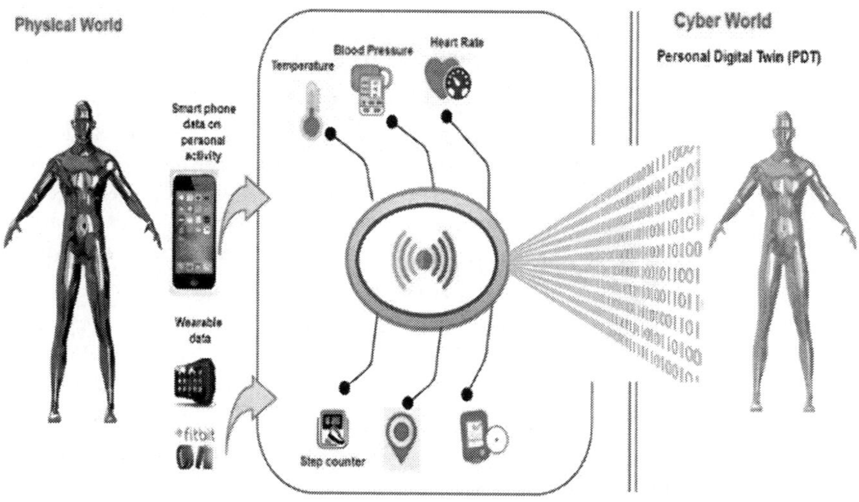

Figure 3.2 The high level of personal digital twin from a personalized healthcare perspective.

3.7 APPLICATIONS IN HEALTHCARE

Since one person is different from the next in a multitude of ways, the majority of treatments designed for the "average patient" are incredibly ineffective for the "actual patient." From unsatisfactory surgery and ineffectual medication to device rejection or replacement, personalized medicine will require the use of digital twins in order to transition from one-size-fits-all treatment. The various ways that digital twin technology will advance medical treatment [10].

1. Diagnosis and treatment decision support—software as a medical device

   Diagnosis will be aided by the patient's digital twin feed from several health data sources, including imaging records, in-person measurements, laboratory results, and genetic data. The patient model will use statistical models to infer the missing parameters and replicate the patient's current state of health as determined by the clinical data that is currently available. For example, noninvasive flow field characterization and diagnostic metric computation are made possible by the coupling of CFD and cardiovascular imaging.
2. Patient monitoring—wearables
   - Digital twin on the cloud will be fed with real-time data via increasingly compact and comfy wearables (sensors). With sufficient knowledge of how diseases progress and ongoing patient data collection through health trackers (biometric, behavioral, emotional, cognitive, psychosocial, etc.), we can create models that identify early symptoms, enabling clinicians and users to diagnose patients before they become ill. In addition, we will be able to assess the efficacy of the medication as it is being administered.
   - A plethora of data sources, including medical records, lab test results, pharmacy data, wellness and disease management data, well-being device-generated data, and social determinants like zip code, local weather, and purchasing behaviors, are currently available to feed our digital twin and customize our risk factors.
   - Surgery simulation—surgery risk assessment

     Surgery by definition is personalized. From the current state to the best outcome, the surgery is tailored to the patient's needs. Personalization is critical to increase intervention success and reduce patient risk. Digital twins will help by simulating an invasive clinical procedure to predict the outcome before the therapy is selected. From medical device selection (position, orientation, dimension, etc.) to surgical variable determination (magnitude, angle, shape, etc.).

3. Medical devices design and optimization—MedTech
   - Two realms converge here. On the one hand, we have the patient's digital twin that has the specific characteristic of the patient and on the other hand, the medical device's digital twin that captures the device design. We can correlate both models to see what happens when a particular device is installed into a specific patient. This is the case of populations that cannot be investigated clinically without harm, such as in patients with rare diseases or pediatric patients.
   - Digital twins are also very useful in optimization tasks like the improvement of a device's performance by running hundreds of simulations with different conditions and different patients. Besides, with the emergence of 3D printing technology, patient digital twins can lead to the personalization of medical devices by creating unique designs for each patient.
4. Drug development and dosage optimization—in silico clinical trials We are able to computationally treat a digital twin with thousands of medications to see which one or ones might work best in that particular situation. Still, this need not end with the medications that are now on the market. We can test novel, potentially effective medications to determine which has a higher chance of success and the ideal dosage by building a virtual cohort of real patients with similar symptoms but distinct phenotypes. Reducing the number of clinical trials required can be achieved by improving the first shoot [11].

   In silico clinical trial will shed light on processes that take years to be observed in vivo or assess the risk of rare cases where a randomized clinical study would need thousands of patients to observe just a few of such cases.

3.8 FUTURE DIRECTIONS

Explore emerging trends and potential future applications of digital twin technology in healthcare, such as virtual clinical trials, remote patient monitoring (RPM), and AI-driven diagnostics.

3.8.1 Virtual clinical trials

The use of digital health technologies—such as mobile devices, mobile apps, remote monitoring devices, and online social interaction platforms—into study design has become a growing trend in the field of clinical trials. Digital health technologies can be utilized in virtual clinical trials to gather data at every phase of the study, enhance trial participant recruitment and retention, facilitate online informed consent, measure clinical endpoints in real time, and continuously monitor adverse events [12].

By enabling trial participants to participate from the comfort of their own homes instead of needing to go to a trial location, digital health technology may improve participant engagement and retention. Engaging patients with mobility challenges or those who reside in remote locations, where it can be difficult to go.

Furthermore, rather than only providing a snapshot of pertinent health information during site visits, data collected through digital health technologies may allow for continuous real-time data collection of endpoints throughout a trial participant's daily life. Information gathered via digital health technology can be used by researchers and healthcare professionals to improve tracking and gain a better knowledge of the impact of treatments and the course of disease.

3.8.2 Remote patient monitoring (RPM)

RPM is a subset of homecare telehealth that enables people to collect patient-generated health data (PGHD) and transmit it to medical practitioners via mobile devices and technology. Typical physiological data that can be gathered with RPM programs are blood pressure, heart rate, weight, and vital signs. A specialized telehealth computer system or software application that can be loaded on a computer, smartphone, or tablet is used to transmit patient data from the point of collection to the doctor's office.

RPM is widely utilized to assist patients in need of elder, post-discharge, or chronic care. It can inform healthcare organizations of possible health risks or maintain patient data between visits by connecting high-risk patients to remote monitoring. Additionally, companies that choose to employ RPM could be used by businesses that want to record workmen's compensation cases, making sure employees are on the right path to return to work.

3.8.3 Examples of remote patient monitoring technology

RPM technology can range from handheld medical devices to online platforms that allow patients to input data. A few examples include:

- Glucose meters for patients with diabetes.
- Heart rate or blood pressure monitors.
- Continuous surveillance monitors that can locate patients with conditions like dementia and alert healthcare professionals of an event like a fall.
- Remote infertility treatment and monitoring.
- At-home tests that can keep substance abuse patients accountable for and on track with their goals.
- Caloric intake or diet logging programs.

3.8.4 How remote patient monitoring works

Although RPM approaches can differ based on the apparatus being utilized or the state being observed, the majority of technologies include comparable parts. The first is a wirelessly enabled sensor that records and stores data related to particular physiological characteristics. A mechanism to link this storage to other sensors, databases of healthcare providers, and relevant apps must also be included.

Applications usually give users an interface via which they may monitor, evaluate, and see treatment recommendations based on data.

RPM devices gather data, which is then transmitted to the appropriate area and kept in a relational database. This makes it possible to examine healthcare organizations using wireless telecommunications data as isolated cases or in relation to a patient's whole medical history. The gadget can frequently notify patients when a healthcare provider has looked over the data or detects an issue that requires the patient to come in.

3.8.5 Benefits of remote patient monitoring

- Increased patient engagement—RPM devices allow patients to play a crucial role in managing and understanding their own health conditions.
- Improved quality of care—RPM gives patients and healthcare providers access to more relevant patient data, thus improving overall quality and value-based care.
- Better access to healthcare—Since RPM allows patients to complete basic health testing on their own, healthcare professionals are allowed to treat more patients.
- Higher levels of education and support—RPM gives patients information and feedback about their personal conditions daily, educating them and providing support.
- Patient assurance—Constant monitoring can give patients a peace of mind that any potential issues will be identified in a timely manner.

3.8.6 AI-driven diagnostics

It is a way to detect insights, ease the diagnostic burden of healthcare workers, and reduce their own risk of infection. Healthcare institutions that have already implemented AI-driven diagnostics are seeing a positive impact—reduced time for diagnosis, higher accuracy in diagnosis, and the ability to monitor patients remotely. These benefits are not only reducing and improving diagnosis but are also making it safer for healthcare workers to provide care. There are three recent examples:

1. **Reduced time for diagnosis**
   A medical data analysis company in Beijing, LinkingMed, is able to diagnose pneumonia, a complication of COVID-19, in less than a minute. The diagnosis is done from analyzing a CT scan, and its test results are accurate 92% of the time, with a test recall rate of 97% [8].
2. **Higher accuracy**
   Many AI diagnostics platforms have been outperforming medical experts, especially on medical imaging tasks. A team of Google and Imperial College researchers recently developed an AI model that can diagnose breast cancer from mammograms. During testing, the tool not only outperformed individual radiologists but it was just as effective as two radiologists working together.
3. **Remote patient monitoring**
   AI-powered remote intensive care unit (ICU) has been introduced by two Israeli hospitals to assist COVID-19 patients [7]. Their platform is taught to anticipate respiratory decline, allowing for early interventions that could potentially improve the course of the patient's treatment. This enables medical personnel to determine the severity of an illness from a distance using a command center. Why are healthcare professionals hesitant to use this kind of technology when it has so many advantages? Fears that medical personnel may be supplanted by AI are among the reasons.

   It's true that a lot of the monotonous duties that healthcare staff must perform could possibly be replaced by AI. These platforms, however, are meant to support, not entirely replace, medical professionals in their decision-making. AI can manage scan backlogs, provide routine or preliminary analysis of health data, and offer insight when a healthcare worker is not available or are limited. Diagnosing patient is a very delicate task. Implementing AI-driven diagnostics throughout a healthcare organization allows healthcare providers to provide a higher level of care in less time than before.

- Orion's NLP Platform comprehends textual data, like doctors' reports, with human-like interpretive intelligence. It connects the diagnosis with MRIs, CT scans, mammograms, and X-rays to train machines. In the end, machines work faster and more accurately, work 24/7, facilitate remote working, and allow clinics to handle more patients in less time.

3.9 REAL-WORLD EXAMPLES OF DIGITAL TWINS IN HEALTHCARE

There are two real-world examples of digital twins in healthcare, showing the new approaches through which this technology is transforming patient care and healthcare administration.

Babylon digital twin for e-medical records

Babylon digital twin is the leading platform that helps individuals see the whole picture of their medical records and other health information. Employing advanced AI technology coupled with sophisticated deep learning techniques, the system provides essential information regarding organ status and diseases' predisposing factors [13].

Currently, the platform focuses on only 20 diseases, but its expansion to capture more than 80 diseases is anticipated in the future. Babylon's digital twin confirms the increasing role of individual health data that enables people to stay on top of their health and well-being.

Hospital ward management digital twin at Mater Hospital Dublin

Mater Hospital Dublin is an example of the transformative nature of digital twinning in healthcare in enhancing the smooth functioning of hospitals and healthcare facilities. Mater Hospital Dublin utilized 3D digital replicas to critically evaluate its daily ward operations with the aim of improving the radiology department. As a result, a significant reduction in patient wait time for critical CT and MRI scans marked a real improvement in patient experience under the digital twin initiative [14].

The integration of workflow-simulated digital twins at the Mater Hospital led to a decrease of about 240 minutes in the wait time for CT or MRI scans. Such optimization contributed to shorter patient turnaround times, resulting in the increase of MRI scan and CT scan capacities by 32% and 26%, respectively.

3.10 CONCLUSION

Digital twin technology holds immense promise for revolutionizing healthcare by enhancing patient care, optimizing medical processes, and advancing medical research. However, successful implementation requires addressing challenges related to data security, integration, and regulatory compliance. Healthcare delivery, operational effectiveness, and patient outcomes can all be greatly enhanced by the use of digital twins, which is a revolutionary development in the field. Digital twins offer a comprehensive and dynamic perspective of individual patients and healthcare systems by utilizing real-time data, sophisticated simulations, and predictive analytics.

REFERENCES

1. Corral-Acero, J., Margara, F., Marciniak, M., Rodero, C., Loncaric, F., Feng, Y., ... & Lamata, P. (2020). The 'Digital Twin' to enable the vision of precision cardiology. *European Heart Journal*, 41(48), 4556–4564.
2. Schwartz, S. M., Wildenhaus, K., Bucher, A., & Byrd, B. (2020). Digital twins and the emerging science of self: Implications for digital health experience design and "small" data. *Frontiers in Computer Science*, 2, 31.

3. Morrison, T. M., Pathmanathan, P., Adwan, M., & Margerrison, E. (2018). Advancing regulatory science with computational modeling for medical devices at the FDA's Office of Science and Engineering Laboratories. *Frontiers in Medicine*, 5, 241.
4. Pappalardo, F., Russo, G., Tshinanu, F. M., & Viceconti, M. (2019). In silico clinical trials: Concepts and early adoptions. *Briefings in Bioinformatics*, 20(5), 1699–1708.
5. Niederer, S. A., Lumens, J., & Trayanova, N. A. (2019). Computational models in cardiology. *Nature Reviews Cardiology*, 16(2), 100–111.
6. Shameer, K., Johnson, K. W., Glicksberg, B. S., Dudley, J. T., & Sengupta, P. P. (2018). Machine learning in cardiovascular medicine: Are we there yet?. *Heart*, 104(14), 1156–1164.
7. Lovell, T. (n.d.). Two Israeli hospitals launch AI-based tele-ICU to support COVID-19 patients. www.healthcareitnews.com/news/emea/two-israeli-hospitals-launch-ai-based-tele-icu-support-covid-19-patients#:~:text=Artificial%20Intelligence-Two%20Israeli%20hospitals%20launch%20AI%2Dbased%20tele%2DICU%20to%20support,detect%20respiratory%20deterioration%20in%20advance
8. Orion Innovation. (n.d.). AI-driven diagnostics strengthen healthcare during pandemic. www.orioninc.com/blog/ai-driven-diagnostics-strengthen-healthcare/#:~:text=A%20medical%20data%20analysis%20company,test%20recall%20rate%20of%2097%25
9. Sahal, R., Alsamhi, S. H., & Brown, K. N. (2022). Personal digital twin: A close look into the present and a step towards the future of personalised healthcare industry. *Sensors*, 22(15), 5918.
10. Katsoulakis, E., Wang, Q., Wu, H., Shahriyari, L., Fletcher, R., Liu, J., ... & Deng, J. (2024). Digital twins for health: A scoping review. *NPJ Digital Medicine*, 7(1), 77.
11. Chen, J., Yi, C., Du, H., Niyato, D., Kang, J., Cai, J., & Shen, X. (2024). A revolution of personalized healthcare: Enabling human digital twin with mobile AIGC. *IEEE Network*, 38(6), 234–242.
12. Chen, J., Shi, Y., Yi, C., Du, H., Kang, J., & Niyato, D. (2024). Generative AI-driven human digital twin in IoT-healthcare: A comprehensive survey. *IEEE Internet of Things Journal*, 11(21), 34749–34773.
13. Babylone. (n.d.). Babylon Health United States. www.babylonhealth.com/us/what-we-offer/chatbot
14. Bland, D. (2018). Hospital ward management digital twin. Challenge advisory. www.challenge.org/insights/digital-twin-hospital-management/

Chapter 4

Treatment and therapy with digital twin technology

Revolutionizing Alzheimer's disease detection and care

Anand Jawdekar and Ayush Kumawat

4.1 INTRODUCTION

Alzheimer's disease is a progressive neurological disorder primarily affecting memory, cognition, and behavior. It is the leading cause of dementia, a condition marked by a decline in cognitive abilities that significantly disrupts daily living. As the disease advances, individuals may encounter memory loss, struggles with language and communication, and alterations in mood and behavior. This condition affects millions worldwide, and its prevalence is expected to increase as the population grows older [1, 2].

Early detection of Alzheimer's disease is critical for multiple reasons. First, it allows for timely interventions that may help slow the progression of the disease and maintain quality of life for longer [3]. Second, it enables individuals and their families to plan for the future and access appropriate support services [4]. However, diagnosing Alzheimer's disease accurately can be challenging, especially in its early stages when symptoms may be subtle [5, 6].

4.2 HOW DIGITAL TWIN TECHNOLOGY COULD HELP IN HEALTHCARE

Digital twin technology presents a promising opportunity for enhancing healthcare outcomes, particularly in the detection and management of Alzheimer's disease. Digital twins are virtual representations of physical objects or systems, developed by integrating data from various sources such as sensors, imaging, and electronic health records (EHRs).

In healthcare, digital twin technology can be applied to create personalized models of patients, including their physiological and neurological characteristics. These models can be continuously updated with real-time data, allowing healthcare professionals to monitor disease progression, predict outcomes, and tailor treatments accordingly.

For Alzheimer's disease, digital twin technology could revolutionize the diagnostic process by providing more accurate and objective methods for

DOI: 10.1201/9781003498117-4

identifying the disease's onset and progression. By analyzing patterns in brain imaging data, such as magnetic resonance imaging (MRI) scans, digital twin models can help detect subtle changes associated with Alzheimer's disease at an early stage, even before symptoms become apparent. This early detection could enable healthcare providers to intervene sooner, potentially slowing the progression of the disease and improving patient outcomes [7].

Furthermore, digital twins can facilitate the development and testing of new therapies by providing a platform for simulating how different interventions may impact individual patients [8]. This personalized approach to treatment could lead to more effective therapies tailored to each patient's specific needs.

Digital twin technology in healthcare can provide numerous benefits:

Personalized medicine and digital twin applications in healthcare

The integration of digital twin technology into healthcare represents a transformative approach to diagnosing, treating, and managing complex diseases, including Alzheimer's. By leveraging real-time data and patient-specific simulations, digital twins enable precise and personalized care, enhancing both clinical and operational outcomes.

Personalized medicine

Digital twin technology supports the shift toward individualized care by creating dynamic, patient-specific models:

- Patient-centric models: Digital replicas of patients simulate their unique physiological and pathological characteristics, allowing clinicians to test potential treatments and predict outcomes with high accuracy.
- Optimized treatment plans: Interventions can be tailored to align with the patient's specific responses, minimizing side effects and enhancing therapeutic effectiveness.

Predictive maintenance in medical equipment

Maintaining the reliability of critical medical devices is essential for uninterrupted care:

- Real-time equipment monitoring: Continuous tracking of medical devices ensures early detection of potential malfunctions, enabling timely interventions.
- Minimized downtime: Predictive analytics reduce equipment downtime, ensuring availability and functionality during critical periods.

Clinical trials and drug development

Digital twins streamline clinical trials, accelerating drug discovery and improving protocol refinement:

- Simulated clinical testing: Virtual trials on digital twin models allow researchers to explore various scenarios, predict potential side effects, and refine study protocols without exposing participants to unnecessary risks.
- Expedited drug development: Simulating drug efficacy and safety on virtual models shortens development cycles and lowers research costs, paving the way for faster therapeutic advancements.

Operational efficiency in healthcare systems

Optimizing hospital workflows and resource management is critical for improving patient care:

- Hospital operations modeling: Digital twins model the dynamics of hospital workflows, aiding in the optimization of patient flow, resource allocation, and overall efficiency.
- Proactive capacity planning: Predictive models anticipate patient influx, enabling hospitals to adjust staffing and resources in real-time to meet demand.

Remote monitoring and telemedicine

Digital twins enhance the capabilities of remote healthcare delivery, promoting proactive and preventive care:

- Continuous health monitoring: Real-time tracking of patient health data allows clinicians to detect anomalies early, reducing the risk of complications.
- Enhanced telehealth consultations: Incorporating digital twin data into telemedicine provides clinicians with a comprehensive view of the patient's condition, resulting in more informed and accurate consultations.

Surgical planning and risk mitigation

The use of digital twins in surgical preparation improves precision and reduces risks:

- Preoperative simulation: Complex surgeries can be planned and practiced on a virtual model of the patient, ensuring optimal approaches and minimizing uncertainties during actual procedures.
- Complication prediction: Potential risks and complications are identified in advance, enabling surgeons to prepare for contingencies effectively.

4.3 UTILIZING MRI IMAGES FOR DETECTION

MRI is a widely used medical imaging technology that employs strong magnetic fields and radio waves to create detailed visualizations of internal body structures. Unlike imaging modalities such as X-rays or CT scans, MRI does not involve ionizing radiation, making it a safer diagnostic tool for patients.

In the context of healthcare, MRI is indispensable for diagnosing and monitoring various conditions, including neurological disorders like Alzheimer's disease. Its ability to generate high-resolution images of the brain enables clinicians to detect abnormalities and monitor changes over time [9].

When applied to Alzheimer's disease, MRI plays a critical role in identifying structural and functional alterations in the brain. These changes often include the shrinkage of key regions associated with memory and cognition, as well as signs of abnormal protein accumulation characteristic of Alzheimer's pathology.

Key techniques in MRI for Alzheimer's detection

1. Structural MRI:
    - Atrophy detection: Identifies shrinkage in critical brain regions, particularly the hippocampus.
    - Volumetric analysis: Quantifies changes in the volume of brain areas linked to Alzheimer's progression.
2. Functional MRI (fMRI):
    - Brain activity mapping: Evaluates variations in brain activity and connectivity, offering insights into functional disruptions caused by Alzheimer's.
3. Diffusion tensor imaging (DTI):
    - White matter integrity: Examines the condition of white matter pathways, which may deteriorate as the disease advances.

Incorporating machine learning and artificial intelligence (AI)
The integration of machine learning and AI with MRI technology has revolutionized the detection of Alzheimer's disease:

- Automated analysis: AI algorithms analyze MRI data to recognize patterns indicative of Alzheimer's progression.
- Feature extraction: Machine learning models extract critical features, such as texture, shape, and volumetric changes, to enable precise classification and prediction.

Benefits of MRI in Alzheimer's detection

- Early diagnosis: MRI can detect subtle brain changes, facilitating diagnosis before noticeable symptoms emerge.

- Non-invasive approach: This technique provides a detailed and safe method to assess brain structure and functionality without exposing patients to harmful radiation.

By combining the high-resolution imaging capabilities of MRI with advanced machine learning algorithms, this approach offers a robust framework for the early and accurate detection of Alzheimer's disease, significantly enhancing diagnostic precision and patient outcomes.

4.4 TRADITIONAL WAYS OF ALZHEIMER'S DISEASE DETECTION

Before the advent of advanced imaging techniques like MRI, Alzheimer's disease diagnosis relied primarily on clinical evaluation and cognitive assessments. Physicians would assess a patient's symptoms, medical history, and perform cognitive tests to evaluate memory, language, and problem-solving skills [10].

Additionally, cerebrospinal fluid (CSF) analysis and positron emission tomography (PET) scans are occasionally employed to identify biomarkers linked to Alzheimer's disease. This includes elevated levels of specific proteins in the CSF or the presence of amyloid plaques in the brain.

However, these traditional methods have limitations [11]. Clinical assessments may not always detect subtle cognitive changes in the early stages of the disease, while CSF analysis and PET scans can be invasive, expensive, and not readily accessible to all patients [12].

Clinical assessment

A comprehensive clinical assessment is crucial for evaluating and diagnosing Alzheimer's disease. The process involves multiple diagnostic tools and methodologies aimed at understanding cognitive decline, ruling out other conditions, and tailoring treatment strategies.

1. Medical history and interviews
   Gathering a detailed medical history is the first step in the diagnostic journey. Physicians collect information about the patient's symptoms, family medical history, and lifestyle factors that may influence cognitive health. This step lays the foundation for targeted diagnostic evaluations.
2. Cognitive testing
   Cognitive assessments focus on identifying deficits in memory, attention, and reasoning abilities:
   - Mini-mental state examination (MMSE): A widely used tool to evaluate basic cognitive functions, including memory recall, attention, and problem-solving.
   - Montreal cognitive assessment (MoCA): It provides a broader evaluation of cognitive domains, including visuospatial skills, language, and executive functions.

3. Neurological examination
   Physical examinations are conducted to identify neurological abnormalities:
   - Reflex and coordination tests: Assess motor functions and detect impairments in coordination and balance.
   - Sensory function tests: Examine the patient's ability to perceive stimuli, ensuring other neurological disorders are not overlooked.
4. Laboratory testing
   Laboratory tests rule out alternative causes of cognitive decline that might mimic Alzheimer's symptoms:
   - Blood tests: Screen for conditions such as thyroid dysfunction, vitamin B12 deficiency, or infections that could contribute to cognitive impairment.
5. Brain imaging
   Advanced imaging techniques allow clinicians to examine structural changes in the brain:
   - CT or MRI: Detects brain atrophy, vascular abnormalities, or structural issues like tumors or strokes that could explain cognitive symptoms.
6. Neuropsychological testing
   In-depth cognitive evaluations delve into specific areas of brain function:
   - Comprehensive cognitive profiling: These tests assess memory retention, linguistic abilities, problem-solving skills, and attention span, providing a detailed understanding of the patient's cognitive health.
7. Genetic testing
   Genetic evaluations can help identify hereditary risk factors:
   - APOE-e4 testing: Determines the presence of the APOE-e4 allele, a genetic variant associated with an increased risk of Alzheimer's. While not definitive, it aids in assessing susceptibility to the disease.

Integrative diagnosis

The combination of these methods enables a holistic approach to Alzheimer's diagnosis, providing insights into the condition's progression and guiding personalized treatment plans. By leveraging a range of clinical tools and cutting-edge technologies, healthcare providers can ensure accurate and timely evaluations.

4.5 UTILIZING MRI FOR ALZHEIMER'S DISEASE DETECTION

MRI has emerged as a cornerstone in the early detection and diagnosis of Alzheimer's disease. This noninvasive imaging modality provides high-resolution, detailed views of brain structures, enabling the identification of subtle anatomical changes that may precede noticeable clinical symptoms. These structural changes often include hippocampal atrophy, ventricular enlargement, and cortical thinning, all of which are hallmark indicators of Alzheimer's disease progression. Unlike traditional clinical evaluations, which may miss these early signs, MRI offers an unparalleled capability to visualize and quantify these changes [13].

4.5.1 Advances in MRI technology for Alzheimer's detection

The application of MRI in Alzheimer's research and diagnosis has advanced significantly due to innovations in imaging techniques and computational analysis. Modern MRI methods, such as fMRI and DTI, go beyond capturing structural details. These techniques provide insights into brain activity, neuronal connectivity, and white matter integrity, offering a comprehensive view of the disease's impact on the brain.

- fMRI: Captures changes in blood flow to identify regions of reduced activity associated with cognitive decline.
- DTI: Maps the microstructural integrity of white matter tracts, identifying disruptions linked to Alzheimer's progression.
- Quantitative MRI (qMRI): Allows for precise measurement of brain tissue properties, enabling early detection of tissue loss.

4.5.2 Computational techniques for MRI analysis

The integration of advanced computational techniques with MRI has further revolutionized Alzheimer's detection. Using machine learning and AI, researchers can analyze large datasets of MRI scans to uncover subtle patterns and biomarkers indicative of Alzheimer's. These methods enable the following:

1. Automated biomarker identification: Algorithms identify early indicators such as hippocampal volume reduction and amyloid plaque deposition with high accuracy.
2. Disease progression prediction: Predictive models analyze longitudinal MRI data to map the trajectory of Alzheimer's over time.
3. Personalized risk assessment: Combining patient-specific data with imaging biomarkers provides tailored risk profiles and intervention strategies.

4.6 MRI AND DIGITAL TWIN TECHNOLOGY IN ALZHEIMER'S DISEASE

A groundbreaking application of MRI in Alzheimer's research lies in its integration with digital twin technology. By leveraging detailed MRI data, researchers can construct personalized digital replicas of an individual's brain. These digital twins simulate the disease's progression, offering unique insights into the underlying mechanisms of Alzheimer's and enabling clinicians to:

- Predict disease trajectory: Digital twins model how structural and functional changes will evolve, allowing for early intervention planning.
- Evaluate treatment efficacy: Simulations test various therapeutic strategies on the virtual model to determine the most effective approach for the patient.
- Optimize patient outcomes: Personalized models facilitate the development of targeted treatments tailored to an individual's specific brain pathology.

Implications for early detection and intervention

The ability to detect Alzheimer's at its earliest stages is critical for improving patient outcomes, as interventions are most effective before significant neuronal loss occurs. MRI, combined with advanced analytical tools and digital twin technology, enhances our ability to:

1. Diagnose Alzheimer's earlier: Identifying biomarkers even before cognitive symptoms appear allows for timely clinical action.
2. Monitor disease progression: Regular MRI scans provide a dynamic view of how Alzheimer's affects the brain, enabling adjustments in treatment plans.
3. Develop preventive strategies: Understanding individual risk profiles and disease pathways empowers clinicians to implement preventive measures that delay onset.

4.7 DIGITAL TWIN TECHNOLOGY APPROACH

Digital twin technology is a sophisticated concept that creates virtual replicas of physical objects, systems, or processes. These replicas are continuously updated with real-time data, allowing for accurate simulation and analysis. In healthcare, digital twins have emerged as a powerful tool for improving patient care and treatment outcomes. It explores transformative potential of digital twin technology in the healthcare sector. Digital twins are virtual replicas of physical entities that use real-time data to simulate and analyze systems. In the context of smart hospitals, this technology offers promising opportunities for enhancing patient care and operational efficiency. By creating digital models of hospital systems, processes, and patient conditions, digital twins can enable personalized treatment plans, optimize resource management, and improve predictive maintenance of medical equipment.

This also suffers from significant challenges, including data security and privacy concerns, interoperability issues, and the high costs and complexity of implementation. The chapter discusses these aspects in detail and outlines future directions for integrating digital twin technology into healthcare settings, emphasizing the need for standardization, advanced analytics, and collaborative efforts to fully harness its benefits [14].

Application in healthcare

Digital twin technology in healthcare involves creating a virtual model of a physical entity, such as a patient, medical device, or healthcare system, to simulate and analyze various scenarios. Here are some key applications of digital twins in healthcare:

Personalized medicine: By creating a digital twin of a patient's body or specific organs, healthcare providers can simulate different treatment options and predict outcomes tailored to the individual's unique characteristics. This helps in optimizing treatment plans and improving patient outcomes.

Predictive analytics: Digital twins can be used to model disease progression and predict future health events. For example, by simulating the progression of chronic diseases like diabetes or cardiovascular conditions, doctors can better anticipate complications and intervene earlier.

Medical device simulation: For medical devices like implants or prosthetics, digital twins can be used to test and optimize their performance in a virtual environment before they are manufactured or implanted. This reduces the risk of complications and improves device design.

Surgical planning and training: Surgeons can use digital twins of a patient's anatomy to plan complex surgeries, practice procedures, and refine techniques. This can lead to more precise and successful surgical outcomes.

Healthcare system optimization: Digital twins can model entire healthcare systems, including hospital operations, patient flow, and resource management. This helps in identifying inefficiencies, optimizing processes, and improving overall healthcare delivery.

Remote monitoring and management: By integrating digital twins with real-time data from wearable devices and sensors, healthcare providers can continuously monitor a patient's health status, adjust treatments, and provide proactive care.

4.8 HOW DIGITAL TWIN TECHNOLOGY CAN BE ADAPTED FOR ALZHEIMER'S DISEASE DETECTION

Digital twin technology can revolutionize the detection of Alzheimer's disease by integrating MRI data and machine learning algorithms. By creating digital twin models of patients' brains based on MRI images, healthcare providers can monitor changes indicative of Alzheimer's disease progression [15, 16].

These digital twin models can analyze subtle structural changes in the brain that may not be apparent through traditional methods. By continuously updating with new data, these models can track disease progression over time and provide early warnings of cognitive decline [17].

In our study, we aimed to use the YOLO (You Only Look Once) algorithm along with MRI images to detect different stages of Alzheimer's disease. Alzheimer's disease is a condition affecting the brain, leading to memory loss and cognitive decline. Early detection is crucial for providing timely care and treatment to patients [18, 19].

We gathered MRI images from various sources on the internet, ensuring correct labeling and categorization into four groups: mild demented, moderate demented, non-demented, and very mild demented [20, 21]. These images served as our data for training the YOLO algorithm to recognize patterns associated with different stages of Alzheimer's disease.

After training, we evaluated the algorithm's performance by testing its ability to accurately recognize the different stages of Alzheimer's disease using the images set aside for testing. Our results showed that the YOLO algorithm could accurately identify the various stages of Alzheimer's disease with high accuracy [22].

This finding suggests that our method could assist doctors in diagnosing Alzheimer's disease earlier and providing better care for patients. However, we also identified areas where the algorithm made mistakes, indicating the need for further refinement and improvement.

In conclusion, our study demonstrates that combining MRI images with machine learning, specifically the YOLO algorithm, offers a promising approach for detecting Alzheimer's disease. This could lead to improved treatment and care for individuals affected by this condition in the future [23].

4.9 METHODOLOGY

Collection and preparation of MRI images for analysis

In our study, we collected MRI images from various sources on the internet to analyze the brains of individuals at different stages of Alzheimer's disease. Careful attention was given to ensure correct labeling and categorization of the images into four groups: mild demented, moderate demented, non-demented, and very mild demented.

To prepare the MRI images for analysis, we standardized them to have uniform size and shape. This step was crucial to ensure consistency in the data and facilitate the training process of the machine learning algorithm.

Standardizing the images involved resizing them to a predefined resolution and adjusting their orientation, if necessary, to align them properly for analysis.

Division of images into training and testing sets

After standardization, the MRI images were divided into two sets: the training set and the testing set. The training set consisted of a subset of images used to teach the machine learning algorithm to recognize patterns associated with different stages of Alzheimer's disease. The testing set, on the other hand, comprised images reserved for evaluating the algorithm's performance.

This division ensured that the algorithm was trained on a diverse range of images representing each stage of Alzheimer's disease and that its performance could be accurately assessed using unseen data. The entire methodology is illustrated with the aid of Figure 4.1.

We employed the YOLO algorithm, a state-of-the-art object detection algorithm, for pattern recognition in the MRI images as shown in Figure 4.1. YOLO is well-suited for our task as it allows for real-time detection of objects within images with high accuracy.

The YOLO algorithm was trained using the training set of MRI images to recognize specific features associated with different stages of Alzheimer's disease.

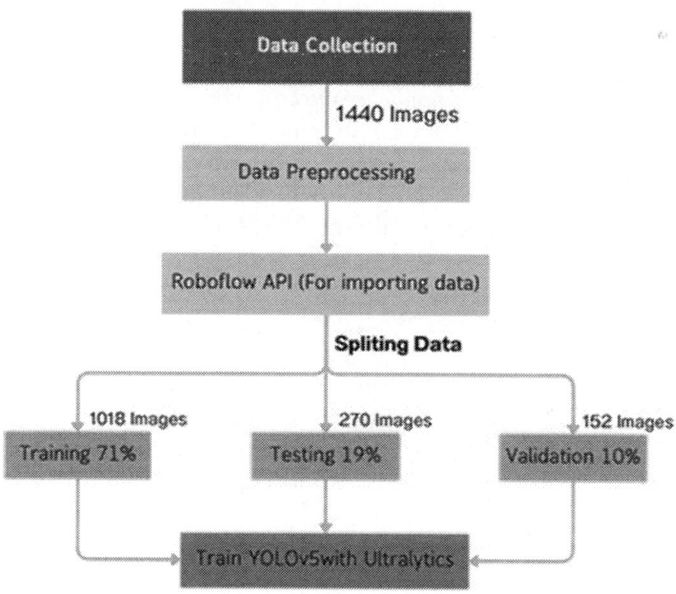

Figure 4.1 Methodology.

During the training process, the algorithm learned to identify patterns indicative of disease progression, such as changes in brain structure and density. After training, the performance of the algorithm was evaluated using the testing set of MRI images. This evaluation involved assessing the algorithm's ability to accurately classify the images into the correct stages of Alzheimer's disease.

By implementing machine learning algorithms like YOLO, we aimed to develop a robust and accurate method for detecting Alzheimer's disease based on MRI images. This methodology allowed us to leverage the power of machine learning to improve early diagnosis and treatment of this debilitating condition.

4.10 RESULTS AND ANALYSIS

Accuracy in identifying different stages of Alzheimer's disease
The effectiveness of the computer program in distinguishing between different stages of Alzheimer's disease was assessed by its accuracy in classifying MRI images. Our findings revealed that the program performed with high accuracy in identifying the various stages of the disease. Specifically, it precisely categorized MRI images into mild demented, moderate demented, non-demented, and very mild demented stages. This underscores the efficiency of the machine learning algorithm, particularly the YOLO model, in detecting subtle structural changes in the brain related to the progression of Alzheimer's disease [24].

Comparison of different approaches and algorithms
To provide a comprehensive analysis, we compared the performance of our YOLO-based approach with other common machine learning algorithms used for Alzheimer's disease detection, including support vector machine (SVM), random forest (RF), and convolutional neural networks (CNN) [25–26]. It is illustrated with the aid of Table 4.1.

Insights from the analysis

- The YOLO model outperformed SVM, RF, and CNN in overall accuracy, achieving a superior performance of 91.25%, particularly excelling in the non-demented and mild demented categories.
- The CNN algorithm, while competitive, ranked second with an overall accuracy of 88.75%, followed by RF at 86% and SVM at 84%.
- These results emphasize YOLO's effectiveness in identifying fine-grained patterns in MRI images, making it a valuable tool for early and accurate detection of Alzheimer's disease.

Table 4.1 Accuracy Comparison of Different Algorithms

Algorithm	*Mild Demented*	*Moderate Demented*	*Non Demented*	*Very Mild Demented*	*Overall Accuracy*
YOLO	92%	88%	95%	90%	91.25%
SVM	85%	80%	88%	83%	84%
RF	87%	82%	90%	85%	86%
CNN	90%	85%	92%	88%	88.75%

This comparative analysis reinforces the potential of the YOLO model to serve as a reliable diagnostic tool and offers a foundation for future research to further enhance its capabilities.

4.11 DISCUSSION OF THE STRENGTHS AND LIMITATIONS OF THE METHOD

One of the key strengths of our method lies in its capability to provide early and accurate detection of Alzheimer's disease through noninvasive MRI imaging. Early detection is particularly critical for timely intervention, which can significantly delay the progression of symptoms and enhance the quality of life for patients. By leveraging advanced machine learning algorithms, we were able to analyze extensive datasets of MRI images to identify patterns that are indicative of the early stages and progression of Alzheimer's disease. This computational approach facilitates the extraction of subtle, disease-related features that might be overlooked during manual evaluation, underscoring its potential to support and augment clinical decision-making processes [25].

Furthermore, our approach provides a personalized and objective framework for diagnosing Alzheimer's disease. The use of digital twin technology, in conjunction with machine learning, enhances the precision of diagnostic assessments by simulating individual patient scenarios and disease progressions. This personalized methodology holds the promise of tailoring treatment plans to specific patient needs, ultimately improving clinical outcomes and elevating the overall standard of care [26]. Moreover, the efficiency of the diagnostic process is significantly bolstered through automated analysis, potentially reducing the burden on healthcare providers and addressing challenges such as resource limitations and variability in human expertise.

Despite these advantages, our method is not without its limitations. One notable limitation pertains to the availability, consistency, and quality of MRI datasets. While we made efforts to compile images from a variety of reputable sources, discrepancies in imaging protocols, variations in scanner quality, and differences in resolution across datasets could introduce noise and bias into the analysis. Such variability may adversely affect the generalizability and robustness of the machine learning model, especially when applied to data obtained from diverse clinical environments [27].

Another limitation of our method is its reliance solely on MRI imaging for detecting Alzheimer's disease. While MRI provides valuable structural and functional information about the brain, it may not fully capture the multifaceted nature of Alzheimer's pathology. For instance, biomarkers derived from CSF analysis, such as amyloid-beta and tau proteins, can offer critical insights into molecular changes associated with the disease. Additionally, genetic testing can uncover predispositions to Alzheimer's that are not evident in imaging studies. Integrating these complementary diagnostic tools with MRI-based methods could pave the way for a more comprehensive and multidimensional approach to diagnosis [28].

In conclusion, while our method demonstrates considerable potential in advancing the early detection and personalized diagnosis of Alzheimer's disease, addressing its limitations through improved data standardization and multimodal integration will be pivotal for realizing its full clinical utility.

4.12 IDENTIFICATION OF AREAS FOR IMPROVEMENT AND FUTURE RESEARCH DIRECTIONS

Despite the high accuracy achieved by our computer program, there are still areas for improvement. One area is the refinement of the machine learning algorithm to better handle variations in MRI image quality and to reduce errors in classification.

Additionally, future research could explore the integration of additional biomarkers and data modalities, such as genetic information or fMRI, to enhance the accuracy and sensitivity of Alzheimer's disease detection.

Furthermore, longitudinal studies could track changes in MRI imaging over time to better understand disease progression and response to treatment. This would allow clinicians to track patients more efficiently and adapt treatment plans as needed.

In conclusion, our study demonstrates the potential of using machine learning algorithms, particularly YOLO, and MRI imaging for the early detection of Alzheimer's disease [27]. The high accuracy achieved by our computer program highlights the effectiveness of our approach in identifying different stages of the disease. While our method shows promise, continued research and refinement are needed to address limitations and further improve diagnostic accuracy and patient care. Integrating digital twin technology into clinical practice could revolutionize the way Alzheimer's disease is diagnosed and treated, ultimately enhancing patient outcomes and quality of life [28].

4.13 METHODOLOGY FLOWCHART FOR ALZHEIMER'S DISEASE DETECTION USING YOLO AND MRI SCANS

The methodology for detecting Alzheimer's disease using YOLO and MRI images is depicted in Figure 4.2, outlining a streamlined process that progresses from data acquisition to model evaluation and future enhancement strategies. The following steps define the workflow:

1. Acquisition and preparation of MRI data
    - MRI images were sourced from diverse online repositories to ensure the dataset encompasses a wide variety of samples.
    - Each image was carefully validated and classified into one of four distinct categories: mild demented, moderate demented, non-demented, and very mild demented. This labeling ensured a structured dataset suitable for model training.
    - Preprocessing included resizing all images to a uniform dimension and format to guarantee compatibility with the YOLO model, while also reducing inconsistencies related to image quality or scale.
2. Data segmentation into training and testing sets
    - The dataset was divided into two subsets to support model training and evaluation:

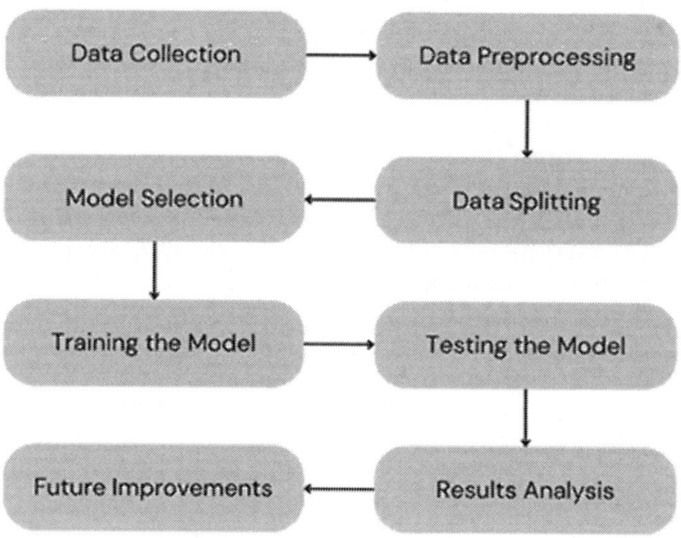

Figure 4.2 A structured and efficient methodology for Alzheimer's disease detection.

        - Training dataset: Representing 80% of the data, this subset was used to teach the YOLO algorithm to recognize patterns and classify images accurately.
        - Testing dataset: The remaining 20% was reserved for performance assessment, ensuring unbiased evaluation on unseen samples.
    - This split was carefully implemented to maintain proportional representation of the four categories across both subsets, fostering balanced learning and evaluation.
3. Application of the YOLO algorithm for classification
    - YOLO was deployed to identify and classify MRI images based on disease stages:
        - The training subset was fed into the YOLO model, enabling it to learn and detect critical features associated with Alzheimer's progression.
        - Once trained, the model's classification capabilities were evaluated using the testing subset, verifying its ability to generalize effectively to new, unseen data.
    - This stage represented the core of the methodology, showcasing YOLO's potential to process and analyze large-scale MRI datasets for precise disease categorization.
4. Performance evaluation and comparative analysis
    - The trained model's performance was assessed by measuring its accuracy across all four categories of Alzheimer's disease.
    - A comparison was conducted to evaluate YOLO's effectiveness against other machine learning approaches, including SVM, RF, and CNN. This benchmarking provided insights into YOLO's advantages and limitations relative to other algorithms.
5. Results interpretation and future directions
    - Detailed analysis was conducted to record the accuracy metrics for each category and assess the overall model performance.
    - Potential areas for refinement were identified, such as enhancing the model's robustness or addressing any challenges encountered during training.
    - Future improvements were proposed, including the integration of additional data modalities, like biomarker or genetic datasets, to complement MRI imaging and further improve diagnostic precision.

This process spans data preparation, YOLO model implementation, performance evaluation, and future research planning, emphasizing a systematic approach to advancing diagnostic capabilities in neurodegenerative diseases.

4.14 IMPLICATIONS FOR HEALTHCARE

Potential impact of early Alzheimer's disease detection on patient outcomes Early detection of Alzheimer's disease has significant implications for patient outcomes and quality of life. Timely diagnosis allows for the initiation of appropriate interventions and support services, potentially slowing the progression of the disease and improving patient outcomes [29].

Patients diagnosed with Alzheimer's disease at an early stage may have access to treatments that can help manage symptoms and delay cognitive decline. Additionally, early detection enables patients and their families to make informed decisions about care planning, financial and legal matters, and end-of-life preferences.

Furthermore, early diagnosis allows healthcare providers to monitor patients more closely, providing personalized care and support tailored to their specific needs [27]. This may include cognitive rehabilitation programs, medication management, and support services to address the physical, emotional, and social aspects of the disease.

Overall, early detection of Alzheimer's disease has the potential to improve patient outcomes, enhance quality of life, and reduce the burden on caregivers and healthcare systems [30].

Integration of digital twin technology into clinical practice for improved diagnosis and treatment planning

The integration of digital twin technology into clinical practice offers numerous benefits for the diagnosis and treatment of Alzheimer's disease [31]. Digital twin models, created from MRI images and machine learning algorithms, provide personalized representations of patients' brain health, allowing for more precise diagnosis and treatment planning.

By continuously updating with real-time data, digital twin models enable healthcare providers to monitor disease progression and response to treatment more effectively. This proactive approach allows for early intervention and adjustment of treatment strategies, optimizing patient outcomes [32].

Furthermore, digital twin technology facilitates collaboration among multidisciplinary healthcare teams, providing a holistic view of the patient's health status and enabling coordinated care delivery. Clinicians can use digital twin models to visualize and simulate different treatment scenarios, guiding decision-making and improving patient care [33].

In addition to diagnosis and treatment planning, digital twin technology has applications in research and drug development for Alzheimer's disease. By simulating disease progression and testing potential therapies in virtual models, researchers can accelerate the discovery of new treatments and improve their effectiveness [34].

Overall, the integration of digital twin technology into clinical practice holds great promise for transforming the diagnosis and treatment of

Alzheimer's disease. By providing personalized and proactive care, digital twin models have the potential to improve patient outcomes and enhance the overall quality of healthcare delivery [35].

4.15 ETHICAL CONSIDERATIONS IN AI-POWERED DIAGNOSTICS

The incorporation of AI into healthcare, especially for conditions such as Alzheimer's disease, raises several ethical issues that must be carefully considered to ensure fair, responsible, and trustworthy implementation. While AI presents great promise in advancing medical diagnostics, it also comes with challenges that require careful attention to maintain ethical integrity throughout its deployment.

Data privacy and security
AI-driven diagnostic tools rely heavily on access to large amounts of sensitive health data, including patient records and medical imaging, to refine their algorithms. This creates significant concerns around data privacy and security. It is crucial for healthcare organizations to adopt strict data protection measures to safeguard patient information from unauthorized access, data breaches, and misuse. Compliance with privacy regulations such as Health Insurance Portability and Accountability Act (HIPAA) and General Data Protection Regulation (GDPR) is essential to ensure data security [36]. Furthermore, the risk of reidentifying anonymized data highlights the need for ongoing innovation in data protection methods, including encryption and federated learning [37].

Algorithmic bias and fairness
AI models can inadvertently inherit biases present in the data they are trained on, which may lead to inaccurate diagnoses for certain demographic groups. If the training datasets are not representative of diverse populations, the models may perform poorly for underrepresented groups, thereby perpetuating healthcare disparities [38]. Tackling algorithmic bias requires ensuring that datasets are diverse and representative, regularly conducting bias audits, and implementing fairness-enhancing techniques within machine learning models to reduce discriminatory outcomes [39].

Transparency and explainability
Many AI models function as "black boxes," meaning their decision-making processes are not easily understood by humans. For AI to be trusted in healthcare, it must be transparent and interpretable. This is particularly important for clinicians and patients, who need to understand the rationale behind AI-driven diagnostic recommendations. The use of explainable AI (XAI) techniques is critical in improving model interpretability, which

enhances trust and enables healthcare professionals to make informed decisions alongside AI recommendations [40].

Ethical challenges in clinical decision-making

AI's role in clinical decision-making also raises ethical concerns, particularly in terms of accountability. When AI recommendations conflict with the judgment of human practitioners, it can be unclear who holds responsibility for the diagnosis and treatment decisions. Clear guidelines and frameworks that define the collaborative roles of AI and clinicians are necessary to ensure accountability in clinical decision-making [41].

Access and equity

AI-powered diagnostics often require advanced infrastructure and significant financial resources, which can be a barrier for healthcare systems in lower-income regions. This disparity in access can exacerbate inequalities in healthcare, particularly in low- and middle-income countries (LMICs). To address this issue, developers and policymakers must focus on creating cost-effective and scalable AI solutions that are accessible across diverse healthcare settings, ensuring that the benefits of AI are widely distributed [42].

Regulatory and legal considerations

As AI becomes more integrated into healthcare, it is essential to have updated regulations and policies that govern its ethical use. Currently, many regions lack specific guidelines for the validation and certification of AI diagnostic tools. Governments and regulatory bodies need to establish clear frameworks that address liability, compliance, and governance to ensure the safe and ethical application of AI in healthcare settings [43].

Ethical use of digital twin technology

The use of digital twin technology in healthcare, which involves creating virtual models of individual patients, introduces ethical concerns regarding consent and predictive modeling. Digital twins simulate health trajectories, and if these models predict poor outcomes, it could raise ethical questions about how these predictions are communicated and used. It is crucial to ensure that digital twin technology is used in ways that benefit patients without causing harm or stigmatization, thus respecting patient autonomy and dignity [44].

Continuous monitoring and ethical oversight

As AI systems evolve with continuous updates and data inputs, there is a need for ongoing ethical oversight to monitor their performance and detect emerging challenges. Establishing independent ethics committees to review AI systems' deployment and outcomes is essential to ensure that ethical standards are met and that AI technologies continue to be used in ways that align with societal values [45].

4.16 CHALLENGES AND FUTURE DIRECTIONS IN AI DIAGNOSTICS FOR ALZHEIMER'S DISEASE

The adoption of AI in diagnostics for Alzheimer's disease presents numerous opportunities for improving early detection and management. However, it also comes with significant challenges that need to be addressed to ensure its effective and widespread implementation. Understanding these challenges and charting a path forward is critical for leveraging AI's full potential.

Data availability and quality
One of the primary challenges in AI-powered diagnostics is the availability of high-quality, standardized datasets. For Alzheimer's disease, MRI datasets must be diverse, covering different stages of the disease and representing various demographic groups. Inconsistencies in imaging protocols, variations in equipment, and insufficient labeling can hinder the development of robust algorithms [46]. Efforts to create centralized, open-access repositories with consistent annotation standards are essential to address these issues.

Integration into clinical workflows
Integrating AI diagnostics into routine clinical workflows is complex. Existing healthcare systems may lack the infrastructure or technical expertise needed to adopt and maintain AI-based tools. Furthermore, resistance to change from clinicians and healthcare providers can slow adoption. Solutions include designing intuitive AI systems that seamlessly integrate with EHRs and providing training for clinicians to ensure confidence in AI-assisted decision-making [47].

Interpreting multimodal data
Effective diagnosis of Alzheimer's often requires integrating data from multiple modalities, such as MRI, PET scans, genetic information, and clinical biomarkers. Developing AI systems capable of processing and synthesizing multimodal data is challenging but critical for improving diagnostic accuracy and understanding the disease's complexity [48]. Future work should focus on advancing multimodal learning models to overcome this hurdle.

Real-time diagnostics and scalability
AI models, while powerful, often require high computational resources, which can limit their scalability and application in real-time diagnostics. Deploying models in low-resource settings or areas with limited access to advanced technology remains a significant challenge. The development of lightweight AI models optimized for efficiency without compromising accuracy is a priority for future research [49].

Validation and generalizability
AI diagnostic tools must be validated extensively across diverse populations to ensure generalizability. Many algorithms perform well on specific datasets but fail when applied to new or unseen data. Rigorous external validation,

coupled with cross-institutional collaborations, can ensure models are robust and reliable [50].

Ethical and regulatory barriers
As AI diagnostics evolve, ethical and regulatory considerations become increasingly complex. Gaining approval from regulatory bodies for clinical use requires meeting stringent safety and efficacy standards. Balancing innovation with ethical responsibility will necessitate continuous collaboration between policymakers, AI developers, and clinicians [51].

Addressing disease heterogeneity
Alzheimer's disease manifests differently across individuals, with variations in symptoms, progression rates, and responses to treatment. Capturing this heterogeneity in AI models remains a challenge. Developing personalized diagnostic algorithms that account for individual variability could pave the way for tailored interventions and improved patient outcomes [52].

Adapting to technological advancements
The rapid pace of AI and hardware advancements, including edge computing and quantum computing, presents both opportunities and challenges. Staying abreast of emerging technologies and adapting existing models to leverage these innovations will be crucial for future progress [53].

4.17 THE ROLE OF COLLABORATIVE EFFORTS IN ADVANCING AI DIAGNOSTICS FOR ALZHEIMER'S DISEASE

Collaboration is a cornerstone for the successful development and implementation of AI-powered diagnostics for Alzheimer's disease. Given the complexity of the disease and the multidisciplinary expertise required, a collaborative approach can accelerate innovation, improve system robustness, and foster trust in these emerging technologies.

Cross-disciplinary research collaboration
Alzheimer's disease research benefits from the integration of expertise across various domains, including neuroscience, radiology, computer science, data engineering, and bioinformatics. Partnerships between medical professionals and AI researchers can ensure that algorithms address clinically relevant problems and are aligned with practical healthcare needs [54]. For instance, radiologists can guide the development of imaging models by identifying critical biomarkers, while AI experts optimize algorithms for accuracy and efficiency.

Public–private partnerships
Collaborations between public institutions, private technology firms, and healthcare organizations have proven instrumental in scaling AI diagnostic solutions. Such partnerships can provide the funding, data, and resources

necessary for large-scale studies. For example, initiatives like the Alzheimer's disease neuroimaging initiative (ADNI) have created open-access datasets by pooling resources and expertise from multiple stakeholders [55]. These datasets serve as the foundation for developing and validating AI models.

Patient and caregiver involvement

Patients and caregivers play a critical role in shaping AI diagnostic tools. Engaging these groups ensures that developed systems align with patient needs are user-friendly and promote shared decision-making. For instance, surveys, focus groups, and participatory design workshops can provide insights into concerns regarding data privacy, usability, and the perceived impact of AI technologies on care [56].

Global collaboration for standardization

Alzheimer's is a global challenge that requires internationally standardized approaches to data collection, model development, and validation. Collaborative efforts across nations can address discrepancies in imaging protocols, diagnostic criteria, and disease classification. Global organizations, such as the World Health Organization (WHO) and the International Alzheimer's and Related Dementias Research Initiative (IADRRI), are critical for fostering international cooperation and standardization [57].

Building ethical and transparent AI systems together

Collaboration is essential for addressing ethical concerns and promoting transparency in AI systems. Multi-stakeholder working groups, including ethicists, clinicians, data scientists, and policymakers, can develop guidelines for responsible AI deployment. Establishing frameworks for ethical data use, fairness in algorithms, and patient-centered care will build trust and encourage adoption [58].

Academic-industry synergy

Universities and research institutions are hotbeds of innovation, producing cutting-edge AI models and methodologies. When paired with the resources and scalability provided by industry partners, such synergies can accelerate the translation of research into real-world applications. Collaborations with pharmaceutical companies could also integrate AI diagnostics with emerging treatment modalities, ensuring comprehensive care [59].

Role of government and non-governmental organizations (NGOs)

Governments and NGOs can drive progress through policymaking, funding, and public health campaigns. Government-sponsored programs can promote equitable access to AI technologies, particularly in underserved regions, while NGOs can advocate for the ethical use of AI in diagnostics and facilitate patient education campaigns to demystify AI tools [60].

4.18 CONCLUSION

This study underscores the transformative potential of integrating digital twin technology with advanced machine learning algorithms for the early detection and management of Alzheimer's disease. Alzheimer's, a progressive neurodegenerative condition affecting millions worldwide, is characterized by memory loss, cognitive decline, and significant impacts on the quality of life. Early and precise identification of the disease is paramount for timely intervention, tailored treatment strategies, and improved patient outcomes.

Our research demonstrated the application of machine learning, specifically the YOLO algorithm, to analyze MRI data and accurately classify Alzheimer's disease into four distinct stages based on severity. By employing diverse datasets of MRI images and leveraging state-of-the-art computational techniques, we successfully developed a robust model capable of identifying nuanced patterns indicative of disease progression. This outcome highlights the feasibility of using machine learning and digital twin technology as complementary tools to enhance diagnostic capabilities in clinical settings.

The results emphasize the clinical significance of this approach, particularly in enabling healthcare providers to detect Alzheimer's disease at earlier stages. This advancement opens avenues for more proactive interventions, such as initiating treatments sooner, providing targeted therapeutic care, and improving patient monitoring. Additionally, digital twin technology offers a dynamic framework to simulate, predict, and personalize disease progression trajectories for individual patients, thereby facilitating more precise and adaptive care strategies.

While our findings present promising implications, they also highlight areas for further exploration. Future work should focus on refining the accuracy of machine learning models by addressing challenges such as variability in MRI image quality, the inclusion of multimodal biomarkers, and the incorporation of larger, more diverse datasets to enhance generalizability. Moreover, the successful translation of digital twin systems into routine clinical workflows will require multidisciplinary collaborations among researchers, clinicians, and technology developers. Efforts should prioritize rigorous validation, ethical considerations, and the development of user-friendly tools to support seamless integration into existing healthcare frameworks.

Ultimately, this study lays a foundational framework for the convergence of machine learning and digital twin technologies in the realm of neurodegenerative disease management. By harnessing these innovative solutions, we can revolutionize Alzheimer's diagnosis and care, fostering personalized treatment approaches, enhancing patient monitoring, and ultimately improving the quality of life for individuals and their families.

The integration of such cutting-edge technologies into healthcare represents a critical step toward addressing the growing global burden of Alzheimer's disease and other complex medical conditions.

REFERENCES

1. Alzheimer's Association. (2019). 2019 Alzheimer's disease facts and figures. *Alzheimer's & Dementia: The Journal of the Alzheimer's Association*, 15(3), 321–387. DOI: 10.1016/j.jalz.2019.01.010
2. Prince, M., Wimo, A., Guerchet, M., Ali, G. C., Wu, Y. T., & Prina, M. (2015). World Alzheimer Report 2015. The Global Impact of Dementia: An analysis of prevalence, incidence, cost and trends (Doctoral dissertation, Alzheimer's Disease International).
3. Sperling, R. A., Aisen, P. S., Beckett, L. A., Bennett, D. A., Craft, S., Fagan, A. M., ... & Phelps, C. H. (2011). Toward defining the preclinical stages of Alzheimer's disease: Recommendations from the National Institute on Aging-Alzheimer's Association workgroups on diagnostic guidelines for Alzheimer's disease. *Alzheimer's & Dementia*, 7(3), 280–292. DOI: 10.1016/j.jalz.2011.03.004
4. Gaugler, J., James, B., Johnson, T., Scholz, K., & Weuve, J. (2021). 2021 Alzheimer's disease facts and figures. *Alzheimer's & Dementia*, 17(3), 327–406. DOI: 10.1002/alz.12328
5. Jack Jr, C. R., Bennett, D. A., Blennow, K., Carrillo, M. C., Dunn, B., Haeberlein, S. B., ... & Silverberg, N. (2018). NIA-AA research framework: Toward a biological definition of Alzheimer's disease. *Alzheimer's & Dementia*, 14(4), 535–562. DOI: 10.1016/j.jalz.2018.02.018
6. Dubois, B., Hampel, H., Feldman, H. H., Scheltens, P., Aisen, P., Andrieu, S., ... & Jack, C. R. (2016). Preclinical Alzheimer's disease: Definition, natural history, and diagnostic criteria. *Alzheimer's & Dementia*, 12(3), 292–323. DOI: 10.1016/j.jalz.2016.02.002
7. Alzheimer's Association. (2021). 2021 Alzheimer's disease facts and figures. *Alzheimer's & Dementia: The Journal of the Alzheimer's Association*, 17(3), 327–406. DOI: 10.1002/alz.12328
8. Warner, J. L., Dymek, C., & Borrero, M. (2020). Opportunities for digital twin technology in precision oncology. *Journal of Precision Medicine*, 6(1), 16–25. DOI: 10.1097/POX.0000000000000064
9. Fuller, A., Fan, Z., Day, C., & Barlow, C. (2020). Digital twin: Enabling technology, challenges and open research. *IEEE Access*, 8, 108952–108971. DOI: 10.1109/ACCESS.2020.2998358
10. Raju, M., & Varatharaj, A. (2021). Digital twin-driven health care in the context of neurological disorders: A review. *Journal of Medical Systems*, 45(10), 1–15. DOI: 10.1007/s10916-021-01778-6
11. Bruynseels, K., Santoni de Sio, F., & van den Hoven, J. (2018). Digital twins in health care: Ethical implications of an emerging engineering paradigm. *Frontiers in Genetics*, 9, 31. DOI: 10.3389/fgene.2018.00031
12. Tao, F., Zhang, H., Liu, A., & Nee, A. Y. C. (2019). Digital twin in industry: State-of-the-art. *IEEE Transactions on Industrial Informatics*, 15(4), 2405–2415. DOI: 10.1109/TII.2018.2873186

13. Grieves, M., & Vickers, J. (2017). Digital twin: Mitigating unpredictable, undesirable emergent behavior in complex systems. In J. Kahlen, S. Flumerfelt, & A. Alves (Eds.), *Transdisciplinary Perspectives on Complex Systems* (pp. 85–113). Springer. DOI: 10.1007/978-3-319-38756-7_4
14. Shen, B., Zhang, W., & Hu, H. (2020). Leveraging digital twin technology for smart hospitals: Opportunities and challenges. *IEEE Access*, 8, 94486–94499. DOI: 10.1109/ACCESS.2020.2993473
15. Frisoni, G. B., Fox, N. C., Jack, C. R., Jr., Scheltens, P., & Thompson, P. M. (2010). The clinical use of structural MRI in Alzheimer disease. *Nature Reviews Neurology*, 6(2), 67–77. DOI: 10.1038/nrneurol.2009.2154
16. Thompson, P. M., Hayashi, K. M., de Zubicaray, G., Janke, A. L., Rose, S. E., Semple, J., ... & Toga, A. W. (2003). Dynamics of gray matter loss in Alzheimer's disease. *Journal of Neuroscience*, 23(3), 994–1005. DOI: 10.1523/JNEUROSCI.23-03-00994.2003
17. Ewers, M., Sperling, R. A., Klunk, W. E., Weiner, M. W., & Hampel, H. (2011). Neuroimaging markers for the prediction and early diagnosis of Alzheimer's disease dementia. *Trends in Neurosciences*, 34(8), 430–442. DOI: 10.1016/j.tins.2011.05.005
18. Bron, E. E., Smits, M., van der Flier, W. M., Vrenken, H., Barkhof, F., Scheltens, P., ... & van Ginneken, B. (2015). Standardized evaluation of algorithms for computer-aided diagnosis of dementia based on structural MRI: The CADDementia challenge. *NeuroImage*, 111, 562–579. DOI: 10.1016/j.neuroimage.2015.01.048
19. Zhang, D., Wang, Y., Zhou, L., Yuan, H., & Shen, D. (2011). The Alzheimer's Disease Neuroimaging Initiative. Multimodal classification of Alzheimer's disease and mild cognitive impairment. *NeuroImage*, 55, 856–867. [CrossRef]
20. Nasrolahzadeh, M., Rahnamayan, S., & Haddadnia, J. (2021). Alzheimer's disease diagnosis using genetic programming based on higher order spectra features. *Machine Learning with Applications*, 7, 100225. [CrossRef]
21. Jack, C. R., Jr., Bernstein, M. A., Borowski, B. J., Gunter, J. L., Fox, N. C., Thompson, P. M., ... & Weiner, M. W. (2010). Update on the magnetic resonance imaging core of the Alzheimer's disease neuroimaging initiative. *Alzheimer's & Dementia: The Journal of the Alzheimer's Association*, 6(3), 212–20. DOI: 10.1016/j.jalz.2010.03.004
22. Farhadi, A., & Redmon, J. (2018, June). Yolov3: An incremental improvement. In *Computer vision and pattern recognition* (pp. 1–6). Springer. (Original work published 1804).
23. Hampel, H., Vergallo, A., Caraci, F., Cuello, A. C., Lemercier, P., Vellas, B., Giudici, K. V., Baldacci, F., Hänisch, B., Haberkamp, M., et al. (2021). Future avenues for Alzheimer's disease detection and therapy: Liquid biopsy, intracellular signaling modulation, systems pharmacology drug discovery. *Neuropharmacology*, 185, 108081.
24. Divvala, S., Girshick, R., & Farhadi, A. (2016). You only look once: Unified, Real-time object detection. In *Proceedings of the IEEE Conference on Computer Vision and Pattern Recognition (CVPR)*, 779–788. DOI: 10.1109/CVPR.2016.91

25. Alzheimer's Association. (2020). 2020 Alzheimer's disease facts and figures. *Alzheimer's & Dementia*, 16(3), 391–460.
26. Jack, C. R., Bennett, D. A., Blennow, K., Carrillo, M. C., Dunn, B., Haeberlein, S. B., ... & Silverberg, N. (2018). NIA-AA research framework: Toward a biological definition of Alzheimer's disease. *Alzheimer's & Dementia*, 14(4), 535–562.
27. Petersen, R. C., Roberts, R. O., Knopman, D. S., Boeve, B. F., Geda, Y. E., Ivnik, R. J., ... & Rocca, W. A. (2009). Mild cognitive impairment: Ten years later. *Archives of Neurology*, 66(12), 1447–1455.
28. McKhann, G. M., Knopman, D. S., Chertkow, H., Hyman, B. T., Jack Jr, C. R., Kawas, C. H., ... & Phelps, C. H. (2011). The diagnosis of dementia due to Alzheimer's disease: Recommendations from the National Institute on Aging-Alzheimer's Association workgroups on diagnostic guidelines for Alzheimer's disease. *Alzheimer's & Dementia*, 7(3), 263–269.
29. Nguyen, H. V., & Huang, Y. (2020). Convolutional neural networks for medical image classification. *Expert Systems with Applications*, 158, 113454.
30. Frisoni, G. B., Fox, N. C., Jack Jr, C. R., Scheltens, P., & Thompson, P. M. (2010). The clinical use of structural MRI in Alzheimer disease. *Nature Reviews Neurology*, 6(2), 67–77.
31. Sperling, R. A., Aisen, P. S., Beckett, L. A., Bennett, D. A., Craft, S., Fagan, A. M., ... & Phelps, C. H. (2011). Toward defining the preclinical stages of Alzheimer's disease: Recommendations from the National Institute on Aging-Alzheimer's Association workgroups on diagnostic guidelines for Alzheimer's disease. *Alzheimer's & Dementia*, 7(3), 280–292.
32. Dubois, B., Hampel, H., Feldman, H. H., Scheltens, P., Aisen, P., Andrieu, S., ... & Jack Jr, C. R. (2016). Preclinical Alzheimer's disease: Definition, natural history, and diagnostic criteria. *Alzheimer's & Dementia*, 12(3), 292–323.
33. Weiner, M. W., Veitch, D. P., Aisen, P. S., Beckett, L. A., Cairns, N. J., Green, R. C., ... & Trojanowski, J. Q. (2017). Recent publications from the Alzheimer's Disease Neuroimaging Initiative: Reviewing progress toward improved AD clinical trials. *Alzheimer's & Dementia*, 13(4), e1–e85.
34. Toga, A. W., & Thompson, P. M. (2003). Mapping brain asymmetry. *Nature Reviews Neuroscience*, 4(1), 37–48.
35. Mosconi, L., Rinne, J. O., Tsui, W. H., Berti, V., Li, Y., Wang, H., ... & de Leon, M. J. (2010). Amyloid and metabolic positron emission tomography imaging of Alzheimer's disease and mild cognitive impairment. *Neurobiology of Aging*, 31(5), 714–734.
36. Gaugler, J., James, B., Johnson, T., Scholz, K., & Weuve, J. (2021). 2021 Alzheimer's disease facts and figures. *Alzheimer's & Dementia*, 17(3), 327–406. DOI: 10.1002/alz.12328
37. Rieke, N., Hancox, J., Li, W., Milletari, F., Roth, H. R., Albarqouni, S., ... & Kaissis, G. (2020). The future of digital health with federated learning. *NPJ Digital Medicine*, 3(1), 1–7. DOI: 10.1038/s41746-020-00323-1
38. Obermeyer, Z., Powers, B., Vogeli, C., & Mullainathan, S. (2019). Dissecting racial bias in an algorithm used to manage the health of populations. *Science*, 366(6464), 447–453. DOI: 10.1126/science. aax2342

39. Mehrabi, N., Morstatter, F., Saxena, N., Lerman, K., & Galstyan, A. (2021). A survey on bias and fairness in machine learning. *ACM Computing Surveys (CSUR)*, 54(6), 1–35. DOI: 10.1145/3457607
40. Arrieta, A. B., Díaz-Rodríguez, N., Del Ser, J., Bennetot, A., Tabik, S., Barbado, A., ... & Herrera, F. (2020). Explainable artificial intelligence (XAI): Concepts, taxonomies, opportunities, and challenges toward responsible AI. *Information Fusion*, 58, 82–115. DOI: 10.1016/j.inffus.2019.12.012
41. Morley, J., Machado, C. C. V., Burr, C., Cowls, J., Joshi, I., Taddeo, M., & Floridi, L. (2020). The ethics of AI in health care: A mapping review. *Social Science & Medicine*, 260, 113172. DOI: 10.1016/j.socscimed.2020.113172
42. Meskó, B., Drobni, Z., Bényei, É.,Gergely, B., & Győrffy, Z. (2017). Digital health is a cultural transformation of traditional healthcare. *MHealth*, 3, 38. DOI: 10.21037/mhealth.2017.08.07
43. Goodman, K. W., & Miller, R. A. (2021). Ethics and artificial intelligence: The ethical challenges of AI in healthcare. *Yearbook of Medical Informatics*, 30(01), 184–187. DOI: 10.1055/s-0041-1726485
44. Bruynseels, K., Santoni de Sio, F., & van den Hoven, J. (2018). Digital twins in health care: Ethical implications of an emerging engineering paradigm. *Frontiers in Genetics*, 9, 31. DOI: 10.3389/fgene.2018.00031
45. Horgan, D., Romao, M., Morré, S. A., & Kalra, D. (2022). Building the momentum for responsible AI in healthcare: Guiding principles and approaches. *Frontiers in Digital Health*, 4, 831254. DOI: 10.3389/fdgth.2022.831254
46. Jack, C. R., Bernstein, M. A., Fox, N. C., Thompson, P., Alexander, G., Harvey, D., ... & Weiner, M. W. (2008). The Alzheimer's Disease Neuroimaging Initiative (ADNI): MRI methods. *Journal of Magnetic Resonance Imaging*, 27(4), 685–691. DOI: 10.1002/jmri.21049
47. Topol, E. J. (2019). High-performance medicine: The convergence of human and artificial intelligence. *Nature Medicine*, 25(1), 44–56. DOI: 10.1038/s41591-018-0300-7
48. Cho, S., Kim, D., Kim, J. H., & Park, C. (2021). Multi-modal deep learning for Alzheimer's disease classification: Combining anatomical and functional imaging. *Frontiers in Neuroscience*, 15, 652286. DOI: 10.3389/fnins.2021.652286
49. Sze, V., Chen, Y. H., Yang, T. J., & Emer, J. S. (2017). Efficient processing of deep neural networks: A tutorial and survey. *Proceedings of the IEEE*, 105(12), 2295–2329. DOI: 10.1109/JPROC.2017.2761740.
50. Esteva, A., Robicquet, A., Ramsundar, B., Kuleshov, V., DePristo, M., Chou, K., ... & Dean, J. (2019). A guide to deep learning in healthcare. *Nature Medicine*, 25(1), 24–29. DOI: 10.1038/s41591-018-0316-z
51. Benjamens, S., Dhunnoo, P., & Mesko, B. (2020). The state of artificial intelligence-based FDA-approved medical devices and algorithms: An online database. *NPJ Digital Medicine*, 3, 118. DOI: 10.1038/s41746-020-00324-0
52. Livingston, G., Sommerlad, A., Orgeta, V., Costafreda, S. G., Huntley, J., Ames, D., ... & Cooper, C. (2017). Dementia prevention, intervention, and care. *The Lancet*, 390(10113), 2673–2734. DOI: 10.1016/S0140-6736(17)31363-6

53. Bohr, A., & Memarzadeh, K. (2020). The rise of artificial intelligence in healthcare applications. *Artificial Intelligence in Healthcare*, 25, 25–60. DOI: 10.1016/B978-0-12-818438-7.00002-2
54. Sweeney, M. D., Kisler, K., Montagne, A., Toga, A. W., & Zlokovic, B. V. (2018). The role of brain vasculature in neurodegenerative disorders. *Nature Neuroscience*, 21(10), 1318–1331. DOI: 10.1038/s41593-018-0234-x
55. Weiner, M. W., Veitch, D. P., Aisen, P. S., Beckett, L. A., Cairns, N. J., Green, R. C., ... & Trojanowski, J. Q. (2015). Impact of the Alzheimer's Disease Neuroimaging Initiative, 2004 to 2014. *Alzheimer's & Dementia*, 11(7), 865–884. DOI: 10.1016/j.jalz.2015.04.005.
56. Peine, A., Faulkner, A., Jæger, B., & Moors, E. (2015). Science, technology and the 'grand challenge' of ageing: Understanding the socio-material constitution of later life. *Technological Forecasting and Social Change*, 93, 1–9. DOI: 10.1016/j.techfore.2014.12.001
57. Hodges, J. R., & Piguet, O. (2018). Progress and challenges in frontotemporal dementia research: A 20-year review. *Journal of Alzheimer's Disease*, 62(3), 1467–1480. DOI: 10.3233/JAD-170973
58. Morley, J., Floridi, L., Kinsey, L., & Elhalal, A. (2020). From what to how: An initial review of publicly available AI ethics tools, methods and research to translate principles into practices. *Science and Engineering Ethics*, 26(4), 2141–2168. DOI: 10.1007/s11948-019-00165-5
59. Rajkomar, A., Dean, J., & Kohane, I. (2019). Machine learning in medicine. *New England Journal of Medicine*, 380(14), 1347–1358. DOI: 10.1056/NEJMra1814259
60. Smith, M., & Hixon, M. (2020). Alzheimer's and dementia: Key policy challenges and the role of technology. *Journal of Health Policy*, 42(4), 231–245. DOI: 10.1016/j.jhealpol.2020.01.003

Chapter 5

Healthcare operations and management using digital twin technology

M. T. Vasumathi, Manju Sadasivan, and Aurangjeb Khan

5.1 INTRODUCTION

The healthcare industry is a multifaceted sector comprising institutions and professionals dedicated to diagnosing, treating, and preventing physical and mental health conditions. This industry includes a vast array of specialties, each focusing on specific treatments, and is organized into primary, secondary, and tertiary care levels. Access to healthcare services is heavily influenced by social and economic conditions, as well as by the policies and management strategies of healthcare services. Efficient healthcare systems require adequate funding, a well-trained and well-compensated workforce, accurate and credible data to inform policies, and well-maintained and effectively managed facilities [1].

Healthcare operations management focuses on the day-to-day operations of healthcare facilities, which directly influence client experiences and organizational objectives. The main aim of healthcare operations management is to secure the necessary funds to maintain the quality and quantity of services. This field includes various disciplines such as administrative, financial, and legal practices. Critical tasks in this area involve controlling expenses, improving the quality of services, managing claims, handling medical billing, managing the revenue cycle, and ensuring compliance and credentialing. Effective healthcare operations management is crucial for overcoming various challenges. For example, implementing advanced technology can improve communication among staff and patients, foster better cooperation among healthcare providers, and reduce or eliminate operational bottlenecks. Healthcare software can support operations management by offering solutions tailored to meet organizational goals and client needs [2].

DOI: 10.1201/9781003498117-5

5.2 GENERAL FUNCTIONS AND ROLES IN HEALTHCARE OPERATIONS MANAGEMENT WITH DIGITAL TWIN APPLICATIONS

The healthcare industry is undergoing a digital transformation, and one of the most promising innovations is the digital twin. A digital twin is a virtual replica of a physical healthcare asset, system, or process that integrates real-time data from various sources. By creating a comprehensive, dynamic model of healthcare operations, digital twins offer a revolutionary approach to optimizing performance and enhancing patient care.

Digital twins provide a comprehensive tool for healthcare operations management, addressing key areas such as predictive maintenance, resource allocation, patient flow, scheduling, financial performance, risk management, capacity planning, supply chain optimization, quality of care, and training. These applications lead to increased efficiency, reduced costs, and better patient outcomes, ultimately enhancing the overall performance of healthcare facilities. By exploiting the capabilities of digital twins, healthcare operations can become more proactive, efficient, and patient-centered [3].

5.2.1 Key functions of health operations enhanced by digital twins

1. Patient flow management: Efficient patient flow is crucial for minimizing bottlenecks and ensuring timely care in healthcare facilities. Digital twins play a significant role in enhancing patient flow management by enabling real-time monitoring and optimization of patient admissions, transfers, and discharges. This technology allows healthcare managers to visualize patient movements throughout the facility, identify potential congestion points, and make data-driven adjustments to improve flow. As a result, waiting times are reduced, and the overall patient experience is significantly improved. With digital twins, healthcare providers can better coordinate care, streamline processes, and ensure that patients receive timely and appropriate treatment, ultimately leading to better health outcomes.
2. Resource allocation: Effective distribution of medical resources and staff is vital for operational efficiency in healthcare settings. Digital twins provide a powerful tool for optimizing resource allocation by analyzing real-time data. By integrating information from various sources, digital twins offer a comprehensive view of resource usage, enabling healthcare managers to make informed decisions about the deployment of medical supplies, equipment, and personnel. This data-driven approach helps reduce waste, maximize utilization, and

ensure that resources are available where and when they are needed most. With digital twins, healthcare facilities can achieve a more balanced and efficient use of their resources, leading to cost savings and improved patient care.

3. Predictive maintenance: Healthcare facilities rely on a wide range of medical equipment, and any downtime can disrupt operations and negatively impact patient care. Digital twins equipped with predictive analytics can identify potential equipment failures before they occur, allowing for proactive maintenance and reducing unexpected downtime. By continuously monitoring the performance and condition of medical devices, digital twins can detect early signs of wear and tear or malfunction. This enables maintenance teams to schedule repairs and replacements at optimal times, minimizing disruptions and ensuring that critical equipment is always operational. The predictive maintenance capabilities of digital twins lead to lower maintenance costs, increased equipment lifespan, and enhanced reliability of healthcare services [4].
4. Performance monitoring: Continuous improvement in healthcare operations requires effective performance monitoring, and digital twins offer a robust solution for this task. By tracking key performance indicators (KPIs) in real time, digital twins provide healthcare managers with valuable insights into the facility's operational efficiency and effectiveness. This continuous monitoring allows for the identification of areas needing improvement and enables data-driven decision-making. With digital twins, healthcare providers can benchmark performance, set targets, and implement strategies to enhance service delivery. This proactive approach ensures that the facility operates at peak efficiency, providing high-quality care to patients while optimizing resources and reducing costs.
5. Operational planning: Operational planning is essential for the strategic management of healthcare facilities, and digital twins offer a powerful tool for this purpose. By simulating different scenarios within the digital twin, healthcare managers can develop and test strategic plans for future operations. This capability allows for the evaluation of various strategies and their potential impacts on the facility. Digital twins enable managers to anticipate challenges, assess risks, and devise contingency plans, enhancing the facility's preparedness and adaptability. With the ability to model and analyze different operational scenarios, healthcare facilities can make more informed decisions, improve response times, and ensure that they are better equipped to handle unforeseen events and changing circumstances [5]. Figure 5.1 provides a brief framework of digital twin intervention in healthcare operations management.

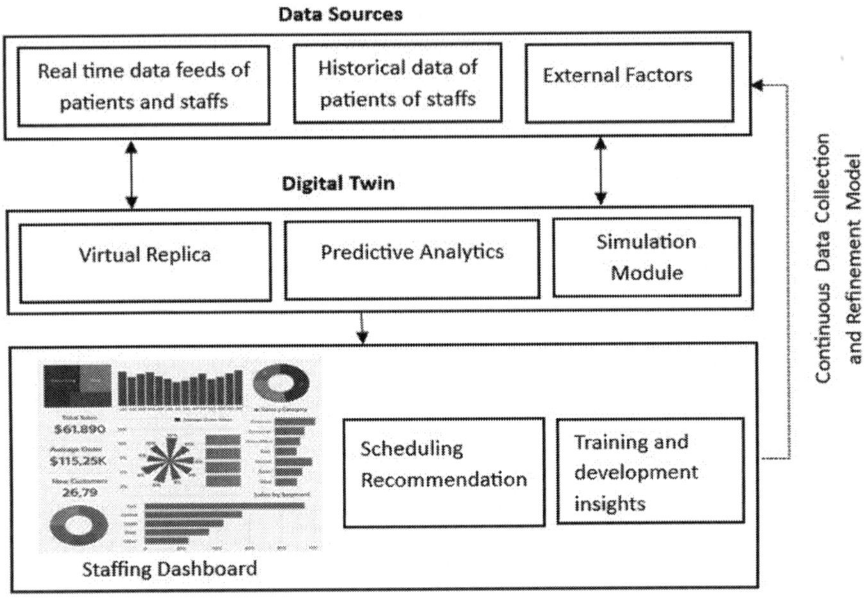

Figure 5.1 Digital twin intervention in healthcare operations management.

5.3 HEALTH OPERATIONS DATA INTEGRATION AND ROLES IN DIGITAL TWIN IMPLEMENTATION

Data integration forms the foundation of a comprehensive digital twin system in healthcare operations by consolidating data from various sources, such as electronic health records (EHRs), medical devices, and administrative systems. This holistic view of healthcare operations enhances decision-making capabilities by providing a centralized platform for accessing and analyzing data. Figure 5.2 provides a comprehensive understanding of the data integration and the roles required for implementing digital twins in health operations.

The successful implementation of digital twins involves collaboration among several key roles. Operations managers identify areas for optimization and define system goals, while clinical staff ensure the system accurately represents clinical workflows to support patient care decisions. IT specialists manage technical aspects, including data integration and system architecture, ensuring security and compatibility with existing infrastructure. Data analysts utilize advanced analytics to uncover patterns and insights, driving informed decision-making. Maintenance engineers ensure accurate representation of physical assets, providing crucial information for predicting and preventing equipment failures. Administrators oversee the system's overall

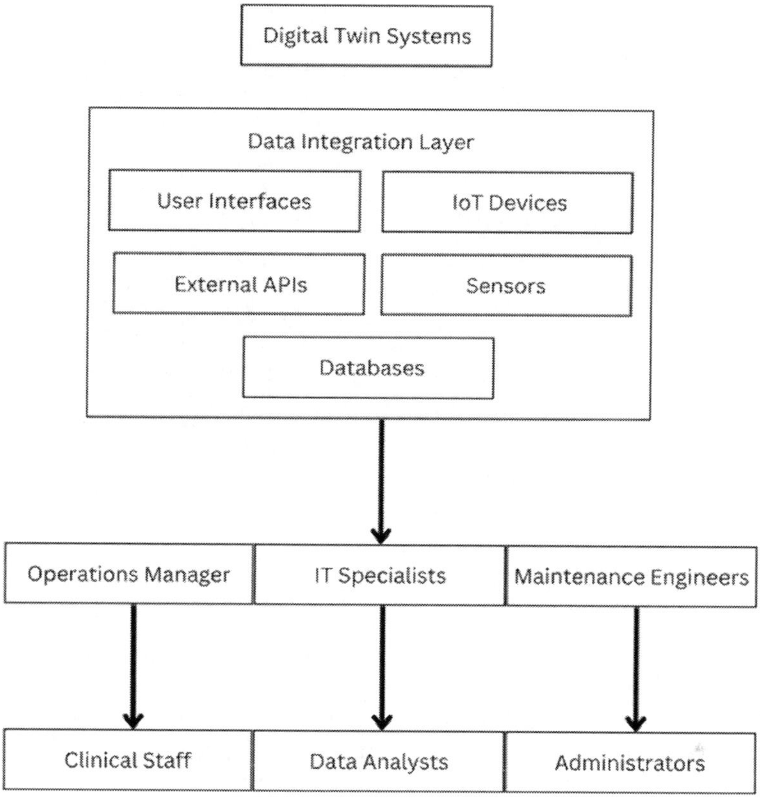

Figure 5.2 Data integration and roles in digital twin implementation.

management, user access, data governance, and regulatory compliance, ensuring effective and efficient use by all stakeholders. By working together, these roles ensure that the digital twin system delivers value and improves patient outcomes [6].

5.4 HEALTHCARE PLANNING AND MANAGEMENT

Digital twins can significantly enhance healthcare planning and management tasks across various domains, as illustrated in Figure 5.3. They enable healthcare organizations to create virtual replicas of facilities, allowing them to test different design scenarios, optimize workflows, and identify potential bottlenecks before investing in physical changes. By simulating the impact of layout modifications, resource allocation, and staffing adjustments, digital twins ensure efficient facility operations and patient

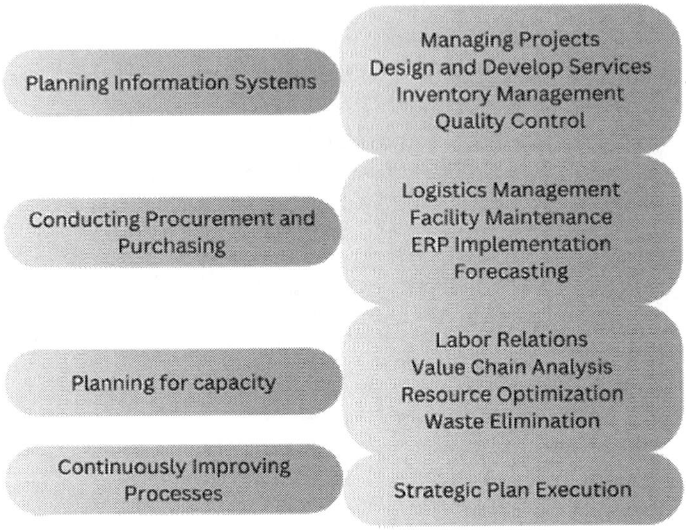

Figure 5.3 Healthcare and planning management.

flow. They can model patient demand, staff availability, and resource utilization to optimize capacity planning, preventing overcrowding and ensuring timely care. Additionally, digital twins provide a safe environment to test process improvement initiatives, streamlining operations and enhancing efficiency. They can also optimize surgical block scheduling by considering interdependencies between operating rooms, staff, and resources, ensuring timely surgical care and efficient resource use. Furthermore, digital twins support growth strategies by modeling the impact of service line expansion, facility growth, and network integration, helping leaders make informed decisions. Leveraging digital twins across these key areas improves planning, optimizes resource utilization, enhances efficiency, and ultimately delivers better patient outcomes [7]. Figure 5.3 illustrates the stages and process involved in the healthcare and planning management.

5.4.1 Planning information systems

1. Managing projects*:* Managing projects in healthcare involves overseeing and coordinating various initiatives to ensure they are completed on time, within budget, and to the required quality standards. Digital twins can play a crucial role by creating virtual models of healthcare projects. For example, a digital twin of

a new EHR system can simulate its implementation across the hospital, allowing project managers to foresee potential issues, optimize workflows, and ensure a smoother rollout. This digital representation helps in testing different scenarios and making data-driven decisions before actual implementation.

2. Helping to design and develop services: Creating and enhancing healthcare services to meet patient needs involves assessing current services, identifying gaps, and innovating new solutions. A digital twin can model a new telehealth service, simulating patient interactions and provider workflows. This helps in understanding the impact of the new service on existing systems, predicting patient outcomes, and optimizing the design before actual deployment. It allows stakeholders to visualize and modify service designs to better meet patient needs and improve care delivery.
3. Managing inventory through the supply chain: Ensuring the availability of necessary medical supplies and equipment involves managing procurement, storage, and distribution processes. Digital twins can create a virtual replica of the supply chain, providing real-time visibility into inventory levels, predicting supply shortages, and optimizing procurement strategies. For instance, an automated inventory management system integrated with a digital twin can simulate demand and supply fluctuations, helping in maintaining optimal inventory levels and preventing stock outs or overstocking.
4. Optimizing quality control: Monitoring and ensuring healthcare services meet established quality standards is crucial for improving patient outcomes and safety. Digital twins can continuously monitor the performance of healthcare processes and equipment, providing real-time data on compliance with quality standards. Regular audits and quality assurance programs can be simulated using digital twins to identify potential quality issues and implement corrective actions proactively. This continuous monitoring and simulation capability helps in maintaining high standards of care.

5.4.2 Conducting procurement/purchasing

1. Managing logistics: Efficiently coordinating the movement and storage of goods within the healthcare system ensures timely delivery and optimal resource allocation. Digital twins can model the entire logistics network, simulating the transportation and storage of medical supplies. This helps in identifying bottlenecks, optimizing routes, and improving overall logistics efficiency. For example, a digital twin can simulate different transportation scenarios to find

the most efficient routes for delivering medical supplies between facilities.

2. Managing and maintaining facilities: Ensuring healthcare facilities are safe, compliant, and well-maintained involves regular maintenance and upgrades. Digital twins can create virtual models of healthcare facilities, enabling predictive maintenance and real-time monitoring. This helps in identifying potential maintenance issues before they become critical, ensuring continuous compliance with safety regulations. For instance, a digital twin of hospital infrastructure can simulate the impact of different maintenance schedules, helping to plan and execute timely upgrades.
3. Conducting enterprise resource planning (ERP): Utilizing integrated software systems to manage and streamline all facets of healthcare operations is essential for efficiency. Digital twins can enhance ERP systems by providing real-time simulations and data analytics. An ERP system integrated with a digital twin can simulate the impact of changes in finance, supply chain, and human resources, allowing for better planning and decision-making. This integration helps in predicting the outcomes of different operational strategies and optimizing resource allocation.
4. Forecasting for planning: Anticipating future needs and trends is essential for efficiently allocating resources and meeting upcoming demands. By simulating various scenarios, digital twins leverage data analytics to forecast patient admission rates, staffing requirements, and resource needs. This powerful capability enables healthcare organizations to make well-informed decisions and proactively prepare for future challenges. For instance, a digital twin can model the potential impact of an upcoming flu season on hospital admissions. By analyzing historical data and current trends, the digital twin can predict the expected influx of flu patients. This information can then be used to strategically allocate staff, ensuring adequate coverage during peak admission periods. Additionally, the digital twin can forecast the necessary supplies and equipment required to handle the increased patient load, allowing the hospital to stock up in advance. By accurately predicting future demands, digital twins help healthcare organizations optimize their resource allocation. This not only ensures that patients receive timely and high-quality care but also helps to minimize waste and inefficiencies. When resources are allocated based on reliable forecasts, hospitals can avoid overstaffing during low-demand periods or running short on critical supplies during high-demand periods [8]. Figure 5.4 illustrates procurement/purchasing and associated tasks.

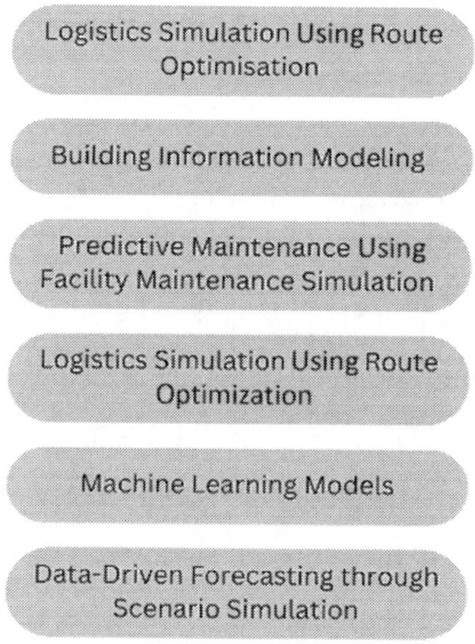

Figure 5.4 Procurement/purchasing and associated tasks.

5.4.3 Planning for capacity

1. Navigating industrial labor relations: Managing the relationship between healthcare management and the workforce involves negotiations, conflict resolution, and labor agreements. Digital twins can simulate the impact of different labor policies and agreements, helping to predict their outcomes and make informed decisions. For instance, a digital twin can model the effects of a new labor agreement on staff productivity and patient care, allowing for better negotiation strategies and conflict resolution.
2. Analyzing the value chain: Examining the full range of activities required to bring a service to market helps in identifying areas for improvement and efficiency. Digital twins can model the entire value chain, providing insights into how different processes are interconnected and where improvements can be made. For example, conducting a value chain analysis using a digital twin can reveal opportunities to reduce costs and improve service delivery, ultimately enhancing patient care.
3. Optimizing resource usage: Ensuring that human, financial, and material resources are used efficiently involves identifying and implementing best practices. Digital twins can simulate resource

usage across different scenarios, helping to identify inefficiencies and optimize processes. For instance, lean management techniques can be tested and refined using a digital twin before actual implementation, ensuring that resources are used effectively to maximize healthcare delivery.

4. Eliminating waste and bottlenecks: Identifying and removing inefficiencies in processes improves overall operational flow. Digital twins can continuously monitor and simulate healthcare processes, identifying waste and bottlenecks in real time. This capability allows for proactive adjustments and continuous improvement. For example, a digital twin can simulate the patient check-in process, identifying delays and suggesting improvements to reduce wait times and enhance patient satisfaction.

5.4.4 Continuously improving processes

Implementing the long-term goals and objectives of the healthcare organization involves aligning daily operations with strategic priorities. Digital twins can simulate the impact of strategic initiatives, providing real-time feedback on their effectiveness. For example, rolling out a new patient care model as part of the hospital's strategic initiative can be simulated using a digital twin to identify potential challenges and optimize the implementation process. This ensures that the strategic plan is executed effectively, aligning with the organization's vision and goals [9].

5.5 BENEFITS OF UTILIZING DIGITAL TWINS IN HEALTHCARE OPERATIONS

Digital twins, which are virtual replicas of physical objects/systems, have been increasingly adopted in healthcare operations. It offers several benefits that enhance efficiency, improve patient outcomes, and streamline the hospital operations. Key benefits of digital twins in healthcare are as follows:

1. Increase predictive maintenance: Digital twins can monitor and predict the performance of medical devices, allowing for timely maintenance and reducing downtime. This ensures that equipment is always available and operational, which is critical in healthcare settings.
2. Improve resource management: By simulating hospital operations, digital twins help in optimizing the use of rooms, beds, staff, and other resources. This leads to improved patient flow and reduced waiting times.
3. Enhance patient care: Digital twins can create detailed models of individual patients, integrating data from various sources like wearable

devices and EHRs. This allows for personalized medicine, where treatments are performed to the unique needs of each patient.

4. Enhance training and education: Digital twins provide a realistic and risk-free environment for medical staff to practice procedures and improve their skills. This leads to better-prepared healthcare professionals and ultimately better patient care.
5. Optimize hospital operations: For better management of hospital operations by modeling hospital workflows, digital twins help identify bottlenecks and inefficiencies. Hospitals can then reengineer processes to improve overall operational efficiency.
6. Optimize diagnostics and monitoring: For optimized diagnostics and continuous monitoring, digital twins can continuously monitor patient vitals and other health indicators, allowing for early detection of potential issues and timely intervention.
7. Simulate complex surgical procedures: For planning and simulation of complex surgeries, surgeons can use digital twins to plan and simulate complex procedures before performing them on patients. This reduces the risk of complications and optimizes surgical outcomes.
8. Actionable insights: For informed decision-making based on data insights, digital twins aggregate and analyze vast amounts of data, providing healthcare administrators with actionable insights that drive better decision-making.
9. Reduce overall operational cost: For the reduction in operational costs, by optimizing various aspects of healthcare operations and improving efficiency, digital twins can help reduce overall operational costs. This can include savings from reduced equipment downtime, better resource allocation, and fewer readmissions.
10. Enhance patient engagement: To enhance patient engagement and satisfaction, patients can interact with their digital twins to understand their health conditions better and manage their own health more effectively. This leads to higher satisfaction and better health outcomes.
11. Accelerate research and development: For accelerated medical research and innovation, digital twins provide a platform for researchers to test new treatments and medical devices in a virtual environment before real-world implementation, speeding up the R&D process [10].

5.6 CHALLENGES AND LIMITATIONS IN IMPLEMENTING DIGITAL TWINS IN HEALTHCARE

Implementing digital twins in healthcare is highly beneficial as we have seen in the previous section but it comes with several challenges and limitations. These obstacles need to be addressed to fully harness the potential of digital twins in healthcare. Some of the primary challenges are as follows.

5.6.1 Privacy and security

Privacy and security are critical concerns when implementing digital twins in healthcare. Digital twins require access to vast amounts of sensitive patient data, including electronic medical records, genetic information, lifestyle data, and real-time health monitoring from wearable devices. Ensuring the privacy and security of this data is paramount, given the stringent regulations such as Health Insurance Portability and Accountability Act (HIPAA) in the USA and General Data Protection Regulation (GDPR) in Europe. Any data breach can have severe consequences for both patients and healthcare providers, leading to identity theft, financial fraud, and reputational damage. To address these challenges, the following approaches can be adopted:

1. Blockchain-based security: Integrating block chain technology can provide tamper-resistant, traceable, and secure storage of medical records for digital twins. Blockchain ensures data integrity and enables fine-grained access control.
2. Searchable encryption: Combining cloud-based storage with post-quantum searchable encryption can allow efficient retrieval of encrypted medical records without compromising privacy.
3. Access control and authentication: Implementing robust access control mechanisms and authentication protocols to regulate who can access and update the digital twin data is crucial.
4. Data minimization: Collecting and storing only the minimum necessary data for the digital twin's functionality can help reduce the risk of data breaches.
5. Transparency and patient consent: Ensuring transparency about data collection and usage, and obtaining explicit patient consent, can build trust and address privacy concerns.

5.6.2 Technologies interoperability issues

For integrating data from diverse sources, healthcare data is often siloed across different systems and formats. Ensuring seamless integration and interoperability between various EHR systems, medical devices, and digital twin platforms is complex and challenging.

5.6.3 High cost of implementation

Developing and deploying digital twins involve substantial costs related to technology infrastructure, software development, and training. This can be a barrier, especially for smaller healthcare providers with limited budgets.

5.6.4 Quality and availability of data

Digital twins rely on high-quality, real-time data to function effectively. Incomplete, outdated, or inaccurate data can lead to erroneous models and predictions, compromising patient care and operational decisions.

5.6.5 Healthcare systems complexity

Creating accurate digital replicas of complex biological systems and healthcare operations is a notable challenge. The human body and healthcare processes are highly complex, and replicating them accurately in a digital twin requires advanced modeling and the simulation techniques.

5.6.6 Resistant to adopt new technologies

Healthcare professionals and administrators may be resistant to adopt new technologies due to concerns about disruption, additional workload, or skepticism about the benefits. Change management strategies are essential to facilitate acceptance and adoption.

5.6.7 Various regulations and ethical issues

The use of digital twins in healthcare must comply with various regulations and ethical standards. This includes issues related to informed consent, data usage, and patient rights. Navigating these regulatory and ethical landscapes can be complex and time-consuming.

5.6.8 Significant technical challenges

Developing a digital twin involves sophisticated technology, including advanced algorithms, machine learning (ML), and real-time data processing. Ensuring these technologies work seamlessly together poses significant technical challenges.

5.6.9 Maintenance and scalability for high amount of data

Once implemented, digital twin systems require ongoing maintenance and updates to remain effective. Additionally, scaling these systems to handle increasing amounts of data and more complex models can be challenging.

5.6.10 Real-time data processing

For digital twins to be effective, we need to process data in real time or near real time. This requires robust computing infrastructure and efficient data processing algorithms, which can be technically demanding [11].

5.7 CASE STUDIES: SUCCESSFUL APPLICATIONS OF DIGITAL TWINS IN HEALTHCARE FACILITIES

Digital twins are successfully implemented in some healthcare facilities especially in the USA, UK, France, and Singapore, demonstrating the potential and effectiveness of the digital twins as highlighted below. This section also highlights the implementation of the digital twins in the healthcare sector:

1. Hospital for Special Surgery (HSS), New York, USA: The Hospital for Special Surgery used digital twins to optimize their orthopedic surgery processes. HSS created digital twins of their surgical procedures and workflows. The digital twins were used to simulate and analyze various aspects of the surgery process, including patient flow, resource utilization, and scheduling. It improved scheduling efficiency to reduce patient wait times and optimized the use of operating rooms and enhanced the ability to predict and manage surgical demand, reducing bottlenecks and increasing overall operational efficiency. It also helped in better resource allocation, ensuring that the right personnel and equipment were available when needed [12].
2. Moorfields Eye Hospital, London, UK: Moorfields Eye Hospital used digital twins to enhance the delivery of eye care services. They created digital twins of patient eyes using detailed imaging data, integrated this data with patient health records, and used advanced analytics to personalize treatment plans. It enhanced diagnostic accuracy by providing a comprehensive view of each patient's eye health. It improved treatment outcomes by tailoring interventions to the specific needs of individual patients and also increased efficiency in patient care by streamlining diagnostic and treatment processes [13].
3. University Hospital of Lille, France: The University Hospital of Lille utilized digital twins to optimize hospital operations and patient care. They developed a digital twin of the hospital's emergency department. They simulated patient flow, staff allocation, and resource usage to identify inefficiencies and areas for improvement.
4. National University Health System (NUHS), Singapore: NUHS implemented a digital twin of their hospital to improve overall management and patient care. They developed a comprehensive digital twin that integrated data from various hospital departments, including patient records, equipment, and facilities. It used artificial intelligence (AI) and ML to analyze data and predict patient admission rates, resource needs, and potential bottlenecks.

5.8 IMPLEMENTATION OF DIGITAL TWINS IN HEALTHCARE

Implementing digital twins for the healthcare sector requires a comprehensive set of hardware and software components to create, manage, and utilize the digital replicas effectively. Key hardware and software requirements are highlighted below.

5.8.1 Servers and storage

High-performance servers are required to handle the computational load and for the real-time data processing and complex simulations. Along with the high-performance server, a large-scale, high-speed storage system is also required to store vast amounts of data generated by sensors, medical records, imaging data, etc. Solutions like NAS (network-attached storage) or SAN (storage area network) are often used.

5.8.2 IoT (Internet of Things) devices and sensors

IoT devices and sensors play an important role in the implementation of the digital twins, as it is the main component for getting the real-time data from the various objects, locations, as well as from the patients, which are the base for creating the digital twins. IoT-enabled medical equipment that can transmit real-time data (e.g., MRI machines, CT scanners, and vital signs monitors). Environmental sensors for monitoring hospital conditions (e.g., temperature, humidity, air quality, smoke, and fire). And the wearable devices for monitoring patients fitness, heart rate, fever, pulse rate, and oxygen level. And to integrate these sensors with the computer system, we needed some microcontroller boards like ESP32 and ESP 8266. These boards are cheaper and capable enough for getting the data from the sensors as well as having wireless connectivity to push the data to the server. Other than these ESP boards, there are lots of options like STM, Arduino, and Raspberry Pi board, which are equally good enough for the same job and all have their own pros and cons [14].

5.8.3 Networking infrastructure

A reliable, high-speed internet and intranet connectivity required for data transmission between devices, servers, and cloud platforms. At the same time wireless access points to support IoT devices and ensure seamless data collection and communication in the system.

5.8.4 Edge computing devices

To process data locally, we need edge servers or gateways, which are to integrate the sensors, collect the data from sensors, and process the data at the local level at the edge layer. It is to reduce the latency and bandwidth usage by handling preliminary data processing before sending it to central servers or cloud platforms. Edge computing devices could be either ESP32, Raspberry Pi, or local servers.

5.8.5 Software requirements

We need to utilize digital twin platforms like Siemens MindSphere, GE Predix, or PTC ThingWorx, which provide tools for creating, managing, and visualizing digital twins. At the same time we need to use a simulation software/tool for modeling and simulating hospital operations, such as AnyLogic or Simul8.

5.8.6 Data integration and management

To integrate data from various sources like EHRs, IoT devices, and legacy systems, a middleware software like Apache Kafka or MuleSoft is required to ensure seamless data flow in the digital twin system. And for storing and managing structured and unstructured data, we need database software like MySQL or PostgreSQL, and NoSQL databases like MongoDB.

5.8.7 Analytics and machine learning platform

We need analytics platforms/tools like SAS, IBM SPSS, or Tableau for analyzing data and generating insights for the required action. We also need ML frameworks like TensorFlow, PyTorch, or Scikit-learn for predictive analytics and for advanced data modeling for the digital twin.

5.8.8 User interface and visualization applications

For a better user interface and visualization, we need software like Power BI, Tableau, or Grafana for creating intuitive and interactive dashboards and visualizations. Web or mobile applications are required for the healthcare stakeholders for the specific hospital management tasks, which can be developed using frameworks like Angular, React, or Flutter.

5.8.9 Privacy and compliance

Solutions for ensuring data privacy and security, including encryption tools, firewalls, and intrusion detection systems, are crucial for the system. At the end, software to ensure adherence to healthcare regulations and standards, such as HIPAA, a US legislation, compliance tools required to be implemented [15].

5.8.10 Architecture of the system

Architecture of the system illustrates the working process and the technologies interoperability for the implementation of the digital twins. Sensors with IoT devices, AI, cloud storage, and XR (extended reality) are the major technologies used for the implementation of the digital twin for any applications as given in Figure 5.5 [11].

5.8.11 Circuit diagram for the IoT devices in the healthcare system for the digital twins

Figure 5.6 illustrates the different IoT devices for different types of data collection from the healthcare system. ESP32 is integrated with heartbeat, oximeter, and temperature sensors, which are directly collecting data from the patients, while the Raspberry Pi module is integrated with webcam and gas/fire sensors to collect the data from the hospital rooms to get the data regarding the beds and patients availability. ESP modules will be integrated with each patient while Raspberry Pi modules will be placed in each room. Data from the ESP and Raspberry Pi modules are collected to the central module through Wi-Fi and will be stored to the local server, while at the same time all required data stored at the cloud server for further visualization

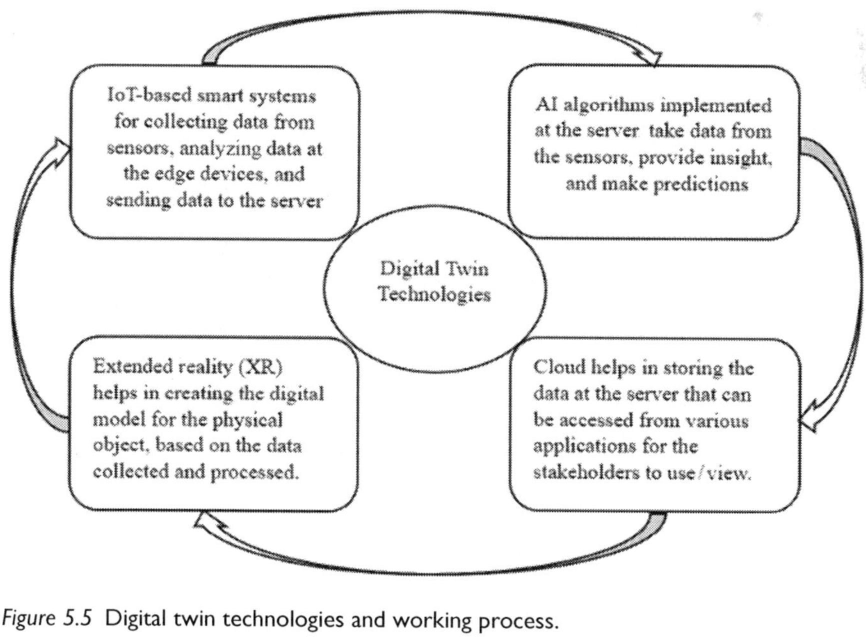

Figure 5.5 Digital twin technologies and working process.

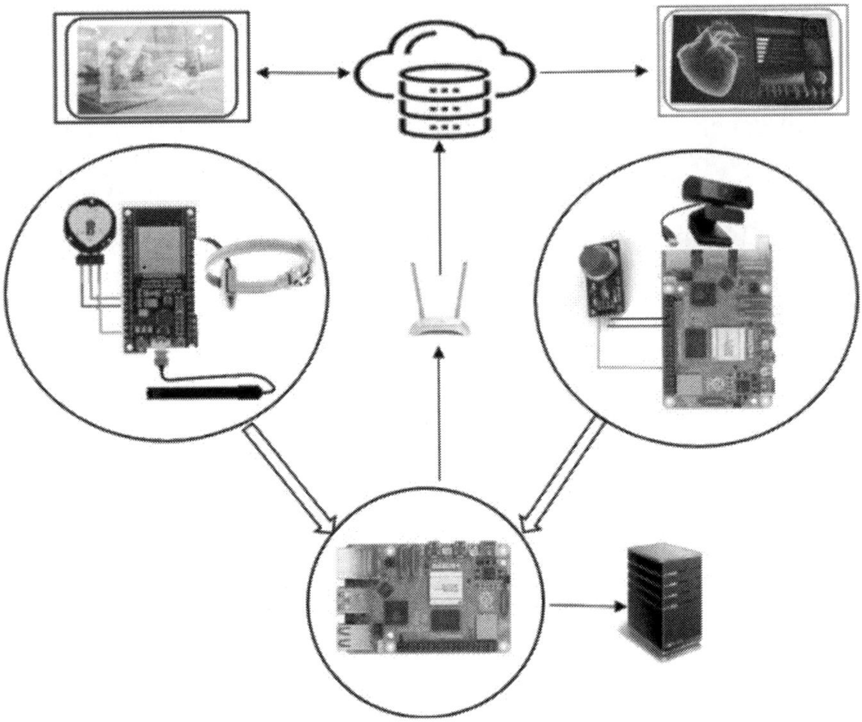

Figure 5.6 IoT devices integration for digital twin-based healthcare system.

and creating the digital twins with the help of XR module. Using the hospital applications, records and results can be accessed from the cloud with security and privacy as per the hospital norms.

5.9 DATA SECURITY AND PRIVACY CONSIDERATIONS IN DIGITAL TWIN IMPLEMENTATION FOR HEALTHCARE

Implementing digital twin in healthcare has many advantages, including better patient outcomes and more efficient operations. Data security, privacy, and the proper implementation of this revolutionary technology must be given top priority as healthcare organizations use digital twins to enhance patient care and streamline operations [16].

5.9.1 Data security and privacy in healthcare

When using digital twins, data security and privacy are crucial due to the sensitive nature of healthcare data:

1. Encryption: Use robust encryption techniques to safeguard data while it's in transit and at rest, making sure that only people with permission can access it.
2. Access controls: To restrict authorized personnel's access to data based on their jobs and responsibilities, implement strict access controls.
3. Audit trails: Ensure thorough audit trails that document all interactions with patient data in order to establish accountability and transparency.
4. Data masking and de-identification: When necessary, anonymize patient data using data masking and de-identification procedures so that it is still accessible for analysis and study.
5. Applicable regulations: Follow the relevant laws protecting the privacy of healthcare data.

5.9.2 Training and adoption strategies

In order to successfully use digital twins, it is imperative that medical professionals receive sufficient training for embracing this cutting-edge technology [17]:

1. Training programs: Provide thorough training courses that teach medical staff the advantages of digital twins and how to use them.
2. User-friendly interfaces: To reduce the learning curve, make sure that digital twin apps have intuitive and user-friendly user interfaces.
3. Continuous education: As technology advances, cultivate a culture of lifelong learning by offering continuing training and assistance.
4. Champion adoption: Find early adopters in your company who can promote the use of digital twins and assist fellow employees in embracing the technology and support them in doing so.

5.9.3 Overcoming implementation challenges

The hurdles can be overcome by the following:

1. Integration complexity: Work together with IT teams to address the challenges of integrating digital twins with current healthcare workflows and systems.
2. Data quality issues: Maintain and enhance data quality on a constant basis to guarantee that digital twins deliver precise insights and assistance.
3. Resource constraints: Make sure you have enough staff and technology available to support the development and upkeep of digital twins.

4. Change management: Create a change management strategy to assist healthcare personnel in adjusting to new procedures and technology with ease.
5. Interoperability: Invest in technologies and standards for interoperability to make sure digital twins can interact with other healthcare systems.
6. Cost management: Make a reasonable budget that includes funds for both the initial setup and continuing upkeep and improvements [18].

5.10 BEST PRACTICES FOR IMPLEMENTING AND MAINTAINING DIGITAL TWIN TECHNOLOGY IN HEALTHCARE OPERATIONS

By providing a dynamic and real-time method to comprehending, replicating, and optimizing numerous healthcare processes and systems, digital twins are completely changing the healthcare sector. A thorough approach is necessary for the implementation and upkeep of digital twin technology in the healthcare industry. Healthcare companies can effectively use digital twin technology to improve patient care, increase operational efficiency, and spur innovation in healthcare delivery by adhering to the following best practices.

5.10.1 Strategic planning and stakeholder engagement

In the healthcare industry, strategic planning entails a thorough evaluation of the organization's strengths, weaknesses, opportunities, and risks. Using this study, plans are developed to help the organization reach its objectives and pinpoint areas for development. Stakeholder engagement is essential to the success of strategic planning. Stakeholder engagement management, that is, effective, involves a multifaceted strategy that includes constant discussions, attentive listening, and teamwork. Early in the planning phase, involve important stakeholders such as patients, IT personnel, and healthcare providers to secure their support and get their views. Make sure that the digital twin strategy is in line with the organization's overarching strategic goals in the healthcare sector.

5.10.2 Data governance and quality management

In the healthcare industry, data governance refers to the process of utilizing collected data to derive additional value and to define the procedures for handling and collecting the data in a secure manner. Data governance encompasses the tactics, personnel, equipment, and procedures used in data management. Healthcare organizations may guarantee data compliance with patient data privacy rules and maintain high-quality data for future analysis by implementing a strict data governance policy. Provide techniques for gathering and combining data from several sources, including patient information, IoT devices, and EHRs. Update digital twin models with real-time data streams to deliver precise and timely insights [19].

5.10.3 Training and education for healthcare professionals

To guarantee that every member of the healthcare team is adequately trained on the use and benefit of digital twin technology, an efficient training program must be in place. To make sure that everyone is collaborating to deliver the greatest care possible, the organization needs to cultivate a culture of safety. In order to keep staff updated on new features, best practices, and technological advancements, continuous training and support must be offered.

5.10.4 Continuous monitoring and improvement of digital twin models

High-performance computing resources must be employed to process and analyze large datasets rapidly and competently. Enhance the predictive and analytical capabilities of digital twins by integrating AI and ML algorithms. Over time, monitoring and improvement of the asset's performance and the efficacy of the optimization measures are required. In order to do this, data collection and analysis may need to continue, and the digital twin and optimization techniques may need to be modified as necessary.

5.11 CURRENT USES OF DIGITAL TWIN TECHNOLOGY IN HEALTHCARE

Healthcare companies may increase patient care, boost productivity, and encourage innovation by utilizing digital twins. This will eventually result in a more adaptable and resilient healthcare system.

5.11.1 Patient care and treatment

Healthcare providers may ensure that each patient receives a customized treatment plan by simulating and predicting the effects of therapies on an individual basis through the creation of digital replicas of patients. With the use of digital twins, complex surgical procedures may be preoperatively planned and simulated more easily. This allows surgeons to plan ahead for any problems and adjust their techniques to improve patient outcomes and safety. These technologies are essential for monitoring chronic illnesses because they provide models of how the diseases advance and allow treatment plans to be modified as conditions change. Individualized

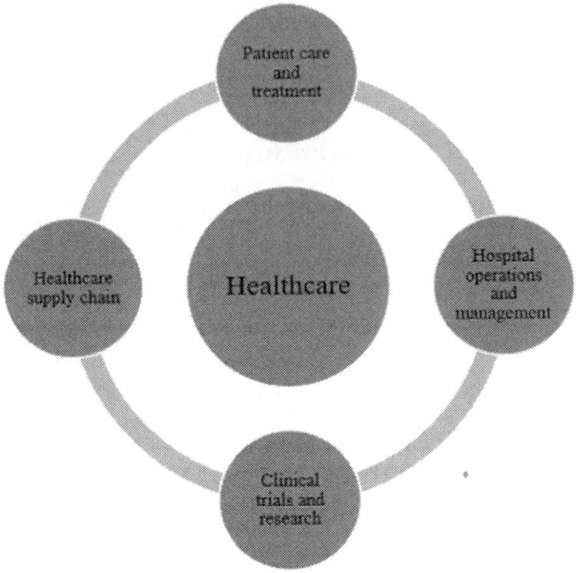

Figure 5.7 Current uses of digital twin technology in healthcare.

specifications are made possible by the use of digital twins in the design of implants and prostheses, guaranteeing the best possible fit and enhanced functionality. Current uses of digital twin technology in healthcare are illustrated in Figure 5.7.

5.11.2 Hospital operations and management

Digital twins use modeling and simulation to determine the best hospital workflows and layouts in an effort to improve patient flow and shorten wait times. With the help of digital twins, healthcare facilities can track and manage their assets more effectively, optimize maintenance plans, and reduce equipment downtime. Digital twins help create containment and prevention techniques that work in healthcare settings by modeling the transmission of infections.

5.11.3 Clinical trials and research

By eliminating the need for lengthy clinical trials, digital twins can speed up drug development by simulating human physiological reactions to medications. In order to assess the results of health interventions and comprehend the patterns of disease transmission, these tools model health dynamics at the population level.

5.11.4 Healthcare supply chain

Digital twins offer insights into healthcare supply chains, assisting with demand forecasting, inefficiency identification, and on-time medical supply delivery. Predictive analytics and real-time monitoring are employed to maintain ideal inventory levels, cutting off surplus and guaranteeing the availability of necessary supplies. Digital twins minimize delays by optimizing delivery routes by simulating many transportation scenarios and taking weather and traffic conditions into account. Disaster scenarios are predicted by digital twins, which makes it possible to create backup plans that guarantee supplies won't stop during emergencies. AI and ML are used by digital twins to predict future supply requirements with great accuracy, optimizing stock levels to minimize waste and shortages. Digital twins ensure the stability of healthcare supply chains by identifying and mitigating risks by modeling the complete supply network.

5.12 FUTURE OUTLOOK AND POTENTIAL DEVELOPMENTS IN DIGITAL TWIN TECHNOLOGY FOR HEALTHCARE OPERATIONS

Digital twins are transforming the healthcare sector by providing a dynamic, real-time method for comprehending, modeling, and improving different healthcare systems and processes. A thorough grasp of the fundamental ideas behind digital twins is necessary before beginning any journey toward their successful implementation in the healthcare industry.

With the potential to completely transform the way healthcare services are provided, tracked, and optimized, digital twin technology has enormous and varied possibilities in the future.

5.12.1 Health monitoring and disease management

Healthcare professionals can track patients' health in real time by combining digital twins with wearable's and the Internet of Medical Things (IoMT). By predicting possible health problems before they worsen and allowing for prompt interventions, this integration lowers the rate of readmissions to hospitals. It enhances patient outcomes and operational efficiencies by enabling healthcare professionals to make data-driven decisions.

Using a comprehensive dataset that includes genetic information and environmental characteristics, the genomic and environmental integration approach creates highly individualized treatment programs. It facilitates preventative care techniques by addressing the patient's current state as well as any future health problems. For executives in the healthcare industry, this represents a shift toward more efficient, precision medicine that might dramatically enhance patient outcomes and satisfaction while also perhaps reducing healthcare costs through an emphasis on early detection and prevention.

Digital twins provide a potent tool for early detection and the application of preventative interventions by simulating the evolution of disease within the distinct physiological setting of each patient. By reorienting the focus from treatment to prevention, this capacity has the potential to improve patient care by lowering the expense of late-stage treatments and possibly lessening the burden of chronic illnesses.

Novel approaches to the diagnosis and treatment of neurological and mental health issues are made possible by the simulation of brain activity and neural connections. For hospital administrators, this entails broadening the area of care to incorporate virtual mental health therapies and cutting-edge, customized neurotherapy, which may enhance patient results and access to mental health services.

5.12.2 Virtual technologies in healthcare

The combination of virtual reality (VR) and augmented reality (AR) technology offers patients customized rehabilitation experiences, gives surgeons 3D visual guidance during surgeries, and improves medical education with interactive training modules. This raises the bar for medical professional training and ensures a better standard of service in addition to increasing surgical accuracy and patient recovery rates [20].

By foretelling the integration of tissues and organs with the patient's body, digital twins are essential in directing the biofabrication process. Furthermore, better epidemic and pandemic preparedness is supported by their capacity to simulate the spread of disease in populations. Executives are promised that these applications will improve public health responses to infectious diseases and transform organ transplantation.

5.12.3 Healthcare operations and sustainability

Through the provision of real-time tracking, stock optimization, and effective logistics, digital twins optimize the supply chain and hospital operations. Through the simulation of healthcare ecosystems, they improve operational efficiency and patient care delivery while enabling more sustainable practices through less waste and carbon emissions.

Resilience of the healthcare system is increased by using digital twins to simulate crisis reactions and strengthen quality control throughout the supply chain. This tactical advantage protects patient outcomes and the reputation of the hospital by enabling hospitals to continue providing high-quality treatment even under challenging circumstances [21].

5.12.4 Global healthcare improvement and ethics

Digital twins have the potential to greatly increase access to healthcare, particularly in impoverished areas, by enabling remote diagnosis and treatments. This technology is essential for attaining healthcare fairness since it optimizes healthcare outcomes and resources, supporting global health initiatives.

Simulating patient experiences helps train healthcare professionals in ethical decision-making and empathy, fostering a patient-centered care culture. For executives, emphasizing these simulations can enhance patient satisfaction and trust, highlighting the institution's dedication to ethical healthcare delivery [22].

5.13 CONCLUSION

Digital twins can easily transform the medical field by addressing challenges that traditional methods cannot fully resolve. These virtual models can mimic the perception and action of any relevant facility in the medical environment, synchronizing their observable state with that of the physical entity (PE). Digital twins offer real-time monitoring, dynamic analysis, and precise treatment for diseases, paving the way for personalized medicine and improved patient outcomes. Despite the need to address technical and ethical issues associated with digital twin technology in healthcare, the progress is promising. The application of digital twins in medicine extends beyond diagnosis and treatment to predicting health and disease states, providing a quantitative understanding of these conditions. As a crucial approach for future medicine, digital twin healthcare will enable precision medicine and make personalized treatment a reality. Moreover, digital twin applications have the potential to optimize healthcare operations management by improving patient flow, resource allocation, equipment maintenance, and overall performance. By integrating real-time data and predictive analytics, healthcare facilities can operate more efficiently and provide better patient care. The interconnected nature of digital twins ensures that each function and role within healthcare operations management works together to create a more efficient, effective, and patient-centered healthcare system.

REFERENCES

1. Jha, R. K., Sahay, B. S., & Charan, P. (2016). Healthcare operations management: A structured literature review. *Decision*, 43(3), 259–279.
2. Dai, T., & Tayur, S. (2020). OM forum—Healthcare operations management: A snapshot of emerging research. *Manufacturing & Service Operations Management*, 22(5), 869–887.

3. Erol, T., Mendi, A. F., & Doğan, D. (2020, October). The digital twin revolution in healthcare. In *2020 4th international symposium on multidisciplinary studies and innovative technologies (ISMSIT)* (pp. 1–7). IEEE.
4. Manchadi, O., Ben-Bouazza, F. E., & Jioudi, B. (2023). Predictive maintenance in healthcare system: A survey. *IEEE Access*, 11, 61313–61330.
5. Talawar, M. P., Pant, H., Sayyed, M. S., Tamboli, M. S., Shaik, M. N., & Ganesan, M. V. (2023). Predictive Maintenance in Healthcare IoT: A Machine Learning-based Approach. *European Chemical Bulletin*, 12(4), 15909–15922.
6. Turab, M., & Jamil, S. (2023). A comprehensive survey of digital twins in healthcare in the era of metaverse. *BioMedInformatics*, 3(3), 563–584.
7. Rivera, L. F., Jiménez, M., Angara, P., Villegas, N. M., Tamura, G., & Müller, H. A. (2019, November). Towards continuous monitoring in personalized healthcare through digital twins. In *Proceedings of the 29th annual international conference on computer science and software engineering* (pp. 329–335).
8. Barbiero, P., Vinas Torne, R., & Lió, P. (2021). Graph representation forecasting of patient's medical conditions: Toward a digital twin. *Frontiers in Genetics*, 12, 652907.
9. Haleem, A., Javaid, M., Singh, R. P., & Suman, R. (2023). Exploring the revolution in healthcare systems through the applications of digital twin technology. *Biomedical Technology*, 4, 28–38.
10. Amardeep Rawat. (n.d.). Digital twins in healthcare – A new era of innovation for businesses. https://appinventiv.com/blog/digital-twins-in-healthcare, April 26, 2024.
11. Attaran, M., & Celik, B. G. (2023). Digital twin: Benefits, use cases, challenges, and opportunities. *Decision Analytics Journal*, 6, 100165.
12. Rogerson, S. (n.d.). OrthoVentions invests in digital twin of skeletons. www.iotm2mcouncil.org/iot-library/news/connected-health-news/orthoventions-invests-in-digital-twin-of-skeletons/
13. Lee, E. L., Barrett, M., Prince, K., Oborn, E., Li, O., & Thomas, P. (2022). *Digital twins and service innovation in designing the Hospital of the Future* (Vol. 1, pp. 1–32). Centre for Digital Built Britain.
14. Farahani, B., Firouzi, F., & Chakrabarty, K. (2020). Healthcare IoT. In F. Firouzi, K. Chakrabarty, & S. Nassif (Eds.), *Intelligent Internet of Things: From device to fog and cloud* (pp. 515–545). Springer. https://doi.org/10.1007/978-3-030-30367-9_11
15. Lutkevich, B. (n.d.). HIPAA (Health Insurance Portability and Accountability Act). www.techtarget.com/searchhealthit/definition/HIPAA
16. McKenna, J. (n.d.). Applying digital twins in healthcare. https://blog.mdpi.com/2024/04/17/digital-twins-in-healthcare/
17. Haleem, A., Javaid, M., Singh, R. P., & Suman, R. (2023). Exploring the revolution in healthcare systems through the applications of digital twin technology. *Biomedical Technology*, 4, 28–38.
18. Albanians, L. (n.d.). A comprehensive guide to implementing digital twins in healthcare. https://medium.com/@Larisa10/a-comprehensive-guide-to-implementing-digital-twins-in-healthcare-dfd832a6f72

19. Prolifics. (n.d.). Data governance in healthcare. https://prolifics.com/us/resource-center/specialty-guides/data-privacy/data-governance-in-healthcare#:~:text=Data%20governance%20in%20healthcare%20is,ensure%20that%20it%20is%20secure
20. Pantelidis, P., Chorti, A., Papagiouvanni, I., Paparoidamis, G., Drosos, C., Panagiotakopoulos, T., ... & Sideris, M. (2018). Virtual and augmented reality in medical education. *Medical and Surgical Education-Past, Present and Future*, 26(1), 77–97.
21. Elkefi, S., & Asan, O. (2022). Digital twins for managing health care systems: Rapid literature review. *Journal of Medical Internet Research*, 24(8), e37641.
22. Moudatsou, M., Stavropoulou, A., Philalithis, A., & Koukouli, S. (2020, January). The role of empathy in health and social care professionals. *Healthcare, MDPI*, 8(1), 26.

Chapter 6

Data security and ethical considerations in healthcare digital twins

Seema Rani and Vijay Hasanpuri

6.1 INTRODUCTION

The pace of healthcare technology development quickly picked up with the arrival of digital twin (DT) technology on the scene [1]. This initiative brought the ability to observe patient care and clinical trials in ways that had previously been unimaginable. DTs has grown into being a key counterpart to healthcare industry by offering the facility of digital copy of various physical entities or mechanisms such as diseases that are living and changing in real time [2]. While there may be the prospect of better healthcare merits, there are a good number of concerns that go along with this, for instance, data security and ethical issues [3]. In this introduction, familiarizing the reader with this issue brings about a detailed assessment of the key issues around data security and ethical consideration in the medical DTs environment [4]. This work basically explores the foundation of the modern methods of data security, how to address ethical complexities associated with informed consent and bias reduction, and the legal and compliance functions within the bounds of healthcare modern ethics. The virtual model of the future in healthcare means a different for us that medical specialists use to know the condition of patients, diagnosing, and treatments [5]. There are many different applications of the word DT that may be as simple as the virtual replica of a single patient or a medical device or as complicated as that of the multitude of organ system. In healthcare, the development of DTs is based on a wide range of information sources, such as electronic health records (EHRs), imaging of the human body, DNA sequences, and actual physiological data that changed with time and wasmodeled individually; these all lead to the emergence of patient-specific and disease-specific dynamics. The digital replicas over and beyond this do not only mirror the clinical static anatomical structure of the human body but also display the dynamic biochemical processes that support both health and disease. Through combining cutting edge technologies, AI and machine learning with intelligent sensors, healthcare DTs provide valuable data on

DOI: 10.1201/9781003498117-6

how individual patients respond to specific treatments and the trajectory of different diseases. Starting from the personalized treatment planning and predictions to virtual clinical trials and medical devices' optimization all of these applications of the DTs tech in healthcare are so vast and diverse so that's why this tech has a huge potential to change the way of practitioners work and improve the outcome for all patients throughout the world [6].

6.2 INTRODUCTION TO DATA SECURITY IN HEALTHCARE DIGITAL TWINS

DT technologies are only about the past few years, integrating into the health industry has sparked off a new age with personalized medicine being data-driven. DTs, the virtual impersonations of the actual objects or systems, have been proven to be capable of reproducing the same factors that are present in the healthcare activities, as well as the research and the programs used in medical treatment planning [7]. Interactive as they are, DTs have the power to unlock what were previously hidden in biological systems and medical devices advancements. Nevertheless, what make the DT technology so important in healthcare is the data security problems that have recent growth. This becomes possible because of the high sensitivity of medical information, as well as the inherent interconnection in modern DT systems, which calls to mind the indispensable significance of strong data security measures [8]. In this part, we move into the depth of data security for healthcare DTs, where we are looking into various types of threats and possibilities for mitigating it, as well as how the landscape of this field evolves. Among key priorities in healthcare information systems, guaranteeing secure data transfer is cardinal in the preservation of patients' confidentiality and privacy. Patient information, which incorporates a plethora of confidential details like medical history, diagnosis, and treatment, is a precious gem for unscrupulous cybercriminals and is being governed by the whole gamut of exclusive regulations for protection [9]. Health information breaches not only undermine the privacy of patients but also undermine the trust which is a critical element in the healthcare systems making such organizations to suffer from financial or reputational loss. Also, the privacy of patient information has to remain a priority as diagnosis and assessment of treatment are all dependent on this integrity of data. Uninvolved and maneuver the registers can give a cause of wrong diagnosis, inadequate treatment and patient unsafety. Consequently, strong data security measures, such as encryption, access controls and intrusion detection system, to protect the confidentiality and integrity of patient data would be a significant and vital step toward building a digital-based healthcare system, where patient cantered care is the top priority [10].

6.3 THE ROLE OF DIGITAL TWINS IN HEALTHCARE

DT technology represents a disruptive trend perhaps the most disruptive in healthcare, facilitated by the advent of emerging technologies to revolutionize patient care, healthcare decisions, and medical research. At the core of the new approach to production, that is, the creation of virtual counterparts – the DTs – of biological systems, medical devices, and "smart" sensors which allow to gather patient data, powered by AI, ML and IOT technologies [11]. Such digital copies act as living simulations and behave in the similar way as they do in real world, with unparalleled fullness of features and details. Based on the integration of heterogeneous data types such as genomic profiles, vitals and lifestyle factors, DTs empower physicians to penetrate granular aspects of an individual patient's physiology and personalize treatments and interventions to their conditions. Such novel individualist focus in healthcare undoubtedly holds great promise to improve the quality and accuracy of treatment, lessen the number of adverse effects that may occur and lead to better outcomes for all patients much sooner [12]. DTs or similitude can capture and analyze data, or information, of patients in real time. These systems help the world of medicine to move into the era of personalized medicine, which recognizes the unique characters and needs of patients. By using AI-powered algorithms, DTs are able to track in real time a wide variety of physiological parameters, which gives caregivers the capability to depart from the traditional one-size-fits-all treatment approach and instead apply the most effective interventions based on the medically needy of each given patient [13]. This could be the development of customized treatments, as a result of adjusting drug doses specifically to genetic markers, or of bespoke counseling recommendations, suited to the unique metabolic profile of a person, and also through the prediction of disease progression relied on real-time data inputs, DTs provide insights that could be the revolution in the medicine. Furthermore, virtual prototypes open up the frontiers of the research and development of new drugs in clinical trials, facilitating ways to reduce the time frame and amounts of money necessary for the design and effectivity of novel therapies [14]. The capability of the models to try new pharmaceutical substances and see their consequences on virtual organ models or patient avatars gives researchers a way to receive essential information about the efficacy of the drug, toxicity, and the way it interacts with other things at a speed that one cannot achieve in a real human organ. This story then not only allows the drug discovery process to be rapidly done but it can also bring about the identification of side effects that may be encountered and serves to optimize the dosing regimens with greater accuracy and efficiency. In fact, DTs are the very tool which signals the advent of a new frontier in precision medicine. Instead of treatment which aligns with the characteristics of the disease, the progression of disease now gets personalized to each patient's unique physiological makeup.

Besides gaining in the areas of personalized medicine and drug development, DTs also come to deliver on the promise of smoothing the healthcare delivery and improve clinical operations efficiency [15]. Healthcare providers can simulate patient care pathways, use of resources, and treatment protocols to find out where the process is suffering from slowdown, long waiting periods, and inefficient resource utilization which may be improved to increase the patient's care and clinical efficiency through the process. Additionally and notably, DTs reinforce healthcare setups to undertake virtual clinical trials, remotely monitor patients, and generally allow for the precise prediction of disease trajectories, therefore paving the way for more proactive and personalized approaches to healthcare [16]. However, along with the possibilities and opportunities of DTs in healthcare, exist some concerns that should be worked upon particularly the ones related to the element of data security, privacy and ethics. DTs which depend heavily on highly sensitive patient data is entrusted to the privacy, integrity and availability of the information is necessary to be on the right side of the patients' trust and which is also for compliance with regulatory requirements. In addition to it an ethical aspects that demands for a solitary patient data protection, fairness in decision-making, bias reduction, and informed consent should be considered so that the benefits of DTs are distributed equally as well as the patient autonomy and rights are respected. Digitally generated twins represent a transformational technology which has the ability to create different patient care, medical research, and health delivery experiences [17]. With the functions of AI, ML, and sensors of IoT being synergized to create digital replicas of biological systems, medical devices, and patient information, DTs facilitate full insight into individual patient physiology. Hence, personalized treatments and custom treatments for every patient's uniqueness are possible via these replicas' usage [14]. DTs can influence the efficiency of the drug discovery processes, which is extremely important for the healthcare field, speed up the delivery and workflow and streamline the clinical operations. Considering that DTs in healthcare may pose many data security and privacy issues, the risks of infringing on patient rights, and the issues around the fair distribution of the emerging technology to all members of society, requires careful consideration [14].

6.4 DATA SECURITY CHALLENGES IN HEALTHCARE DIGITAL TWINS

Technology has revolutionized healthcare in myriad possible ways, though these advances are not immune to the security hazards and flaws. The digital parallel world is increasingly getting connected by means of integrating medical devices and internet things, which makes whole space extremely vulnerable to the hackers' attacks. From the reality of accidents caused by unauthorized access and data breaches to the threats inflicted on the confidentiality, integrity and availability of the information about patients by ransomware attacks and insider risks, the healthcare institutions everywhere are facing the variety of the cybersecurity problems [18]. The leading data security challenge when it comes to healthcare DTs is the confidentiality of the most sensitive medical information. The sensitive nature of patient data, such as EHR, diagnostic images, genomics sequence has created a lucrative market for cyber attacks, where hackers aim either to gain financially or can use otherwise malicious purposes. Additionally, the system attribute of the ecosystem of DTs leads to the fact that any violation of one system means the spillover of this process to the whole healthcare system. As a result, strict measures like encryption, access controls and intrusion detection systems will be assumed to be included in the list of safeguards of patient data and prevent unauthorized access or the willingness to disclose personal information [19]. The second difficulty could be giving appropriate impeccability and veracity to healthcare data in DT environment. Besides, as healthcare organizations more and more entrust DTs with clinical decision support systems and treatment planning process, the precision and dependability of the underlying data begin to be the cornerstone of that approach. Any malicious interference or modification of medical records and simulation data will surely result in a sharp rise of risks done to patient safety besides the care delivery procedure. Data integrity is also fundamental for compliance with regulations, including avoiding being found liable if data is corrupted. Healthcare institutions must make sure that the data lifecycle of a patient remains unchangeable and correct, starting with collection and storage and ending with transmission and analysis. This implies the provision of validation tools, checksum creations, and integrity expiations to guarantee the data will not be illegally changed or doctored. Healthcare DTs require to go through with the compliance of the regulations associated with them which comprise the Health Insurance Portability and Accountability Act (HIPAA) in the United States and the General Data Protection Regulation (GDPR) in the European Union. This regulation doesn't only tighten the screws on the management of patient records in terms of their handling, storage, and communication, yet, it also results in a hefty responsibility on the healthcare institutions to implement top-notch data security measures [20]. HIPAA can be reference as it regulates the administrational, physical, and technical safeguards of the ePHI – confidentiality, integrity, and availability. Furthermore, GDPR regulations necessitate that healthcare organizations apply appropriate technical and management procedures that ensure the security and privacy of personal data, which in turn includes health information. Failure of the compliance with these laws and regulations would bring heavy fines, legal responsibility and damage to their reputation, which makes the organizations to build a robust data security system and be sure about regulatory compliance. Another considerable point of concern is the continuously changing threat landscape and the rising level of sophistication of cyber attacks that result in major obstacles for healthcare organizations when it comes to protecting patients' data and securing the DT environment. Ransomware the latest trend in the global cybercrime has evolved into a big problem for the healthcare industry, as cyber criminals try to attack weak systems and demand payment in exchange. Through these types of cyber-attacks, some diseases can get out of healthcare systems control, patient care becomes compromised and the safety of patients is at stake – all calling for proactive solutions to deal with the attacks and reduce their possible aftermath (prevention, detection and reaction). Furthermore, insider risks are increasingly a big concern to healthcare data security, where the employees, contractors, or trusted individuals serve on dispensing with security, due to being either wittingly or unwillingly malicious [21]. Healthcare organizations have to meet the stringent access controls, employee training programs, and monitoring features to prevent the risk of insider threats and verify the security of patient none medical records.

Digital dualizing in healthcare gives us broad possibilities to make medical care better, to facilitate the clinical decision-making process, and to boost the research activity. On the other hand, they play an important role in the protection of data's security, privacy and adoption of the regulatory compliance too. Healthcare entities need the maximum level of data security. Authenticity of the healthcare data must be intact and maintained. All the legal and regulatory requirements are important to follow in order to safeguard the patients' confidentiality and maintain the highest level of ethical conduct [22]. Further, the use of proactive approaches, for instance, employee training, threat intelligence sharing, and incident response planning among others are inevitable in reducing the risk attributed to cybercrime and protecting the patient's data in the contemporary healthcare setting with accelerating trend of interconnectedness and digitalization. To this end, one needs to confront the difficulties associated with data security head-on and implement a multi-faceted strategy for data security. In other words, dovetailing DTs with privacy protection and the maintenance of data integrity can make them more powerful.

6.5 MITIGATION STRATEGIES FOR DATA SECURITY

To counter the complications of data security in healthcare DTs, the organizations need to employ a multi-angle approach that incorporates both technical and organizational measures plus regulations. Key strategies for mitigating data security risks include: Key strategies for mitigating data security risks include:

Encryption and data masking:
It stands to be the most appropriate measure of ensuring security of healthcare data through data encryption both at rest and utilizing the transit in the healthcare DT environments. Encryption is a vital defense, because it especially prevents patient information from going into unreadable hands by changing it (converting it) into code that no one can decode without the code key (decryption key). At a rest, encryption provides a guarantee that patient record stored on servers, databases, and other storage systems remains in the pocket of unauthorized people even with the breach of security or physical theft. Via a means of data encryption with strong security algorithms, codes like Advanced Encryption Standard (AES) or RSA, Healthcare Organizations can avoid data breaches as well as stay compliant by the regulatory framework like the Health Insurance Portability and Accountability Act (HIPAA) and the General Data Protection Regulation (GDPR). Additionally, encryption at rest helps to especially safeguard patient privacy and confidentiality, deeply instilling trust and confidence among patients and all stakeholders in the system as well as maintaining the security of their personal medical information [23]. Furthermore, using encryption protocols to protect transit data is an extremely important link in the chain security process that ensures the secure transmission of patient information between systems, devices, and healthcare providers. Data of patients may get exposed at public networks or cloud environments or even third-party platform while on transit thus open for any eavesdropping by wicked hackers. By encrypting in-transit data using secure communication protocols such as Transport Layer Security (TLS) or Hypertext Transfer Protocol (HTTP), healthcare institutions can create encryption protocols whose primary operation is to prevent intercepting and tampering with information by unauthorized parties. Also, the utilization of encryption in transit will prevent forces of the man-in-the-middle, where the intent of intermission is not communication between two parties. With that, healthcare organizations get to ensure the confidentiality and integrity of patient data through the use of encryption while in transit, thus from the stage when the data is stored in EHR systems to the time when it is accessed by medical devices and from remote patient monitoring platforms usage. To add to that, applying data masking for obfuscating patient data is an additional necessary security method that has to be facilitated to limit the number of unauthorized accesses [24] The human body: A DT of the cyber physical systems. Data masking involves the substitution of real data elements e.g. patient names, social security numbers or medical record numbers etc. with imaginary or encoded values ensuring the continuity in the format and structure of the original data. Through masking confidential information, healthcare providers may limit access to protected data exclusively to such individuals or systems which genuinely need it, thus ensuring patients' Confidentiality and reduced the probability of data breaches or intentional

disclosures. For example, a data masking technique can be employed which helps prevent misusers to access and breach the security of the valuable data bits. Through obfuscating patient data using data masking techniques such as tokens, pseudonymization, or shuffling, healthcare organizations are creating textual data that cannot be traced back to patients. This information remains useful as it can be performed for medical research, analytics, and quality improvement initiatives. Apart from this, deploying encryption protocols and data masking techniques is a vital step considered not only for the protection of patient data but also for achieving compliance with the specific industry regulations and standards. Regulations like the Hipaa and GDPR impose technical and organizational measures to accomplish the effectuality of privacy, integrity, and the availability of health information. Industry "best practices" like encryption and data masking, are considered a prerequisite in regulatory papers and guidelines while using sensitive data, and they are often mentioned as a requirement or recommendation [25]. By putting into operation encryption implication and data masking, the healthcare organizations can be epitomized as the institutions that care about protecting patient privacy and confidentiality, thus ticking off the risk of penalties from the regulators, legal liabilities, and reputational harm which is related to data breaches or non-compliance with the regulations.

Indeed, correct advanced encryption protocols and information masking methods are those which will enable a trustworthy guard for both the confidential medical data at rest and in transit within healthcare DT ecology. Indeed data encryption is a very essential element of maintaining confidentiality and integrity of patient's information. In add it also involves techniques called data masking to limit access to sensitive information that can harm patient's identities. Through the usage of encryption protocols and data masking, health organizations can greatly reduce the incidence of data breaches and thus, maintain compliance with the regulatory body requirements. In addition, such a system demonstrates feelings of trust and confidence toward the security of the personal health information of the patients and stakeholders [26]. In addition to encryption and data mining, data masking, which has been acknowledged as the best practice in the industry for protecting sensitive data and makes an essential part of the whole security strategy for healthcare DT environments?

Access controls and authentication

Super granular access control and a robust authentication approach which any healthcare organization is supposed to follow in order to prevent any unauthorized access to the sensitive healthcare data and to ensure the security of the DT environment from the database breaches. Pixel-level access controls enable the companies to implement specific permissions, denying anyone who is not authorized to access the data or perform the pre-defined functions unless they are willing to go through the role and privilege procedures. Applying data-level access controls means that patient info browser becomes accessible only to people who really need it for their job, and does not let unauthorized persons viewing or altering it, thus reducing the risk of data leakage or theft. Concerning with the fine-grained access controls, it is of the importance in related to compliance with the Regulatory Requirements consisting of the Health Insurance Portability and Accountability Act (HIPAA) and the General Data Protection Regulation (GDPR), that deal with the implementation of a strong control to maintain the integrity of patient privacy. A central feature of the access control is the secure identity authentication procedures, which verify ID login of individuals before authorizing their access to confidential data in the healthcare system. MFA – multi-factor authentication is a widely used login method which takes you further and requires multiple identification means like password, biometric data or a numerical code sent to a mobile device before providing an access. The MFA's requirement of multiple kinds of authentications pushes up the security of user accounts and protects the latter from the unauthorized access caused by the stolen credentials or the identity theft. Implementing MFA systems of access control to e-twin environments, with an emphasis on remote access or privilege based accounts with high privileges is a mandate for healthcare organizations. Role-based access control (RBAC) comes in handy as another mode of access control in which roles are assigned to users based on the responsibilities and the relevancy of the access of a particular information. RBAC helps department to give role a name, like a clinician, nurse, or administrator, and then assign as an access to each role based on duty and requirements. RBAC gives permissions that match the affected user roles so that only personnel with the right jobs to have their access limited to the data or system resources that they should not have. In addition, RBAC makes the access management process simpler which is effected by centralized permission management and reduction of administrative efforts that are usually spent on assigning permissions to individual users. The RBAC systems are a must for healthcare organizations and they have to be implemented to strengthen their policy of least privilege and to lower the chances of data breaches or unauthorized access. It becomes important to hire privileged access management (PAM) solutions to simplify the assignment and tracking of permissions for privileged accounts as such accounts have elevated permissions and access to data and system resources. PAM (Privileged Access Management) solutions ensure organizations to secure privileged accounts by means of password management, session monitoring, and access restrictions, therefore lowering the possibility of both insider threats and outer attacks aimed at high privileges accounts. Through secretive PAM solutions, healthcare organizations can exercise efficient access controls, track the privileged jobs activity in real time and detect and respond quickly to certain access or suspicious behavior. In addition to this, the PAM solutions also help in regulatory requirements, as it provides audit trails and other logs that are used to trace privileged account activity and maintain a level of accountability in terms of access to sensitive data. In the final word, implementing granular access control in the first place and equipping the healthcare organizations with robust authentication system is significant to secure sensitive Healthcare data and to protect the DT environment from the unauthorized access. Permissions can be assigned such that user roles and privilege define the administrators of sensitive data and system resources. permission is the mechanism that is used for the purpose of roles and privilege to be the administrators of the sensitive data and system resources Authentication tools, such as two-factor authentication, role-based access control and privileged access management solutions, are among things that are not forgotten when implementing strong user account security and reducing the risk of data breach or unauthorized access. Adopting these access control mechanisms will ensure health records being protected and confidentiality is maintained by the health system and therefore compliance to the regulatory requirements is ensured and integrity and confidentiality of data within DT environments is maintained.

Network segmentation and intrusion detection

Decomposition of DT networks and implementation of IDPS are essential security measures that help in organization cybersecurity and limitation of intrusion by cyber threats in DT environments. The DT network, which is an amalgam of interlinked systems, devices and storage archives form a wider security concern where malicious actors try to exploit the vulnerability and gain unauthorized control on the data. Through fragmenting the DT network and deploying the IDPS solutions, healthcare organizations can, therefore, counter breaches by containing potential, repel attackers' lateral movement, as well as the threat detection and response in real time. Segmentation of a network encompasses the technique of dividing the big network into series of isolated segments or zones each that has its own kind of rules and restrictions. Implementing segregated digital network twins the healthcare providers ultimately limit the area of possible penetrations and do not let the attackers move on with their lateral actions to get access to sensitive data or vital systems. Twinning networks, like in healthcare organizations, could be segmented based on administrative and functional department's boundaries [27]. This means that the clinical system in one department can be separated from that of another one. For the IoT devices, they should be isolated from the core network infrastructure. Besides that, organizations will be able to create micro-segmentations to divide the network communications even further and can use access restrictions based on certain criteria like the identity of the user, the type of a device or application. Implementing Intrusion Detection and Prevention Systems (IDPS) is the other crucial strategy to improve the DT network's defense system and detect any clue of unlawful act or an attempt for unauthorized access. The

IDPS solutions watch network traffic in real-time scanning data packets for suspicious behavior, for instance known incident signatures, traffic that is peculiar, or attempts of unauthorized access. This way, by installing IDPS solutions at the "hotspots" of the network, e.g., at network perimeters, between network segments or on critical servers and endpoints, healthcare organizations can effectively prevent and stop potential threats from getting access to patients' data or disrupt healthcare services. The fact that the ITDS systems can see the activities in the network in real time and provide alarms about the possible cyber attacks to the security staff is among the important features of the solution. Linking data from several sources, e.g. network log, system logs, etc., improvement in the process of determining the seriousness and the potentials for cause, IDPS (Intrusion Detection and Prevention Systems) solution can prioritize information based on their significance and effect on the organization. This offers the security staff enough time to investigate the root cause of the breach which allows for faster response to security incidents, to make and implement remediation measures that limit the threat and keep its impact from spreading. Furthermore, IDPS systems might automate reactions for security breaches such as traffic blocking, device quarantining, etc. or incidents handling by means of policy-based rules defined previously. In addition to this, the IDPS solutions are the crucial part of the compliance with the rules of software development as they provide audit logs, reporting capabilities together with logging tools which enable healthcare organizations to prove their adherence to the standards of good practice and requirements of local and international regulations. Laws such as the Health Insurance Portability and Accountability Act (HIPAA) and The General Data Protection Regulation (GDPR) have mandated to institutions to implement proper safeguards in order to shield patient data and make sure that the confidentiality, even integrity and availability of the healthcare information is achieved. Introducing IDPS systems into the deployed healthcare environments means enhanced security stance, regulatory compliance and at the same time maintenance of patients' trust in the institution's security measures of the personal health information. In the conclusion, the key strategies considered to be of vital significance for healthcare organizations are segmenting DT networks and deployment of intrusion detection and prevention systems (IDPS) for the purpose of strengthening the network security and minimizing the risk of hacking attacks within DT environments. Network segmentation allows organizations to take potentially Hazardous attacks or attackers laterally moving, whereas IDPS make network activity in real time is responsive seeing and allow proactive detection and response to security breaches. Considering the implementation of these precautionary measures, healthcare institutions will be able to mitigate data breach risks, adhere to the compliance rules, and preserve confidential information integrity and accessibility inside the DT environments.

Data loss prevention (DLP)

Data loss prevention (DLP) solutions constitute an important aspect for healthcare providers inheriting the task of safeguarding healthcare data as well as struggling against unauthorized data passes and exfiltration events within virtual healthcare analogs / health twins. DLP solutions facilitate a collection of approaches and means, notably monitoring, Unauthorized data loss or leakage will be spotted and addressed everywhere, such as email, websites, files transfer and removable storage devices. Through implementing DLP solutions, healthcare organizations can adopt policies and uphold the strict controls to prevent unauthorized disclosure of patients' information while ensuring the conformance to regulations and the corresponding risks of data breaches and other compliance violations are minimized. In the same time, we are exploring one of main roles by DLP solutions is to check outgoing network packets in real time and ensure that no sensitive information is being send outside (or to the internet). DLP solutions are using the advanced content inspection technology, which includes keyword matching, regular expressions, and data fingerprinting. These components are used for the data classification and assignment of the policies and rules based on the predefined criteria. This allows companies to fail an unauthorized disclosure of patient prescription histories, diagnostic images, patient demographics, and other very sensitive health data to external entities or unauthorized third parties. Through investigating of network traffic that transmits data, DLP law keepers bring visibility to data flows whereby they seemingly make organizations able to pinpoint and respond instantly to any potential security problems or compliance violations before they turn into big data breaches. Furthermore, DLP solutions allow for governments to keep an eye on outbound network traffic, as well as enforce confidentiality policies to make sure data stay safe from unauthorized access and interception during transfer. Encryption as a mediatory function in securing the patients' personal information by changing the plain data into encrypted data by applying the cryptography algorithms that causes unreadability of data to the nonauthorized parties. DLP solutions can mandate encryption policies to have sensitive data encrypted before it's going out from the organization network. Encryption can be done for many types of data such as email, web or file transfer. The encryption policies can help healthcare organizations in retaining the privacy and intactness of patient data, they will be able to fulfill the regulatory discipline such as HIPAA and GDPR and will minimize the risk of data breaches or unpermitted access to the information while it is during the transmission. In addition, DLP solutions provide a critical function by analyzing data traffic inside the environment of virtual twins, which aim to identify suspicious behaviour that signals data leaks or an inside threat. DLP solutions, by examining the traffic patterns, behaviour of the users and the user logs, can easily identify taking the data in large size, abnormal access to the data and access attempts without authorization, and notify security incident or compliance violation. The DLP options will instantly send signals to security offices through alerts and notifications so that they can handle the security incidents on a timely manner. Secondly, the SIEM and other security tools can collect knowledge for one face via integration between DLP devices. Furthermore, it will show a picture of a corporation across multiple sources.

By way of this, DLP solutions arm organizations in the sectors of healthcare with relevant features for reports and analytics that help them draw inferences about prevalent trends in data use complications, violations, and security. DLP solutions are able to form unique reports and charts to tell what happened in data breach cases, what policy was broken and what regulations are caused will help company in decision making. Moreover, DLP solutions are also useful for fast and efficient incident response and threat investigation since the auditable event logs and information about data breaches such as time and location of weapons helps in smooth prosecution of guilty party and prevent future occurrence of security breaches. Healthcare systems should make Data Loss Prevention (DLP) tools mandatory for any domain which has access to sensitive health data and DT environments to stop unauthorized forwarding or illegal information export. DLP solutions not only enabling organizations to inspect outgoing network traffic, but also checking that encryption policies is in place and breaching attempts, such as data exfiltration or recognized employees in their affairs, are detected. Organizations engaged in fulfilling healthcare responsibilities can offer privacy and compliance by implementing DLP as a security solution. It assists in defending patients' data, complying with regulatory requirements, and protecting data from security breaches or regulatory violations. Moreover, DLP applications have leverages reporting and analytic features which feeds valuable data regarding the usage trends, compliance status, and security incidents thereby empowering the organizations to make necessary decisions and implement proactive actions to strengthen their security posture.

Continuous monitoring and incident response

Ensuring a strong monitoring program is mandatory for healthcare companies for efficient detection and response to security incidents in digital reality by its means. Today's protean threat environment where cybercriminals become bolder and employ more advanced security techniques warrants for proactive monitoring of network activity, system logs as well as security events that give vital indicators toward prevention of escalation of suspected malicious activities to full-blown data breach or difficulty in compliance with security policies. Security monitoring program which is well developed and steadfast comprises different activities and implements different technologies including Security Information and Event Management (SIEM), performance of continuous vulnerability assessments and incident response procedure to provide comprehensive and real time visibility into the organization's security situation. At the core of the security monitoring process stands SIEM (Security Information and Event Management) solution which serves as a centralized point of aggregation, correlation, and analysis of security events coming from all the network sources within the organization. SIEM machine assimilates logs from on the network network, endpoint devices, and security tools, hence enables security officials to have a holistic view of the organization security posture and takes prompt actions as soon as an unlikely event is spotted. SIEM systems basing on the linkages of information from different sources can pinpoint abnormal activity or pattern that could suggest security threat or fraudulent activities. Moreover, SIEM systems constitute algorithms and reporting features that make transcendence to security events analysis, alert prioritization, and automatic adjustment of incident response processes possible. Besides SIEM systems' deployment, performing regularly safety audits is a vital part of a good monitoring process. Vulnerability scanning includes network mapping, system configurations analysis and application assessment in order to identify known vulnerabilities, misconfigurations and weaknesses that attackers may leverage to steal sensitive data or disrupt vital service availability. Vulnerabilities should be identified and prioritized based on their level of unresponsiveness and effects on citizens' security system with the aim of taking immediate action as a measure to remediate the security gaps and improve the organization's defense against cyber threats. Regularity vulnerability assessments have to be adhering to best practices and guidelines of the industry in order to be effective for the security posture of the organization as potential threats increase every day. On the other hand, creating a response and recovery plan for security violations is also a crucial action for the organizations in the healthcare industry to limit the size of the adverse effects in case of an incident. The response procedure prescribes those steps and actions should be taken in the event of a security incident, such as detection, analysis, isolation, elimination, and effort of recovery. Through defining the part, the duty, and play the security team escalates against response procedures to respond quickly and effectively to the security incidents, reduce the impact on patient care and operations, and hence restore normalcy as quickly as possible. Crisis response procedures must undergo frequent evaluations, drills, and updates to ensure their efficacy and continuing viability in guarding against the latest and newly discovered threats and occurring attacks. Additionally, such an active security monitoring should comprise of threat intelligence feeds as well as threat hunting and advanced analytic skills, which will facilitate timely detection and mitigation of new threats and zero-day vulnerabilities. Threat intelligence feeds are the primary source of current and relevant information on discovered threats, vulnerabilities, as well as the tactics used in perpetration and spreading of unauthorized activities. Organizations can rely on that, and they can stay ahead of the curve by proactively defending against potential security risks. While threat hunting, security professionals conduct active scanning of both internal and external networks, infrastructure systems, and applications for indications of potential intrusions, including disruptive IOCs that might have avoided conventional protective mechanisms. Integration of alarm intelligence feeds, "pestverlens" hunting capabilities, and superior analytics helps to stance healthcare institutions to despatch speedily and eventually of data breaches and operations that may affect the patient care and survive. In brief, the development of a reliable security monitoring mechanism is meaningful for healthcare establishment in that it helps the institution in addressing security incidents in real time within the DT infrastructures. Not only of SIEM systems but also regular vulnerability scan and incident response procedure deployment security officers in healthcare organizations are able to monitor their networks, identify potential data security threats with a aim to reduce the risk of data breaches or compliance violation. Firstly, augmenting threat intelligence feed information, threat hunting capabilities, and advanced analytics into the cyber security monitoring platform allows organizations to always remain one step ahead of while allowing them to protect healthcare data more effectively and stop zero day vulnerabilities from occurring in their environments that are based on DTs.

Through applying these mitigation measures the healthcare organizations can be more precise in their security postures and provide the data patient with troublesome surrounding cyber threats. Date securing becomes a primordial feature of healthcare DTs's developmental and operational procedures. Through recognising security challenges and weaknesses digital platforms have, organizations will be better suited to implement high security measures for data storage, data integrity, and to comply with regulations. Utilizing encryption, access controls, virtual network segregation, and incident response procedures can be a mitigating strategy to avoid threats emerging from the cyber realm and to create a secure space for the introduction of DTs which will contribute in achieving better patient results and medical researches.

6.6 ENSURING DATA SECURITY

In the delicately-balanced world of healthcare DTs, there is a care to safeguard the integrity and sensitivity of medical data that patients must do. The present part highlights the modern mechanisms and tactics used to preserve data of healthcare in virtual twin frameworks, with cryptography and access controlling being among the main security measures [27].

6.6.1 Encryption for data protection

Encryption provides the key to a healthcare organization's armoury of privacy, with this vital tool keeping the patient's sensitive data secure against those who do not have access or are intercepting the information. For this reason the application in both data at rest and data in transit perfectly strain the risk of data leaks. Thus, the privacy of this information within DT environment would be strictly secured. At the bottom of it, encryption changes the plain text data into cipher text and then the key is used to encipher the data; using such complex algorithms, it becomes incomprehensible or unreadable to unauthorized individuals or entities without the corresponding decryption key. In the healthcare arena, where the privacy and security of patient dates are beyond doubt, encryption acts as a cornerstone to preserving the electronic health records (ERHs), x-ray images and other clinical information from prying eyes and malicious intruders In contrast, advanced encryption algorithms, e.g. AES and RSA, are commonly employed in healthcare DT sphere as they ensure high-level cyber health and reliability. Among all the variants of encryption known to mankind, AES has been proved to be the winner. AES is a transportation of the sensitive data and has been highly effective as against the different cryptographic attacks such as brute-force attacks and cryptographic weakness. In the same manner, RSA encryption which is built on a mathematical foundation of public-key cryptography serves as a secure form of encryption that enables the process of encrypting and decrypting data with the help of keypair asymmetry, which enables safe transport of information and data exchange between parties. Moreover, the healthcare organizations aim to provide a full-cycle data protection by deploying encryption solutions to encrypt data during transit in order to reliably secure information during inter-device, inter-system and other forms of transmission. By applying the TLS or SSL encryption protocols on the data in transit, healthcare organizations can implement secured communication channels which are able to withstand – possible interceptions by attackers. If end-of-the-end encryption is also given, it helps in increasing the security of the data as the data is in an encrypted form from the very beginning and throughout the entire period, whether it is being generated, transmitted, or stored, thereby preventing cyber-attacks and the unauthorized access. Consequently, the employment of the encryption techniques brings compliance with regulations and good practices of the healthcare industry that are dedicated to the protection of patients secret and privacy. Regulations, for example, HIPAA in the United States and the GDPR regulation in the European Union require organizational aides to be applied that are capable of securing electronic protected health information (ePHI) and personal data including encryption during storage and transmission of data. Adherence to them, apart from the fact that would keep these organizations from legal and state penalties, also encourages the trust and confidence among patients and stakeholders that they are safe with their own medical information. Besides the merely complying enforcement, encryption also acts as a preventive tool for lessening the risks of data leaked and building the safety in general among the healthcare institutions. The healthcare industry however remains a main point of interest for cybersecurity actors who exploit weaknesses in digital twining operations to steal sensitive information, disrupt vital nodal points or extort organizations for financial gain. Healthcare institutions owe their patient safety and operations to reliable encryption protocols which vendors implement. By doing this the adverse influence of the cyber attacks is insured. Additionally, encryption technologies' development is consistently ongoing to combat security threats that emerge due to the shifting of computing technology. Inventions including homomorphic encryption, quantum-resistant cryptography, and secure multiparty accumulation are going to be valuable means of protecting the confidentiality of health-related information in DT ecosystems. Homomorphic encryption among others allow the said computation on encrypted data without having to decrypt it; this can prevent the problem of being hacked especially where information is in a cloud system. Similarly, quantumn proofed cryptography is the technology that tries to devise the cryptography algorithms which are quantum computer proofed so that the traditional cryptographic methods are broken down by the quantum computer systems. In summing up, encryption is the irreplaceable means of safeguarding healthcare data from an unauthorized access and intercept through DT spaces. Through enabling encryption of data at rest and in transit using sophisticated encryption algorithms such as AES and RSA, healthcare organizations can effectively seize interception of data and preservation of patient privacy with the aim of fulfilling regulatory requirements too. Moreover, security technology is the main factor in implementing trust and confidence among patients and stake-holders, through which the digital health technology is spreading well with unlimited opportunities and healthy future of the healthcare sector.

6.6.2 Access controls and role-based permissions

Roles-based access control and permission levels are among the pillars required for upholding data security and prevention of unjustified disclosure of healthcare data within DT environment In a period, when data breaches are the most dangerous modes of endangering patient privacy and organizational security, healthcare organizations must implement preventative measures to control access to delicate information and reduce the risk of those information disbursement without authorization [28]. RBAC stands as the key approach, it enables healthcare organizations to assign users with specific roles and inherited rights based on their position, variance in operations and the concept of privileges escalation. Through building up the user's specific access rights using the role assignment, RBAC ensures that the user only has access to information needed for the fulfilment of their functions, thus lowering the probability of any unauthorized usage. RBAC works in accordance with least privilege that postulates that by default, a user should be granted only the minimum amount of authority to complete his/her duties effortlessly. Through implementing this idea healthcare entities will be able to prevent many data leakage cases and breaches by limiting access to data for people whom this sensitive data doesn't relate with. To illustrate, for the clinicians to be able to deliver service better they may need records of patients and images necessary for the diagnosis and the support staff may only need important features such as scheduling and billing. RBAC gives authorized units the authority to make access permissions based on managerial roles and ensuring that each user has the right access level for the performance of his primary job responsibilities without violating the confidentiality and security of patient data. Also, MFA i.e. multi factor authentication features as avenge implementation of multi-factor authentication (MFA) further improves access controls by requiring users to provide multiple forms of verification before risky data access. The MFA factor brings an additional measure of security alongside alternative authentication methods that use passwords, which limits field exposure and takes care of possible hijacks by unauthorized persons through compromised identity data. Customers could be prompted for factors above the authentication credentials, like a biometric scan, hardware keys, or one-time passcodes (OTPs) sent to their mobile devices, resulting to an extra means of barring unauthorized access. The healthcare organizations will be able to shorten access controls and protect the data of healthcare information from unauthorized divulgence as well as exploitation of the existing data through implementation of MFA. As well as RBAC and MFA, the healthcare providers must also implement strong identity and access management processes that are end-to-end and handle the account lifecycle, set of access privileges, and permissions within the DT settings. IAM is the collective term that brings together the procedures, policies and technology that manages user identity databases; ensures that users are authentic; and restricts access to specific resources and applications. The attacker could introduce fraudulent users into the system that have access to sensitive data. They can also act as users who have lost their roles and hence might gain access to restricted resources illegally. This includes tasks such as user provisioning, de-provisioning, role assignment, access certification, and access recertification, all of which are critical mechanisms of maintaining the integrity and security of access controls over time. Through practices of IAM guidance, healthcare organizations will be able to ensure that while access privileges are being given it will be done in time, hence reducing the specter of uncertified user access and data leaks owing to inconsistencies or improperly configured authorizations. Additionally, hospitals should undertake periodic assessment and auditing of access controls, with the aim of finding and fixing any loopholes, which can potentially increase security threats. Periodic access review, in its turn, provides an opportunity to review the access rights of users, to reveal the accounts that are no longer used or even have been left during the user changes of their positions, as well as any unauthorized changes of permissions. Through regular access reviews, healthcare institutions are able to not only verify that access controls continue to be fit for purpose in regards to the business mandates, regulatory requirements, and best practices, but can also adapt to the changes. Furthermore, intrusion detection from access audits gives the adequate perception of what is going on and what users are doing, making quick response to malicious activities or to them becoming intrusions possible in real time. Therefore, the issue of data privacy with respect to DTs in healthcare organizations will be manageable only when proper access controls and role-based permissions are implemented to deny access and disclosure of sensitive medical data within virtual environments. IAM (Identity and access management) and RBAC (role-based access control) processes, in conjunction with multi-factor authentication (MFA), can be used to put in place a strict granularity in access control to patient records, medical information and other private data of the organization while minimizing the threat of internal breaches and data leaks. These together can be done periodically to ensure that access reviews and audits increase the overall effectiveness; looking for possible loopholes or any security flaw can be identified and corrected. Through a planned security system which involves data controls for access, healthcare organizations are able to protect patient privacy, maintain compliance of specific regulations, and ensure that their stakeholders' trust and confidence in the secure nature of their personal health information is well kept.

6.6.3 Blockchain technology for data integrity

Blockchain technology for data security and integrity gives a ground-breaking innovation through the invention of a decentralized and immutable way to administer healthcare data within DT realm [29]. Blockchain technology is basically a distributed ledger, which runs in a fully transparent and immutable form recording data of millions of transactions taking place across the network of nodes. Through this decentralized structure, each entity is independent of the others and cannot have the control over the whole network making the deletion of data or access of unauthorized parties almost impossible. Through the lens of healthcare with the data of patients with authenticity and integrity being beyond importance, blockchain technology is such that it presents great potential for the integrity and immutability of medical records, diagnostic images, and other healthcare data exchanged across the DT platforms. The main advantage of the blockchain technology is that it gives you a chance to create an unchangeable, audited history of all healthcare data that is available up to date and can be verified as authentic. With each dealing being crypto-linked to the previous one, the result is a chain of blocks whose content doesn't change and can't be tampered with without the agreement of all the network participants. This incomparable uniqueness of the blockchain technology guarantees that all data once being recorded are still unchangeable and publicly verifiable, offering a reliable series of history for the whole data exchange. Healthcare institutions can better control their transparency, accountability, and trust in the integrity of healthcare data with the help of blockchain technology, which reduces the risks at the cost of data interception, impersonation, or manipulation. Additionally, the smart contracts which allow for the use of predefined rules and conditions that are encoded into the blockchain enable the use of different smart contracts. Smart contracts enable automated verification and implementation of data access policies for healthcare data sharing within DT settings, making sure of the authentication of the authorized users and/or entities [30]. For instance, smart contracts can be put into force as a means of obtaining data access that is subsequently regulated by the agreed criteria of roles, agreements and regulations. As a result, smart contracts automatically enable data access policies and data enforcement, which make processes of access control smoother, better, and safe with low error risk and no need for monitoring. Actually, the blockchain system is decentralized, while this quality boosts resilience and reliability therefore it is extremely resistant to single points of failure or an attack. While centralized databases (which are susceptible to cyber-attacks and data breaches, reply system failure) distribute their data among the multiple nodes in peer-to-peer fashion, one entity cannot obtain control over the entire network. To begin with, the lower level of processing makes the blockchain capable of wiping out the vulnerabilities, bringing in effectiveness and recovering function of the sensitive information in it thus limiting down the possibilities of errors. In case of a network outage or cyber-attacks, blockchains can constantly run and keep moral integrity of medical data within DT cultures. Besides that, for the healthcare system there are benefits to access, use and exchange of large amounts of health data. The blockchain technology provides a highly secure and systematized platform for data exchange and sharing that enables doctors and patients to interoperate conveniently, regardless of what technology or platform the others use. The healthcare industry could utilize blockchain networks for trusted sharing of medical records, diagnostic images, and other healthcare data with partners via the networks and it will leverage collaborative studies, seamless coordination of care and population health management initiatives. Such multi-sidedness in healthcare brings out the innovation and efficiency needed to use DT technology at its best, when track and trend patient's data to get better healthcare outcomes. Therefore, in the final part, blockchain technology provides a framework of a blockchain technology for assuring the decentralized nature of data stuffing and preventing data tampering for healthcare data within DT ecosystems. Blockchain technology entails recording data transactions in a transparent and unchangeable registry, which makes it the best-suited data solution because it reduces the risks of data tampering and dishonesty. The adoption of smart contracts as the mechanism for smart policy application will ensure the appropriate verification and enforcement of data access policies. This in turn, adds value to data security and data governance. In addition, the decentralized nature of blockchain networks strengthens resilience and stability that results in it being the ideal platform for complex applications, including healthcare data management. The healthcare organizations can break the barriers of trust, transparency and collaborating through the blockchain technology. In the end, patients will benefit, and the delivery of care will get advanced.

6.6.4 Secure data sharing and interoperability

Securing data exchange and interoperability connect the building blocks of multiparty cooperation across healthcare providers, researchers, and other parties, utilizing DT environments consistently in the processes, and still guarding patient privacy and safety of such information. In the time when the diffusion of Electronic Health Records (EHRs), the diagnostic images and other holes which make up the electronic medical information have taken a new turn, the capability to smoothly transfer and share healthcare information across distinct systems and services is essential for the delivery of the coordinated and patient-cantered care [31]. Establishing of standard protocols and the interoperability framework that have FHIR (Fast Healthcare Interoperability Resources) and DICOM (Digital Imaging and Communications in Medicine) as the main pillars support the care smoothness flowing in there and throughout the whole healthcare ecosystem involving variety of systems and applications. HL7 FHIR and DICOM is popular interoperability standards in the healthcare industry, with models for data format, exchange, and communication protocol for sharing clinical, neuroradiology, and imaging data across healthcare systems, devices, and applications. One of the major strengths of HL7 FHIR is its modern and flexible construction of data representation and exchange. It allows organizations to easily integrate and interoperate healthcare systems that may normally be disconnected in a seamless way and across various systems and platforms. Moreover, DICOM uses the same format and communication protocols for transmitting and exchanging images and data associated with the images, which helps in achieving interoperability between diverse imaging modalities, PACS and even the applications related to imaging. In addition, the application of secure data exchange means as a measure is also a mandatory component because it is needed to deliver the confidentiality, integrity, and security of healthcare data in transmission from systems and endpoints. Secure channels for the transmission of the sensitive healthcare data across networks are assured by the use of encrypted APIs (application program interfaces) and secure messaging protocols which prevent the detonation of data that may ensue unauthorized access, interception, or tampering. The API encryption uses cryptographic techniques that help encrypt the data payload as well as to authenticate the communication between systems, while the secure messaging protocols including HL7 Secure Messaging guarantee the compliance of privacy and security regulations by electronic data exchange between healthcare facilities. In this regard, the implementation of industry best practices and security standards such as Transport Layer Security (TLS) and Secure Sockets Layer (SSL) assists in improving the safety of data exchange since both of them work by encrypting data in transit and authorized communication between systems. Sometimes, this means they must bootstrap small business operations from scratch, addressing logistical challenges and understanding the nuances of local markets. Utilizing both TLS and SSL protocols, healthcare providers can significantly cut down their chances of experiencing data breaches when clients' information is in transit. These boundaries prevent unauthorized access, interception, or tampering of healthcare data during transmission thus keeping patients' data private and intact during the process. Besides this, care in implementing access controls, data governance policies and audit trails is very needed to provide accountability and transparency in healthcare data sharing and interoperability efforts. Access control is an important feature in healthcare organizations that enables them to define who can access or even share critical healthcare information and restricting it to only authorized entities (i.e. individuals or organizations) with permission. Data governance policies set directions and processes for controlling and securing personal healthcare data across the entire lifecycle of the data, from creating data to transmitting, storing it onwards, while audit trails continuously save the record of access, sharing and the modification of data, so that organizations can trace the data usage and enforce compliance with the regulations. Finally, data security and interoperability are of great significance for establishing cooperation between providers of healthcare services, biomedical researchers, and other actors, and it is important to protect data and patient privacy within DT environments. Standards based approaches and interoperability mechanisms which are built on top of platforms like HL7 FHIR and DICOM enable us to smoothen data exchange between different systems or platforms and to provide compatibility, consistency, interoperability in various heterogeneous environments. Furthermore, the deployment of the secure data interchange solutions, like as encrypted APIs and secure messaging protocols, results in data transmission between networks and endpoints being secured, with the patient confidentiality and integrity being preserved during the entire data exchange process. Developing uniform best practices for the industry, information security standards, legal frameworks for governance, helps promote trustworthiness, transparency and responsibly of healthcare organizations for healthcare data sharing and interoperability, which is a key driver to the patient-centered care delivery and improved patient outcomes.

6.6.5 Continuous monitoring and threat detection

Regular drops and known attack signatures implication to the data protection in the healthcare DT environment is the integral part of the defending system framework. Healthcare sector is inevitably more dependent on digital technologies like big data, cloud computing, and electronic health records to provide patients with care and offer security for the storage of medical information [32]. This naturally raises the need for privacy and security as to untreated cyber threats. Intrinsic surveillance should be continuous, this means, 100% of traffic going through systems, logging & user activity is being monitored in real time, so whenever something bad happens, it is responded to in an appropriate way, minimizing the risks of data breaches, unauthorized access, and other malicious activities. Alongside with sensors, cameras, and people count systems, the heart of machine learning lies in the Security Information and Event Management (SIEM) technical design. SIEM systems are the centralSystems providing the data collection, correlation and analysis of security information from multiple sources including, but not only, the organization's wireless networks. Collecting all logs, sensors statistics and security devices data into one, the SIEM system summarizes, accumulates and contextualizes this information for the company's security staff to get a detailed view of company security status, allowing fast response to cyber incidents. SIEM systems, through the use of its advanced analytics and correlation engines, enable the detection of unique patterns, suspicious and malicious activities, and probable intrusion, which is what empowers the administration to be preemptive and take measures that limit the scope of damage from a security breach, or an attack. Alongside the SIEM systems, the IDPS represents another tool that is of upmost importance in the ongoing monitoring and identification of the arising threats within healthcare twin systems. Situation-specific IDPS solutions perform the analysis of traffic in the network and determine the intrusions such as unauthorized access, infections with malware, and Denial-of-Service (DoS) attacks in real time. Through flow of network data packets and behaviouristic pattern analysis, IDPS solutions could preempt and respond to security threats before they accomplish their goals of compromising critical services or disrupting operations. IDPS capability is more than just analyzing traffic and profiles; it can now configure features to automatically block or shutdown traffic which it detects to be suspicious, preventing cyber-incident from escalating into full blown breaches. Intelligent machines incorporating the results of machine learning and AI algorithms in their operation, instantly carry out the role of hunting for threats and predicting future attacks, thus bringing the possibility of responding to security threats before they happen not only in theory but in reality. Machine learning algorithms that analyze large data of security respond to security patterns and trends, which has allowed security teams to prioritize their second response to the most critical security. Furthermore, the AI algorithms can be trained to utilize relational data and historical information to foresee security incidents and security deficiencies that could appear in an organization in the future, hence, the organization can take proactive measures and minimize the risks before they occur. Another function is the staying informed of caring on both the existing and coming threats that result in compliance with regulatory requirements and also the health sector standards for data security and privacy. These legislations, such as the Health Insurance Portability and Accountability Act (HIPAA) in the United States and the General Data Protection Regulation (GDPR) in the European Union, ask for the implementation of a strong security processes. It is to protect sensitive patient's data from unauthorized access, revelation or the change. Through using of the advanced security monitoring tools and both proactive and reactive threat detection mechanisms, the healthcare organizations will show their strict compliance with regulations' requirements and avoid penalties and legal liabilities related to damages or incidents of information security. Moreover, the ability to track ongoing as well as to discover threats helps healthcare organizations to better combat cyber attacks. Real-time detection and response to security risks will prevent the consequences impact on healthcare companies, threat of data loss, and operation interruption. Thus the continuous monitoring of the organization's networks allows it to conduct post-incident analysis as well as forensic investigations in order to identify the causes behind the security failures and to take appropriate actions to avoid they keep happening. Last but not least, persistent monitoring and major threats means the attitudes which ensure a proactive approach in healthcare DT sector data safety. Through using sophisticated security monitoring devices such as SIEM Systems and IDPS Solutions the healthcare organizations are capable of spotting and dealing with incidents immediately, reducing the probability of data breaches and unauthorized data entry. The inclusion of machine learning/AI algorithms into daily operations makes proactive works such as threat hunting and predictive analytics possible. This makes threat mitigation much easier and in most cases, it's done before a security threat escalates and does significant damage. Regular checking and risk assessment accompanied with regulator ties not only help the healthcare organizations to comply with security regulation but also help the organizations to be more resilience and competent to respond to security issues very powerfully. Through applying proactive, continuous monitoring and threat detection, healthcare organizations are better protected and can continue to attack sensitive patient data, maintain confidence in stakeholders, and ensure the integrity of their DT environment without interruption.

In summary, the safeguarding of patient data in the healthcare's digital simulations is the more multifaceted the approach, which would compromises encryption, access controls, blockchain technology, secure data sharing and the use of monitoring applications. Admiring state-of-art security measures and using the latest technology, healthcare systems will defend personal patient data, keep information integrity, and keep the highest expectations of confidentially and faith in the digital period.

6.7 LITERATURE REVIEW

Jørgensen et al. (2024) [33] has addressed in this paper the numerous concerns pertaining to the security, privacy, safety, and reliability of DTs and their use in healthcare. Using a comparative conflict analysis, the security, safety, privacy, trust, and operational requirements for Internet of Things DTs were implemented.

Khapekar et al. (2024) [34] examined the complex interaction between AI and DTs, showing how DT skills are improved by AI-driven data analytics. The findings are supported by real-world case studies provided by the authors, who show how this integration maximises operating savings, reduces downtime, and improves product quality. In this framework, privacy and ethical issues are discussed. The main conclusions show how AI-driven data analytics give DTs real-time insights, predictive modelling abilities, and informed decision assistance. Researchers should investigate methods to make AI models clear and comprehensible, and businesses are encouraged to leverage these synergies to obtain a competitive edge.

Armeni et al. (2022) [35] highlighted the current uses of DTs in a variety of healthcare domains, including clinical trial design, hospital operations, and precision medicine, in order to determine the opportunities and obstacles preventing or promoting a wider and quicker spread of these technologies. Lastly, talk about the most recent research, potential applications and challenges, and offer suggestions to support the further advancement of DT's use in healthcare.

Wickramasinghe et al. (2022) [36] has looked into a Black Box classification as one potential method for using DTs in the context of individualised treatment for uterine cancer. This essay, which combines three important fields – clinical, digital health, and computer science – presents one of the earliest initiatives to employ DTs in this way.

Liu et al. (2019) [37] proposed a cloud healthcare system framework based on DT healthcare (CloudDTH). This is a unique, generalised, and expandable framework for personal health management, particularly for the elderly, that works in a cloud environment to monitor, diagnose, and predict various aspects of an individual's health utilising wearable medical devices, among other gadgets. The goal of CloudDTH is to create interaction and convergence between virtual and real locations in medicine. As a result, a DTH model is put into practice and a novel notion of DT healthcare (DTH) is put forth and explored. After that, a CloudDTH reference framework built on DTH is developed, and its primary enabling technologies are investigated. Lastly, a case study for real-time supervision and the viability of a few application scenarios are shown.

Chakshu et al. (2019) [38] suggested a method to use a linked blood flow and head vibration model to determine the degree of carotid stenosis from a human face video. An attempt has been made to correlate the proportion of carotid blockage with noninvasive footage of a patient's face using this semi-active DT model. A mild head vibration is caused by the carotid arteries' pulsatile blood flow. This vibration is used in the current investigation as a potential marker of the severity of carotid stenosis. In the current work, a head vibration model related to blood flow forces with or without occlusion has been proposed. Numerous virtual head vibration data for varying levels of occlusion are produced by the model. A computer vision technique is used with human face videos to identify the in vivo head vibration. The virtual vibration data produced by the combined computational blood flow/vibration model is compared with the in vivo vibrations. To determine the best fit between the in vivo and virtual data, the in vivo vibration is compared to the virtual data.

Lauzeral et al. (2019) [39] emphasises parts of DT models in the medical context that can be simulated using computer. It specifically addresses the requirement for quick and precise simulators for the mechanical response at the tissue and organ scale, as well as the capacity to incorporate patient-specific anatomy from medical imaging in order to identify the subtle differences between typical anatomical models. The researcher suggested an automated process for building mechanical liver models that are capable of real-time function and have patient-specific shape. The technique relies on the extraction of pertinent anatomical features from a database of medical photographs using Statistical Shape Analysis, followed by Model Order Reduction to compute an explicit parametric solution for the mechanical reaction as a function of these features. It was decided to use a non-intrusive sparse sampling of the feature space in conjunction with a Finite Element solver to generate low-rank solutions through Sparse Subspace Learning. To generate a parametrized representation of the liver architecture, a database containing 385 three-dimensional liver shapes that were taken from medical pictures was used to train the statistical shape model in the application described in the research. The lower order model then employed this parametrization as well as an extra parameter characterising the breathing motion in linear elasticity as input. The high fidelity Finite Element models constructed from liver pictures omitted from the training dataset consistently agree with the results. Nonetheless, the researchers noted in the discussion how challenging it is to have compact shape parametrizations because of the high diversity of the shapes in the dataset and they suggested possible solutions to this problem.

Croatti et al. (2020) [40] discussed how agents and Multi-Agent Systems (MAS) technologies can be integrated with DTs in the healthcare industry. Following an overview of the use of DTs in healthcare, the researcher provided a first case study and talked about their vision for agent-based DTs in this paper. The agent-based DTs are used to handle severe traumas.

Hirschvogel et al. (2019) [41] demonstrates a high degree of concordance with in vivo data and accurately forecasts increases in left ventricular pressure and stroke volume as ventricular support rises. Moreover, the DT provides insight into quantities that no experimental setup can adequately capture or that are not accessible at all. In conclusion, the model is a very useful tool for the dimensioning of new VAD technologies and potential heart failure treatment plans since it can relate integral hemodynamic variables to local tissue mechanical deformation. The provided in silico twin expands the range of quantities of interest and makes in vivo research easier to access.

Bruynseels et al. (2018) [42] employed the theory of "DTs," according to which one would eventually have access to extremely detailed biophysical and lifestyle data on an individual. This viewpoint reinterprets "normality" or "health" as a collection of behaviours that are consistent for a given person against the backdrop of behaviours seen in the general population. This viewpoint will also influence what constitutes augmentation and therapy, as the "asymptomatic ill" and life extension by anti-aging medication are two examples of how this might be demonstrated. These modifications result from the process used to derive meaning when measurement data is provided. In particular, patterns in the data and the interpretations applied to them may serve as the foundation for moral distinctions. The ramifications of DTs for society and ethics are examined. DTs suggest a data-driven strategy for medical treatment. Through the implementation of equalising enhancing initiatives, this method can serve as a social equaliser and potentially yield substantial societal benefits. However, as a DT may not be a technology that everyone can use and because patterns found in a population of DTs may result in discrimination and segmentation, it can also be a cause of inequality.

Zoltick and Maisel (2023) [43] The numerous laws, rules, and regulations that have been underlined are important to take into account for any new and cutting-edge technology, but they are especially important for a technology as vast and all-encompassing as the DT ecosystem. Such a technology, being in its early phases of existence and relying in many ways on a combination of current technologies and innovations, has the contradiction of being open vs proprietary, and all the hybrids in between. Legally speaking, it takes into account intellectual property rights, such as the protection of trade secrets, patents, and copyrights, and weighs those rights against the advantages and safeguards provided by contract law. Regulatory and ethical issues arise from the DT's broad applicability to a variety of technologies and fields, including healthcare, banking, education, aviation, power plants, nuclear reactors, and many more. When utilising the DT ecosystem in these and other contexts, data must be gathered, processed, generated, and transmitted while adhering to privacy and cybersecurity regulations and ethical considerations that call for careful evaluation of potential bias, reliability, and transparency in the technology employed.

Al-Dalati (2023) [44] offer the most cutting-edge approaches and strategies that may be utilised to effectively safeguard patients and healthcare providers by creating a framework for privacy and trust in addition to a cybersecure one for DTs. A number of solutions, including intelligent Intrusion Detection Systems (IDS), effective authentication techniques, secure communication channels, privacy by design, increased trust through block chain integration, and improved adherence to current relevant standards, will be recommended.

Saeed et al. (2024) [45] highlights the need of classifying data and understanding the level of sensitivity of the data being created and used. It is stressed that robust security measures are required to protect data from unauthorised access and breaches, including access controls, authentication protocols, and encryption techniques. In order to provide further assurances regarding data security and compliance, the chapter emphasises the importance of continuous monitoring, auditing, and risk assessment protocols. It looks at the effective use of routine audits, proactive risk assessments, and real-time monitoring to identify and mitigate security issues.

Aluvalu et al. (2023) [46] offered a cutting-edge technique that uses computer image processing to recognise patients' faces and aid physicians in patient care. The biometric that serves as an authentication mechanism for cloud-based digital health record access. The technique of communication utilised to acknowledge the insurance company, the family, and the professional advisor. With a success rate of over 80%, the empirical results effectively validated the unique approach that was suggested. In order to work together with the Digital Health Record, E-H-S, Expert Adviser, and other expert systems in the future, this article suggests developing an intelligent expert system. while providing care for anonymous patients in the emergency room.

6.8 ETHICAL CONSIDERATIONS

Ethics is one of the main thing in the creation and use of DT technology in healthcare because patients will not be safe in terms of autonomy, privacy and wellbeing. This section provides ethics in healthcare DTs, starting with informed consent, data possession, the reasons for and against bias reduction, and fairness issues in DT implementations.

6.8.1 Introduction to ethical considerations

Ethics of healthcare DTs has its roots in the fundamental philosophies of autonomy, beneficence, non-maleficence and justice called the four pillar of ethics in medicine. The functioning of these principles lay the basis and cultivate the idea of the ethical behavior of healthcare professionals and institutions, and make sure that the patient's rights are respected and the ethical difficulties are resolved reasonably. Besides being an issue that a DT deals with, ethics is also a wide spectrum in the context of DTs that include informed consent and data privacy, fairness of algorithms in decision-making, and equity of access to healthcare services among other. These ethical nuances whatever they might be them, contribute to outlining the ethical terrain of healthcare DTs, as a means to guarantee them the standard of ethics at the patients' center and in the interest of social responsiveness. At the core every medical application there is a natural ethical consideration – the autonomy principle, which enables persons to have full knowledge of their own health status and their own choices regarding medical procedures. The informed consent acts as a foundation for ethical conduct of healthcare, so that patients are empowered with proper knowledge of what they are getting into when it comes to taking part in DT procedures and sharing their private data. In order to be ethically responsible for the DT of the patients, the organization must get an explicit consent from patients prior to collect, store or share their health information within the digital world, with respect for each people' autonomy and privacy. Supplementation of the healthcare team efforts with risk-benefit analysis education for patients would ensure that they comprehend the possible consequences and his or her input to the program by empowering them to participate knowledgeably. In the same way, ethical issues surrounding healthcare DTs evolve around the principles of beneficence and non-maleficence which are that care providers must act toward their patient's best interest and at no cost of doing any harm. The healthcare organizations must also stand firm in the legal responsibility to promote the objectives of using patient data and DT technologies through upgrading patient treatments and the healthcare system. Besides, effective data security means that patient privacy is protected and the integrity of DT applications is duly considered, while all these measures are tested and approved to minimize improper use, adverse events, and unintended consequences. However, when it comes to algorithms and AI in DT settings, healthcare professionals must also be aware of the possible ethical implications. The ethicality should be safeguarded when there is potential bias or discrimination, and permission of the patient should be asked for everything. Furthermore, the decision should be accountable, transparent and in alignment with the patient interest. In addition, the ethical aspects centering around healthcare DTs focus on the zweeness principle which highlights the fact that healthcare resources should be spread equally and fairly among the individuals in the society. Healthcare organizations should guarantee that these initiatives go hand in hand with efforts to guarantee equity and inclusivity, which would have covered areas such as disparities in access to healthcare services and resources among different populations. This could mean adopting measures to address uneven digital divide among members of our community who might not have a chance to use DT technology as it can bring the benefits along. Also one should note that in the same time healthcare organizations should look at possible dangers of utilization of DTs that can increase existing inequalities such as difference in data access to healthcare or bias usage algorithmic deciding. The healthcare industry can utilize a social justice perspective while seeking the solutions in some problematic questions such as digital divide in healthcare services. As a summation, principles of autonomy, beneficence, non-maleficence and justice are the major guidelines for ethical considerations in healthcare DTs, which ensure the rights of patients are taken into account and any dilemma is resolved fairly and compassionately. Data privacy issues like at informed consent and fairness in algorithmic decision making are the major issues that need to be considered while the ethical structure of digital healthcare is ethically responsible. Such ethical guidelines act as a roadmap environmental directing ethical obligation, patient-centric care, and social responsibility institutions thus helping them computer assisted in delivery of healthcare services and treatments improvements and patients' outcomes.

6.8.2 Informed consent and data ownership

Compliance with the informed consent principle is a necessary feature of an ethical medicine practice. It is a very vital part and the fundamental one in the context of healthcare DTs. DT technology, which makes use of patient's data to develop virtual representations for laboratory and medical studies, emphasizes the role of informed consent even more while working toward achieving medical science breakthroughs. The patients own this basic right to be very well aware about the collection, use and disclosure of their health information, and can consent in using their health information in DT applications by them just having to provide explicit consent. As the authenticity of DT concept is under scrutiny, the healthcare organizations must adopt procedures that are fully transparent enabling patients to be firmly informed about all aspects of their involvement in these initiatives. As the research topic is concerned at its crux, informed consent is the name of communicating the aim, risks, benefits and alternatives related to the DT programs to the patient. This data should be given out in plain and comprehensible language that is devoid of pressure or manipulation so that patients can perceive the pros and cons and choose the way that reflects their values and strikes a balance among available alternatives. Besides having patients obtain access for asking queries, clarity, and withdrawing their plastic at anytime without fears of catching problems or negative effects, healthcare institutions must guarantee this. Secondly, areas of ethics are uncovered by the fact that ownership of personal information is an issue to be considered in cases of healthcare DTs, because patients need to be sure to have the ability to control access to health details and still retain a right to own their data. The situation remains that though health organizations may use and process patients information for diverse objectives including DT development of the patients, the patients must however, be self-powered and in control of their health information. The Healthcare institutions shall set the minimum of rules and regulations on the ownership of data rights and then define the part played by the patients and organizations in the preparation and protection of health data. One of the major elements involved in data ownership is the principle that patients exercize their rights based on the personal autonomy, which says that they have the right to decide on who has access to them and how this information will be used. Healthcare facilities must be able to protect patient autonomy by setting up things that patient can control that is they can modify their health data and erase it when they are not comfortable with it. This may take the shape of imposing reliable data access protection, like patient portals or secure online platforms, which allow patients to monitor their health records, add and correct personal information and manage consent options. Also, healthcare organizations should provide for HIPAA (acronym for Health Insurance Portability and Accountability Act) in United States and GDPR (General Data Protection Regulation) in European Union which are regulatory requirements that govern proper privacy of patients and handling of health data which should be secure. This is to say that transparency along with accountability cannot be neglected by ethical data practices in healthcare DTs means. Health organizations should be open about how the healthcare data are collected such as the kind of data monitored, and the purpose of information gathering. It is also essential to protect such data and only sharing it with the relevant parties with consent from the patient. In addition to this, organizations should adopt in-depth data governance structures, which not only make resource management and data access more transparent but also provide safeguards against data expiration. This includes auditing and monitoring data access and utilization. Through transparency and accountability, healthcare organizations can create a trusting community among patients, as such will promote ethical data practices and ensure the safety and security of health information the virtual shadow of the patients portray. Conclusively, informed permission and data ownership are the main ethiccal issues that should be taken into account when building healthcare DTs and patients should be empowered and remain fully in control of their own health information. Through arranging for clear consent processes and designer to the patients' autonomy rights, healthcare institutions can give patients a chance to exercise their decision-making power regarding their involvement in DT programs. Maintaining transparency and adhering to the principles of data ownership in DT set-ups is also an essential factor. It can be done through making the policies strikingly clear and implementing strong data governance practices. Nonetheless, choosing consent and ownership of data is the technical way by which healthcare organizations can develop trust, transparency, and accountability in utilizing DT technology for the improvement of patients care as well as the progression of medical sciences.

6.8.3 Bias reduction in digital twins

Ethical concerns about algorithmic bias are encountered at when healthcare DTs are examined, as the biases of an algorithm can repeat the inequalities in the way of healthcare delivery and patients' outcomes. These biases can stem from multiple sources, such as biases in the data trained algorithms have, biases embedded in the process of designing and implementing algorithms, and bias in decision-making processes healthcare humanizes the profession. Without these biases being adequately assessed, the resulting inequitable treatment may enlarge the set of health disparities and create distrust among patients who use DT technology. Hence, healthcare organizations should focus on putting in places the strategies that deal with biases associated with the DT apps, make inspiration and transparency in algorithmic decision making, and ensure diversity and inclusiveness are in data collection and algorithm invention. Although the bias in healthcare DTs mainly appears during data preparation for the machine learning algorithms training, it can lead to serious errors. Bias may be an unavoidable outcome of data collection errors, for instance, when certain kind of people are intentionally kept out or there are insufficient sample to represent a homogeneous feature of a larger population. Therefore, it results in distorted models and other wrong predictions. In order to alleviate this, healthcare institutions should rely on robust data preprocessing skills such as biases spotting and corrections in the training data. This could range from applying methods, such as data augmentation, oversampling of underrepresented groups, and removal of biasing features or variables which would furthermore impede fairness in the outcomes. Moreover, groups need to put emphasis on diversity and inclusivity in data set collection initiatives aiming at using a wide variety of demographic groups and disorder types in order to make sure algorithms are trained in the representation and correction of the data. Moreover, a base may breed from the structural features and procedures of machine learning systems. Algorithmic bias can simply be adopted by various organizations, including giving preference to a certain culture, amplifying the current level of inequality in healthcare access and outcome or reproducing stereotypes and discriminatory practices. Healthcare organizations must be championing the transparency of algorithms that can be achieved by constructing the algorithms decision-making procedures in a well-documented way involving the underlying assumptions, data sources and the exact way to train and evaluate algorithms. Organizations can make the transparency a priority to enable stakeholders to evaluate the fairness and reliability of algorithm and identify the bias factors that may undermine the correctness of the healthcare decisions. Additionally, continuous checking and the evaluation of the algorithm performance is so critical for finding and lowering biases of DT applications. Healthcare institutions need to secure surveillance systems for perennially tracking the outcomes produced by algorithms and the medical impact and healthcare delivery improvement. It entails undertaking periodic evaluations of algorithmic decision-making processes, ensuring the precision and impartiality of predictions across diverse demographic groups, and collecting feedbacks from the stakeholders to know the areas of improvement. Through proactive measurement of algorithms' performance and immediate cleansing of opportunities of biases, healthcare organizations provide that DT applications uphold their ethical standards and offer equal access to healthcare services for patients from all societal strata. Furthermore, an employer should ensure diversity and inclusivity in the collection of datasets and also in the design of the algorithms to reduce the biases and to make the decision-making model fair in healthcare. Healthcare institutions should put diversity at the head of their data sets appropriation and make sure it includes all the ethnicities of their patient group, covers all the health conditions and situations. Besides, inclusivity must be incorporated in the algorithm development processes, involving different stakeholders; including patients, caregivers, and community representation in the algorithm design, validation, and evaluation stages. Through mix of perspectives and experiences, healthcare organizations can unveil and eliminate biases, execute the justice through the process of decision-making of healthcare and credibility in adopting DT technology between patients and other stakeholders. We conclude that in the context of healthcare DTs, bias reduction has been an ethical consideration as artifical intelligence may express prejudice and bias that cause disparities in healthcare delivery and outcomes. DT technology promotion is implemented via biases reduction in applications and algorithmic decision-making transparency. Accountable algorithms and equity patients' data collection or development are key elements to ensure healthcare organization trustworthiness. Through the application of bias reduction strategies in the medical field, healthcare organizations can be able to benefit from DT technology to ensure positive patient outcomes, at the same time provide more benefits to the society and advance medical research through equity and social justice.

6.8.4 Fairness in digital twin applications

Promoting fairness within the DT applications in healthcare is of the utmost importance to create more open and equitable access to vital services and sources of knowledge. The notion of justice, with bases in distributive justice, procedural justice, and social equity, provides the fairness considered necessary to minimize bias, unfair practices and perpetuation of disparities in healthcare. It puts the emphasis on supplying careers care according to patients' needs, not their race, gender, socioeconomic status or belonging to any other population groups. However, healthcare companies have to with great responsibility develop and implement DTs applications with fairness at their hearts taking into consideration the impact algorithmic decisions could have on marginalized groups and applying measures to prevent discrimination and disparities in accessing healthcare for all. At the core of fairness, in the case of DT implementations, is the virtue of distributive justice, represented by equitable access to healthcare for everyone in the society whether rich or poor. This is performing mathematical algorithms and decision-making processes which are, first of all, for patients. They must be created so that a resource will be allocated according to how much the patient is in a critical condition rather than the social and economic factors. The inclusion of a needs-based approach to the distribution of resources within healthcare organizations will at the same time take care of disparities in access to care and the delivery of the appropriate treatment and support to patients, regardless of their social and economic status. Moreover, procedural justice extends its role in the quality assurance of DTs by providing platforms for transparent, accountable, and engagement of rights holders in decision-making processes. Procedural justice is about the fact that the healthcare organizations should set procedures that are clear and should be based on the rule of transparency, should be characterized with the involvement of the stakeholders, and may be finally resolved by the fair and justly manner. By incorporating patients, caregivers, and community representatives in creating and putting into effect DT applications healthcare institutions can build confidence and reliability in the welfare and honesty of decision-making processes involving healthcare. Additionally, societal justice is associated with the rule that these DT applications should be implemented to ensure that systemic barriers are eradicated and that no inequality is occurred between healthcare services and resources. To reduce health inequalities, healthcare organizations have to pinpoint and mitigate the structural inadequacies that affect patients' health outcomes, covering such issues as geographical access to healthcare facilities, social determinants of health, and biases at the systemic level in healthcare delivery. Through establishing mechanisms that achieve the demolition of the barriers and the promotion of social equity, healthcare organizations provide a system that is tailored to suit everyone patient; irrespective of their circumstances or background. Also, being transparent and having clear accountability increases trust and confidence among patients and communities in healthcare decisionmaking processes. Healthcare organizations should guarantee that algorithms are not only transparent but also explainable, meaning that citizens should be given a clear information about how healthcare resources are distributed and decisions are made. With this transparency, accountability is promoted and patients are able to understand why the algorithm takes certain decisions, therefore they can speak for themselves regarding their medical puzzle and be involved with shared medical decision making processes. Lastly, it is crucial that there is impartiality in DT services in healthcare in order to ensure that equity in accessing healthcare services and resources. Applying principles of distributive justice, procedural justice and social equity in health system enable you to develop DT applications focusing on the patient's needs and generally reducing the inequalities experienced in healthcare delivery and outcome. Maintaining honesty and openness in every healthcare decision-making procedure is crucial for the creation of an equitable, trustworthy and accountable system for all patients and communities, therefore producing a healthcare system that is fair, transparent and responsive to the needs of the entire community. Efforts to make DT technology benefit community fairness and equity are the main direction through which healthcare institutions can obtain the advantage of DT technology to proceed health equity and make better patients' outcomes for all.

Finally, ethical issues are key to defining the role of healthcare DTs in terms of patient experience, organization procedures, and societal norms. The healthcare organization must adhere to the principles of respect for autonomy, beneficence, non-maleficence and justice when it faces the ethical dilemmas and advances the responsible utilization of DT technology in healthcare. Transparency in the consent process, data ownership, bias reduction and fairness are the ethical building blocks of digital applications in healthcare which will keep healthcare organizations at the top in terms of moral principles and create credibility and confidence in the system among the patients, healthcare providers and stakeholders.

6.9 LEGAL AND COMPLIANCE ISSUES

The new battlefield of health data DTs is the intricate matrix that entails legal and regulation necessities in ensuring compliance and managing the legal implications of any health data breach. This article investigates the legal and compliance affairs related to the DT tech use in the field of healthcare, overviews the existing law regulations and standards effective to patient data gathering, storage and transportation.

6.9.1 Overview of legal landscape

Politics, ethics, and technology are the top three laws that regulators and healthcare groups operating in the digital world must comply with while obtaining patients' consent, mitigating the risks of stolen data and preserving professional conduct. In the America, the violation of patients' healthy information privacy is heavily confronted with Health Insurance Portability and Accountability Act (HIPAA). The Health Insurance Portability and Accountability Act (HIPAA) is also responsible for imposition of sanctions on the organizations that do not fully comply. Application of European Union's General Data Protection Regulation (GDPR) is also worth noting. This regulation contains very strict requirements about processing and managing personal data, which includes healthcare data, in the EU and beyond. Furthermore, other international standards for example ISO/IEC 27001 for information security management and ISO 13485 for quality management systems in healthcare are esorted, which help in developing the regulatory framework that would ensure legal compliance and quality standards.

6.9.2 Compliance considerations

Legal and regulatory compliance orders, constituting a serious challenge for healthcare organizations are one of the barriers to implementation of the DT technology. By far the most important compliance related issues concern data sovereignty, because it stipulates the applicable laws governing storage and processing of health data. Data protection laws and regulations in healthcare are used for health facilities to comply with the legal frameworks in individual jurisdictions, with the understanding of cross-border data transfer restraints and data localization requirements. Moreover, the healthcare DTs should adhere to industry-accepted and certificated specifications, such as HITRUST (Health Information Trust Alliance) and SOC 2 (Service Organization Control 2) standards to prove that their implementation is styled in a manner that is compliant with security and privacy requirements. Such certifications prove exclusive compliance of an organization to industry best practices and regulatory standard requirements. This factor excites patients, partners and regulating authorities.

6.9.3 Managing legal risks

The healthcare organizations also have to undertake smart risk management on the legal side of things that are related to the deployment of DT. Out of various legal risks, data breaches and other security incidents, which can incur large financial penalties as well as, reputational loss and other legal troubles, are among the most common ones. Healthcare bodies must implement rigorous data security mechanisms comprising encryptions, access controls and breach responding procedures so that the risk of data breaching and loss of patients' information will be reduced. Additionally, healthcare entities are required to develop rules and processes for data governance, data transfer, and consent administration to ensure compliance with relevant legal and ethic regulations. This covers the fact that consent forms have to be given to patients when collecting, using and sharing their confidential data, as well as allowing patients to exercise their privacy rights provided by the data protection rules such as the right of access, rectification and erasure of the personal data.

6.9.4 Ethical considerations

Not only that along with the legal and regulatory requirements, ethical aspects of DT technology should be addressed by healthcare organizations as well. These include being open about data collection and processing processes, lowering the risk of discrimination and bias in computing-based decision-making platforms, and giving all patients equal access to healthcare services and resources. Incorporating ethical principles such as beneficence, non-maleficence, autonomy, and justice can play an important role in the DT plans that various healthcare organizations may have by upholding the highest ethical conduct standards and promoting trust among patients, providers, and stakeholders.

There is the wrap-up for the legal and compliance issues that affect healthcare DTs. It involves a deep knowledge of laws, regulations, and industry standards, or risk management strategies and ethics. Meeting with legal requirements, attaining compliance of the industry standards, and maintaining legal risks management, as well as addressing ethical issues, the healthcare organizations will be able to avoid legal liabilities, increase the patient's trust, and promote responsible and ethical use of DT technology in healthcare.

6.10 PROPOSED ALGORITHM: DATA SECURITY AND ETHICAL CONSIDERATIONS IN HEALTHCARE DIGITAL TWINS

Algorithm 1. Algorithm for data security and ethical considerations in healthcare digital twins

Input: Legal and regulatory requirements
| – Assess compliance
| – Define ethical framework
| – Conduct risk assessment
| – Implement data security measures
| – Address ethical considerations
| – Monitor and evaluate

Step 1: Assess legal and regulatory requirements

- Decipher the applicable laws, regulations as well as the expected provision of privacy and security in healthcare data governance and care of health data.
- Ascertain the law, regulations, HIPAA, GDPR, and specific protocols (e.g., HITRUST, SOC 2) associated with business industry.

Step 2: Define ethical framework

- Establish an ethical guideline on which the autonomy, beneficence, non-maleficence, and justice principles will be applied.
- Ethical perspectives need to be considered, these instances being informed consensus, data ownership, bias reduction, and fairness in DT applications.

Step 3: Conduct risk assessment

- Find out security threats and ethical dilemmas healthcare DTs may be prone to.
- Assessive the effects of data breaches, algorithmic biases, and privacy violations on patient safety and as far as reputation of an organization is a matter of concern.

Step 4: Implement data security measures

- Use various encryption systems, control access, and intrusion detection systems to keep patient information safe.
- Provide secure and interoperable data transfer by means of a robust protocol suite complemented by encryption methods.
- Put in place data governance policies and procedures that will help preserve data integrity and information security.

Step 5: Address ethical considerations

- Obtain advertisement of human appointment for the collection, practice, and delivery of patients health information in DT technology.
- Specify data ownership rights and enable patients by making means to access, change, and delete health information which is of their choice.
- Include the use of bias reduction strategies including data preprocessing and algorithmic transparency for the sole purpose of addressing the bias problems in DT applications.
- Encourage fairness and equality in healthcare decision-making cycles by analyzing how algorithms affect weak societies.

Step 6: Monitor and evaluate

- Periodically test and audit data security and ethical compliance by conducting auditing surveys.
- Analyze the efficacy of security measures, code of ethics and safety system provided to counter risks, misuse and promote responsibility in using DT.
- Revise and update processes and procedures proactively to account for evolving threats and ethical issues.

The Figure 6.1 illustrates the steps involve in the data security and ethical considerations in healthcare DTs. Healthcare DTs have a flowchart for ensuring secure and ethical use of patient data in the privacy, integrity and ethics. The chart starts by evaluating the legal and regulatory expectations and then leads the healthcare organizations through the development of an ethical frame, risk analysis, data protection measures, while addressing the ethical aspects. Different stages in the diagram show each critical step in the process, from defining compliance requirements to evaluating effectiveness of safeguards and ethical frameworks. The guidelines provided in this flowchart will help healthcare organizations systematically and purposefully find their way through the data security and ethical landscape

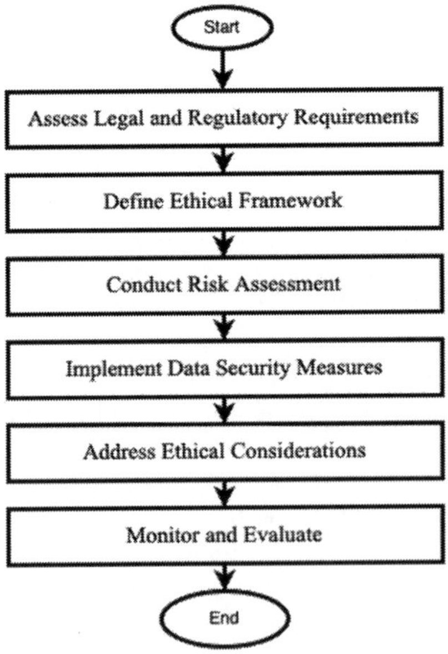

Figure 6.1 Flowchart of data security and ethical considerations in healthcare digital twins.

of DT usage in healthcare, and therefore build trust, transparency, and accountability.

6.11 STRATEGIES FOR ADDRESSING DATA SECURITY AND ETHICAL CONCERNS

Here are some strategies for addressing data security and ethical concerns in healthcare DTs:

1. Data encryption and access controls:
    - Implementation of strong encryption methods for protection of all the data (both at rest and whilst in transit) should be considered.
    - Employ a strict access control for allowing only those personnel to have access to the private data.
    - Employ multifactor authentication mechanisms to fortify the security in the use of user access.
2. Data minimization and anonymization:
    - Keep and store as the least data amount needed as for the goal only.
    - Consider anonymizing or pseudonymize the patient data when required to fulfill data protection mission.
    - Make sure to have a tight policy and kind of a doctrine for data maintenance and erasure so that you are quite sure that there is no unauthorized data access.
3. Regular security audits and monitoring:
    - Perform proactive security audits and tests on a regular basis so as to detect weaknesses and cyber-security hazards.
    - The mechanism of continuous network monitoring and response to the security incidents at real time should be considered.
    - Design programs to counter security incidents and also facilitate their recovery by means of corrective action taken immediately.
4. Compliance with regulations and standards:
    - See to it that all healthcare data security and privacy laws () and regulation () such as HIPAA (Health Insurance Portability and Accountability Act) in US () and GDPR (General Data Protection Regulation) in Europe are complied to.
    - Familiarize yourself with the upcoming changes of policies and reshape your organizational procedures or guide accordingly to sustain compliance.
5. Ethical use of data:
    - Setting up ethical guidelines and principles for the gathering, use and exchange of a patient's data in healthcare DT system.

- In order to execute effectively the transparency and accountability in the use of data, planning for open communication to patients is significant about how their data will be used and shared.
- Assure that data is used with patience of the patients, who deserve to be autonomous, to be respected, and not to be infringed on their rights of privacy.

6. Stakeholder engagement and education:
   - Interaction with the community consisting of healthcare providers, patients, technology developers, and policymakers concerning the data safety and ethical questions arising in the use of healthcare DTs is a necessity.
   - Train medical staff, both professionals and teams, for preventing data breaches and practices of ethical data usage.
   - Maintain the culture of the given organization at all the functional levels from people to accountability of security.
7. Collaboration and information sharing:
   - Interact with other healthcare establishments, academic institutions, and other related private entities in an effort to communicate and share the best strategies of handling security risks and ethical concerns.
   - Join industry activities and working groups that are concerned with data security and medical ethics and to remain on top of emerging ideas and discoveries.

6.12 FUTURE DIRECTIONS AND EMERGING TRENDS

Here's an exploration of future directions and emerging trends in healthcare DTs, along with potential advancements in data security measures and ethical frameworks, as well as areas for further research and development:

6.12.1 Emerging trends in healthcare digital twins

- **Personalized healthcare:** DTs are going to be frequently commissioned for building personalized image of patients and this will facilitate therapies that are targeted specifically and prove to be really efficient in providing the result.
- **Real-time monitoring and intervention:** Breakthroughs in sensor technology, especially data monitoring for DTs, provide the means for the continuous monitoring of patients' health. This can detect health issues early and provide timely interventions.
- **Integration with AI and machine learning:** DTs will be laced with AI and machine learning algorithms, which in turned feed on

information and improve predictive capabilities to ensure a more precise and effective healthcare delivery.

- **Virtual clinical trials:** Healthcare digital twins will change the way clinical trials are conducted it will mimic in the virtual form how the drugs or other interventions will really affect the virtual patient which will speed up the process and reduce the duration of the traditional trials and make the research work for developing new treatments faster.
- **Interoperability and data exchange:** Development of the standardization and interoperability to help DT systems link up with the electronic health records (EHRs) and other healthcare information technology (IT) systems will enhance the comprehensive patient care and the population health management by facilitating the integration.

6.12.2 Advancements in data security measures

- **Homomorphic encryption:** Using the volume approaches in the computational operations, the homomorphic encryption techniques will offer the ability for calculations on encrypted data without decrypting it therefore ensuring the data security and privacy.
- **Blockchain technology:** The blockchain made missions with data storage provide the safe and immutable records of health data. Hereby this storage enables transparency, integrity, and traceability among transactions that take place inside a DT network.
- **Differential privacy:** Data will be analyzed using privacy-preserving procedures to avoid the risks of disclosing sensitive patients' data while still enabling researchers to derive useful conclusions from aggregated data, hence protecting privacy and confidentiality of patients.
- **Zero-trust security architectures:** Zero-trust security models will be closely observed so that only authorized access is permitted and authenticated users are in charge of the cyber health DT environments, thus preventing anonymous access.

6.12.3 Enhancements in ethical frameworks

- **Ethical AI and algorithmic transparency:** The ethical directive and framework will be formulated for the purpose of providing transparency and accountability through the engineering and deployment of AI algorithms in healthcare DT systems, which is considered the main challenge in minimising algorithm bias and ensuring fair outcomes.
- **Patient-centered ethical principles:** Such ethical standards will aim at patient-oriented principles like autonomy, and dignity, which is made possible through patients having the power over their health information, and also to make decisions on its application.

- **Multistakeholder collaboration:** Ethical frameworks can be used to reinforce the need for multi-stakeholder cooperation and include ones that show a special interest in the ethical challenges that are related to the healthcare DTs and creating trust, transparency, as well as accountability among all the stakeholders.

6.12.4 Areas for further research and development

- **Security of edge computing in healthcare:** Scientists will be required to mark the safety of edge computing solutions in order to avoid compromising data security and privacy between edge units and centralized health DT systems.
- **Ethical considerations in AI explainability:** Besides that there should be more research directed to problems related to explainability and interpretability of AI algorithms exploited in health service twin systems as we want to guarantee that AI can explain the results of its decision making for clinicians and patients.
- **Privacy-preserving data sharing:** Academic efforts will be concentrated on developing privacy-protection techniques allowing for secure sharing of healthcare data between different stakeholders while also ensuring patients secret and other information, ultimately enabling collaborative research, data-driven healthcare innovation.
- **Human-centric design of digital twins:** Research will investigate the human-centered design foundations for the healthcare DTs. Humanized approach will be used in terms of patients' and healthcare professionals' perspective, focusing on resolving problems with usability, effectiveness, and ethical issues.

By exploring these future directions and emerging trends, healthcare organizations can anticipate challenges and opportunities associated with the adoption of DT technology and develop strategies to ensure the responsible and beneficial use of these innovative tools in healthcare.

6.13 CONCLUSION

There are two main challenges that relate to data security and ethical options in healthcare DTs: defending the patient confidentiality as well as integrity and well-being; additionally promoting trust, transparency, and accountability in the use of technology in healthcare. During all of this work, we have seen the DT technology full of depths, from giving protection to patient's data against hacking and cyber-attacks to solving complex ethical problems like getting consent from patients and reducing bias. Through the application of a theory that entail both legal and regulatory regime, government regulations system, ethical principles development, risk assessment and management, data security measures, ethical considerations, and monitoring and evaluation, healthcare organizations can successfully mitigate risks, promote respectful utilization of DT technology, and maintain the highest standing of patient care and ethical values. It is vital, therefore, for all the stakeholders across the healthcare system to team up, innovate, and give priority to safeguarding of data and morality in the creating and deploying of the DTs for healthcare purposes with a view to working for the advancement of personalized medicine, improving health outcome,s and innovation of a culture of trust and accountability in healthcare.

REFERENCES

1. Hassani, H., Huang, X., & MacFeely, S. (2022). Impactful digital twin in the healthcare revolution. *Big Data and Cognitive Computing*, 6(3), 83.
2. Singh, M., Fuenmayor, E., Hinchy, E. P., Qiao, Y., Murray, N., & Devine, D. (2021). Digital twin: Origin to future. *Applied System Innovation*, 4(2), 36.
3. Jones, D., Snider, C., Nassehi, A., Yon, J., & Hicks, B. (2020). Characterising the digital twin: A systematic literature review. *CIRP Journal of Manufacturing Science and Technology*, 29, 36–52.
4. Kritzinger, W., Karner, M., Traar, G., Henjes, J., & Sihn, W. (2018). Digital twin in manufacturing: A categorical literature review and classification. *Ifac-PapersOnline*, 51(11), 1016–1022.
5. Anshari, M., & Hamdan, M. (2022). Enhancing e-government with a digital twin for innovation management. *Journal of Science and Technology Policy Management*, 14(6), 1055–1065.
6. Qi, Q., Tao, F., Hu, T., Anwer, N., Liu, A., Wei, Y., ... & Nee, A. Y. (2021). Enabling technologies and tools for digital twin. *Journal of Manufacturing Systems*, 58, 3–21.
7. Tao, F., Zhang, H., Liu, A., & Nee, A. Y. (2018). Digital twin in industry: State-of-the-art. *IEEE Transactions on Industrial Informatics*, 15(4), 2405–2415.
8. Sun, T., He, X., & Li, Z. (2023). Digital twin in healthcare: Recent updates and challenges. *Digital Health*, 9, 20552076221149651.
9. Elayan, H., Aloqaily, M., & Guizani, M. (2021). Digital twin for intelligent context-aware IoT healthcare systems. *IEEE Internet of Things Journal*, 8(23), 16749–16757.
10. Haleem, A., Javaid, M., Singh, R. P., & Suman, R. (2023). Exploring the revolution in healthcare systems through the applications of digital twin technology. *Biomedical Technology*, 4, 28–38.
11. Erol, T., Mendi, A. F., & Doğan, D. (2020, October). The digital twin revolution in healthcare. In *2020 4th international symposium on multidisciplinary studies and innovative technologies (ISMSIT)* (pp. 1–7). IEEE.
12. Khan, S., Arslan, T., & Ratnarajah, T. (2022). Digital twin perspective of fourth industrial and healthcare revolution. *IEEE Access*, 10, 25732–25754.
13. Sahal, R., Alsamhi, S. H., & Brown, K. N. (2022). Personal digital twin: A close look into the present and a step towards the future of personalised healthcare industry. *Sensors*, 22(15), 5918.

14. Corral-Acero, J., Margara, F., Marciniak, M., Rodero, C., Loncaric, F., Feng, Y., ... & Lamata, P. (2020). The 'digital twin'to enable the vision of precision cardiology. *European Heart Journal*, 41(48), 4556–4564.
15. Jimenez, J. I., Jahankhani, H., & Kendzierskyj, S. (2020). Health care in the cyberspace: Medical cyber-physical system and digital twin challenges. In M. Farsi, A. Daneshkhah, A. Hosseinian-Far, & H. Jahankhani (Eds.), *Digital twin technologies and smart cities. Internet of Things*. Springer. https://doi.org/10.1007/978-3-030-18732-3_6
16. Yang, D., Karimi, H. R., Kaynak, O., & Yin, S. (2021). Developments of digital twin technologies in industrial, smart city and healthcare sectors: A survey. *Complex Engineering Systems*, 1(1), N–A.
17. Angulo, C., Gonzalez-Abril, L., Raya, C., & Ortega, J.A. (2020). A proposal to evolving towards digital twins in healthcare. In I. Rojas, O. Valenzuela, F. Rojas, L. Herrera, & F. Ortuño (Eds.), *Bioinformatics and biomedical engineering. IWBBIO 2020*. Lecture Notes in Computer Science, vol. 12108. Springer. https://doi.org/10.1007/978-3-030-45385-5_37
18. Zhang, J., Li, L., Lin, G., Fang, D., Tai, Y., & Huang, J. (2020). Cyber resilience in healthcare digital twin on lung cancer. *IEEE Access*, 8, 201900–201913.
19. Vats, T., Singh, S. K., Kumar, S., Gupta, B. B., Gill, S. S., Arya, V., & Alhalabi, W. (2023). Explainable context-aware IoT framework using human digital twin for healthcare. *Multimedia Tools and Applications*, 83(22), 1–25.
20. Alazab, M., Khan, L. U., Koppu, S., Ramu, S. P., Iyapparaja, M., Boobalan, P., ... & Aljuhani, A. (2022). Digital twins for healthcare 4.0 – Recent advances, architecture, and open challenges. *IEEE Consumer Electronics Magazine*, 12(6), 29–37.
21. Zheng, Y., Lu, R., Guan, Y., Zhang, S., & Shao, J. (2021, June). Towards private similarity query based healthcare monitoring over digital twin cloud platform. In *2021 IEEE/ACM 29th International Symposium on Quality of Service (IWQOS)* (pp. 1–10). IEEE.
22. Faleiro, R., Pan, L., Pokhrel, S. R., & Doss, R. (2022). Digital twin for cybersecurity: Towards enhancing cyber resilience. In *Broadband communications, networks, and systems: 12th EAI international conference, BROADNETS 2021, Virtual Event, October 28–29, 2021, Proceedings 12* (pp. 57–76). Springer International Publishing.
23. KeshmiriNeghab, H., Jamshidi, M., & KeshmiriNeghab, H. (2022). Digital twin of a magnetic medical microrobot with stochastic model predictive controller boosted by machine learning in cyber-physical healthcare systems. *Information*, 13(7), 321.
24. Barnabas, J., & Raj, P. (2020). The human body: A digital twin of the cyber physical systems. *Advances in Computers*, 117(1), 219–246.
25. Pirbhulal, S., Abie, H., & Shukla, A. (2022, June). Towards a novel framework for reinforcing cybersecurity using digital twins in IoT-based healthcare applications. In *2022 IEEE 95th vehicular technology conference (VTC2022-Spring)* (pp. 1–5). IEEE.
26. Hamzaoui, M. A., & Julien, N. (2022). Social cyber-physical systems and digital twins networks: A perspective about the future digital twin ecosystems. *IFAC-PapersOnLine*, 55(8), 31–36.

27. Shaikh, E., Al-Ali, A. R., Muhammad, S., Mohammad, N., & Aloul, F. (2023). Security analysis of a digital twin framework using probabilistic model checking. *IEEE Access*, 11, 26358–26374.
28. Saad, A., Faddel, S., Youssef, T., & Mohammed, O. A. (2020). On the implementation of IoT-based digital twin for networked microgrids resiliency against cyber attacks. *IEEE Transactions on Smart Grid*, 11(6), 5138–5150.
29. Huang, S., Wang, G., Yan, Y., & Fang, X. (2020). Blockchain-based data management for digital twin of product. *Journal of Manufacturing Systems*, 54, 361–371.
30. Liu, K., Yan, Z., Liang, X., Kantola, R., & Hu, C. (2024). A survey on blockchain-enabled federated learning and its prospects with digital twin. *Digital Communications and Networks*, 10(2), 248–264.
31. Hasan, H. R., Salah, K., Jayaraman, R., Omar, M., Yaqoob, I., Pesic, S., ... & Boscovic, D. (2020). A blockchain-based approach for the creation of digital twins. *IEEE Access*, 8, 34113–34126.
32. Stergiou, C., & Psannis, K. (2022). Digital twin intelligent system for industrial internet of things-based big data management and analysis in cloud environments. *Virtual Reality & Intelligent Hardware*, 4(4), 279–291.
33. Jørgensen, C. S., Shukla, A., & Katt, B. (2023, September). Digital twins in healthcare: Security, privacy, trust and safety challenges. In *European symposium on research in computer security* (pp. 140–153). Springer Nature.
34. Khapekar, S. H., Wankhade, S., Sawai, S., Agrawal, S., & Jaronde, P. (2024). AI-driven data analytics within digital twins: Transformative potential and ethical consideration. In S. Ponnusamy, M. Assaf, J. Antari, S. Singh, & S. Kalyanaraman (Eds.), *Digital twin technology and AI implementations in future-focused businesses* (pp. 61–69). IGI Global.
35. Armeni, P., Polat, I., De Rossi, L. M., Diaferia, L., Meregalli, S., & Gatti, A. (2022). Digital twins in healthcare: Is it the beginning of a new era of evidence-based medicine? A critical review. *Journal of Personalized Medicine*, 12(8), 1255.
36. Wickramasinghe, N., Jayaraman, P. P., Forkan, A. R. M., Ulapane, N., Kaul, R., Vaughan, S., & Zelcer, J. (2021). A vision for leveraging the concept of digital twins to support the provision of personalized cancer care. *IEEE Internet Computing*, 26(5), 17–24.
37. Liu, Y., Zhang, L., Yang, Y., Zhou, L., Ren, L., Wang, F., ... & Deen, M. J. (2019). A novel cloud-based framework for the elderly healthcare services using digital twin. *IEEE Access*, 7, 49088–49101.
38. Chakshu, N. K., Carson, J., Sazonov, I., & Nithiarasu, P. (2019). A semi-active human digital twin model for detecting severity of carotid stenoses from head vibration – A coupled computational mechanics and computer vision method. *International Journal for Numerical Methods in Biomedical Engineering*, 35(5), e3180.
39. Lauzeral, N., Borzacchiello, D., Kugler, M., George, D., Rémond, Y., Hostettler, A., & Chinesta, F. (2019). A model order reduction approach to create patient-specific mechanical models of human liver in computational medicine applications. *Computer Methods and Programs in Biomedicine*, 170, 95–106.

40. Croatti, A., Gabellini, M., Montagna, S., & Ricci, A. (2020). On the integration of agents and digital twins in healthcare. *Journal of Medical Systems*, 44(9), 161.
41. Hirschvogel, M., Jagschies, L., Maier, A., Wildhirt, S. M., & Gee, M. W. (2019). An in silico twin for epicardial augmentation of the failing heart. *International Journal for Numerical Methods in Biomedical Engineering*, 35(10), e3233.
42. Bruynseels, K., Santoni de Sio, F., & Van den Hoven, J. (2018). Digital twins in health care: Ethical implications of an emerging engineering paradigm. *Frontiers in Genetics*, 9, 31.
43. Zoltick, M. M., & Maisel, J. B. (2023). Societal impacts: Legal, regulatory and ethical considerations for the digital twin. In N. Crespi, A.T. Drobot, & R. Minerva, (Eds.), *The digital twin* (pp. 1167–1200). Springer International Publishing.
44. Al-Dalati, I. (2023). Digital twins and cybersecurity in healthcare systems. In A. E. Saddik (Ed.), *Digital twin for healthcare* (pp. 195–221). Academic Press.
45. Saeed, M. M. A., Saeed, R. A., & Ahmed, Z. E. (2024). Data security and privacy in the age of AI and digital twins. In S. Ponnusamy, M. Assaf, J. Antari, S. Singh, & S. Kalyanaraman (Eds.), *Digital twin technology and AI implementations in future-focused businesses* (pp. 99–124). IGI Global.
46. Aluvalu, R., Mudrakola, S., Kaladevi, A. C., Sandhya, M. V. S., & Bhat, C. R. (2023). The novel emergency hospital services for patients using digital twins. *Microprocessors and Microsystems*, 98, 104794.

Chapter 7

The future of digital twin technology in healthcare

Ashwani Kant Shukla, Raj Shree, Ravi Prakash Pandey, Vivek Shukla, and Karm Veer Arya

7.1 INTRODUCTION

The technology of digital twins is completely transforming our comprehension and interaction with the tangible realm, encompassing various entities, actions, and structures. This innovative technology is reshaping the way we perceive and connect with the physical world. A digital twin is a virtual representation or duplicate of a tangible object, structure, or operation. Through the use of up-to-date information and advanced data analysis, a digital model is generated to facilitate the observation, evaluation, and imitation of the corresponding physical entity. This innovation permits a thorough comprehension and enhancement of the real-world counterpart's efficiency, characteristics, and upkeep requirements. In the healthcare sector, digital twins are leveraged to develop customized models of patients, medical equipment, and healthcare infrastructures [1]. Digital twins are advanced models that mimic the complexities of biological systems, including patient-specific traits and medical processes. They utilize a range of data inputs, such as electronic health records (EHRs), imaging scans, genetic information, and sensor readings, to tailor diagnostic and therapeutic strategies for individual patients.

Digital twins in healthcare are centered around the different elements involved in their conceptual framework. The physical aspect pertains to the actual entities, objects, systems, or procedures that are duplicated in a digital format. Within the healthcare sector, these physical entities encompass patients, organs, medical equipment, medical facilities, and medical procedures. The digital twin acts as a virtual representation of the physical object. It includes in-depth details of the entity's anatomy, physiology, and behavior, obtained from real-time data and computational models. Digital twins use various data sources and advanced analytics to gather, assess, and display intricate healthcare information. This encompasses a wide range of data sources, including organized data from EHRs, medical imaging, and lab tests, as well as unstructured data from sources like wearable sensors, genomics, and environmental factors. In addition,

DOI: 10.1201/9781003498117-7

digital twins offer the capability for instant monitoring and simulation of patients' health conditions, medical equipment functioning, and operational processes within healthcare facilities. In addition to providing assistance with predictive modeling and simulations for disease progression, treatment outcomes, and operational workflows, they also offer support for various components within a complex ecosystem. This ecosystem encompasses healthcare providers, patients, medical devices, Internet of Things (IoT) sensors, and data analytics platforms. By integrating these elements, they facilitate the seamless flow of information and data necessary for effective decision-making and healthcare management [2]. This environment allows for the seamless sharing of information, fostering teamwork, and enabling more informed choices throughout the entire healthcare system.

Over the last few years, there has been a significant evolution in digital twin technology, which can be attributed to the progress made in data analytics, IoT connectivity, and computational modeling methods. Initially created for industrial use, digital twins have now become popular in a wide range of sectors, such as manufacturing, aerospace, automotive, and healthcare. Digital twins are widely utilized in the manufacturing industry to generate virtual duplicates of production facilities, equipment, and logistical processes. Companies in this sector harness digital twin technology to anticipate maintenance requirements, refine operational processes, and uphold product quality standards. Through the continuous monitoring of machinery performance and the simulation of various production scenarios, digital twins empower manufacturers to take a proactive approach to maintenance, reduce instances of downtime, and enhance the efficiency of resource allocation. Digital twins have become indispensable tools in the aerospace and defense sectors, serving essential functions such as design validation, performance optimization, and predictive maintenance for a wide range of aircraft, satellites, and defense systems. Within these industries, digital twins are utilized by aerospace engineers to replicate flight scenarios, evaluate structural soundness, and forecast potential equipment malfunctions, ultimately bolstering safety measures, dependability, and operational effectiveness in the aerospace field. Similarly, in the realm of automotive manufacturing, digital twins are instrumental in facilitating product development, conducting rigorous testing procedures, and refining vehicle performance metrics. Automobile manufacturers develop digital replicas of vehicles, engines, and automotive parts for the purpose of simulating driving scenarios, analyzing fuel consumption, and testing safety functionalities [3]. Utilizing immediate data sourced from interconnected vehicles and IoT sensors, these digital replicas facilitate remote troubleshooting, foresighted maintenance, and software upgrades via wireless transmission. Digital twins are revolutionizing the energy and utilities industry by facilitating predictive maintenance, grid optimization, and the seamless integration of renewable energy sources. Energy firms are developing digital replicas of power plants, transmission networks, and renewable energy facilities to oversee their operations, anticipate equipment malfunctions, and enhance energy generation. Through the simulation of grid activities and the incorporation of renewable energy sources, digital twins streamline resource allocation processes and assist in the transition toward eco-friendly energy infrastructures. Digital twin technology is transforming the landscape of healthcare by enhancing patient care, managing medical devices, and streamlining healthcare operations. Medical professionals utilize digital twins to construct individualized representations of patients, medical equipment, and clinical processes. These virtual copies facilitate tailored diagnostics, treatment strategies, and remote monitoring of patients' well-being. Through the simulation of disease advancement, treatment effectiveness, and operational procedures, digital twins elevate clinical decision-making, elevate patient results, and enhance the efficiency of healthcare provision.

The potential of digital twin technology in revolutionizing healthcare delivery, improving patient outcomes, and enhancing operational efficiency in healthcare institutions is significant. By capturing the distinctive attributes and health profiles of patients, digital twins facilitate personalized medicine approaches. Digital twins enable personalized healthcare interventions by integrating a variety of data sources, including genetic information, medical imaging, and real-time sensor data. The increasing availability of wearable sensors and IoT devices allows for remote monitoring of patients' health and vital signs through digital twins. Healthcare professionals can use digital twins to monitor patients' physiological metrics, medication compliance, and lifestyle choices in real time. Taking a proactive stance allows for the prompt identification of health problems, timely actions, and ongoing tracking of long-term conditions [4]. The use of digital twins is transforming the field of surgical care through the facilitation of strategic planning, simulations, and training for intricate surgical processes. Doctors can make use of digital copies of patients' body structures to envision surgical scenarios, rehearse surgical methods, and predict any possible obstacles. This contributes to enhanced surgical accuracy, lowered risks during operations, and better safety outcomes for patients. Digital twins use cutting-edge analytics and machine learning (ML) to predict disease progression and treatment results. Through studying patient data over time, genetic factors, and environmental influences, digital twins help categorize risks, develop early treatment plans, and personalize healthcare strategies. This proactive method boosts healthcare efficiency and enhances patient results. Digital twins enhance healthcare efficiency by simulating various clinical processes, managing resources, and monitoring patient movement within medical facilities. Through digital twin technology, hospital administrators have the opportunity to improve bed utilization, staff allocation, and inventory management of medical equipment. By simulating different operational scenarios and forecasting changes in demand, digital twins help healthcare organizations simplify their processes, reduce expenses, and boost overall effectiveness. The use of digital twins is essential for overseeing and upkeeping medical devices in healthcare settings. Biomedical engineers can develop digital replicas of equipment such as MRI machines, ventilators, and infusion pumps to oversee their functioning, predict maintenance requirements, and optimize their usage. Taking a proactive stance helps to reduce the amount of time that equipment is out of commission, uphold adherence to regulations, and improve safety for patients [5]. Digital twins are effective assets for advancing healthcare studies, fostering creativity, and supporting efforts to enhance quality. Capturing the benefits of digital twins enables researchers to carry out simulations of clinical trials, explore how diseases progress, and experiment with new methods of treatment. The availability of comprehensive patient information over time, along with the ability to create models through computation, allows digital twins to speed up the process of making scientific breakthroughs, make it easier to test hypotheses, and fuel progress in the field of medical technology and clinical practice [6].

7.2 ARCHITECTURE AND COMPONENTS OF DIGITAL TWINS IN HEALTHCARE

Digital twins are becoming increasingly popular in the field of healthcare as a promising avenue for innovation. These virtual replicas mirror real-world entities like systems, processes, or individuals, presenting a wide range of possibilities for revolutionizing various aspects of healthcare. The potential benefits of digital twins in healthcare are immense, as they have the ability to completely overhaul personalized medicine, streamline treatment processes, elevate medical education, and refine training techniques. Healthcare providers can improve patient representations in a virtual environment by using personalized data like genetic information, medical history, lifestyle factors, and environmental influences [7]. Digital twins can help create customized treatments, interventions, and care plans for each patient, leading to better outcomes and higher satisfaction. Personalized medicine is a key use for healthcare digital twins, allowing professionals to simulate treatment impacts, predict results, and adjust therapy plans. For instance, digital twins can assist oncologists in determining the best chemotherapy regimen based on a patient's genetic profile and tumor characteristics [8]. Similarly, in the field of cardiology, digital twins can be used to simulate the effects of different medications or interventions on a patient's heart function, allowing for personalized treatment planning and optimization. Another key application of healthcare digital twins is in surgical planning and simulation. Surgeons can use virtual replicas of patients' anatomy to plan and rehearse complex surgical procedures before performing them in real life. By simulating different surgical techniques and scenarios, surgeons can anticipate potential challenges, optimize surgical approaches, and minimize risks. This not only enhances patient safety but also improves surgical outcomes and reduces the likelihood of complications [9].

7.2.1 Digital twins healthcare components

Exploring the intricate layers of technology and data integration is necessary to understand the components and architecture of healthcare digital twins [10, 11]. This detailed overview examines the different components, how they interact, and the important architectural considerations needed to develop and deploy healthcare digital twins.

7.2.1.1 Data acquisition and integration

Data serves as the foundational component of digital twins in every aspect. In the realm of healthcare, digital twins rely heavily on a diverse array of data sources, including EHRs, medical imaging results, and data from wearable devices, genetic information, environmental data, and more. The collection of this data involves the intricate task of gathering, combining, and consolidating these different sources to build a cohesive infrastructure that forms the backbone of the digital twin.

7.2.1.2 Data storage and management

Healthcare data, once obtained, must be securely stored and effectively managed to ensure its confidentiality and integrity. This process involves implementing advanced data storage systems like databases, data lakes, or cloud-based storage platforms that can effectively handle vast amounts of both structured and unstructured data. Managing healthcare data also involves performing essential tasks such as data cleansing, normalization, and indexing to maintain high data quality and accessibility for authorized users.

7.2.1.3 Data processing and analytics

Data processing and analytics play a crucial role in the development and utilization of healthcare digital twins. These technologies are vital for generating insights and providing decision support in the healthcare industry. Utilizing a combination of analytical techniques such as ML, statistical analysis, and predictive modeling, healthcare professionals can extract valuable patterns, trends, and correlations from the vast amount of data available. Furthermore, advanced analytics algorithms are employed to simulate the behavior of digital twins, predict potential outcomes, and optimize interventions for better patient outcomes.

7.2.1.4 Simulation and modeling

In healthcare digital twins, the ability to simulate and model is crucial as it enables the creation of virtual versions of real-life entities and situations. This process entails the creation of mathematical models and computational simulations that accurately depict how the digital twin behaves, its characteristics, and its interactions within its surroundings. The range of simulation methods varies from basic mathematical models to elaborate, physics-based simulations that replicate intricate physiological processes at a cellular or molecular level.

7.2.1.5 User and visual interface

The user interface and visualization components of healthcare digital twins provide interfaces for users to interact with and interpret the digital twin's outputs. This includes developing intuitive user interfaces, dashboards, and visualization tools that present data, insights, and simulation results in a clear and actionable manner. Visualization techniques may include 2D and 3D graphics, interactive charts, heatmaps, and immersive virtual reality (VR) environments.

7.2.1.6 Integration with external systems

Healthcare digital twins often need to interact with external systems and devices to access real-time data, exchange information, and integrate with existing healthcare infrastructure. In order to achieve this, it is essential to have smooth integration with various healthcare IT systems, including electronic medical record systems, medical devices, IoT sensors, and other technologies. The utilization of standardized interfaces and protocols like HL7 FHIR and DICOM greatly assists in promoting interoperability and facilitating the exchange of data among diverse systems.

7.2.1.7 Security and privacy

In healthcare digital twins, ensuring the security and confidentiality of patient information is crucial due to the sensitivity of the data and the risks associated with breaches or unauthorized entry. To address these concerns effectively, strong security measures such as encryption, access controls, authentication methods, and audit trails should be put in place.

The implementation of these protocols is intended to ensure the protection of data confidentiality, integrity, and accessibility within the digital twin framework. It is crucial to adhere to regulations such as Health Insurance Portability and Accountability Act (HIPAA) and General Data Protection Regulation (GDPR) in order to safeguard patient confidentiality and fulfill regulatory obligations.

7.2.1.8 Scalability and performance

Healthcare digital twins require meticulous planning to effectively manage the growing volume of data and computational requirements. It is essential to develop flexible architectures and leverage infrastructure resources that can seamlessly adapt to evolving demands. Strategies such as parallel processing, distributed computing, and caching play a crucial role in improving system performance and guaranteeing prompt responsiveness. Figure 7.1 illustrates the digital twins healthcare components.

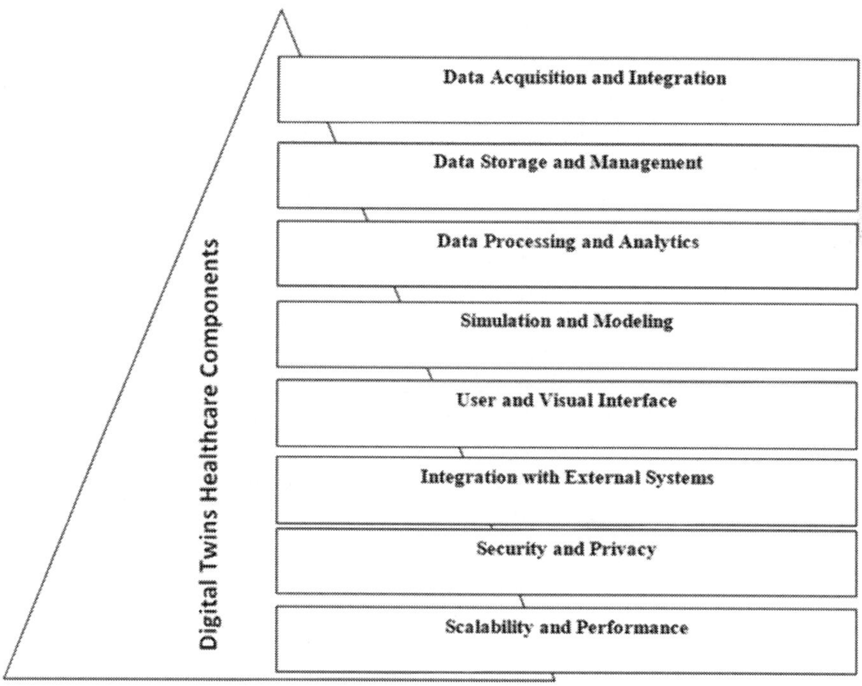

Figure 7.1 Digital Twins Healthcare Components.

7.2.2 Design of healthcare digital twins

The architecture of healthcare digital twins is characterized by a distributed, modular design that incorporates various components working together to create, simulate, and interact with the digital twin. While specific architectures may vary depending on the use case, requirements, and technology stack, typical healthcare digital twin architecture may include the following layers [12, 13].

7.2.2.1 Data ingestion layer

The digital twin ecosystem heavily relies on the data ingestion layer to oversee the acquisition, collection, and importing of data from diverse origins. This layer encompasses a range of interfaces that allow access to EHRs, medical imaging databases, wearable technology, IoT sensors, and external data repositories. The methods used for data ingestion can vary, including batch processing, real-time streaming, and event-driven architectures, each tailored to handle different types of data streams effectively.

7.2.2.2 Data processing and analytics layer

The layer of data processing and analytics is a crucial component that includes various functionalities for processing, analyzing, and extracting valuable insights from the data that has been ingested. These functionalities encompass tasks like data preprocessing, which involves actions such as cleansing, normalization, and transformation to ensure the data is in a usable format. Additionally, this layer incorporates advanced analytics algorithms that are essential for tasks such as pattern recognition, anomaly detection, and predictive modeling. Various tools and techniques, such as ML models, statistical methods, and domain-specific algorithms, are employed within this layer to generate meaningful insights and predictions based on the data. These tools play a vital role in extracting valuable information from the data and uncovering patterns and trends that can be used for decision-making purposes. This layer acts as a bridge between raw data and actionable insights, transforming the data into useful information that can drive business decisions and strategies.

7.2.2.3 Simulation and modeling layer

The responsibility of the simulation and modeling layer is crucial as it involves creating an intricate virtual representation of the digital twin. This is achieved through the development of intricate mathematical models, computational simulations, and algorithms. By combining these elements, a detailed and accurate replication of the behavior, characteristics, and interactions of the digital twin with its physical counterpart in the real world is achieved. Cutting-edge simulation engines, numerical solvers, and optimization algorithms play a key role in accurately replicating a wide variety of scenarios such as physiological processes, medical procedures, and treatment outcomes. These advanced tools and techniques enable the simulation and modeling layer to provide a realistic and comprehensive insight into how the digital twin behaves and interacts within its environment.

7.2.2.4 User interface and visualization layer

The user interface and visualization layer provide interfaces for users to interact with and visualize the digital twin's outputs. This includes developing user-friendly interfaces, dashboards, and visualization tools that present data, insights, and simulation results in a clear and actionable manner. Visualization techniques may include 2D and 3D graphics, interactive charts, heatmaps, and immersive VR environments.

7.2.2.5 Integration and interoperability layer

The layer that focuses on integration and interoperability plays a crucial role in ensuring a smooth flow of communication and data exchange between the healthcare digital twin and various external systems, devices, and data sources. This includes establishing connections with electronic medical record systems, medical devices, IoT sensors, and other healthcare IT systems by utilizing standardized interfaces and protocols. Various data exchange mechanisms like HL7 FHIR, DICOM, REST APIs, and message queues are employed to promote interoperability and facilitate seamless data sharing among diverse systems within the healthcare environment.

7.2.2.6 Security and privacy layer

Securing patient information in the digital twin system used in healthcare is crucial for protecting the privacy and security of sensitive data. This involves implementing strong security measures like encryption, access controls, authentication mechanisms, and audit trails. These measures are necessary to safeguard the confidentiality, integrity, and accessibility of patient information within the digital twin system in healthcare settings. The guidelines outlined in regulations like HIPAA, GDPR, and other data privacy laws, healthcare organizations can maintain patient confidentiality and adhere to legal standards. These measures are essential in preventing unauthorized access, breaches, or tampering of patient data, ultimately safeguarding the overall integrity of the healthcare system.

7.2.2.7 Infrastructure and deployment layer

The infrastructure and deployment layer provides the underlying infrastructure resources and deployment environment for hosting and running the healthcare digital twin solution. This includes cloud computing platforms, on-premises servers, container orchestration systems, and other infrastructure components required to support the scalability, availability, and performance of the digital twin system. DevOps practices, automation tools, and monitoring solutions are used to manage and maintain the infrastructure and ensure optimal system performance [14].

Healthcare digital twins signify a revolutionary change in the way healthcare services are provided, tailored, and perceived. These digital twins make use of cutting-edge technologies like artificial intelligence (AI), ML, and the IoT to facilitate personalized healthcare, surgical preparation, medical learning, scientific investigations, and pharmaceutical advancements. Healthcare digital twins are designed with a distributed and modular architecture, with different components collaborating to build, simulate, and engage with the digital twin effectively. Although there are obstacles like ensuring data privacy, ensuring interoperability, and managing scalability, the advantages of healthcare digital twins are immense. It present numerous possibilities to elevate patient outcomes, elevate the quality of care, and promote innovation in healthcare delivery.

7.2.3 Data sources and integration healthcare digital twins

Data sources and their integration are essential components in the creation and functionality of healthcare digital twins. These digital twins, which are virtual representations of actual entities, heavily rely on a wide range of data sources to effectively replicate patient physiology, disease advancement, treatment outcomes, and medical procedures. This extensive examination will focus on the multitude of data sources utilized in healthcare digital twins, the obstacles associated with integrating these data, and potential strategies to navigate and surmount these challenges [15–17].

7.2.3.1 Data sources for healthcare digital twins

Healthcare digital twins are virtual replicas of individual patients, organs, or even entire healthcare systems, constructed to simulate and predict outcomes, optimize treatments, and enhance decision-making. To build robust healthcare digital twins, an array of data sources must be tapped into. These sources span patient records, medical imaging, genomic data, real-time monitoring, and more. The comprehensive overview of these data sources:

- *EHRs:* EHRs are repositories of detailed and extensive information regarding a patient's medical background, including their past health conditions, diagnoses, prescribed medications, results from laboratory tests and imaging procedures, as well as proposed treatment strategies. When these data from EHRs are seamlessly incorporated into healthcare digital twins, they offer a valuable and extensive pool of patient-specific information that can be utilized for the purpose of creating sophisticated models and simulations in healthcare.
- *Medical imaging:* Medical imaging techniques, including X-rays, CT scans, MRI, and PET scans, offer comprehensive insights into the anatomy and physiology of patients' organs and tissues. By incorporating these imaging data into digital replicas of patient anatomy, healthcare professionals can generate precise anatomical models for the purposes of surgical preparation, disease detection, and therapy supervision.
- *Genomic data:* Genomic data, including DNA sequences, gene expression profiles, and single nucleotide polymorphisms (SNPs), provide insights into patients' genetic predispositions, hereditary diseases, and pharmacogenomics. Incorporating genomic data into healthcare digital twins allows for personalized medicine approaches based on patients' genetic profiles, optimizing treatment efficacy and minimizing adverse reactions.
- *Wearable devices and sensors:* Wearable technology, including smart watches, fitness trackers, and medical-grade sensors, plays a crucial role in collecting immediate and comprehensive data on patients' well-being. This information spans from vital signs and activity levels to sleep patterns and physiological parameters, providing a detailed insight into an individual's health. By merging the data gathered by wearable devices with digital twins, healthcare professionals can establish a system for constant monitoring of patients' health conditions. This integration allows for the early identification of any irregularities or deviations, prompting timely intervention strategies to be put in place.
- *IoT devices:* IoT devices, including connected medical devices, home monitoring systems, and ambient sensors, generate streams of data related to patients' health and environmental conditions. Integrating IoT data into digital twins provides real-time insights into patients' living environments, lifestyle factors, and social determinants of health, enhancing the holistic understanding of their health status and care needs.
- *Clinical trials and research databases:* Clinical trials databases, research repositories, and public health datasets contain valuable information on disease prevalence, treatment outcomes, epidemiological trends, and therapeutic interventions. Integrating data from

clinical trials and research databases into digital twins facilitates evidence-based decision-making, supports hypothesis testing, and drives innovation in healthcare delivery and medical research.

- *Healthcare interoperability standards:* Healthcare interoperability standards play a vital role in connecting different healthcare systems and platforms by allowing the smooth sharing of patient data. These standards include Fast Healthcare Interoperability Resources (FHIR), Digital Imaging and Communications in Medicine (DICOM), and Logical Observation Identifiers Names and Codes (LOINC). Healthcare organizations can ensure that information from various sources is integrated effectively into digital twins by adhering to these standards. This will result in more personalized and comprehensive care for patients. Ultimately, data-driven decision-making is supported and the overall quality of patient care is enhanced.

7.2.3.2 Data integration in healthcare digital twins

Data integration lies at the core of developing effective healthcare digital twins, which are virtual representations of real-world patients, organs, or healthcare systems. These digital replicas rely on the seamless aggregation, harmonization, and analysis of diverse healthcare data sources to provide personalized insights, optimize treatments, and enhance decision-making. However, the integration process is fraught [18–21] with challenges stemming from data complexity, interoperability issues, regulatory constraints, and ethical considerations:

- *Semantic interoperability:* Adopting standardized terminologies, ontologies, and vocabularies facilitates semantic interoperability across different healthcare data sources, enabling consistent representation and interpretation of data elements. Semantic interoperability standards such as Systematized Nomenclature of Medicine Clinical Terms (SNOMED CT) and Standard Nomenclature of Clinical Drugs (RxNorm) promote harmonized data exchange and integration in digital twins.
- *Application programming interfaces (APIs) and integration platforms:* APIs and integration platforms provide standardized interfaces and protocols for accessing, querying, and exchanging data between healthcare systems, devices, and applications. API-based integration enables seamless connectivity and data interoperability across heterogeneous data sources, reducing integration complexity and accelerating time-to-market for digital twin solutions.
- *Data virtualization and federation:* Data virtualization and federation techniques allow for unified access to distributed data sources

without physically consolidating data into a central repository. Virtualized data access enables real-time querying, aggregation, and analysis of data from disparate sources, providing a holistic view of patient information while minimizing data movement and duplication.

- *Event-driven architecture (EDA):* EDA facilitates real-time data integration and processing by enabling asynchronous communication and event-driven workflows. EDA leverages event streaming platforms, message queues, and event-driven microservices to decouple data producers from consumers, enabling scalable, resilient, and responsive data integration in healthcare digital twins.
- *Data governance frameworks:* Implementing data governance frameworks, developing comprehensive data management policies, and upholding effective data stewardship practices are essential to enhance the quality, purity, and adherence to regulations at every stage of the data life cycle. The establishment of a strong data governance framework is crucial in ensuring that data integration processes are in accordance with regulatory guidelines, ethical norms, and industry best practices for the ethical usage of data in healthcare digital twins.
- *ML and AI:* ML and AI techniques such as natural language processing (NLP), pattern recognition, and predictive modeling can automate data integration tasks, identify data relationships, and uncover hidden insights from complex healthcare datasets. AI-powered data integration accelerates data preprocessing, normalization, and enrichment processes, enhancing the efficiency and effectiveness of data integration in healthcare digital twins.
- *Blockchain for data sharing:* Blockchain technology offers decentralized, immutable, and transparent ledger systems for securely sharing and exchanging healthcare data among stakeholders. Blockchain-based data sharing platforms enable patient-centric control over data access, traceability of data transactions, and auditability of data sharing activities, fostering trust and transparency in data integration for healthcare digital twins.

7.2.3.3 Challenges of data integration in healthcare digital twins

The process of incorporating data into healthcare digital twins is met with a variety of obstacles that arise from the intricate nature of healthcare systems, strict regulations, difficulties in interoperability, and ethical concerns. Overcoming these hurdles is essential for maximizing the benefits of digital twins in the healthcare sector. An in-depth analysis of the primary challenges includes the following [22]:

- *Data heterogeneity:* Healthcare data is highly heterogeneous, varying in structure, format, semantics, and quality across different sources and systems. Integrating heterogeneous data sources into digital twins requires addressing data normalization, standardization, and harmonization challenges to ensure consistency and interoperability.
- *Data volume and velocity:* Healthcare data is characterized by high volume, velocity, and variety, posing challenges for data storage, processing, and analysis. Integrating large volumes of streaming data from real-time sources such as wearable devices and IoT sensors requires scalable infrastructure and efficient data processing pipelines to handle the data influx in a timely manner.
- *Data quality and completeness:* The healthcare industry faces challenges related to the accuracy and completeness of data, such as missing information, errors, and discrepancies, which could potentially impact the effectiveness of digital twin models and simulations used in healthcare. In order to mitigate these risks and ensure the trustworthiness and accuracy of data, it is imperative to implement thorough data cleaning, validation, and enhancement procedures as an integral part of the data preparation process before integrating it into digital twin frameworks.
- *Data privacy and security:* The field of healthcare data is subject to stringent regulations that are strict and specific when it comes to privacy and security. These regulations, such as the HIPAA and the GDPR, are designed to safeguard patient information by mandating the utmost confidentiality and preventing any unauthorized access or disclosure of sensitive data. When it comes to integrating data into digital twins, it becomes imperative to establish robust security protocols to fortify the protection of information. This involves implementing encryption techniques, access controls, and other measures to ensure that sensitive data remains safeguarded. By adhering to these rigorous security practices, healthcare organizations can guarantee that they are in full compliance with regulatory requirements, thus maintaining the confidentiality and security of patient data at all times.
- *Data governance and consent:* The successful management of healthcare data for digital twin applications is dependent on the establishment of strong data governance policies, frameworks for managing consent, and ethical considerations. In order to ensure that healthcare data is utilized effectively in digital twin applications, it is crucial to have comprehensive policies in place that govern how the data is collected, stored, and shared. Consent management frameworks play a key role in ensuring that individuals have control over how their healthcare data is used and shared in digital twin applications. Ethical considerations are essential in guiding the

responsible and appropriate use of healthcare data in digital twin applications, taking into account the potential consequences and implications of using this data. Overall, effective management of healthcare data for digital twin applications requires a multifaceted approach that includes robust data governance policies, consent management frameworks, and ethical considerations.

Healthcare digital twins rely heavily on data sources and integration to create virtual replicas of real-world entities in healthcare settings. These digital twins allow for simulation and interaction, enabling personalized medicine, surgical planning, medical education, and research. By combining various data sources like EHRs, medical imaging, genomic data, wearable devices, IoT sensors, and clinical research databases, healthcare digital twins enhance the quality of care provided to patients. To effectively integrate these diverse data sources, healthcare organizations must address challenges such as data heterogeneity, volume, quality, privacy, and governance. This can be achieved through the implementation of strategies like semantic interoperability, API-based integration, data virtualization, event-driven architecture, data governance, ML, and blockchain technology. These approaches ensure that the data used in digital twin applications is standardized, secure, and accessible to all relevant parties. As healthcare organizations continue to leverage data integration in digital twin applications, they gain valuable insights that can lead to improved patient outcomes and innovation in healthcare delivery and research. This not only benefits individual patients but also contributes to advancements in the healthcare industry as a whole.

7.3 EMERGING IN DIGITAL TWIN TECHNOLOGY

The emergence of digital twin technology is seen as a major advancement with potential to revolutionize various industries like manufacturing, healthcare, smart cities, and agriculture. A digital twin is a computer-generated replica of a physical entity that allows for constant monitoring, assessment, and simulation. In recent years, digital twin technology has seen the emergence of trends impacting its development. One significant trend is the integration of IoT devices and sensor data. IoT devices installed in physical assets gather real-time data on factors like temperature, pressure, vibration, and location. Organizations can gain better insight into asset performance by using collected data in digital twins [23]. This leads to predictive maintenance, operational optimization, and data-driven decision-making. IoT-enabled sensors connected to machinery are beneficial for monitoring equipment in the manufacturing sector. Sensors collect data for digital twins to help manufacturers anticipate breakdowns, plan maintenance, and streamline production. AI and ML are important for enhancing digital twin capabilities. AI algorithms analyze data from digital twins to detect trends, anomalies, and insights. ML algorithms are essential for digital twins to improve predictive accuracy in healthcare by analyzing patient data and medical images to simulate diseases and customize care plans. This technology helps expedite medical research and reduce healthcare costs.

A growing trend in digital twin technology is the use of edge computing for immediate data processing. Edge computing involves processing data close to where it is generated, such as on IoT devices or sensors. This approach reduces latency, enhances data security and privacy, and improves digital twin performance. Edge computing in smart cities helps with real-time monitoring of traffic, energy usage, and environmental factors. Data from IoT sensors in the city is processed locally to help authorities make informed decisions quickly. Digital twin technology is also used more to tackle environmental and resilience issues [24]. Digital twins allow organizations to simulate different scenarios to make better decisions. In agriculture, digital twins can optimize farming practices and reduce environmental impact. Farmers can improve efficiency and mitigate climate change effects on crop yields. Interoperability and standardization are becoming more important as digital twin technology evolves. Interoperability refers to the ability of digital twins to easily share data with different systems, platforms, and devices, regardless of the provider or technology used. Standardization involves creating common frameworks, protocols, and data models to ensure consistency and interoperability among various digital twin applications. It is crucial to promote interoperability and standardization to enhance collaboration, seamless integration, and expansion of digital twin technologies across various industries and sectors. Through the implementation of uniform guidelines and protocols, companies can fully unleash the power of digital twins to promote creativity, productivity, and environmental responsibility. The advancement of digital twin technology is quickly progressing due to trends like the merging of IoT and sensor information, implementation of AI and ML, utilization of edge computing for instant processing, importance placed on sustainability and resilience, and emphasis on interoperability and standardization. By embracing and utilizing digital twins, organizations will open up new possibilities for creativity, improvement, and change in different sectors.

7.3.1 IoT integration and real-time data streaming

Digital twin technology is important in Industry 4.0. It changes how industries work with systems. A digital twin is a virtual copy of a physical object or system that simulates the real thing. This technology is more effective when combined with IoT and real-time data streaming, offering opportunities for optimization and better decision-making in various industries. The IoT connects physical and digital realms to enable communication between devices, sensors, and systems. Companies can access real-time data on resources, processes, and surroundings by integrating IoT devices with digital twins. Sensors powered by IoT can monitor various factors such as temperature, pressure, and vibration, providing detailed information on asset performance. In manufacturing, IoT sensors in machinery collect data for digital twin simulations. This integration helps with predictive maintenance by detecting anomalies in real time. Addressing issues early can improve asset reliability and productivity [25]. Real-time data streaming feeds live data into digital twin models to keep simulations accurate. Organizations can use advanced analytics and ML to optimize data and improve the accuracy of their digital twins. An example is the use of digital twins in smart cities, where IoT sensors are integrated into urban infrastructure for detailed city modeling. Real-time data streaming from sensors allows accurate simulations of traffic flow, air quality, energy consumption, and other important factors. This helps decision-makers allocate resources effectively, enhance public services, and prevent disruptions beforehand [26]. Digital twins, IoT integration, and real-time data streaming improve efficiency and drive innovation in organizations. Digital twins offer a complete view of assets and processes, enabling predictive analytics for informed decision-making. Furthermore, this trio of technologies encourages collaboration and innovation among engineers, data scientists, and domain experts. They work together in a digital environment to improve models, processes, and drive innovation [27].

Using digital twins with IoT and real-time data has great potential, but there are challenges. Security and privacy are key concerns, leading to the need for strong cybersecurity measures to protect sensitive information. Furthermore, interoperability issues can complicate connecting IoT devices, which highlight the need for uniform protocols to aid integration. Companies must also manage and govern data to maintain the reliability and integrity of data used in digital twin models. Data silos and fragmentation hinder information flow, impacting predictive analytics and decision-making. Integrating digital twins, IoT, and real-time data boosts productivity. Organizations can leverage these technologies for insights, efficiency, and growth in a connected data-driven world. In order to fully benefit from this collaboration, it is important to address the obstacles and factors that come with implementing these technologies.

7.3.2 Artificial intelligence and machine learning in digital twins

Digital twins are virtual replicas of physical objects or systems. They are important in various sectors due to IoT technology and advanced simulation techniques. With AI and ML, digital twins transform how we design, monitor, and optimize complex systems. A digital twin is a virtual copy of a physical entity or operation that is constantly updated with real-time data. It enables detailed analysis and simulations without affecting the actual system. AI and ML are essential in boosting the abilities of digital twins. AI and ML are used in predicting maintenance issues beforehand. The algorithms use historical and real-time data to predict equipment failures and allow for proactive maintenance. Sensors in machinery gather data for analysis and prediction to prevent expensive downtime and ensure consistent equipment performance. ML algorithms are utilized to examine the gathered data in order to recognize patterns that may suggest potential issues that could arise in the future, prompting quick and effective interventions when necessary. Additionally, the use of AI-powered anomaly detection further improves the precision of digital twins by highlighting any discrepancies or anomalies that deviate from the anticipated behavior. AI algorithms play a crucial role in identifying anomalies in energy usage patterns within a structure or detecting abnormalities in the functionality of a wind turbine. They have the ability to swiftly spot issues that need further examination, enabling prompt corrective measures to be taken. In addition, AI and ML play a significant role in enhancing digital twins through optimization. These advanced technologies can sift through massive amounts of data to pinpoint inefficiencies and suggest optimal settings to boost overall performance. For example, in energy systems, ML algorithms can enhance the efficiency of power grids by constantly adjusting variables like generation, transmission, and distribution based on current demand and environmental conditions. Moreover, the use of AI in simulation and scenario modeling has revolutionized the capabilities of digital twins. These technological advancements allow digital twins to accurately simulate a wide range of potential scenarios, providing stakeholders with valuable insights into the potential outcomes of different decisions. This functionality is particularly beneficial for urban planners, as it enables them to assess the potential impact of infrastructure changes and policy implementations on crucial aspects such as traffic flow, air quality, and energy consumption. By offering a detailed and comprehensive analysis of various what-if scenarios, digital twins empower stakeholders to make well-informed decisions that support sustainable development goals [28].

AI-driven digital replicas have the ability to completely transform the landscape of personalized healthcare and patient treatment in the healthcare industry. These cutting-edge twins harness patient information and physiological models to generate lifelike representations of each individual's health experiences, enabling accurate forecasts of disease advancement and the customization of treatment plans. They allow healthcare professionals to experiment with treatment protocols for individual patients virtually. AI and ML technology improve digital twins' capabilities. However, integrating these technologies poses challenges such as data privacy and security issues. Strong cybersecurity measures and adherence to privacy laws are necessary for analyzing sensitive data. There is a vital need to prioritize data security and protect personal privacy when using digital twin technology. Biases in AI algorithms can perpetuate inequalities and lead to inaccurate results if not addressed. The complexity of AI and ML models in digital twins poses obstacles in terms of transparency and interpretability. In order for all individuals participating in the process to trust the information provided [29], it is crucial for them to fully understand how these models produce their results. Enhancing the transparency of AI algorithms and promoting openness in how decisions are made is key in fostering trust and accountability.

7.3.2.1 The role of AI and ML

AI and ML play crucial roles in enhancing the capabilities and effectiveness of digital twins in several ways [30–32]:

- *Predictive maintenance:* Predictive maintenance is one of the key areas where AI and ML are widely utilized in digital twins. These technologies leverage historical and current data collected from sensors attached to various machinery and equipment to detect patterns that may signal upcoming malfunctions. By employing predictive analytics, organizations can adopt a proactive approach to maintenance, ultimately leading to decreased downtime, cost savings, and improved overall operational effectiveness.
- *Anomaly detection:* AI-powered anomaly detection enhances the accuracy of digital twins by flagging deviations from expected behavior. Whether its detecting irregularities in energy consumption patterns of a building or identifying anomalies in the performance of a manufacturing process, AI algorithms can quickly identify issues for further investigation, facilitating timely corrective actions.
- *Optimization:* AI and ML algorithms analyze vast datasets to identify inefficiencies and recommend optimal configurations for improved performance. Whether it's optimizing energy consumption in buildings, streamlining production processes in manufacturing plants, or maximizing the efficiency of supply chain logistics, AI-driven optimization enhances the functionality and efficiency of digital twins.
- *Simulation and scenario modeling:* AI-driven simulation and scenario modeling enable digital twins to simulate various what-if scenarios, helping stakeholders anticipate the consequences of different decisions. AI-powered simulations offer valuable insights for making informed decisions, whether it be urban planners evaluating the effects of changes in infrastructure or healthcare professionals refining treatment protocols.

The integration of AI and ML technologies within digital twins presents a vast range of possibilities across various industries. These opportunities span predictive maintenance, optimization, personalized healthcare, and urban planning, among others. In order to fully harness the potential of AI-powered digital twins, challenges like data privacy, security, bias, and transparency in models must be addressed. By effectively navigating through these obstacles, companies can tap into the transformative power of AI and ML to drive innovation and improve productivity in the era of digital twins.

7.3.3 Blockchain for data security and privacy

Blockchain technology is becoming increasingly popular for its decentralized nature and its ability to provide a secure and unchangeable record of transactions. This technology is now being carefully scrutinized for its potential to enhance data security and privacy in digital twin applications. By utilizing blockchain, organizations can address challenges related to data reliability, ensuring the authenticity of information and managing access control more effectively. This, in turn, helps build trust and confidence among all stakeholders involved, while also ensuring compliance with regulatory requirements. The implementation of blockchain technology offers the opportunity to improve the security protocols and secrecy of data within digital twins, while also allowing for a more comprehensive exploration of its wide-ranging uses, benefits, and challenges. Digital twins serve as virtual replicas of physical entities or processes, relying on real-time data from sensors, IoT devices, and other sources to enable ongoing monitoring, analysis, and informed decision-making. Nevertheless, there exist various obstacles linked to safeguarding and maintaining the confidentiality of this information. One of the obstacles includes the vulnerability of centralized storage systems to potential cyber threats, unauthorized access, and data breaches. These weaknesses jeopardize the security and secrecy of sensitive data. Additionally, there are additional worries regarding matters like data ownership, verification, and traceability, which further complicate these challenges.

7.3.3.1 Role of blockchain in enhancing data security and privacy

Blockchain technology, with its decentralized and distributed ledger system, has various strengths that make it well-suited for addressing concerns regarding data security and privacy in the realm of digital twins.

- *Immutable data storage:* Blockchain technology, known for its decentralized and distributed ledger system, possesses multiple capabilities that render it particularly effective in tackling issues related to data security and privacy within the context of digital twins.

- *Decentralization and distribution:* Distributing data across a decentralized network of nodes, blockchain technology effectively eliminates the vulnerability of single points of failure, making it more difficult for data to be manipulated or accessed without authorization. Through consensus mechanisms, all participants in the network must agree on the validity of transactions, thereby improving data security and creating a resilient defense mechanism against potential cyberattacks.
- *Enhanced authentication and access control:* Blockchain technology allows for the establishment of strong authentication protocols and precise access control measures through the use of smart contracts. These contracts, which are automatically executed without the need for human intervention, are designed to uphold preestablished regulations and restrictions, thereby guaranteeing that only approved individuals are able to view or alter particular information within the virtual replication environment.
- *Data ownership and traceability:* Blockchain technology enables clear and traceable ownership of data through a secure and verifiable system of recording data transactions and origins. Every piece of data is linked to a distinct cryptographic identifier that allows stakeholders to track its history and ownership from inception to completion. This functionality not only promotes responsibility and openness but also resolves issues surrounding data control and adherence to regulations.

The potential of blockchain technology in improving data security and privacy in digital twins is vast and widely recognized across different industries. With the use of its decentralized and unalterable ledger, businesses have the ability to tackle issues surrounding the integrity, verification, and control of data, ultimately building confidence among those involved and meeting regulatory standards effectively. Despite the challenges and complexities associated with blockchain adoption, its potential benefits for digital twin applications justify further exploration and investment in this transformative technology. As blockchain continues to evolve and mature, its integration with digital twins is poised to revolutionize data management, collaboration, and innovation in the digital era.

7.4 CHALLENGES AND SCOPE IN DIGITAL TWINS

Digital twins are completely transforming a wide range of industries by generating virtual versions of physical systems, processes, or products. This groundbreaking technology has the potential to revolutionize the way businesses operate and interact with their surroundings. The adoption and impact of digital twins differ across various sectors, presenting a mix of obstacles and potential benefits. One of the key challenges companies face when implementing digital twins is the intricate task of merging data from different sources. In order to create accurate simulations of real-world conditions, digital twins depend heavily on data collected from a variety of sensors, IoT devices, and other sources. However, aligning different sources of data and guaranteeing their accuracy and uniformity can be a complex task that requires careful attention to detail. This process involves implementing strong data management protocols and utilizing advanced analytical tools to derive valuable conclusions from a range of data sources. An additional obstacle lies in ensuring the confidentiality and protection of digital twin data, as these virtual duplicates frequently include confidential details related to physical resources, operations, and individuals. It is essential to shield this information from cyber threats and unauthorized entry in order to uphold credibility and prevent potential security breaches. It is crucial to implement strong encryption, strict access controls, and adherence to data protection laws in order to effectively address security vulnerabilities related to digital twins. One major challenge that needs to be overcome in order to fully harness the capabilities of digital twins is interoperability. This obstacle arises from the fact that many companies utilize various software platforms, protocols, and standards, which hinders the smooth exchange of data between different systems. To achieve interoperability, there is a need for collaboration across industries to establish open standards that will facilitate seamless integration and communication within digital twin ecosystems [33].

Although there are obstacles to overcome, digital twins present a wide range of possibilities for promoting innovation and enhancing business results. One significant potential lies in the realm of predictive maintenance, in which digital twins analyze up-to-date data to predict potential equipment malfunctions and enhance maintenance planning. This proactive approach allows organizations to foresee and address problems before they happen, resulting in decreased downtime, lower expenses, and improved asset efficiency. Additionally, digital twins shine in the field of optimization and simulation. By developing digital models of manufacturing processes or distribution networks, companies have the ability to replicate various situations and pinpoint areas for improvement. This simulation allows for well-informed decision-making, which ultimately aids in maximizing productivity, resource efficiency, and overall operational success. In addition, digital twins play a crucial role in fostering product development and customization by offering valuable insights into consumer behavior and preferences. Through the analysis of data obtained from digital twins utilized in real-world settings, businesses can obtain valuable information about how customers engage with their products. This knowledge can be instrumental in informing enhancements to product design, as well as in creating personalized marketing campaigns and tailored customer experiences.

This process helps companies to adapt their strategies and offerings to better align with customer needs and preferences, ultimately enhancing customer satisfaction and loyalty. In addition, digital twins provide the capability for assets, operations, and infrastructure to be monitored and controlled remotely. This feature is especially beneficial in sectors such as energy, utilities, and transportation, where it is crucial to have remote access to important systems. Through the remote monitoring and control enabled by digital twins, companies can enhance safety measures, streamline operations, and effectively adapt to shifting circumstances. Furthermore, digital twins serve as a robust tool for fostering innovation and enhancing efficiency in diverse industries. Despite facing obstacles like data integration, security issues, and the need for interoperability, there are significant benefits to be gained from utilizing digital twins in various industries. These benefits include the ability to predict maintenance needs, optimize processes, foster product innovation, and enable remote monitoring. By overcoming the challenges associated with digital twins and capitalizing on the opportunities they offer, businesses can enhance their efficiency, productivity, and overall competitiveness in the modern digital landscape [34].

7.4.1 Regulatory compliance and ethical considerations

It is crucial to prioritize regulatory compliance and ethical considerations when implementing digital twins to ensure responsible and ethical deployment that adheres to laws and regulations. This chapter will delve into the important aspects of regulatory compliance and ethical considerations in relation to digital twins. To begin with, regulatory compliance entails adhering to laws and regulations governing the protection, security, and use of data. Different areas around the world have their own set of rules and regulations when it comes to data protection, such as the GDPR in the European Union and the California Consumer Privacy Act (CCPA) in the United States. These regulations place strict requirements on the collection, handling, and storage of personal information. Digital twins often involve the collection and analysis of vast amounts of data, which could potentially include personal information of individuals. It is imperative for companies to ensure compliance with relevant data protection laws to protect the privacy of individuals and avoid legal liabilities. It is also crucial to emphasize that regulatory compliance extends to industry-specific guidelines governing the use of digital twins in sectors such as healthcare, manufacturing, and transportation. In the healthcare sector, digital twins have the potential to replicate patient physiology and model disease progression. It is essential for these applications to adhere to regulations like the HIPAA in the United States, which mandates the protection of patient health information.

Ethical considerations play a crucial role in the development and deployment of digital twins. An essential ethical concern is the potential presence of bias in the data used to train and operate digital twins. Biases, whether intentional or unintentional, have the power to produce unjust results and exacerbate existing inequalities. It is crucial for organizations to be diligent in identifying and mitigating biases in data sources and algorithms when utilizing digital twins to ensure fair and impartial outcomes. The fundamental ethical principles of transparency and accountability are essential in the integration of digital twins. Therefore, organizations must be forthcoming about the data collection process, its utilization, and the algorithms employed for analysis. Furthermore, it is imperative for organizations to implement mechanisms to ensure accountability and provide means for redress in cases where digital twins result in adverse outcomes or harm to individuals and communities. Additionally, ethical dilemmas arise regarding the implications of digital twins on employment and labor practices. While digital twins have the potential to boost efficiency and productivity, they may also lead to job displacement or alterations in work dynamics. Organizations need to address the ethical ramifications of these changes and adopt proactive measures to lessen negative impacts, such as initiatives for reskilling and upskilling affected employees. Moreover, ethical considerations extend to the environmental impacts of it. Developing and maintaining digital twins requires a lot of computing resources and energy, which can harm the environment. Companies need to reduce the carbon footprint of digital twin technologies through energy-efficient computing methods, sustainable practices, and responsible resource management [35]. To ethically deploy digital twins, regulatory compliance and ethical considerations are essential. Ensuring digital twins comply with laws and regulations, address biases, promote transparency and accountability, and minimize negative effects on employment and the environment. These steps help organizations maximize the benefits of digital twins while maintaining ethical standards.

7.4.2 Interoperability and data standardization

Digital twin technology relies on interoperability and data standardization to ensure smooth integration and communication across various systems and platforms. The importance of interoperability and data standardization in digital twins is explored. Interoperability allows different systems, devices, or applications to exchange data and work together seamlessly. Interoperability in digital twins allows virtual replicas to interact with different components, sensors, and software systems. It is vital for maximizing the potential of digital twins by enabling data sharing and collaboration across industries. The primary challenge is the fragmentation of technologies and standards. Many organizations use systems that may not be compatible with digital twin platforms. Different industries have unique requirements for digital twin implementations. Industry stakeholders are developing open standards for digital twins to improve interoperability.

The standards outline data formats, interfaces, and protocols for interoperability. Using open standards helps organizations achieve compatibility and smooth data exchange for digital twins, fostering collaboration and innovation in various industries.

Data standardization is important for interoperability in digital twin environments. It involves defining consistent formats for data organization. Standardized formats make data easily accessible and usable across systems. This is crucial in digital twins for integrating and analyzing diverse data sources. Standardizing data formats improves data quality and consistency, reducing errors from different data sources. Common data standards help streamline integration processes, speed up decision-making, and enhance accuracy in digital twin simulations. Data standardization allows for scalability and extensibility in digital twin implementations. With standardized data formats, organizations can easily add new sensors or devices to digital twin environments without major modifications or custom integrations. Organizations can adjust digital twin solutions to match business needs and technological progress. Interoperability and data standardization are important for digital twin technology, promoting collaboration and efficiency. Using open standards and common data formats can help maximize the benefits of digital twins for better operations, decision-making, and growth [36].

7.4.3 Scalability and infrastructure requirements

It is important for digital twins to be scalable and have strong infrastructure for successful implementation. These virtual replicas should be able to handle more data, support complex simulations, and offer real-time insights on a large scale. Scalability refers to the ability of a digital twin system to handle increasing workloads, data volumes, and user needs while maintaining efficiency and reliability. It is important for managing data and computations as digital twins are used more in complex environments. Achieving scalability with digital twins is primarily hindered by the copious amounts of data generated from diverse sources like sensors and IoT devices. This data plays a critical role in developing accurate simulations and models of real-world systems or processes. As the quantity of interconnected devices and sensors expands, so too does the volume of data produced, highlighting the need for adaptable storage and analysis techniques to effectively handle the surge of information.

Cloud computing offers versatile and adjustable infrastructure solutions for digital twins by providing immediate access to diverse computing resources, storage choices, and networking capabilities. This advanced technology enables users to seamlessly expand or reduce capacity according to their requirements, guaranteeing the utmost performance and effectiveness for digital twin applications. It provides flexibility for organizations to adjust resources based on workload needs. This allows for the deployment of digital twins that can adapt to changing data volumes and computational needs. Edge computing is essential for scaling digital twins in situations where real-time data processing is important. Edge computing moves computation and data storage closer to where data is created, which improves speed and efficiency. Using edge computing, organizations can use digital twins in different locations while maintaining high performance. Digital twins can also handle complex simulations on large systems or networks. Digital twins are becoming more complex, requiring increased computational power for efficient simulations. Scalable computing resources like parallel processing are crucial for handling these complex simulations. Scalability in digital twins includes supporting more users and various uses. Digital twins need to serve engineers, operators, analysts, and decision-makers in different industries. Scalable interfaces, visualization tools, and collaboration features are necessary for various user needs. Scalability and infrastructure are crucial for digital twin design and deployment. Using cloud, edge, and scalable resources helps build flexible digital twin solutions for operational needs [37].

7.4.4 Cost–benefit analysis

Cost–benefit analysis is an essential tool used to assess the economic viability and potential returns of investing in digital twins. It involves calculating the costs and benefits involved in implementing this technology to help organizations make well-informed decisions regarding their investments. By evaluating the costs and benefits associated with deploying digital twins, organizations can determine the feasibility of investing in this technology and strategize on ways to optimize its value [38].

7.4.4.1 Costs

Costs associated with digital twins include initial investments in hardware, software, and infrastructure; data acquisition and integration expenses; ongoing maintenance and support; and training programs. Additionally, organizations may incur costs related to scalability, customization, and compliance with regulatory requirements:

- *Initial investment:* The deployment of digital twins entails upfront costs associated with acquiring hardware, software, and infrastructure components. This includes purchasing sensors, IoT devices, computing resources, and digital twin platforms or software solutions. Additionally, there may be costs related to system integration, customization, and implementation consulting services.

- *Data acquisition and integration:* Collecting and integrating data from various sources, such as sensors, enterprise systems, and third-party applications, incurs costs. Organizations may need to invest in data acquisition technologies, data cleansing, and integration tools to ensure that data is accurate, consistent, and accessible for digital twin simulations and analyses.
- *Infrastructure and computing resources:* Digital twins require scalable infrastructure and computing resources to support real-time data processing, complex simulations, and analytics. Organizations may incur costs associated with deploying cloud computing resources, edge computing infrastructure, or high-performance computing clusters to meet the computational requirements of digital twin applications.
- *Training and education:* Training employees and stakeholders on how to use digital twin technology effectively is essential for maximizing its value. Organizations may need to invest in training programs, workshops, or certification courses to build the necessary skills and expertise to operate and leverage digital twins successfully.
- *Maintenance and support:* Ongoing maintenance and support are necessary to ensure the reliability, performance, and security of digital twin environments. This includes software updates, security patches, troubleshooting, and technical support services. Organizations may incur recurring costs associated with maintaining and supporting digital twin systems over their life cycle.

7.4.4.2 Benefits

Digital twins offer a wide range of advantages such as enhancing operational efficiency by identifying areas for improvement, predicting maintenance needs to prevent breakdowns, minimizing risks by simulating potential scenarios, speeding up innovation and product development processes, and enabling informed decision-making based on data analysis. Moreover, they empower organizations to optimize the allocation of resources, enhance customer satisfaction through personalized experiences, and gain a competitive edge by utilizing real-time data and predictive analytics for strategic planning:

- *Operational efficiency:* Digital twins offer a transformative solution for organizations looking to enhance their operations and maximize efficiency across different areas. These virtual models provide valuable real-time data on how assets are performing, the dynamics of processes, and how resources are being utilized. This allows organizations to pinpoint areas of inefficiency, identify bottlenecks, and uncover potential opportunities for improvement. By leveraging this information, organizations can achieve cost savings and increase productivity.

- *Predictive maintenance:* Digital twins offer significant advantages through their capacity to support predictive maintenance techniques. These virtual replicas can forecast potential equipment breakdowns, detect necessary maintenance tasks, and enhance maintenance planning by examining data gathered from sensors and IoT devices in real time. Embracing this proactive maintenance strategy can effectively lower downtime, prolong the lifespan of assets, and decrease overall maintenance expenses.
- *Risk mitigation:* Digital twins are utilized by organizations to gain a comprehensive insight into the risk factors and potential disruptions that may arise in their operations. Through the simulation of various scenarios and the evaluation of how they could affect performance, safety, and compliance, digital twins allow organizations to pinpoint and address risks in a more efficient manner. Employing a proactive risk management strategy, digital twins have the ability to avert expensive accidents, penalties from regulations, and harm to their reputation.
- *Innovation and product development:* Digital twins play a crucial role in driving innovation and improving product development processes. By allowing for quick prototyping, simulation, and testing of novel ideas and designs, digital twins enable organizations to streamline their product development life cycle. Companies can leverage digital twins to refine product concepts, validate design choices, and better predict customer preferences. This results in faster time-to-market, cost savings in the development phase, and a boost in product quality and competitiveness for the organization.
- *Data-driven decision-making:* Digital twins have revolutionized the way organizations make crucial choices by harnessing real-time insights and predictive analytics. With access to data generated through digital twin simulations, organizations can streamline operations, allocate resources efficiently, and identify key areas for investment. These data-driven decisions ultimately enhance the accuracy, flexibility, and speed of decision-making processes, translating into more favorable business results.

7.4.4.3 Cost–benefit analysis framework

Organizations can perform a thorough cost–benefit analysis of digital twins by adhering to a systematic framework that includes the following essential steps [39]:

- *Identify costs and benefits:* Enumerate all the costs associated with the development and maintenance of digital duplicates, along with the potential benefits they offer in terms of improving operational efficiency, mitigating risks, promoting innovation, and streamlining decision-making processes.

- *Quantify costs and benefits:* Determine the financial impact of costs and benefits by attaching specific monetary values to each one within a designated time frame. This process may require estimating expenses through various means such as procurement quotes, vendor proposals, or standard industry benchmarks. Additionally, quantify the benefits by utilizing metrics that evaluate elements like cost reduction, revenue increase, or mitigation of risks.
- *Calculate net present value (NPV):* In order to assess whether investing in digital twins is financially viable, it is crucial to calculate the NPV of both the costs and benefits involved. NPV factors in the idea of the time value of money by adjusting future cash flows to their present value using a discount rate. This analysis allows decision-makers to assess the profitability of the investment over a period of time and make well-informed choices about moving forward with its implementation.
- *Perform sensitivity analysis:* Performing sensitivity analysis allows organizations to assess how variations in uncertain variables, such as fluctuations in technology expenses, market dynamics, or operational efficiency, can influence the outcomes of a cost–benefit analysis. This exercise enables businesses to gauge the resilience of their investment choices across a range of potential scenarios.
- *Make informed decisions:* Employ the insights gained from the cost–benefit analysis to make informed decisions regarding the possible investment in digital twins, effectively prioritize investments, and identify the most beneficial strategies to optimize the return on investment from digital twin deployments.

The cost–benefit analysis is an essential method for assessing the economic viability and potential return on investment of adopting digital twin technology. It allows organizations to carefully evaluate the costs and advantages of implementing digital twins, enabling them to make well-informed financial decisions, allocate resources efficiently, and fully capitalize on the benefits of this innovative technology.

7.5 FUTURE DIRECTIONS AND TRENDS IN DIGITAL TWINS

The future of digital twins holds immense potential to revolutionize industries and foster innovation in a wide range of fields. There are several key areas of focus and potential advancements that are reshaping the landscape of digital twins [40–43].

7.5.1 AI and machine learning integration

The fusion of AI and ML with digital twins is poised to revolutionize decision-making by enabling a higher degree of intelligence and autonomy. Through the utilization of AI algorithms, the vast troves of data produced by digital twins can be meticulously analyzed to unveil intricate patterns, fine-tune processes, and forecast future occurrences with enhanced precision. This integration is set to elevate the functionalities of digital twins, allowing for the provision of on-the-spot insights, flexible control mechanisms, and anticipatory guidance, laying the groundwork for the emergence of autonomous systems and self-adjusting procedures.

7.5.2 Digital twin ecosystems and interconnected systems

The advancement of digital twins is moving toward the creation of interconnected ecosystems where numerous digital twins can communicate and work together to accurately simulate intricate systems and networks. These digital twin ecosystems will enable the seamless blending and cooperation between various fields, including smart cities, industrial supply chains, and healthcare networks. By illustrating the relationships and connections between different components, companies can obtain a more comprehensive understanding of the dynamics within a system, better manage resource distribution, and enhance coordination among interconnected systems.

7.5.3 Edge computing and real-time processing

Edge computing is set to have a significant impact on the development of digital twins in the coming years. Through the utilization of edge computing, real-time data processing, analysis, and decision-making can take place at the network's edge. By positioning digital twins closer to where data is generated, companies can decrease latency, lower bandwidth needs, and improve responsiveness in environments that are subject to constant changes. This advancement allows for the implementation of applications like real-time monitoring, predictive maintenance, and autonomous control to run with improved efficiency and effectiveness, even in settings with limited resources or bandwidth.

7.5.4 Digital twins for sustainability and resilience

The use of digital twins is expected to grow rapidly as they are deployed to tackle sustainability issues and improve resilience in the midst of environmental threats and disturbances. Companies have the opportunity to employ digital twins to model and predict the effects of climate change analyze and improve the use of resources, and plan and build environmentally friendly infrastructure and urban settings. Moreover, digital twins offer the potential for organizations to create robust strategies for withstanding the impacts of natural calamities, disruptions in the supply chain, and unexpected incidents by forecasting various scenarios and assessing response plans ahead of time.

7.5.5 Human-digital twin interaction

The development of digital twins in the future will entail a higher level of cooperation between individuals and virtual representations of actual systems or procedures. Enhanced visualization methods, augmented reality (AR), and VR technologies will provide users with the ability to engage with digital twins in an instinctive manner, view intricate data in immersive settings, and obtain a more profound understanding of system functions. This interaction between humans and digital twins gives users the capability to analyze hypothetical situations, carry out virtual experiments, and make educated choices based on immediate feedback, resulting in increased productivity and effectiveness in decision-making.

7.5.6 Blockchain for trust and data integrity

Blockchain technology has the potential to revolutionize trust, transparency, and data integrity within digital twin ecosystems. Through the use of blockchain-based distributed ledgers, companies have the ability to securely document and time-stamp various transactions, data exchanges, and interactions among digital twins. This helps to establish the origin and history of data, ensuring its permanence and providing a reliable audit trail. As a result, stakeholders can place greater trust in the information being shared within decentralized digital twin networks.

The future prospects of digital twins are shaped by the amalgamation of AI and ML, the advancement of interconnected ecosystems, the embrace of edge computing and real-time processing, the emphasis on sustainability and resilience, the transformation in human-digital twin interface, and the implementation of blockchain to ensure trust and data integrity. These upcoming developments have the capability to completely transform various industries, streamline operations, and catalyze innovation in this digital age.

7.6 CONCLUSIONS

Digital twins are considered a revolutionary technology that has the ability to bring about significant changes in various sectors. The research findings show that digital twins can bring about numerous advantages, including enhancing operational efficiency, enabling predictive maintenance, and facilitating better decision-making by providing real-time data and analysis.

These digital replicas allow companies to streamline their operations, minimize downtime, and manage risks effectively by replicating intricate systems and situations. Nevertheless, there are various obstacles to overcome in the realm of digital twins, such as the complexities associated with integrating data, ensuring security measures are in place, and establishing interoperability standards. In addition, the evolution of digital twins requires the integration of AI and ML, the creation of interconnected ecosystems, and the utilization of edge computing for instantaneous data processing. It is expected that digital twins will play a pivotal role in addressing sustainability issues and strengthening resilience against environmental threats. Furthermore, there are anticipated developments in human-digital twin interactions and the utilization of blockchain technology to ensure the integrity of data. Digital twins have the ability to bring about significant changes in various industries by allowing for more intelligent, interconnected, and effective operations. Companies that adopt digital twin technology have the opportunity to outperform their competitors by utilizing up-to-date information, improving the distribution of resources, and strengthening their decision-making skills in a constantly changing and challenging business landscape.

Digital twins in the healthcare sector provide numerous possibilities for customizing patient care, monitoring patients from afar, and utilizing predictive analytics to improve treatment outcomes. Additionally, these digital replicas can be leveraged by healthcare providers to enhance operational efficiency, streamline processes, and facilitate predictive maintenance in various medical facilities. Policy makers, on the other hand, may encounter difficulties concerning data privacy, security, and adherence to regulations when dealing with digital twins. However, they can also benefit from innovative solutions and economic growth by implementing supportive policies and standards that foster the development and utilization of digital twin technology. Future studies need to concentrate on further developing AI algorithms to improve their predictive abilities. Additionally, efforts should be made to enhance interoperability standards for better integration and to explore the potential applications of AI in fields like sustainability and resilience. Professionals in the field should give importance to data governance, security measures, and user-centric design to fully leverage the benefits of digital twin technology. It is crucial for collaboration between educational institutions, businesses, and policymakers to navigate ethical, legal, and regulatory hurdles, and to fully unleash the innovative and societal potential of digital twin technology.

REFERENCES

1. Barricelli, B. R., Casiraghi, E., & Fogli, D. (2019). A survey on digital twin: Definitions, characteristics, applications, and design implications. *IEEE Access*, 7, 167653–167671.

2. Corral-Acero, J., Margara, F., Marciniak, M., Rodero, C., Loncaric, F., Feng, Y., ... & Lamata, P. (2020). The 'digital twin' to enable the vision of precision cardiology. *European Heart Journal*, 41(48), 4556–4564.
3. Tao, F., Zhang, M., Liu, Y., & Nee, A. Y. (2018). Digital twin driven prognostics and health management for complex equipment. *CIRP Annals*, 67(1), 169–172.
4. Grieves, M., & Vickers, J. (2017). *Digital twin: Mitigating unpredictable, undesirable emergent behavior in complex systems*. In J. Kahlen, S. Flumerfelt, & A. Alves (Eds.), *Transdisciplinary perspectives on complex systems: New findings and approaches* (pp. 85–113). Springer. https://doi.org/10.1007/978-3-319-38756-7_4
5. Psaty, B. M., Dekkers, O. M., & Cooper, R. S. (2018). Comparison of 2 treatment models: Precision medicine and preventive medicine. *Jama*, 320(8), 751–752.
6. Li, L., Lei, B., & Mao, C. (2022). Digital twin in smart manufacturing. *Journal of Industrial Information Integration*, 26, 100289.
7. Peirlinck, M., Costabal, F. S., Yao, J., Guccione, J. M., Tripathy, S., Wang, Y., ... & Kuhl, E. (2021). Precision medicine in human heart modeling: Perspectives, challenges, and opportunities. *Biomechanics and Modeling in Mechanobiology*, 20, 803–831.
8. Madabhushi, A., & Lee, G. (2016). Image analysis and machine learning in digital pathology: Challenges and opportunities. *Medical Image Analysis*, 33, 170–175.
9. An, J., Chua, C. K., & Mironov, V. (2021). Application of machine learning in 3D bioprinting: Focus on development of big data and digital twin. *International Journal of Bioprinting*, 7(1), 342.
10. Tao, F., Zhang, H., Liu, A., & Nee, A. Y. (2018). Digital twin in industry: State-of-the-art. *IEEE Transactions on Industrial Informatics*, 15(4), 2405–2415.
11. Qi, Q., & Tao, F. (2018). Digital twin and big data towards smart manufacturing and industry 4.0: 360 degree comparison. *IEEE Access*, 6, 3585–3593.
12. Bagaria, N., Laamarti, F., Badawi, H. F., Albraikan, A., Martinez Velazquez, R. A., & El Saddik, A. (2020). Health 4.0: Digital twins for health and well-being. In A. El Saddik, M. Hossain, & B. Kantarci (Eds.), *Connected health in smart cities* (pp. 143–152). Springer.
13. Schroeder, G. N., Steinmetz, C., Pereira, C. E., & Espindola, D. B. (2016). Digital twin data modeling with automationml and a communication methodology for data exchange. *IFAC-PapersOnLine*, 49(30), 12–17.
14. Sermesant, M., Delingette, H., Cochet, H., Jaïs, P., & Ayache, N. (2021). Applications of artificial intelligence in cardiovascular imaging. *Nature Reviews Cardiology*, 18(8), 600–609.
15. Eleftheriou, O. T., & Anagnostopoulos, C. N. (2022). Digital twins: A brief overview of applications, challenges and enabling technologies in the last decade. *Digital Twin*, 2, 2.
16. He, X., Qiu, Y., Lai, X., Li, Z., Shu, L., Sun, W., & Song, X. (2025). Towards a shape-performance integrated digital twin for lumbar spine analysis. *Digital Twin*, 1, 8.

17. Aubert, K., Germaneau, A., Rochette, M., Ye, W., Severyns, M., Billot, M., ... & Vendeuvre, T. (2021). Development of digital twins to optimize trauma surgery and postoperative management. A case study focusing on tibial plateau fracture. *Frontiers in Bioengineering and Biotechnology*, 9, 722275.
18. Chakshu, N. K., Sazonov, I., & Nithiarasu, P. (2021). Towards enabling a cardiovascular digital twin for human systemic circulation using inverse analysis. *Biomechanics and Modeling in Mechanobiology*, 20(2), 449–465.
19. Jung, A., Gsell, M. A., Augustin, C. M., & Plank, G. (2022). An integrated workflow for building digital twins of cardiac electromechanics—A multi-fidelity approach for personalising active mechanics. *Mathematics*, 10(5), 823.
20. Liu, Y., Zhang, L., Yang, Y., Zhou, L., Ren, L., Wang, F., ... & Deen, M. J. (2019). A novel cloud-based framework for the elderly healthcare services using digital twin. *IEEE Access*, 7, 49088–49101.
21. Li, X., Lee, E. J., Lilja, S., Loscalzo, J., Schäfer, S., Smelik, M., ... & Benson, M. (2022). A dynamic single cell-based framework for digital twins to prioritize disease genes and drug targets. *Genome Medicine*, 14(1), 48.
22. Popa, E. O., van Hilten, M., Oosterkamp, E., & Bogaardt, M. J. (2021). The use of digital twins in healthcare: Socio-ethical benefits and socio-ethical risks. *Life Sciences, Society and Policy*, 17, 1–25.
23. Hernigou, P., Safar, A., Hernigou, J., & Ferre, B. (2022). Subtalar axis determined by combining digital twins and artificial intelligence: Influence of the orientation of this axis for hindfoot compensation of varus and valgus knees. *International Orthopaedics*, 46(5), 999–1007.
24. Davies, J., Martinec, M., Delmar, P., Coudert, M., Bordogna, W., Golding, S., ... & Crane, G. (2018). Comparative effectiveness from a single-arm trial and real-world data: Alectinib versus ceritinib. *Journal of Comparative Effectiveness Research*, 7(9), 855–865.
25. Wu, C., Lorenzo, G., Hormuth, D. A., Lima, E. A., Slavkova, K. P., DiCarlo, J. C., ... & Yankeelov, T. E. (2022). Integrating mechanism-based modeling with biomedical imaging to build practical digital twins for clinical oncology. *Biophysics Reviews*, 3(2), 021304-1–021304-23.
26. Stahlberg, E. A., Abdel-Rahman, M., Aguilar, B., Asadpoure, A., Beckman, R. A., Borkon, L. L., ... & Zervantonakis, I. (2022). Exploring approaches for predictive cancer patient digital twins: Opportunities for collaboration and innovation. *Frontiers in Digital Health*, 4, 1007784.
27. Twin, I. D. (2023). IBM digital twin. www.ibm.com/products/maximo/predictive-maintenance?cm_sp=ibmdev-_-developer-articles-_-product
28. DigiTwin. (2022). Medical augmented intelligence and DigiTwin. www.mai.ai/digitwin/
29. Insel, T. R. (2017). Digital phenotyping: Technology for a new science of behavior. *JAMA*, 318, 1215–1216.
30. Bruynseels, K., Santoni de Sio, F., & Van den Hoven, J. (2018). Digital twins in health care: Ethical implications of an emerging engineering paradigm. *Frontiers in Genetics*, 9, 31.
31. Ferdousi, R., Laamarti, F., Hossain, M. A., Yang, C., & El Saddik, A. (2022). Digital twins for well-being: An overview. *Digital Twin*, 1, 7.

32. Ahmed, H., & Devoto, L. (2021). The potential of a digital twin in surgery. *Surgical Innovation*, 28(4), 509–510.
33. Al-Ali, A. R., Gupta, R., Zaman Batool, T., Landolsi, T., Aloul, F., & Al Nabulsi, A. (2020). Digital twin conceptual model within the context of internet of things. *Future Internet*, 12(10), 163.
34. Jimenez, J. I., Jahankhani, H., & Kendzierskyj, S. (2020). Health care in the cyberspace: Medical cyber-physical system and digital twin challenges. In M. Farsi, A. Daneshkhah, A. Hosseinian-Far, & H. Jahankhani (Eds.), *Digital twin technologies and smart cities. Internet of Things* (pp. 79–92). Springer.
35. Garg, H., Sharma, B., Shekhar, S., & Agarwal, R. (2022). Spoofing detection system for e-health digital twin using EfficientNet Convolution Neural Network. *Multimedia Tools and Applications*, 81(19), 26873–26888.
36. De Benedictis, A., Mazzocca, N., Somma, A., & Strigaro, C. (2022). Digital twins in healthcare: An architectural proposal and its application in a social distancing case study. *IEEE Journal of Biomedical and Health Informatics*, 27(10), 5143–5154.
37. Newrzella, S. R., Franklin, D. W., & Haider, S. (2022). Three-dimension digital twin reference architecture model for functionality, dependability, and life cycle development across industries. *IEEE Access*, 10, 95390–95410.
38. Shamanna, P., Saboo, B., Damodharan, S., Mohammed, J., Mohamed, M., Poon, T., ... & Thajudeen, M. (2020). Reducing HbA1c in type 2 diabetes using digital twin technology-enabled precision nutrition: A retrospective analysis. *Diabetes Therapy*, 11, 2703–2714.
39. Angulo, C., Gonzalez-Abril, L., Raya, C., & Ortega, J. A. (2020, April). A proposal to evolving towards digital twins in healthcare. In *International work-conference on bioinformatics and biomedical engineering* (pp. 418–426). Springer International Publishing.
40. Erol, T., Mendi, A. F., & Doğan, D. (2020, October). Digital transformation revolution with digital twin technology. In *2020 4th international symposium on multidisciplinary studies and innovative technologies (ISMSIT)* (pp. 1–7). IEEE.
41. Thiong'o, G. M., & Rutka, J. T. (2022). Digital twin technology: The future of predicting neurological complications of pediatric cancers and their treatment. *Frontiers in Oncology*, 11, 781499.
42. Xie, S., Zhu, S., & Dai, J. (2021, September). Feasibility study of intelligent healthcare based on digital twin and data mining. In *2021 international conference on computer information science and artificial intelligence (CISAI)* (pp. 906–911). IEEE.
43. Pires, F., Cachada, A., Barbosa, J., Moreira, A. P., & Leitão, P. (2019, July). Digital twin in industry 4.0: Technologies, applications and challenges. In *2019 IEEE 17th international conference on industrial informatics (INDIN)* (Vol. 1, pp. 721–726). IEEE.

Chapter 8

Emerging technologies in digital twin

Reflections on self-leadership and addiction recovery

V. Pietiläinen, V. V. Saari, and R. Rusko

8.1 INTRODUCTION

This chapter focuses on the emerging technologies in digital twins applied to self-leadership strategies related to addictive worldviews and behavior. Typically, digital twins are associated with technology [1]. However, the massive contemporary invasion of artificial intelligence (AI) has enlarged the application possibilities of digital twins. The Guo et al. [2] mention the following application possibilities for digital twins: a smart factory in industrial production, a digital model of life in the medical field, construction of the smart city, security guarantee in the aerospace field, and immersive shopping in the commercial field. Furthermore, the use of digital twins has recently increased in healthcare [3].

Several emerging technologies of digital twins are based on AI. Natural language processing (NLP) technologies, such as ChatGPT, are especially topical. This chapter maps the various emerging technologies of digital twins, focusing on qualitative technologies and especially on AI's NLP technologies. Furthermore, this chapter expresses the possibility of using linguistic-based digital twins (from now on, LBDT) in the field of healthcare, a perspective that is rarely studied in the literature [4]. The chapter is not interested in healthcare as an institution. The focus is on a person's (e.g., a client) self-direction and agency. This is natural, as in LBDT, the practical emphasis is relationships between human beings and AI.

In the context of health care, it is suggested that carefully planned digital twins may replace healthcare professionals in the branch of individual therapists, for example [5]. At the current stage of development, however, the chapter takes a critical stance toward the clinical use of LBDT. One question, among others, is how the digital twin would learn the therapeutic framework. Or what would be the responsibility and accountability of the digital twin in therapeutic events? This leads the chapter into the concept of self-leadership, which has proven to be an effective approach to personal challenges and life situations [6]. Conversely, self-leadership is not a clinical concept, although it has presumable positive health outcomes.

 DOI: 10.1201/9781003498117-8

The chapter considers addictions and addictive behavior as one of the most prevalent health challenges in contemporary societies. It argues that people are generally addicted to something at some level, mainly because of the explosion of stimuli in everyday life. Addictive behavior may be associated with the increased use of social media, but the chapter does not exclude, for example, alcohol abuse or gambling as manifestations of addiction.

The chapter adapts a self-leadership perspective to addiction rather than a clinical one. That is, the chapter proposes that addiction is something more general to late postmodern humanity than an individual clinical problem. An idea of *homo addictus* can be defined as "intoxication of senses" or "as an intensification or exaltation of sensory pleasure tending toward an extreme of insensibility" [7].

Following the establishment of the research framework, the chapter addresses the question of *how LBDT affects the self-leadership process of addiction redundancy*. The structure of the chapter is as follows: The literature review begins with an introduction to the digital twin and LBDT. Then, it examines how the concept of self-leadership and its strategies are related to addiction and addictive behavior. After that, the chapter introduces an LBDT case. In the first part of the case, the chapter describes how the self-leadership strategies are applied as a framework to train the LBDT. In the second part of the case, the chapter highlights how the LBDT engages in the self-leadership process of eliminating addictions and addictive behavior. The chapter concludes with the case's implications for digital twin and self-leadership research and practice.

8.2 THE CONCEPT OF A DIGITAL TWIN

Digital twin – definitions and perspectives

The literature has several different understandings and definitions of digital twins. The logic of digital twins comes from physical twins, such as physical replicas. The Apollo 13 program, for example, used physical replicas in the 1970s when NASA reproduced the spacecraft's settings on Earth to address potential problems and challenges [8].

The use of physical replicas has not been restricted to the area of aerospace technology. Prototypes are also physical replicas. They are used in several branches, such as product designing, exploring difficulties in the production process before mass production, and the software industry [9]. Thus, physical twins, physical replicants, and prototypes have similar aims and features to digital twins. Following the perspectives of the seminal book of Gelernter, they all are some kinds of "Mirror Worlds" [10]. According to Türkyilmaz [11], Mirror Worlds of Gelernter (1993) reflects the idea of the digital twin, actually without naming the concept of "digital twin" but using terms such as computer or twin processes. After the book of Gelernter (1993), the next step in the path of digital twin discussions was introduced by

Michael Grieves in 2002, when he gave a speech about the physical product, which has two spaces: real space and virtual space [12]. This duality is the most vital feature of digital twins. Siddique and colleagues [8] see that the digital twin is based on three elements: Real-time and automatic data flow, physical twin, and digital model/simulation.

The definitions of digital twins have two main approaches. One approach expresses the role of quantitative data and probabilistic simulations of a system or equipment [13–15], another approach is focused on the digital representation (virtual replicas) of a real-world physical object, which focuses on the object itself as a developing technology that enables complex interaction between physical objects and their virtual replicas [16–17, 11].

According to Liu and colleagues [18], contemporary developing technologies, such as the Internet of Things (IoT), Big data, AI, CAM, CAD, CAE, FEA, PDM, wireless sensor networks, edge computing, cloud computing, and the fifth-generation cellular network (5G), are improving possibilities for digital twin applications. However, the integration of the physical world and the digital world needs still more effort. For example, Liu et al. (2021) see that the full strategic advantage of this integration is not exploited to its full extent. Noteworthy is the same metaphor of "World" for digital twins (and replicators) between the studies of Liu and colleagues [18] and Gelernter [19].

According to Tao and colleagues [20], the digital twin can perform monitoring, simulation, prediction, and optimization, among others. These capabilities are mainly related to quantitative measuring. Thus, using digital twins is associated with quantitative methods and analysis. The situation has changed due to AI and mainly due to NLP technologies of AI, such as ChatGPT, Claude, Meta Llama, Microsoft Bing Chat, and Google Gemini, among others [21].

Contemporary natural language technologies are based on conversational agents, a concept already used in the 1960s. Still, conversational agents have developed quickly to today's generative models, such as ChatGPT [22]. Overall, digital twin research has expanded rapidly during recent years: the number of papers published per year during the digital twin was two in 2014, seven in 2015, and 2934 in 2021 [22].

The use and role of digital twin in healthcare: The practical and conceptual use of digital twins is multifaceted in healthcare. De Benedictis and colleagues (2023) find four sectors of healthcare where the use of digital twins is or will be, important. These sectors are patient treatment, physicians and surgeons training and practice, the pharmaceutical industry, and public health management. The patient treatment sector contains four components: predictive, preventive, personalized, and participative medicine. According to De Benedictis et al. [23], the participatory component may make patient treatment efficient by bringing various applications from hospitals and clinics to workplaces, homes, and schools. It considers each patient to be unique, taking into account their genetic heritage, lifestyle, and environmental factors [23].

In the sector of physicians and surgeons of digital twins, training is based on a real-time replica of a patient, which can improve surgical training for residents and assist physicians in surgical practice [23]. Digital twins have also been exploited to develop the competent use of the robotic system for surgeons [24].

De Benedictis and colleagues [23] notice two types of pharmaceutical industry: the pharmaceutical production process, which focuses on smart manufacturing, and drug discovery and development. The role of digital twins in drug discovery and development is especially important in data management, that is, in the integrated information from various scientific and clinical sources [25].

The role of digitizing and algorithms as decision-makers has been emphasized, especially in the field of healthcare. The use of dichotomy between decision support algorithms (DSA) and decision-making algorithms (DMA), for example, is strongest in the field of healthcare [26]. Similarly, the position of the digital twin has been carefully considered related to other levels of healthcare in some studies of digital healthcare [23, 27].

Both of these studies position the use of digital twins similarly, even using the exact figure named "Digital Twin high-level conceptual architecture." The digital twin layer in this digital twin architecture is surrounded by several other layers, such as the security layer, service layer, data layer, physical twin layer, and connectivity layer [23, 27]. The digital twin layer contains four parts: human–machine interface (HMI), reasoning, modeling, and feedback. It has direct linkages to all of the other layers. It is the core of the digital twin architecture and contains the digital replica of the physical system. According to Somma and colleagues [27], the digital twin layer is based on modeling functionalities, knowledge extraction, feedback generation, and HMI, which allow direct interaction with end-users.

To the user of the digital twin, the connectivity layer is essential: it enables online communication and interaction, that is, intra-twin communication between the digital twin and the physical twin. Furthermore, the connectivity layer handles inter-twin communication between other virtually replicated physical entities [27].

Generally, emerging digital twin technologies have changed the possibilities and visions of healthcare systems – some studies even name the noticed progression of healthcare as a "revolution" [28, 29]. Haleem and colleagues [29] find large-scale effects of the digital twin in the healthcare system, such as patient health, data facts, cost reduction, patient autonomy, qualitative services, societal disruptions, benefits, and risks (environmental and technology push get avoided). The digital twin of the patient seems to have revolutionary features. Healthcare systems may collect various individual healthcare information together, which constructs a digital twin of the patient [29]. Demand for this kind of technology is topical and even overwhelming in the medical industry. At its best, this technology means cost-savings and improved treatment outcomes for the patient [29]. On the other hand, the efficient use of the digital twin needs very speedy data transfer between the digital twin and the physical twin. Furthermore, the entity may contain hundreds of distant sensors with unstable networks. This challenges the data security protocols and systems of digital twins in healthcare [28, 29]. The general progress of digital twin technology has effects on healthcare, which is especially challenging for digital twin applications due to the inter-individual variability of the patients and the need to take ethical and philosophical perspectives into account [30]. Furthermore, the healthcare sector has large entities that need a mass of real-time information flows, such as hospitals and local and national networks between hospitals. However, some studies of healthcare digital twins introduce the concept of smart hospital digital twin [31–33]. According to Jemaa and colleagues [32], a smart hospital digital twin environment needs strong collaboration between internal and external stakeholders, such as clinical personnel, administration, and technology providers.This chapter considers the recent development of NLP technologies, which has enabled digital twins based on the linguistic capabilities of the technology. The most advanced LBDTs, such as ChatGPT, can construct various avatars with different values and knowledge, representing multiple societal, firm, municipality, or city stakeholders. This feature makes possible political or social digital twins. Before making societal decisions, the user can test the social effects of the societal change among different stakeholders, varying the constructed environment of avatars (stakeholders). The great benefit of LBDTs is the accessibility and ease of use of technology. Contemporary digital twin discussions are missing several potential roles and possibilities for digital twins based on NLP technologies. This study makes the initiative to fill this gap in the context of self-leadership and addiction redundancy.

8.3 SELF-LEADERSHIP STRATEGIES, ADDICTIVE MIND, AND BEHAVIOR

Self-leadership has more than 40 years of research tradition. As the name suggests, self-leadership shifts the focus of leadership from influencing others to influencing oneself. Carl Manz (1986) introduced self-leadership as a concept derived from intrinsic motivation theory [34], socio-cognitive theory [35], and control theory [36]. Self-leadership has several purposes in its multidimensional background. At the heart of the theory are the strategies that can positively affect oneself [37]. Self-leadership utilizes control theory to influence one's behavior, especially to make undesirable problems and tasks more tempting. Intrinsic motivation theory, on the other hand, is associated with the search for meaning in work – and life in general.

The socio-cognitive theory relates to both purposes [38]. The most recent turn in the self-leadership approach incorporates emotions into strategies with two main propositions. First, the self-leadership process suffers when a person cannot reveal their authentic feelings. For example, a customer service representative might try to be polite even though a customer is yelling at them. Second, self-leadership is perceived as significantly more effective and meaningful when a person experiences positive emotions while trying to accomplish something. Conversely, negative emotions during performance increase the likelihood of avoiding that task in the future [39].

Researchers have identified many benefits of high-level self-leadership skills. For example, self-leadership is associated with positive career development, job satisfaction, stress reduction, and emotional regulation [40]. In the context of avoiding negative behaviors, self-leadership is associated with reducing self-punishment and undesirable habits [38]. This chapter explores the potential positive effects of self-leadership on addiction: the chapter is particularly interested in self-leadership, reduced addiction, and LBDT opportunities. The concept of self-leadership has yet to be widely associated with LBDT. However, predictive technology is widely deployed to support work-life situations, such as customer self-direction in banks, online stores, and hospitals. The chapter scrutinizes key self-leadership strategies from an addiction reduction perspective and then adds an LBDT dimension to the examination.

Self-leadership theory introduces three main strategic frameworks that can be applied to addictions. First, behavioral strategies emphasize direct and indirect views of one's action [41]. The former is a person's conscious decision to reduce an addiction. For example, one may formulate an action plan in which they describe the situations in which the addiction is involved and then the actions to avoid these situations or replace the addictive behavior. The action plan can include both short-term and long-term goals. It might also include the endeavors to prevent self-punishment and reward desirable behavior. The latter view addresses environmental cues associated with addictive behavior [41]. One can create cues that support desirable actions. For example, if classical music distracts from addictive behavior, one can surround them with cues that facilitate listening to music. One can also hide the negative cues in the environment, for example, making cigarettes or alcohol visually unavailable, which is assumed to lead to addictive behavior.

The second strategy concept expands intrinsic motivation. It seeks to identify those things that make life meaningful. The assumption is that if the meaningfulness of life is increased, there will be no room for addictive behavior. In particular, the logic is that an inner locus of control during action increases the feeling of competence. This leads to self-determination, a willingness to engage in action again. Finally, the action begins to feel meaningful; it has gained a purpose. As a strategy, the sense of natural reward is enhanced when one can identify dimensions or patterns in one's actions that evoke positive emotions [38]. For example, composing music may be an alternative to addictive behavior, such as drinking alcohol. The process of composing may involve both natural reward and avoidance dimensions. Creating a melody might feel rewarding, but developing the melody into a complete song might feel like a chore. In this case, the natural rewarding solution might be for the person to focus only on the melody and the good feeling it gives, ignoring the end product of the process.The third and most sophisticated concept of strategy concerns constructive cognitive patterns. It emphasizes two dimensions. First, visual imagery has been found to be very effective in self-leadership. In other words, if a person can summarize goals in an internal visual image, they are more likely to be achieved [42]. For instance, a person may create an image that exaggerates the negative consequences of addiction, such as an image of a smoker's polluted lungs or a heavy drinker's damaged liver. Similarly, effort can be put into creating a positive image of an alternative behavior to addiction. Second, internal visual imagery can be strengthened through self-talk. Self-leadership proposes that self-talk is always present in people's minds, but they do not necessarily recognize it. As a result, self-punishing talk characteristically dominates the mind. By consciously paying attention to internal speech, self-punishing talk can be made visible, and alternative, more positive patterns of this speech can be created [38]. For example, a person can intuitively write down their thoughts when an addictive behavior is occurring, in progress, or coming to an end, and try to understand the cognitive logic and intervene.

Despite the effectiveness of self-leadership strategies, the theory can be criticized for being strongly individual-centered. In principle, the strategies do not consider how individual goals and purposes relate to the common good and the environment. Some researchers associate high-level self-leadership skills with ethical leadership [43, 44]. However, these studies do not address the relationship between strategies and ethics. Bracht and associates [45] partially fill the gap by emphasizing the intrapreneurial perspective of self-leadership, which links personal actions and aspirations to the broader development of society or the organization. They also highlight the link between self-leadership, personal values, and authenticity. This chapter suggests that self-leadership strategies might work for addiction reduction. However, addictive behavior is often multi-dimensionally linked to personal history. For example, Dingle and associates [46] describe how addicted individuals may experience a loss of identity or personal values during the onset of addiction. The chapter suggests that this dimension of addiction requires an understanding of a person's life context and history, in addition to self-leadership strategies. Therefore, the chapter adds personal values and their connection to a common good as a fourth strategy or "meta-strategy" of self-leadership.

8.4 RESEARCH DESIGN

As a principle of research design, the chapter carefully considered the transparency of LPDT planning and training. In the research literature, the concept of AI transparency is still partially fragmented and evolving. Here, the chapter availed a three-dimensional framework to approach transparency in LPDT design. First, as a virtue, transparency is a norm or standard to be followed. Second, as a relation, transparency reveals the audience of the action. That is, to whom transparency is justified. Third, at a systemic level, it addresses an institutional context that includes organizational or governmental regulations, rules, and legal requirements for transparency [48, 49].

As a virtue, the chapter examined the standards related to ChatGPT as a basis for development. This level of transparency was considered the most challenging, as the algorithm was developed elsewhere than this chapter. At worst, such broad LBDTs can be defined as "black boxes" because they "process humanly unmanageable amounts of data in humanly incomprehensible ways, resulting in unknown biases in the resulting decisions" [50]. In this chapter, the potential limitations of ChatGPT had to be accepted as such to allow the algorithm to be used as intended by the research question. Regarding transparency, the chapter highlighted a user perspective. That is the self-leadership dimension that would be personally valuable and motivating. Finally, as the system is transparent, attention is paid to the academic audience, and the theoretical framework is justified and well-grounded. Next, the chapter describes the LBDT training process from the perspective of the transparency principles.

The chapter availed self-leadership strategies and a "meta-strategy" as a framework for generating LBDT. Here, the LBDT is a "mirror" or a "sketch" of the potential self-leadership state related to addiction, constructed with the tailored ChatGPT. The endeavor was to reflect the individual's starting point concerning the self-leadership question. More specifically, an empathetic design, employing design thinking and participatory modeling, was vital to the LBDT development process. The approach included direct engagement with individuals who have an addiction and social challenges to ensure the tool was tailored to their specific needs and realities. The LBDT demo, titled The Arctic Self Leadership Architect (from now on ASLA), represents a synthesis of advanced AI and deep human-centered research. It was created by partnering with Ville-Veli Oy (second author) and the University of Lapland (first and third authors). The ASLA's genesis was motivated by the desire to utilize the users' extensive expertise in living well, creativity, predictive technology, and the researchers' knowledge to create something profoundly useful for humanity. The case of ASLA focuses on the connection between digital and physical twins (Figure 8.1). However, this does not rule out the possibility of combining ASLA with other digital systems and digital twins in the future.

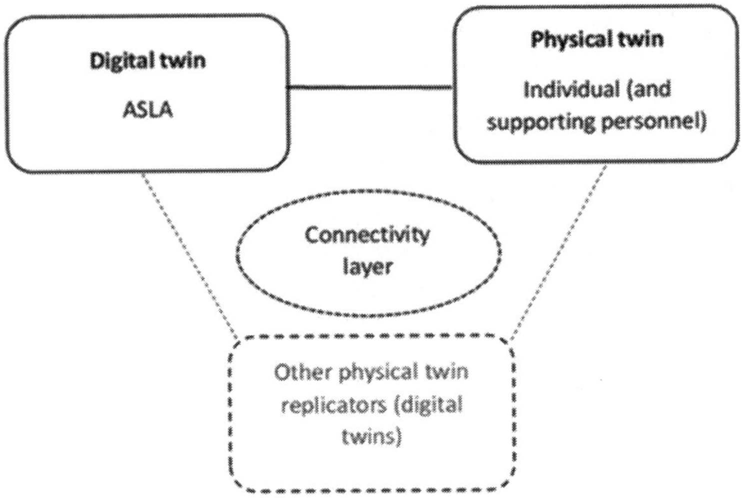

Figure 8.1 Digital twin of ASLA.

The ASLA creation consisted of the following dimensions:

- *Prototype development:* Through iterative cycles of prototyping and feedback, the cognitive models within the GPT were refined to accurately reflect and support the users' mental and emotional landscapes.
- *Technical development:* The practical development of the GPT involved programming the AI with knowledge of self-leadership strategies (including the meta-strategy) and the capability to adapt and respond to diverse user inputs guided by theoretical frameworks and participatory cognitive models of its future users.
- *Feedback and refinement:* Continuous testing with academic peers and target users provided ongoing feedback, crucial for refining the AI's functionalities and ensuring its effectiveness.

First, a design scientific approach was chosen, supported by a simulation of GPT creation. A more advanced GPT was used for the simulation of GPT creation. All AI systems utilized in the ASLA creation were OPENAI tools running on GPT4. For this, OPENAI offers a GPT creation toolkit that, when enhanced with already employed GPT, gives rise to very highly functioning GPTs like ASLA.

Second, creating the ASLA GPT included a thorough review of relevant and appropriate self-leadership and addiction recovery theories. The original concept of self-leadership [36], the revised self-leadership questionnaire [41], the self-leadership reviews [40, 51, 37, 38], the emotional perspective of self-leadership [39] were incorporated into the framework to name the essential theoretical viewpoints. The framework was elucidated as cognitive, natural reward, behavioral, and meta-strategies in the context of addiction recovery.

Third, the modeling of some of the tools within the ASLA GPT was done in a participatory manner with persons known to the authors who have experienced addiction problems, allowing for more practical adaptation and testing of the tools where they are most needed.Fourth, the development of the basic framework of ASLA was evaluated in a joint creation session with George, the more advanced GPT. The basic framework of ASLA was further enhanced with meta-strategic alliances or core values copied from its creator (the second author). This gave birth to the artifact: a basic blueprint of ASLA, albeit with limited capabilities and needing more participatory modelled tools.

Fifth, the blueprint based on ASLA was then remodeled into a GPT configuration. OpenAI has easy-to-use tools for creating GPTs from configurations and can help beginners design GPTconfigurations. In this process, the more advanced GPT, George, replaced the OpenAI´sinbuilt guide for GPT creation, thus allowing for more advanced iterative design scientific principles to be utilized in the design and testing of ASLA.

Sixth, the GPT algorithm was trained after configuration. This was done using the design science method of participatory modeling of the future ASLA by asking relevant questions of the GPT. After getting a good understanding of how it works, a training discussion with George took place. Together with George, the more advanced GPT and the developer (the second author) looked at the basic configuration of ASLA and assessed the theoretical framework of self-leadership provided by researchers at the University of Lapland.

Seventh, after mapping and structuring the theoretical framework together with George, the authors were ready to update the configurations of ASLA basic to ASLA (Demo). At this point, the authors concluded that ASLA had the potential to be valuable in addiction recovery.

Eighth, rigorous ASLA (DEMO) testing took place and was used in various settings. As the test results indicated, small increments were made to the ALSA configurations. Ultimately, the research team was ready to test the ASLA (DEMO) against the research question. The results will be presented in the next section.

As the meta-strategies in using ASLA were participatory and designed from the current starting point of the user's cognitive capabilities, the paths co-developed with ASLA are non-deterministic of their nature, thus allowing for higher user freedom and dynamics of play. The relationship between self-leadership strategies and meta-strategy was carefully considered during development. As a result, ASLA logic emphasizes both dimensions.

First, ASLA attempts to capture some general ideas about the user's life situation to identify personal values or worldviews. Second, ASLA focuses more specifically on self-leadership strategies and specific cognitive, emotional, or behavioral patterns to elaborate the appropriate and often unique approaches to addiction redundancy.

8.5 OUTCOMES

As a starting point, ASLA asks for contextual information to outline the user's meta-strategy. It attempts to understand the most appropriate approach for the user to explore self-leadership (Figure 8.2). The first option, "Help me know and experience myself as an important person," predicts a situation where the user feels vulnerable and fragile. The second option, "Tell me about yourself and what to do! What is important to you?" predicts a situation in which a person is curious about their life but may experience difficulty making choices or prioritizing issues against each other. The third option, "Help me with a challenge, so that is fun!" suggests that the user already has an idea of the challenge in mind that could be worked on in a way that does not feel like a burden but is motivating. The final fourth option, "Tell me a joke about yourself!" further emphasizes the informal side of the self as a development dimension.

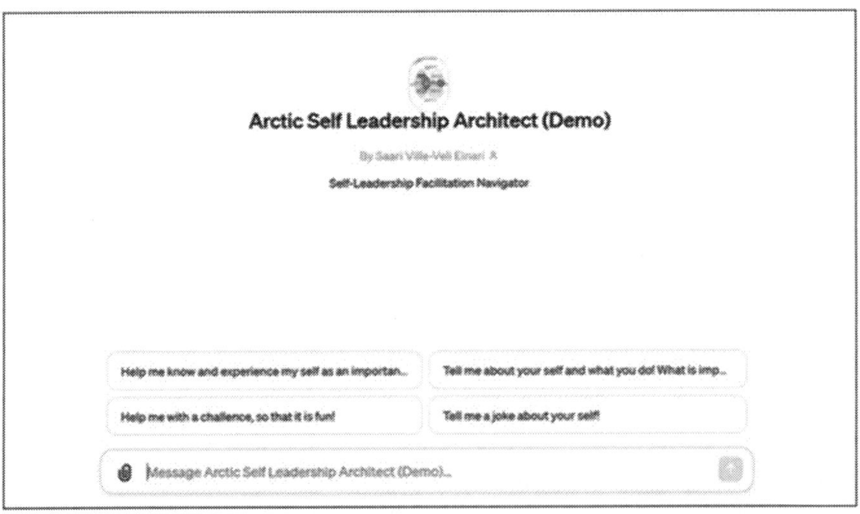

Figure 8.2 The session opening window in Arctic Self Leadership Architect (Demo) (ASLA), an emerging digital twin technological tool for self-leadership and addiction recovery.

ASLA is designed to provide immediate support once the user has chosen their self-leadership approach. In this case, the user has identified their challenge as "I drink too much coffee and get nervous. Also, when not drinking coffee, I get a headache." ASLA quickly analyzes the challenge, offering a range of strategies and highlighting the motivational aspect (Figures 8.3 and 8.4).

After the initialization phase, ASLA is given a glimpse of the user's cognitive state. From this glimpse, ASLA has mapped various meta-strategies that might fit the user's recovery process well. The user is presented with multiple cognitively aligned meta-strategies that can help the user start the recovery process. In this example, the user felt curious to know more about step 2 in the list of suggested meta-strategies. Thus, an element of user-driven engagement toward the implementation of meta-strategies emerged and illustrated with the aid of Figure 8.5.

In the next phase, the user looks at the suggestions that seem most promising to them. Here, the proposition "maybe through a colorful chart of daily journal with stickers for caffeine-free days" was selected for further investigation. Again, ASLA begins the analysis, but with a more restricted focus. It suggests specific ways to incorporate the chosen self-leadership strategy, including process setting, tracking, rewarding, and tips for success. (Figures 8.6 and 8.7).

As the user has engaged in jointly tailoring a path of recovery or self-leadership challenge, ASLA co-creates a plan with the user. To keep up with the plan and implement user-designed steps toward better health, it is suggested that the user-ASLA self-leadership plan is supported by a real person, social worker, mentor, or friend. This caters to the real-world application of joint innovations toward better health for the user.

After testing the action plan, the user can use ASLA to refine the chosen strategy. As a result, the potential bottlenecks of the action plan can be reframed. The user can also go back to the beginning and choose a different perspective (meta-strategy) of self-leadership or vary the self-leadership strategies under investigation, and together with ASLA or a physical person, map a more comprehensive and holistic plan toward a better life.

8.6 DISCUSSION

ASLA contributes to the research and practice of digital twin and self-leadership in two ways. Regarding the digital twin concept, LBDT is a promising branch of human-centered research. The basic premise of health care is a treatment that leads to clinical solutions [52]. From that perspective, the nature of addiction is something that should be treated. The chapter does not question clinical interventions for addiction. However, it does suggest that the addictive worldview and behavior is something more general for a

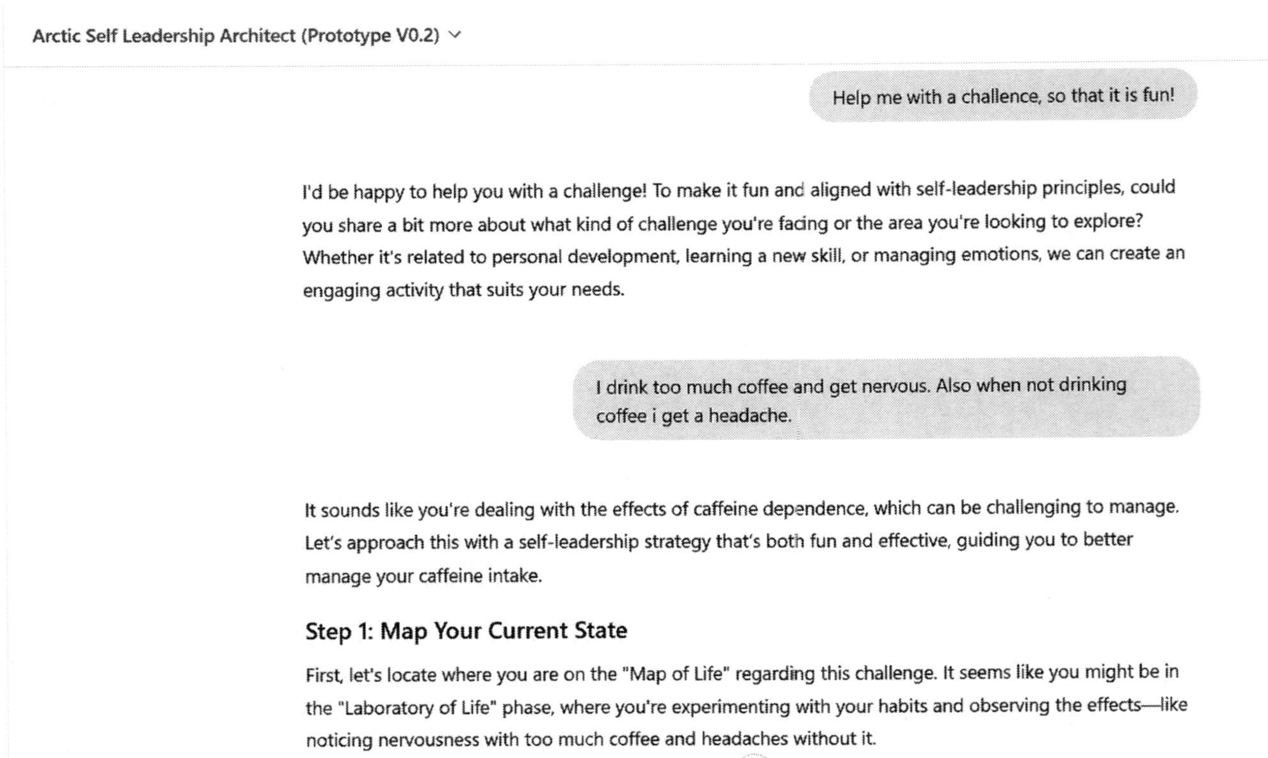

Figure 8.3 Starting a self-leadership mentoring session, getting to know the service. Participatory mapping of self-leadership/addiction challenges. They are jointly evoking participatory mapped meta-strategies and choosing a path.

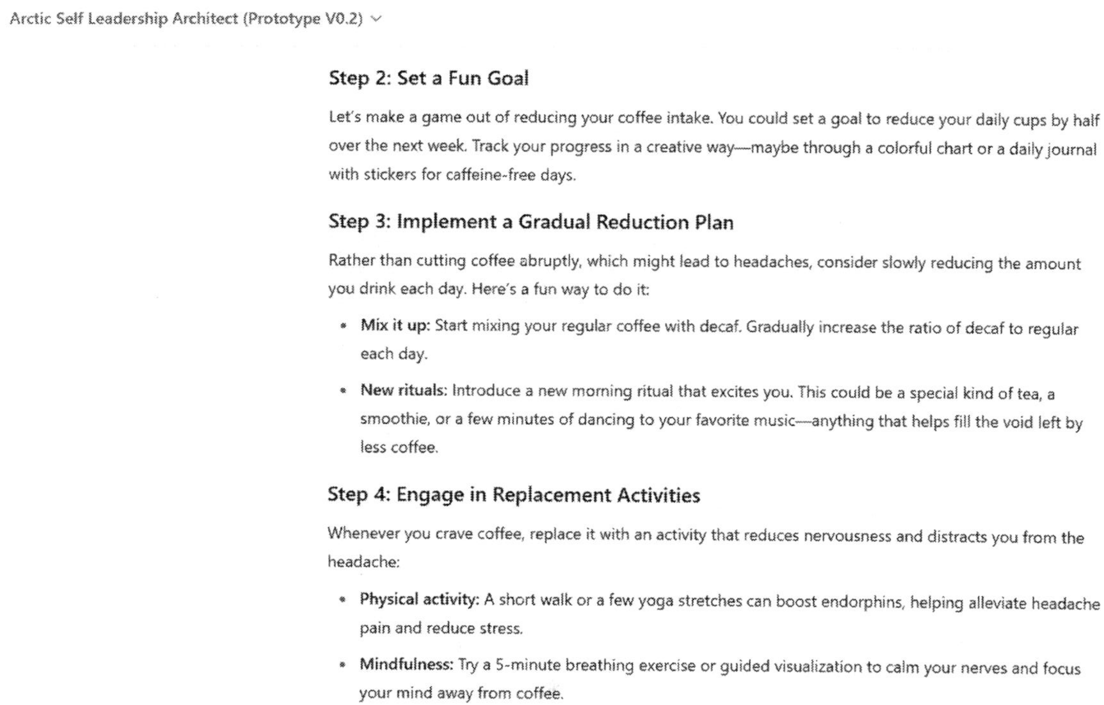

Arctic Self Leadership Architect (Prototype V0.2)

Step 2: Set a Fun Goal

Let's make a game out of reducing your coffee intake. You could set a goal to reduce your daily cups by half over the next week. Track your progress in a creative way—maybe through a colorful chart or a daily journal with stickers for caffeine-free days.

Step 3: Implement a Gradual Reduction Plan

Rather than cutting coffee abruptly, which might lead to headaches, consider slowly reducing the amount you drink each day. Here's a fun way to do it:

- **Mix it up:** Start mixing your regular coffee with decaf. Gradually increase the ratio of decaf to regular each day.
- **New rituals:** Introduce a new morning ritual that excites you. This could be a special kind of tea, a smoothie, or a few minutes of dancing to your favorite music—anything that helps fill the void left by less coffee.

Step 4: Engage in Replacement Activities

Whenever you crave coffee, replace it with an activity that reduces nervousness and distracts you from the headache:

- **Physical activity:** A short walk or a few yoga stretches can boost endorphins, helping alleviate headache pain and reduce stress.
- **Mindfulness:** Try a 5-minute breathing exercise or guided visualization to calm your nerves and focus your mind away from coffee.

Figure 8.4 Review of various mapped meta-strategies and implementation of meta-strategic alliances to overcome user challenges.

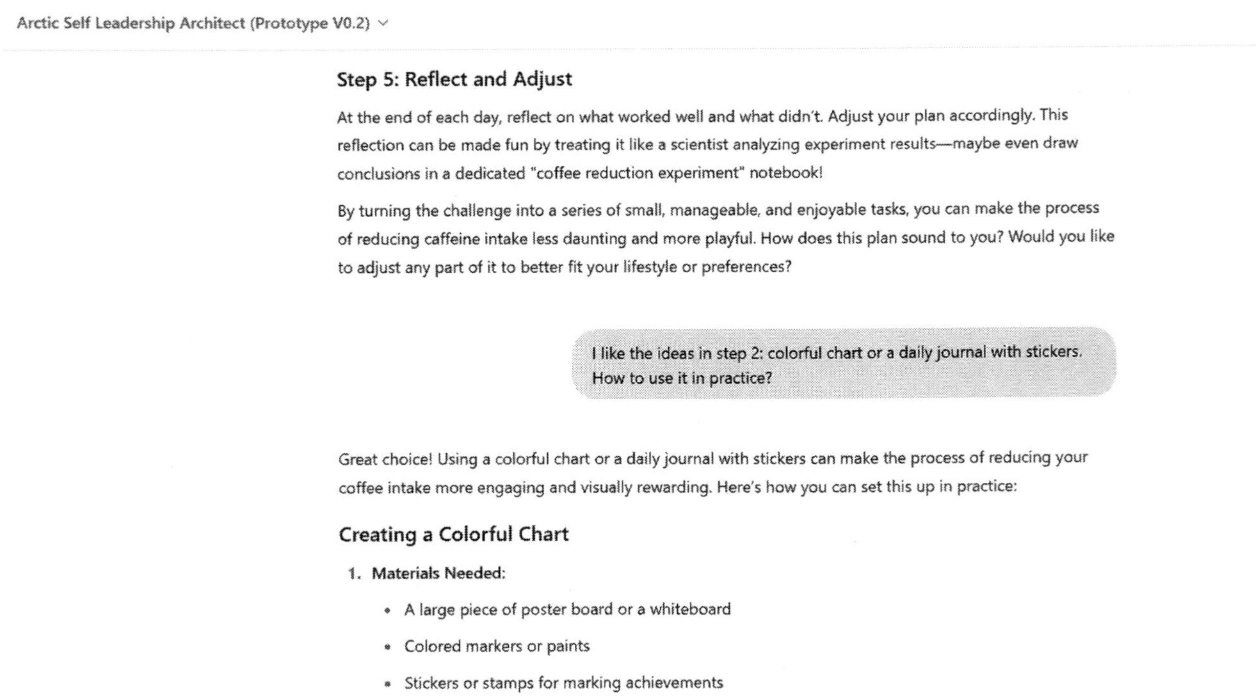

Figure 8.5 Continuing the meta-strategic mapping and allowing the user to choose which path to utilize. Co-innovation of user-aligned meta-strategic recovery implementation for overcoming challenges.

Arctic Self Leadership Architect (Prototype V0.2)

2. **Design the Chart:**
    - Divide the chart into columns for each day of the week.
    - Label each column with the date.
    - Have rows for different times of the day or simply one box per day depending on how often you typically drink coffee.
3. **Tracking:**
    - Every time you skip a coffee or replace it with a decaffeinated option, place a sticker or make a colorful mark in the corresponding box.
    - Use different colors for different actions, like one color for no coffee at all, another for half-caff, and another for decaf.
4. **Rewards:**
    - Set milestones, such as one week, two weeks, etc. When you reach a milestone without exceeding your coffee limits, reward yourself with something enjoyable unrelated to food or drink, like watching a favorite movie or buying a small gift for yourself.

Using a Daily Journal with Stickers

1. **Materials Needed:**
    - A notebook or journal
    - Fun stickers (stars, happy faces, etc.)
    - Colored pens or markers
2. **Set Up the Journal:**

Figure 8.6 Facilitation of a practical step-by-step meta-strategy implementation activity for overcoming a challenge.

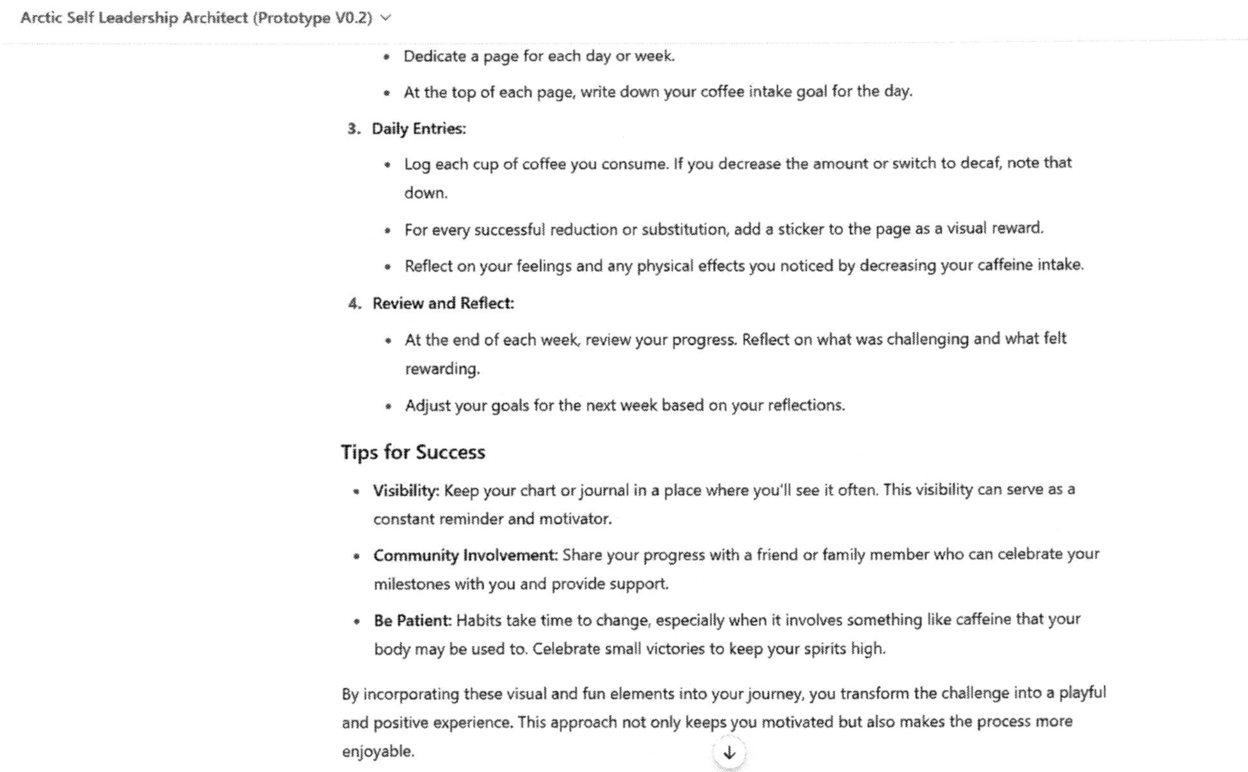

Arctic Self Leadership Architect (Prototype V0.2)

- Dedicate a page for each day or week.
- At the top of each page, write down your coffee intake goal for the day.

3. **Daily Entries:**
   - Log each cup of coffee you consume. If you decrease the amount or switch to decaf, note that down.
   - For every successful reduction or substitution, add a sticker to the page as a visual reward.
   - Reflect on your feelings and any physical effects you noticed by decreasing your caffeine intake.
4. **Review and Reflect:**
   - At the end of each week, review your progress. Reflect on what was challenging and what felt rewarding.
   - Adjust your goals for the next week based on your reflections.

Tips for Success

- **Visibility:** Keep your chart or journal in a place where you'll see it often. This visibility can serve as a constant reminder and motivator.
- **Community Involvement:** Share your progress with a friend or family member who can celebrate your milestones with you and provide support.
- **Be Patient:** Habits take time to change, especially when it involves something like caffeine that your body may be used to. Celebrate small victories to keep your spirits high.

By incorporating these visual and fun elements into your journey, you transform the challenge into a playful and positive experience. This approach not only keeps you motivated but also makes the process more enjoyable.

Figure 8.7 Continuing the personalized step-by-step program utilization and providing the user with further tips for facilitating a successful journey toward a better life.

late post-human society than an individual clinical problem. Self-leadership as a concept shifts the study of addiction toward agency and strategic action.

The self-leadership tradition has approached addictions through strategies that focus on cognitive thought patterns, natural rewards, and behavior [37]. However, self-leadership research has scarcely adopted an LBDT perspective in general and on phenomena such as addiction. In addition, the revised self-leadership questionnaire [41] addresses a person's view on the strategies level but does not combine them against various self-leadership challenges. The results of this study demonstrate how LPDT can produce user-designed, multiple approaches and specific action plans related to the self-leadership phenomena of addictive worldviews and behaviors.

The chapter's literature review showed the high speed of digital technology development and its multifaceted reflections on the opportunities of digital twins generally, especially in healthcare. The glaring feature of these discussions is that several sources name the new situation and opportunities of digital twins in healthcare as a "revolution" [28–29]. This interpretation is very typical in the contemporary literature of digital twin healthcare: In addition to the two studies above, this term has been used in the headline of the digital twin healthcare study by Erol, Mendi, and Doğan [53], Hassani, Huang and MacFeely [54], and Chen and colleagues [55] among others.

However, the fast adaptation of new digital technology in the digital twins of healthcare causes several challenges. These challenges are both technical and ethical. Among technical challenges is data security, which is linked with ethical problems, too. As mentioned, multifaceted healthcare systems may collect confidential individual healthcare information together, which constructs a digital twin of the patient [29].This may cause complex information security challenges – especially in cases where the connectivity layer contains inter-twin communication between several digital twins or physical twins [56, 27]. However, the implemented experiment with ASLA was based on the relatively simple connection between ChatGPT-based digital twin and physical twin. ASLA, as a healthcare product, makes it possible to connect large healthcare systems with several digital and physical twins, and other actors of healthcare.

8.7 CONCLUSION

As an example of emerging technologies of digital twins in healthcare, this chapter proposes a theory and practice branch combining LBDT and self-leadership. Literature review considers wider range of digital twin technologies in healthcare, their opportunities and challenges, but in order to introduce new potential of this field, chapter introduced one more in-depth case. According to the brief demonstration presented in this chapter, LBDT, trained by an appropriate theoretical framework, effectively outlines self-leadership as a concept and a detailed strategy. Concurrently, LBDT expands the agency of the third party (the AI) in the self-leadership process. As the role of LBDT is likely to increase significantly shortly, there is a growing need to understand the new agency thoroughly.

Limitations and further research

Further research on the subject of participatory user engagement, development of meta-strategic methodologies, value-based research, modeling, and emergent development of digital twin technologies requires cooperation across the science and societal structures. A multidisciplinary research design with a focus on meta-strategies might provide the necessary tools to support the sustainable development of methodologies needed as well as tools and artifacts such as ASLA, fostering a more significant societal understanding, application, and effect of meta-strategic alliance in scientific discoveries as well as real-world practices, decision-making, and sustainable outcomes.

A potential limitation of the research is that LBDT itself may be experienced as addictive. Predictive algorithms are in many ways associated with dependency and addiction in the era of homo addictus. From this perspective, the idea of reducing addiction through addictive technology is a potential risk. At the very least, the chapter suggests this would be a dimension to explore further in the future. The case study presented in this chapter provides an example of how critical people in real life can be involved in the self-leadership process in addition to LBDT.Future research on research principles, human meta-strategic alliances, and the ethical utilization of human virtues in developing AI models is suggested. A multidisciplinary approach to scientific endeavor is required to assess the multidimensionality of the capabilities of human-computer interaction in its essence. Thus, it is recommended that emphasis be placed on the utilization of research design methods, such as design science research, automation, intervention methods, and the science of serious simulation games, as such have been fruitful inspirations to develop the research project, as well as its artifact, ASLA.

The design of new scientific principles and methodologies also has value in international scientific collaborations, where a decentralized aspect of research in the evolution of human capacity to develop and create methods and tools for better health can play a significant role in designing ethically sound societies of the future.

Epistemology, more research on the "self" is needed because LBDT involves a self-leadership process. The current self-leadership research tradition does not sufficiently recognize this connection, and the human-technology discussion is also limited in the digital twin research. However, the discussion of human experience and AI is ongoing in other research traditions and a philosophy of science. As we explore these innovations and their applications, we respectfully acknowledge the opportunity to contribute to a burgeoning philosophy of technology – one that thoughtfully considers the evolving relationship between self and digital agency, thus calling upon the new generation for help in designing a new philosophy of technology.

REFERENCES

1. Keathley, H., Enos, J., & Parrish, M. (2020). Types of digital twins and application possibilities in product management. In *Proceedings of the American Society for Engineering Management 2020 International Annual Conference, Huntsville.*
2. Guo, J., & Lv, Z. (2022). Application of digital twins in multiple fields. *Multimedia Tools and Applications*, 81(19), 26941–26967.
3. Haleem, A., Javaid, M., Singh, R. P., & Suman, R. (2023). Exploring the revolution in healthcare systems through the applications of digital twin technology. *Biomedical Technology*, 4, 28–38.
4. Aydın, Ö., & Karaarslan, E. (2022). OpenAI ChatGPT generated literature review: Digital twin in healthcareIn Ö. Aydın (Ed.), *Emerging computer technologies*, 2.
5. Roose, K. (2022). The brilliance and weirdness of ChatGPT. *The New York Times*, 5.
6. Goldsby, M. G., Goldsby, E. A., Neck, C. B., Neck, C. P., & Mathews, R. (2021). Self-leadership: A four decade review of the literature and trainings. *Administrative Sciences*, 11(1), 25.
7. Connor, S. (2012, October 12). *Homo Addictus. Investigating the intoxication of the senses: Pleasure, poison and perception, 1600–Present, CRASSH.* University of Cambridge.
8. Siddique, S., Haque24, M. A., Rifat, R. H., George, R., Shujaee, K., & Gupta, K. D. (2023, December). Cyber Security issues in the industrial applications of digital twins. In *2023 IEEE symposium series on computational intelligence (SSCI)* (pp. 873–878). IEEE.
9. Carr, M., & Verner, J. (1997). *Prototyping and software development approaches.* Department of Information Systems, City University of Hong Kong, Hong Kong, 319–338.
10. Gelernter, D. (1993). *Mirror worlds: Or the day software puts the universe in a shoebox... How it will happen and what it will mean.* Oxford University Press.
11. Türkyilmaz, S. (2022). Industrial applications of the digital twin: Literature review. *International Review.*
12. Grieves, M., & Vickers, J. (2016). *Mitigating unpredictable, undesirable emergent behavior in complex systems (excerpt).* Florida Inst. Technol. Tech. Rep.
13. Glaessgen, E., & Stargel, D. (2012, April). The digital twin paradigm for future NASA and US Air Force vehicles. In *53rd AIAA/ASME/ASCE/AHS/ASC structures, structural dynamics and materials conference 20th AIAA/ASME/AHS adaptive structures conference 14th AIAA* (p. 1818).

14. Shafto, M., Conroy, M., Doyle, R., Glaessgen, E., Kemp, C., LeMoigne, J., & Wang, L. (2010). Draft modeling, simulation, information technology & processing roadmap. *Technology Area*, 11, 1–32.
15. Ríos, J., Hernández, J. C., Oliva, M., & Mas, F. (2015). Product avatar as digital counterpart of a physical individual product: Literature review and implications in an aircraft. *Transdisciplinary Lifecycle Analysis of Systems*, 657–666.
16. Canedo, A. (2016, October). Industrial IoT lifecycle via digital twins. In *Proceedings of the eleventh IEEE/ACM/IFIP international conference on hardware/software codesign and system synthesis* (p. 1).
17. Hu, W., Zhang, T., Deng, X., Liu, Z., & Tan, J. (2021). Digital twin: A state-of-the-art review of its enabling technologies, applications and challenges. *Journal of Intelligent Manufacturing and Special Equipment*, 2(1), 1–34.
18. Liu, M., Fang, S., Dong, H., & Xu, C. (2021). Review of digital twin about concepts, technologies, and industrial applications. *Journal of Manufacturing Systems*, 58, 346–361.
19. Gelernter, D. (1993). *Mirror worlds: Or the day software puts the universe in a shoebox.How it will happen and what it will mean.* Oxford University Press.
20. Tao, F., Xiao, B., Qi, Q., Cheng, J., & Ji, P. (2022). Digital twin modeling. *Journal of Manufacturing Systems*, 64, 372–389.
21. Biswas, S. S. (2023). Potential use of chat gpt in global warming. *Annals of Biomedical Engineering*, 51(6), 1126–1127.
22. Schöbel, S., Schmitt, A., Benner, D., Saqr, M., Janson, A., & Leimeister, J. M. (2024). Charting the evolution and future of conversational agents: A research agenda along five waves and new frontiers. *Information Systems Frontiers*, 26(2), 729–754.
23. De Benedictis, A., Mazzocca, N., Somma, A., & Strigaro, C. (2022). Digital twins in healthcare: An architectural proposal and its application in a social distancing case study. *IEEE Journal of Biomedical and Health Informatics*, 27(10), 5143–5154.
24. Hagmann, K., Hellings-Kuß, A., Klodmann, J., Richter, R., Stulp, F., & Leidner, D. (2021). A digital twin approach for contextual assistance for surgeons during surgical robotics training. *Frontiers in Robotics and AI*, 8, 735566.
25. Subramanian, K. (2020). Digital twin for drug discovery and development – The virtual liver. *Journal of the Indian Institute of Science*, 100(4), 653–662.
26. Rusko, R., Koivisto, S. A., & Jestilä, S. (2023). Algorithms as decision-makers. In *Analytics enabled decision making* (pp. 23–44). Springer Nature.
27. Somma, A., De Benedictis, A., Esposito, C., & Mazzocca, N. (2024). The convergence of digital twins and distributed ledger technologies: A systematic literature review and an architectural proposal. *Journal of Network and Computer Applications*, 103857.
28. Khan, S., Arslan, T., & Ratnarajah, T. (2022). Digital twin perspective of fourth industrial and healthcare revolution. *IEEE Access*, 10, 25732–25754.
29. Haleem, A., Javaid, M., Singh, R. P., & Suman, R. (2023). Exploring the revolution in healthcare systems through the applications of digital twin technology. *Biomedical Technology*, 4, 28–38.

30. Venkatapurapu, S. P., DeWitt, M. T., Behar, M., & D'Alessandro, P. M. Digital twins for proactive and personalized healthcare–Challenges and opportunities. *Handbook of Digital Twins*, 1, 888–902.
31. Rasubala, V. C., & Tjahyadi, H. (2022, September). Digital twin roles in public healthcare. In *2022 1st International conference on technology innovation and its applications (ICTIIA)* (pp. 1–5). IEEE.
32. Jemaa, M. H., Jemili, F., Charfeddine, A. M. R. I., Msolli, M. A., & Korbaa, O. (2023). Digital twin for a human heart using deep learning and stream processing platforms. PREPRINT (Version 1) available at *Research Square*, https://doi.org/10.21203/rs.3.rs-3359965/v1
33. Han, Y., Li, Y., Li, Y., Yang, B., & Cao, L. (2023). Digital twinning for smart hospital operations: Framework and proof of concept. *Technology in Society*, 74, 102317.
34. Deci, E., & Ryan, R. (1980). The empirical exploration of intrinsic motivational processes. In L. Berkowitz (ed.), *Advantages in experimental social psychology* (p. 13). Academic Press.
35. Bandura, A. (1986). *Social foundations of thought and action* (pp. 23–28). Prentice-Hall.
36. Manz, C. C. (1983). *The art of self-leadership: Strategies for personal effectiveness in your life and work*. Prentice-Hall.
37. Harari, M. B., Williams, E. A., Castro, S. L., & Brant, K. K. (2021). Self-leadership: A meta-analysis of over two decades of research. *Journal of Occupational and Organizational Psychology*, 94(4), 890–923.
38. Steward, G., Courtright, S., & Manz, C. (2011). Self-leadership: A multi-level review. Measurement of Self-leadership. *Journal of Management*, 37(1), 191–196.
39. Manz, C. C., Houghton, J. D., Neck, C. P., Fugate, M., & Pearce, C. (2016). Whistle while you work: Toward a model of emotional self-leadership. *Journal of Leadership & Organizational Studies*, 23(4), 374–386.
40. Goldsby, M. G., Goldsby, E. A., Neck, C. B., Neck, C. P., & Mathews, R. (2021). Self-leadership: A four decade review of the literature and trainings. *Administrative Sciences*, 11(1), 25.
41. Houghton, J. D., & Neck, C. P. (2002). The revised self-leadership questionnaire: Testing a hierarchical factor structure for self-leadership. *Journal of Managerial Psychology*, 17(8), 672–691.
42. Tzortzaki, A. M. (2022). Developing compassionate self-leadership: A conceptual framework for leadership effectiveness in the digital age. *Journal for Global Business Advancement*, 15(3), 272–296.
43. Alves, J. C., Lovelace, K. J., Manz, C. C., Matsypura, D., Toyasaki, F., & Ke, K. (2006). A cross-cultural perspective of self-leadership. *Journal of Managerial Psychology*, 21(4), 338–359.
44. Steinbauer, R., Renn, R. W., Taylor, R. R., & Njoroge, P. K. (2014). Ethical leadership and followers' moral judgment: The role of followers' perceived accountability and self-leadership. *Journal of Business Ethics*, 120, 381–392.
45. Bracht, E. M., Junker, N. M., & van Dick, R. (2018). Exploring the social context of self-leadership – Self-leadership-culture. *Journal of Theoretical Social Psychology*, 2(4), 119–130.

46. Bracht, E. M., Junker, N. M., & van Dick, R. (2018). Exploring the social context of self-leadership – Self-leadership-culture. *Journal of Theoretical Social Psychology*, 2(4), 119–130.
47. Dingle, G. A., Cruwys, T., & Frings, D. (2015). Social identities as pathways into and out of addiction. *Frontiers in Psychology*, 6, 1795.
48. Meijer, A. (2014). Transparency. In M. Bovens, R. E. Goodin, & T. Schillemans (Eds.). *The Oxford handbook of public accountability* (pp. 507–524). Oxford University Press.
49. Felzmann, H., Fosch-Villaronga, E., Lutz, C., & Tamò-Larrieux, A. (2020). Towards transparency by design for artificial intelligence. *Science and Engineering Ethics*, 26(6), 3333–3361.
50. Haresamudram, K., Larsson, S., & Heintz, F. (2023). Three levels of AI transparency. *Computer*, 56(2), 93–100.
51. Knotts, K., Houghton, J. D., Pearce, C. L., Chen, H., Stewart, G. L., & Manz, C. C. (2022). Leading from the inside out: A meta-analysis of how, when, and why self-leadership affects individual outcomes. *European Journal of Work and Organizational Psychology*, 31(2), 273–291.
52. Roose, K. (2022). The brilliance and weirdness of ChatGPT. *The New York Times*, 5.
53. Erol, T., Mendi, A. F., & Doğan, D. (2020, October). The digital twin revolution in healthcare. In *2020 4th international symposium on multidisciplinary studies and innovative technologies (ISMSIT)* (pp. 1–7). IEEE.
54. Hassani, H., Huang, X., & MacFeely, S. (2022). Impactful digital twin in the healthcare revolution. *Big Data and Cognitive Computing*, 6(3), 83.
55. Chen, J., Yi, C., Du, H., Niyato, D., Kang, J., Cai, J., & Shen, X. (2024). A revolution of personalized healthcare: Enabling human digital twin with mobile AIGC. *IEEE Network*, 38(6), 234–242.
56. Wang, Y., Su, Z., Guo, S., Dai, M., Luan, T. H., & Liu, Y. (2023). A survey on digital twins: Architecture, enabling technologies, security and privacy, and future prospects. *IEEE Internet of Things Journal*, 10(17), 14965–14987.

Chapter 9

Exploring the future of digital twin ecosystems

Anand Jha and Sanjay Patsariya

9.1 INTRODUCTION

What is digital twin (DT)?

A digital twin (DT) can be defined as the digital replica of a real thing. The real thing can be shown in a virtual environment, like a computer-created world. This virtual environment (digital copy) is constantly updated with information from different sources [1].

DTs have rapidly evolved from theoretical concepts to practical tools that revolutionize how industries operate and innovate. Originally pioneered in manufacturing and later adopted across sectors such as healthcare, transportation, and construction, DTs are virtual images of physical systems, objects or processes etc. The DTs are synchronized in real time with their physical counterparts, leveraging data from IoT devices, sensors and other sources to offer insights, optimize operations, and simulate scenarios. Hence, DTs represent objects throughout their development and progression lifecycles.

In the manufacturing sector, DTs are used at every step of making a product. They help to optimize a product by simulating that product to predict how it's made before real models and machines are built [2].

However, a DT is more than just a digital copy of a physical system or object. It is a detailed representation that aims to precisely reflect the real-world system in real-time. It analyzes how the system works and uses advanced simulation, machine learning, and other emerging technologies to gain insights for better decision-making. The analytical and predictive capabilities of a DT distinguish it from being a mere physical replica.

Why DT?

DT leads the Industry 4.0 revolution using advanced data analytics and IoT connectivity. DT was a critical constituent of the Made in China 2025 plan. This plan aims to develop intelligent control systems, industrial software applications, fault diagnosis software, and sensor and communication

DOI: 10.1201/9781003498117-9

protocols. The goal is to create real-time connections, accurately identify and interact with manufacturing equipment and products, and implement intelligent control systems [3]. DT will contribute significantly for the economic growth. According to Market Research Future, the DT market is projected to reach $35 billion by 2025 [4]. A combined report from the Fraunhofer Institute and the industry group Bitkom estimated that Germany's digital transformation market could grow to €267 billion by 2025 due to Industry 4.0 [5].

DT with Internet of Things (IoT) can be used for proactive maintenance and fault detection in manufacturing and smart cities. IoT's rich data provides essential resources which assist in identifying anomalies in patient care, detect faults in various systems, and contribute to effective traffic management in smart cities [6,7,8]. Due to such reasons, DT has also been a focus of academia.

DT history

In the 1960s, NASA, the National Aeronautics and Space Administration, came up with the idea of a "twin." During the Apollo program in the 1970s, NASA built digital copies of space vehicles on Earth. DTs depict the condition of spacecraft equipment throughout the mission [9]. This DT was used to debug flight issues in real-time. NASA replica was the first application of the "twin" concept. This idea of "twin" worked well throughout the Apollo-13 mission. The Apollo-13 malfunctioned, and the NASA team on the Earth presumed that the conditions were the same as on Apollo-13. This helped them bring the spacecraft and astronauts back to Earth safely [10].

In the year 2005, Michael Grieves introduced the term "Digital Twin" during the product lifecycle management (PLM) course. He defined the "DT" as "virtual digital representation equivalent to physical products." Around 2010, NASA and John Vickers utilized the DT as a virtual model of a physical system [11,12].

In the year 2012, NASA successfully applied the DT concept to create a digital replica of a health management system and related fleet data of a flying machine. This twin leads to unmatched safety and reliability levels [11,13]. The use of DT in the manufacturing sector can be credited to the arrival of IoT. Specific DT frameworks was developed by manufacturing giants such as GE and Siemens. Such DT platforms help in real-time monitoring, inspection, and maintenance [14]. Figure 9.1 presents a brief timeline of the history of the DT development.

Defining DT

There are multiple DTenabling technologies such as sensing, modeling, data storage and management, communication, connection and data

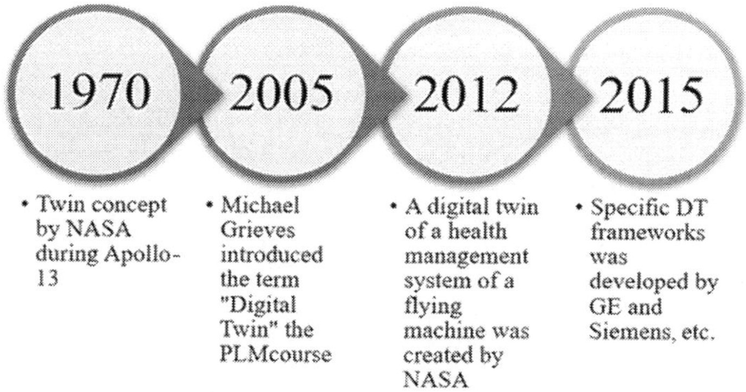

Figure 9.1 Digital twin development history.

analytics, and so on. Each one of them is also evolving. This results in the new application domains of DT technology; hence definition of DT is also evolving to accommodate new capabilities of these enabling technologies [15].

Michael Grieves defined the DT as the "virtual digital representation equivalent to physical products" in 2005 [16]. In 2012, NASA defined DT as "an integrated multi-physics, multi-scale, probabilistic simulation of an as-built vehicle or system that employs the best available physical models, sensor updates, fleet history, etc., to mirror the life of its corresponding flying twin" [11]. This definition of DT made aerospace field a significant research area of the DT. Later in 2015, the word "vehicle" was substituted by the word "product," to widen the definition of DT to include broader applications [17].

Different application areas defined DT differently. For example, for IoT; DT is a defined as the dynamic digital representation that captures the past and present behavior of a physical entity, enabling optimized business outcomes. For manufacturing industry, DT is defined as a virtual replica of a physical production system which enables system optimization, monitoring, diagnostics, and prognostics through the integration of AI, machine learning, software analytics, and vast amounts of system data [18]. For design engineering DT is defined as a comprehensive digital representation of all parts of a product development lifecycle by integrating physical, virtual data, and interaction between them [19].

There are various definitions of DT which are general in nature, that is, they do not cater to a specific industry or field. For example, DT is a virtual copy of a real-world system that gets regular updates on the real system's performance, maintenance, and health status throughout its physical system's lifetime [20]. Another general-purpose definition of DT is that a DT is a digital version of a real object or machine which makes use of integrated simulations and service details." [21,22].

Hence, it is perplexing to have aaccepted DT definition which serves the purpose of all application areas of DT. However, all definitions have revealed that the DT is characterized by three essential components of DT – (1) the physical entity, (2) virtual model, and (3) connection between them. The connection is a real-time one and used to exchange information between a virtual system and a physical system using a real-time data connection, in order to map the virtual system to the physical system.

Digital model versus digital shadow versus DT

Digital model

A digital model is a virtual static representation of a physical object, system, or process. It's a simplified, abstracted, and static representation, often used for design, simulation, analysis, and visualization purposes [23]. Digital models are typically created to study specific aspects of a system or process, and they might not be updated in real-time. Digital model is typically created using CAD software or other modeling tools. Digital model focuses primarily on the object's geometry, structure, and functional properties.

Examples of digital models include the static representations of physical entities, such as building blueprints or product designs. A key characteristic of digital models is the absence of automatic real-time data synchronization with their physical counterparts. This means that changes made to the physical object are not automatically mirrored in the digital model, and vice versa. The digital model remains a static representation, disconnected from the physical system's evolution.

Digital shadow

A digital shadow is a virtual dynamic depiction of a physical object, system, or process that is updated periodically [23], but this flow of information is one-way between the digital and physical object. Digital shadow collects data periodically from the physical entity to mirror its current state. If the physical object changes, the digital object changes too. But the digital object doesn't change the physical object.

Digital shadow serves as a digital replica of the physical asset, providing insights into its performance and conditions. It is a more detailed and accurate representation than a digital model, but still not as comprehensive as a DT. Digital shadows are often used for monitoring, analysis, and optimization.

Digital twin

An advanced digital representation that combines the static properties of a digital model with the dynamic data of a digital shadow. A DT is a virtual, real-time, and dynamic replica of a physical object, system, or process system that continuously exchanges data in both directions. This bidirectional data flow ensures that any changes made to the physical entity are reflected in the DT, and vice versa [23]. This DT requires information to flow to-and-fro between the real world and itself dynamically. The two-way steady real-time connection and transfer of data between the virtual and physical objects (systems) facilitate the optimization of ML and simulation algorithms. This further helps in analyzing and predicting the forthcoming state of the real system andoptimizing the same which results in accelerated decision-making [24].

It's a highly detailed and accurate depiction that mirrors the physical counterpart's behavior, performance, and state. A DT enables simulation, prediction, and behavior optimization of the physical entityby continuously learning and adapting based on real-world data [24]. A digital twin is used for a diverse range of applications such as predictive maintenance and optimization, product development, real-time analysis, real-time monitoring, simulation and testing, and process optimization, personalization and customization. Key differences between them are:

- **Level of detail**: Digital model (simplified) < Digital shadow (detailed) < Digital twin (highly detailed)
- **Update frequency**: Digital model (static) < Digital shadow (periodic) < Digital twin (real-time)
- **Purpose**: Digital model (analysis, prediction) < Digital shadow (monitoring, optimization) < Digital twin (real-time monitoring, prediction, personalization)

The Figure 9.2 illustrates the difference between digital model, digital shadow and DT.

In essence, digital models are simplified representations such as a blueprint, digital shadows are real-time snapshot with periodic updates, and DTs are real-time, dynamic replicas that mirror their physical counterparts. A DT is a living, evolving depiction capable of predicting future states.

DT in healthcare

The DT concept is revolutionizing the field of medicine, particularly in precision medicine, cancer care, individualized training, and personal well-being. In healthcare, DT applications are transforming: (1) hospital

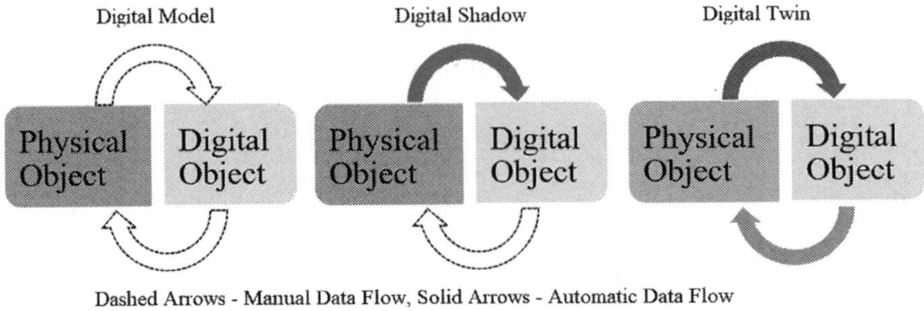

Figure 9.2 Difference between digital model, digital shadow, and digital twin.

management and facility design, (2) workflow development and decision-making, and (3) individualized therapy and personalized patient care, treatment planning, and post-treatment care [22,24]. DTs can be tailored to a person's unique state of wellness or illness, enabling personalized diagnosis, treatment planning, care, and survivorship.

The buddinguse-cases of DTs in healthcare are vast. These use-cases promises to redefine the way we approach patient care, disease management, and healthcare delivery. DTs can be deployed in silico clinical trials, medical device development, drug discovery, care coordination, and surgical planning. To recognize the bursting potential of DTs, comprehensive patient data, or "deep digital phenotypes," is essential for creating truly individualized models since each individual is unique and requires a personalized approach.

By creating highly detailed and dynamic digital counterparts, healthcare providers can gain unprecedented insights into complex biological systems, optimize treatment plans, and improve patient outcomes [25].

9.2 EMERGING TECHNOLOGIES IN DTS

Artificial intelligence (AI)

In addition to DTs, another pivotal technology that holds immense potential for escalating the performance of manufacturing systems and Industry 4.0 is AI. AI is the linchpin that transforms a static digital model into a dynamic, predictive DT. It imbues the DT with intelligence, enabling it to learn, adapt, and make decisions [26]. As artificial intelligence (AI) technology advances and becomes more cost-effective, it can be integrated into production systems to assist manufacturers with intricate decision-making and enhance business processes. In particular, ML is a sub-domain of AI that let computers learn from data and make decisions on their own.

Hence, AI and its sub-domainsplay key roles in enhancing DTs. AI-powered DTs can learn from data, dynamically adapt their behavior, and predict outcomes with greater accuracy. These technologies can optimize energy usage in buildings, predict failures in industrial machinery, and even simulate patient responses to medical treatments based on individual health data.

Such AI technologies are listed below with examples:

- **Machine learning:** Develops predictive models to anticipate system behavior and optimize performance. Models are developed via learning or training process. The learning process requires large volume of data of both structured and unstructured nature. These datasets can be obtained from a business or a factory within a timeframe [26]. Machine learning can further be supervised learning, unsupervised learning and reinforcement learning. An example of machine learning task is predicting equipment failures in manufacturing using historical maintenance data.
- **Deep learning:** Deep learning is revolutionizing the capabilities of DTs, transforming them from static representations into dynamic, intelligent entities. Deep learning enables DTs to recognize complex pattern for advanced analytics and decision-making. Using deep neural networks visual recognition of parts can be done in DT to enable the robotic manipulation of complex parts [27]. An example of this is identifying anomalies in sensor data to detect potential issues in infrastructure. Key Roles of deep learning in DTs include:

  1. Enhanced predictive modeling
  2. Improved data analysis
  3. Real-time optimization
  4. Virtual sensing
  5. DT creation

- **Natural language processing (NLP):** NLP is a key component in the evolution of DTs. It facilitates human–machine interaction and knowledge extraction from textual data. NLP enables them to understand, interpret, and respond to human language. This integration enhances the interaction between humans and DTs, making them more accessible and effective. Lately, text mining techniques have made significant advancements, aiding in the extraction of valuable intuitions from textual data [28].

Leading-edge NLP models can be built on the transformer architecture. Such architecture is symbolized by an encoder-decoder structure [29]. These models can be sued for various purposes in DTs, for example, generating reports and insights from sensor data using natural language.

Internet of Things (IoT) and edge computing

The proliferation of IoT sensors embedded in physical assets facilitates continuous data collection, which is crucial for real-time updates of DTs. The "Internet of Things" (IoT) refers to the devices connected to the internet. It is an attempt to make "things" intelligent and the making them capable of interacting and collecting information from their environment. The "things" in IoT may be computing devices, mechanical machine, digital machines, objects, animals or people that have unique identifiers (UIDs). Such things can transfer data over a network without requiring human-to-human or human-to-computer interaction and this is what makes them intelligent.

The term "Internet of Thins" was first coined by Kevin Ashton in the late 1990s [30]. His idea was to interconnect all things with the aim to track and monitor everything we do which is an essential requirement of smarter world. Thebasic idea of inter-connecting all devices lets developers track and monitor what we do. It makes the world smarter. Figure 9.3 depicts this idea of IoT.

Figure 9.3 Idea of IoT for a smart world.

IoT devices proliferation is witnessing a sizeable growth. There were about 17 billion IoT devices in 2018 [31]. However, by the year 2025, it is predicted that about 75 billion devices will be in use making IoT industry worth over $5 trillion [32]. The IoT adds data that can be used by DTs employed in manufacturing, health care, automotive, urban management and other industries.

Edge computing processes data closer to the source, minimizing latency and facilitating quicker real-time analysis and decision-making within DTs. The integration of IoT and edge computing is mostly valuable in industries requiring instant responses, such as autonomous vehicles and smart grids. For instance, analyzing sensor data on-site to trigger immediate actions, such as adjusting equipment settings.

IIoT

IIoT evolved from IoT, focusing on industrial applications. While IoT definitions vary, IIoT specifically targets industrial productivity improvements. Similar to IoT, IIoT significantly enhances manufacturing processes. By connecting devices and empowering real-time data analysis, IIoT optimizes performance, boosts production, reduces costs, and minimizes waste [33].

Advancements in big data, cloud computing, AI, and ML have enabled the processing of vast amounts of production data. This has fueled the growth of the Industrial Internet of Things (IIoT), specifically tailored for industrial applications.

Research has explored using side channels like acoustic and magnetic emissions to monitor legacy manufacturing equipment without sensors. This approach, combined with digitalization advancements, has led to the development of smart manufacturing systems. A case study focused on building a DT for Fused-Deposition Modeling (FDM) using IoT sensors demonstrates the ability to collect and analyze data streams, such as acoustic, power, and magnetic output, to accurately detect anomalies [34].

5G connectivity

The rollout of 5G networks significantly enhances the capabilities of DTs. 5G technology can improve mobile broadband, machine communication, and ensure reliable, low latency data transmission. The 5G technology based on the ultrareliable low latency communication (URLLC), enhanced mobile broadband (eMBB) and massive machine type communication (mMTC) achieves high speed, wide coverage and low latency communication. This technology supports real-time streaming of vast amounts of data from IoT devices to DTs, facilitating seamless interactions and enhancing responsiveness. Industries like healthcare and manufacturing can benefit from enhanced connectivity for remote monitoring and control [35].

Augmented reality (AR) and virtual reality (VR)

Augmented reality (AR) and virtual reality (VR) technologies enrich user interfaces by overlaying DT data onto the physical environment or providing immersive virtual environments for simulation and training. These technologies (AR and VR) enhance decision-making processes by providing intuitive visualizations and interactive experiences. For instance, AR can guide maintenance technicians through complex procedures using real-time data overlays.

The growth of AR and VR in DT are being accelerated by the developments in Industry 4.0, IoT and IIoT [36]. The increasing complexity of devices due to IoT has led to the adoption of DTs for training purposes. By creating virtual representations of these devices, manufacturers can develop interactive training modules. These DTs, when integrated with AR or VR, allow users to explore 3D models, access real-time status data, and follow step-by-step instructions, effectively simulating on-the-job training scenarios [36].

VR aims to replace the way we see the world with a computer-generated world [37]. AR, on the other hand, adds to our experience of the real world [38]. It lets us interact with physical objects through the Internet of Things (IoT) and gives us more information about them [36].

VR replaces the real world with a simulated environment [37], while AR enhances the real world with digital elements [38]. AR facilitates communication with physical objects through IoT integration and provides supplementary context-aware data about the physical objects [39]. Using AR, the technicians can see how to fix the DT. They can do this interactively.

A novel concept termed "eGastronomic things," essentially DTs of food-related devices and processes was proposed by [36]. Similar to the Internet of Things (IoT), these digital replicas are constructed by deploying IoT sensors to collect data from physical gastronomic equipment. To illustrate the concept, the authors use an ice cream machine, demonstrating how its DT can be leveraged to optimize performance through real-time monitoring and maintenance.

Within the domain of DT, the AR and VR can facilitate:

1. **Immersive visualization:** Immersive visualization meanscreating interactive 3D environments for system inspection and analysis. For example, overlaying digital information on real-world equipment for maintenance guidance.

2. **Remote collaboration:** AR/VR enables real-time collaboration between experts in different locations. For example, virtual inspections and repairs on remote equipment can be conducted using AR/VR.
3. **Training and simulation:** AR/VRprovide realistic training scenarios for operators and technicians. For example, equipment failures can be simulated with the aid of AR and VR in a virtual environment for training purposes.
4. **Increased efficiency:** Tasks can be performed more quickly and accurately with the aid of AR and VR.
5. **Enhanced decision-making:** Immersive experiences can lead to better decision-making by providing deeper insights.

Blockchain

The blockchain has numerous potential applications in DTs. The blockchain is decentralized system records data across multiple computers in a series of interconnected blocks. Each block is secured with a unique cryptographic hash, containing details such as timestamp and transaction information. This ensures data integrity and transparency. The concept of block chain is shown in Figure 9.4.

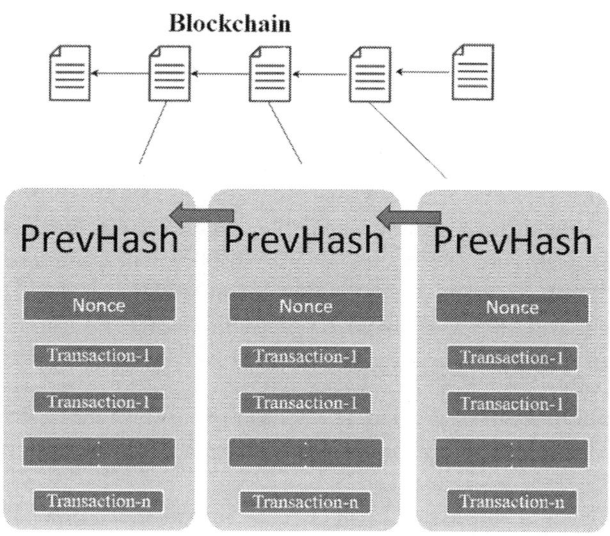

Figure 9.4 Block chain in digital twin.

Blockchain technology is beneficial to create DTs for complex supply chains, such as those in the aircraft industry. Research, like that in [7], has explored using blockchain to secure DTs in additive manufacturing. By integrating blockchain with a DT, the authors proposed a novel approach to monitor and control aerospace manufacturing processes, leveraging blockchain's security and transparency benefits.

Blockchain technology has progressed beyond its initial application and has got is application in latest domains such as IoT, IIoT, DTs, and so on. Blockchain technology offers significant advantages when combined with DTs, enhancing data security, transparency, and trust. Here are some key potential uses:

Data integrity and security:

- **Data integrity through immutable records:**Blockchain ensures that data stored within the DT is tamper-proof and immutable, providing a high level of security.
- **Data provenance:** Tracks the origin and history of data, enhancing trust and accountability.
- **Protection against data manipulation:** Prevents unauthorized modification of data, safeguarding the integrity of the DT.

9.3 DT AND HEALTHCARE INDUSTRY

DTs are virtual depictions of physical objects, systems, or processes that can be used to simulate, predict, and optimize their behavior. DTs can change how we do patient care, medical research, and public health. DTs empower practitioners to advise patients on disease prevention and preparedness [40].

DTs are precise virtual replicas of real-world entities. Health DTs are virtual representations of patients, constructed from genetic, multimodal, and real-time health data. Leveraging healthcare data, these models can accurately simulate patient conditions. By identifying early disease indicators, DTs empower individuals to proactively manage their health, including detecting potential cancer relapses. Additionally, they can analyze lifestyle patterns to warn users of unhealthy behaviors [41]. They drive precision medicine by offering personalized and dynamic health profiles. These virtual models enable healthcare providers to simulate treatments, predict disease progression, and deliver tailored interventions based on individual patient characteristics.

Proactive patient care, enhanced by DTs, improves quality of life. AI and ML-powered DTs leverage real-time data from cloud platforms to accurately predict health outcomes [42]. DTs offer an interactive and user-friendly healthcare experience. Patients actively participate in their health journey, fostering healthier lifestyles. By processing medical data, DTs enhance transparency and trust between patients and physicians, leading to improved overall healthcare experiences.

9.4 EMERGING TECHNOLOGIES IN HEALTHCARE DTS

The integration of DT technology with other advanced technologies, like AI and IoTenriches its competences. AI analytics can enhance the insights derived from DTs by processing large datasets to identify patterns and outcomes that inform clinical decisions [43]. Furthermore, IoT devices contribute to the real-time data streams necessary for maintaining accurate DTs [40].

This section walks through the application of emerging technologies in the creation and utilization of DTs within the healthcare sector. Here are some emerging technologies in DTs with a focus on healthcare:

- Artificial intelligence
- Internet of Things (IoT)
- Augmented reality (AR) and virtual reality (VR)
- Blockchain

Artificial intelligence (AI)

Machine learning and AI are essential for DTs in healthcare. They optimize model development, enable data-driven simulations, and enhance predictive capabilities for personalized treatments and risk identification

AI-powered DTs in healthcare leverage advanced analytics and real-time monitoring of vast health datasets from electronic health records and wearables. This integration optimizes DT creation and updates, ensuring they accurately reflect patient conditions or medical system dynamics.

The convergence of AI and DT technology is poised to revolutionize healthcare. By enabling deeper insights into patient health, AI will refine DTs for personalized medicine and optimize operational efficiency. This synergy will drive advancements in predictive healthcare, better diagnosis and treatment planning, ultimately improving patient outcomes.

AI can be used for:

1. **Real-time patient monitoring**
2. **Predictive analytics**
3. **Genomic data analysis**
4. **Precision medicine**
5. **Personalized medicine and treatment plans**
6. **Drug response prediction**
7. **Drug discovery**
8. **Simulation and surgical planning**

Real-time patient monitoring

AI-powered DTs enable continuous monitoring of patient health data, facilitating proactive disease management. By analyzing data in real-time, these digital representations offer personalized treatment insights based on the patient's current condition. This approach is especially valuable for chronic diseases where timely interventions are critical for improved outcomes.

Predictive analytics

AI-powered DTs excel at early disease detection and risk prediction through advanced data analysis. By leveraging comprehensive patient data, these models forecast potential complications and recommend preventive actions. This predictive approach optimizes resource allocation and enables timely disease management [33]. For example, predictive analytics can be used for predicting patient readmissions based on electronic health record data and lifestyle factors.

Genomic data analysis

By integrating genetic data, DTs enable in-depth genomic analysis, identifying genetic markers and disease susceptibilities. AI algorithms can analyze vast amounts of genomic data to recognize genetic markers linked with diseases and treatment responses. This information simplifies the development of personalized treatment plans based on individual genetic profiles.

Precision medicine

The convergence of AI and DT technology creates significant implications for precision medicine. For example, through the use of AI-driven insights derived from DTs, clinicians can make more informed treatment decisions that are customized to patients' needs, thus enabling more effective interventions. Additionally, these technologies facilitate the identification of optimal treatment pathways by simulating various scenarios and outcomes based on individual patient data, ultimately leading to improved patient health and reduced healthcare costs [44].

Personalized medicine and treatment plans

AI and DTs collaborate to create highly personalized treatment plans. By analyzing individual genetic, lifestyle, and environmental data, AI recommends optimal interventions. By combining complex AI models with diverse genetic and non-genetic data, precision medicine can leverage data-driven insights to inform decision-making. This requires an AI and

DT-based system capable of real-time data capture, analysis, and simulation to support accurate clinical judgments [45]. This tailored approach boosts treatment effectiveness, minimizes side effects, and enhances overall patient well-being. Utilizing AI, tailored treatment plans can be created based on individual patient data. For example, creating personalized drug regimens based on genetic makeup and disease biomarkers.

Drug response prediction

Utilizing artificial intelligence (AI) in conjunction with DTs has shown promising results in predicting patient responses to treatments. For example, the DT model has been employed to forecast treatment response to neoadjuvant therapy in patients with triple-negative breast cancer, where it successfully integrated quantitative MRI data with mathematical modeling. This enabled a more tailored approach to therapy, optimizing treatment outcomes based on individual patient characteristics [46].

Drug discovery

The integration of artificial intelligence (AI) and DT technology holds significant promise for transforming drug discovery processes. DTs are virtual representations of physical systems that can simulate, analyze, and predict outcomes, allowing researchers to explore various scenarios without the need for extensive physical trials. By utilizing AI algorithms within these DTs, pharmacologists can develop more precise models that enhance the understanding of disease mechanisms and drug interactions. An example may be identifying potential drug candidates by simulating their interactions with target proteins.

Simulation and surgical planning

The integration of artificial intelligence (AI) with DT technology is making significant strides in surgical planning and simulation. DTs serve as high-precision virtual replicas of physical systems, enabling accurate modeling of surgical environments and patient-specific anatomical features [47]. AI enhances these simulations by allowing for more sophisticated analyses and predictions of surgical outcomes, which can optimize preoperative planning.

DT technology can be utilized to create realistic surgical simulations, aiding in various aspects of surgical procedures. By integrating mixed reality (MR) and 5G cloud computing, healthcare professionals can visualize and interact with highly detailed virtual models, which mimic real anatomical structures. This not only enhances training for surgical teams but also helps in refining surgical techniques tailored specifically to individual patient needs

AI-driven DTs enable realistic surgical simulations for planning and training. By leveraging 3D modeling of patient anatomies, healthcare providers can:

- Simulate surgical procedures in a virtual environment
- Anticipate and overcome challenges before entering the operating room
- Refine techniques through precise and repeated practice

This innovative approach leads to:

- Improved surgical outcomes
- Reduced operation times
- Enhanced patient safety during complex procedures

Internet of Things (IoT)

Technological advancements have spurred innovation across sectors like agriculture, manufacturing, education, and healthcare. The IoT is a prime example of this progress, introducing new tools and methods to revolutionize industries such as healthcare and DT.

The IoT is revolutionizing the healthcare sector through its integration with DT technology. DTs create virtual depictions of physical entities, permitting for real-time monitoring and management of healthcare systems and patient care. The integration of IoT and DT enhances the capability to process vast amounts of data from medical devices and sensors, facilitating improved healthcare delivery and operational efficiency [48,49].

Real-time patient monitoring and decision-making

IoT along with sensor technology can be used to gather data from patients' wearables and medical devices, creating a more comprehensive DT. IoT devices such as smartwatches and fitness trackers, are essential for collecting real-time health data that fuels DT models. By tracking vital signs and physical activity, these wearables enable continuous monitoring and analysis of patient health.

IoT-enabled DTs facilitate continuous patient monitoring and tracking of patient vital signs by collecting data from varied sources, such as wearable devices and medical instruments. This real-time data lets healthcare professionals to make well-versedchoices swiftly. By leveraging these technologies, healthcare providers can anticipate health issues and condition changes, enabling proactive intervention [40,50]. The continuous monitoring enables real-time patient data collection, in-depth health analysis and proactive care and intervention.

Remote patient monitoring

DTs, enriched by IoT data, facilitate predictive analytics, allowing for the anticipation of health crises and the optimization of care plans. This proactive approach to healthcare empowers patients to manage their conditions effectively while reducing the burden on healthcare systems. DT and IoT enables remote care and management of chronic diseases. For example, monitoring patients with diabetes or heart failure through connected devices.

Personalization of healthcare services

The combination of IoT and DT technology allows for the personalization of healthcare services. By simulating individual patient profiles, practitioners can tailor treatment plans that are uniquely suited to each patient's needs and conditions. This individualized approach ultimately leads to improved treatment outcomes [51].

Wearable devices

The integration of wearable devices with theIoT has significantly transformed healthcare. Expanding and combining wearable technology with IoT to monitor both physical and mental health will accelerate the development of more comprehensive and innovative DTs in healthcare [52, 53].

In the future, we may use wearable technology to study changes in the muscles and bones of people who have trouble moving or are paralyzed. Wearable devices gather real-time health data such as data on vital signs, physical activity, and environmental exposures, enabling constant patient monitoring. This allows for timely interventions based on vital signs and health metrics. Future wearables will be smaller, more comfortable, and capable of transmitting data directly to cloud-based DTs.

The combination of wearable devices and DTs not only enhances patient care but also reduces the need for in-person visits. Implantable Devices provides continuous monitoring of internal physiological parameters. By employing real-time datafrom wearable and implantable devices and integrating this data with electronic health records to create a comprehensive patient profile [54]. Applying data analytics on this data, healthcare professionals can adjust treatments and prescriptions based on individual responses, leading to improved health outcomes [55, 56]. Furthermore, this approach supports proactive healthcare measures, focusing on prevention rather than reaction, thereby improving quality of life for patients.

Augmented reality (AR) and virtual reality (VR)

DT technology is emerging as a pivotal component in the integration of AR and VR within healthcare. By creating a digital replica of physical entities, practitioners can analyze real-time data and simulate procedures in a controlled environment. The integration of DT and AR/VR fosters improved decision-making and personalized patient care. [57].

The prominent use-cases of VR/AR in DT are:

1. **Medical education and training**
2. **Enhancing patient understanding through immersive experiences**
3. **Surgical planning and simulation**
4. **Patient education and engagement**

Medical education and training

The combination of AR/VR and DTs facilitates advanced training methods for healthcare staff. For instance, immersive VR, when used with DTs, enables healthcare staff to train in a realistic and interactive environment that mimics real-life situations they might face in clinical practice. This improves the learning experience for healthcare professionals. An example would be providing immersive training scenarios for medical students and residents. Another example includes the use of immersive VR for onboarding medical personnel and staff, fostering engagement and reducing training time compared to traditional methods. Participants often report a higher preference for VR methods over low-fidelity training modalities.

Enhancing patient understanding through immersive experiences

Utilizing AR and VR in conjunction with DTs can enhance patient comprehension by offering realistic simulations of medical procedures or health conditions. Patients can visually explore their anatomy, simulate the effects of treatment options, and understand potential outcomes in a safe environment, thus improving their confidence and engagement [58].

Surgical planning and simulation

Utilizing DTs alongside AR/VR technology enhances surgical training by allowing for hands-on practice in a risk-free environment. This method can lead to improved preparation for surgeries, resulting in better patient outcomes and minimized procedural complications overall.

The integration of DT technology with AR and VR provides immersive simulation environments for surgical planning. By employing VR, surgeons can navigate through 3D simulations of the anatomy and surgical procedures, which can reduce cognitive load and enhance understanding of complex scenarios. Enhancing surgical precision and reducing complications through virtual practice. For example, creating realistic simulations of complex surgical procedures.

While the integration of DTs with AR/VR offers transformative opportunities for surgical simulations, challenges such as high operational costs and the necessity for skilled personnel to manage and implement these technologies remain.

Patient education and engagement

Augmented reality (AR) and virtual reality (VR) have become instrumental in transforming patient education and engagement within the healthcare sector. These technologies facilitate immersive and interactive experiences that cater to diverse learning styles, leading to better understanding and retention of information among patients. An as example, consider using AR to visualize complex medical information.

By simulating real-time patient data, DTs allow for tailored educational experiences that empower patients to engage more actively in their treatment processes [59]. This holistic approach increases patient understanding of their health conditions and enhances their decision-making abilities regarding treatment options. Healthcare providers are increasingly developing AR and VR-based educational programs to provide patients with essential information about their health. These programs can include guided tours of anatomical structures, visual explanations of treatment procedures, and interactive discussions with avatars in the metaverse, all designed to promote active learning and retention [60].

Blockchain

Blockchain can be used to secure and manage the data used to create DTs. The Blockchain within the field of healthcare DT can be used for ensuring patient privacy and data integrity, supply chain movement of medical products and better collaboration among healthcare professionals.

Data security and privacy

By integrating blockchain technology, the DTs can ensure the integrity, security, and traceability of patient data, which is vital for accurate diagnoses and effective treatment plans. Blockchain's decentralized nature enhances data security, addressing concerns regarding unauthorized access and data tampering [61,62]. Protecting patient data through secure and immutable record-keeping. For example, blockchain can ensure the confidentiality of electronic health records.

Supply chain transparency

Blokchain can be deployed to track the movement of medical products to prevent counterfeits and ensure quality. For example, verifying the authenticity of medications and medical devices.

Collaboration and resource management through interoperability

Utilizing blockchain in DT fosters collaboration among healthcare professionals by providing a secure platform for information sharing. This collaborative approach is essential during crises, such as pandemics, where resource management becomes critical. Blockchain enables the effective distribution and utilization of medical resources like ventilators and personnel by linking dynamic DTs of both patients and healthcare assets to enhance pandemic response [63]. Blockchain facilitates seamless data exchange between healthcare providers. For example, secure sharing of patient information across different healthcare systems.

Addressing cybersecurity challenges

The implementation of blockchain technology alongside DTs significantly mitigates cybersecurity risks inherent in healthcare systems. By securing patient data through blockchain's immutable ledger, healthcare providers can safeguard sensitive information from cyberattacks and data breaches. This dual approach ensures that patient privacy is prioritized while maintaining the operational efficiency of health services [62].

9.5 APPLICATIONS OF DTS IN HEALTHCARE

DT technology has been increasingly adopted within the healthcare industry due to its ability to create virtual replicas of physical medical assets or processes. In medicine, the idea of personalized treatment is becoming more popular. This is especially true in areas like precision medicine, cancer care, personalized training, and personal well-being [20].

DTs have broad applications in healthcare, spanning from hospital administration and design to personalized patient care. They can be tailored for both wellness and illness management, supporting personalized diagnosis, treatment plans, and post-treatment care. Potential applications extend to in silico clinical trials, medical device development, drug discovery, care coordination, and surgical planning. Creating patient-specific DTs requires comprehensive data collection to capture unique individual characteristics.

This DT approach has the potential to significantly enhance patient outcomes, streamline healthcare procedures, and optimize the management of medical equipment [64]. By bridging the gap between the physical and digital realms, DTs can facilitate advanced monitoring and diagnostic capabilities, ultimately improving the effectiveness of treatment strategies [64,65].

One prominent application of DTs is in the management of chronic diseases such as diabetes, where they can be utilized for personalized treatment plans and monitoring patient health in real time [66]. Furthermore, DTs enable the development of model-based systems for healthcare applications, including intelligent management of medical equipment [67]. Such implementations can lead to influential advancements in understanding disease progression and enhancing patient-specific interventions [66]. DTs can be used to simulate clinical trials, reducing the need for animal testing and human subjects.

The key applications of DTs in health care are:

1. **Patient monitoring and management**
2. **Personalized medicine and treatment**
3. **Drug discovery and development**
4. **Chronic disease management**
5. **Accelerating clinical trials**
6. **Supporting regulatory compliance**
7. **Surgical planning and simulation**

Patient monitoring and management

DT technology has been increasingly applied in healthcare to develop innovative solutions for patient monitoring. By creating a virtual representation of patients, healthcare providers can simulate real-time data related to health metrics, which leads to more effective monitoring strategies. Healthcare providers such as doctors can now get more information about their patients' health than ever before. They can collect data from many sources, like electronic health records, wearable devices, and medical imaging. This helps them understand the patient's condition better and give them the best possible care. This application not only enhances the ability to track vital signs but also allows for precise adjustments in treatment plans when necessary, such as providing early warnings [68,69].

Personalized medicine and treatment

DTs are instrumental in advancing personalized medicine, where treatment approaches are customized to fit the unique characteristics of individual patients. This technology allows for the simulation of potential treatment outcomes based on a patient's virtual representation, thereby aiding in the prediction of responses to treatments. Tailoring treatment plans based on individual patient responses and predicting treatment outcomes. The personalized strategies derived from DTs lead to improved outcomes and the optimization of therapeutic processes [70].

DTs in drug discovery and development

DTs are revolutionizing the pharmaceutical industry by offering unprecedented opportunities to accelerate drug discovery, development, and commercialization. By creating virtual representations of patients, drugs, and biological systems, researchers can simulate and predict drug behavior, optimize clinical trials, and improve patient outcomes. This innovative approach helps in understanding how specific drugs affect biological systems and facilitates more efficient experimentation by mimicking real-life scenarios during drug discovery [71].

The integration of DTs into drug discovery processes allows researchers to create detailed simulations of molecular interactions, streamlining the identification of optimal drug candidates. This methodology enables the investigation of how different molecular properties impact clinical outcomes [46].

Chronic disease management

The concept of DTs has gained considerable traction in the management of chronic diseases, as it allows for highly personalized healthcare solutions. This technology creates virtual representations of patients, enabling healthcare providers to monitor and manage various chronic conditions more effectively.

Accelerating clinical trials

DTs play a crucial role in enhancing the efficiency and effectiveness of clinical trials. They can represent individual patients, which aids in personalizing treatment plans, monitoring patient responses, and predicting outcomes based on simulated scenario [58]. DTs optimize clinical trials by identifying ideal patient populations, simulating various trial designs, tracking patient responses in real-time, and even conducting virtual trials before human studies.

Supporting regulatory compliance

The use of DTs in drug development also aligns with regulatory requirements by providing a robust framework for data collection and analysis. This compliance is vital for ensuring that drug development meets safety and efficacy standards set by governing bodies [71].

Surgical planning and simulation

- **Integration of DT technology in surgery:** DT technology is increasingly being integrated into surgical planning and simulation to create a virtual representation of a patient's anatomy, which allows for personalized surgical procedures. This technology combines real-time data from various sources, enabling surgeons to visualize complex anatomical structures before operating. Such immersive simulations can improve the precision of surgical interventions, ultimately leading to better patient outcomes and reduced complications [41,72].
- **Enhancing telemedical simulations:** A digital-twin-enabled Internet of Medical Things (IoMT) system provides significant advancements in telemedical simulations for surgical procedures. By employing mixed reality and 5G cloud computing, this approach allows for detailed and interactive modeling of surgical environments, which can enhance the training for medical professionals and improve the overall quality of surgical education. This facilitates remote collaborative approaches, enabling surgeons to engage in real-time consultations and simulations regardless of geographical limitations [41, 72].
- **Optimizing trauma surgery:** In trauma cases, DTs assist in optimizing surgical techniques and postoperative management through tailored simulations. By modeling cases such as tibial plateau fractures, DTs allow surgeons to visualize the injury comprehensively and strategize their approach effectively. This specific focus on patient pathology and condition significantly enhances the overall surgical experience [72].
- **Improving surgical training and education:** The implementation of DT technology in surgical simulators has revolutionized medical training. By providing high-fidelity simulations that replicate real-life surgical challenges, trainees can practice and hone their skills in a risk-free environment. This method of education not only prepares future surgeons for a variety of scenarios but also builds their confidence before they operate on live patients [70].

9.6 CONCLUSION

The evolution of DT technology signifies a transformative shift in the manufacturing sector, particularly as it aligns with the principles of Industry 4.0. The evolution of DTs is fueled by advancements in simulation techniques, data integration, and user interface technologies. With the evolution of such technologies, DTs will play an increasingly vital role in optimizing operations, predicting outcomes, and fostering innovation across diverse sectors. Leveraging AI, IoT, and blockchain, organizations can achieve new breakthroughs, streamline operations, and outpace competitors. DTs facilitate enhanced monitoring, predictive maintenance, and optimization of manufacturing processes, which contribute significantly to productivity and operational efficiency.

The healthcare industry stands to benefit immensely from the integration of emerging technologies into DT development. In healthcare, DT applications have seen promising growth, particularly in personalized care and training simulations. The adoption of immersive virtual reality combined with DTs has proven to be effective for clinical on boarding and training, leading to a more efficient workforce with high rates of acceptability. Moreover, the integration of these technologies allows for real-time monitoring and management of health conditions, showcasing their immense potential for improving patient outcomes.

Thus, the confluence of DT technology with manufacturing, Industry 4.0 principles, and healthcare applications not only enhances operational performance but also paves the way for innovative solutions that cater to the dynamic requirements of various sectors. This ongoing technological advancement solidifies the role of DTs as a cornerstone for future healthcare delivery.

REFERENCES

1. Fuller, A., Fan, Z., Day, C., & Barlow, C. (2019). DT: Enabling technology, challenges and open research. *IEEE Access*, 8, 108952–108971.
2. Negri, E., Fumagalli, L., & Macchi, M. (2017). A review of the roles of digital twin in CPS-based production systems. *ProcediaManuf*, 11, 9.
3. State Council of China. (2015). Made in China 2025, available at: www.gov.cn
4. Future, M. R. (2019). DT market is estimated to grow at a CAGR of 42.54% from 2018–2025, available at: www.marketresearchfuture.com/press-release/digital-twin-market
5. Lee, J., Bagheri, B., & Kao, H.-A. (2015). A cyber-physical systems architecture for Industry 4.0-based manufacturing systems. *Manufacturing Letters*, 3, 18–23.
6. Bilberg, A., & Malik, A. A. (2019, April). Digital twin driven human–robot collaborative assembly. *CIRP Annals*, 68(1), 499–502.
7. Mandolla, C., Petruzzelli, A. M., Percoco, G., & Urbinati, A. (2019, August). Building a digital twin for additive manufacturing through the exploitation of blockchain: A case analysis of the aircraft industry. *Computers in Industry*, 109, 134–152.
8. Mohammadi, N., & Taylor, J. E. (2017, November). Smart city digital twins. In *2017 IEEE Symposium Series on Computational Intelligence (SSCI), Honolulu, HI* (pp. 1–5). IEEE.

9. Rosen, R., Von Wichert, G., Lo, G., & Bettenhausen, K. D. (2015). About the importance of autonomy and DTs for the future of manufacturing. *IFAC-Papersonline*, 48, 567–572.
10. Douthwaite, J. A. et al. (2021). A modular digital twinning framework for safety assurance of collaborative robotics. *Frontier Robot AI*, 8, 758099.
11. Glaessgen, E., & Stargel, D. (2012, April 23–26). The DT paradigm for future NASA and U.S. Air Force vehicles. In *AIAA/ASME/ASCE/AHS/ASC Structures, Structural Dynamics and Materials Conference AIAA/ASME/AHS Adaptive Structures Conference AIAA, Honolulu.*
12. Piascik, B. et al. (2010). *Materials, structures, mechanical systems, andmanufacturing roadmap – Technology Area 12, NASA, draftedn.*
13. Tuegel, E. J., Ingraffea, A. R., Eason, T. G., & Spottswood, S. M. (2011a). Reengineering aircraft structural life prediction using a DT. *International Journal of Aerospace Engineering*, 2011, 14.
14. ElianeFourgeau, E. G., Adli, H., Fernandes, C., & Hagege, M. (2016). System engineering Workbench for multi-views systems methodology with 3d experience platform. The aircraft radar use case. *Complex Systems Design and Management Asia*, 426, 269–270.
15. Qi, Q., Tao, F., Hu, T., Anwer, N., Liu, A., Wei, Y., Wang, L., & Nee, A. (2021). Enabling technologies and tools for DT. *Journal of Manufacturing Systems*, 58, pp. 3–21.
16. Grieves, M., & Vickers, J. (2017). DT: Mitigating unpredictable, undesirable emergent behaviro in complex systems. In F. J. K. E. Al (Ed.), *Transdisciplinary Perspectives on Complex Systems*. Springer International Publishing.
17. Rıos, J., Hernandez, J. C., Oliva, M., & Mas, F. (2015). Product avatar as digital counterpart of a physical individual product: Literature review and implications in an aircraft. *Advances in Transdisciplinary Engineering*, 2, 657–666.
18. Liu, Z., Meyendorf, N., & Mrad, N. (2018). The role of data fusion in predictive maintenance using DT. In D. E. Chimenti & L. J. Bond (Eds), *44th Annual Review of Progress in Quantitative Nondestructive Evaluation, AmerInst Physics* (Vol. 37). Melville.
19. Tao, F., Sui, F., Liu, A., Qi, Q., Zhang, M., Song, B., Guo, Z., Lu, S. C.-Y., & Nee, A. (2019). DT-driven product design framework. *International Journal of Production Research*, 57, 3935–3953.
20. Madni, A. M., Madni, C. C., & Lucero, S. (2019). Leveraging DT technology in model-based systems engineering. *System*, 7, p. 7.
21. Vrabic, R., Erkoyuncu, J. A., Butala, P., & Roy, R. (2018). DTs: Understanding the added value of integrated models for through-life engineering services. *Procedia Manufacturing*, 16, 139–146.
22. Bjornsson, B. et al. (2019). Digital twins to personalize medicine. *Genome Medicine*, 12, 4.
23. Paredis, R., Gomes, C., & Vangheluwe, H. (2021). Towards a family of digital model/shadow/twin workflows and architectures. In *International Conference on Innovative Intelligent Industrial Production and Logistics.*
24. Rasheed, A., San, O., & Kvamsdal, T. (2020). Digital twin: Values, challenges and enablers from a modeling perspective. *IEEE Access*, 8, 21980–22012.

25. Zhang, P., & KamelBoulos, M. N. (2023). Generative AI in medicine and healthcare: Promises, opportunities and challenges. *Future Internet*, 15(9), 286.
26. Ahuett-Garzaa, H., & Kurfess, T. (2018). A brief discussion on the trends of habilitating technologies for Industry 4.0 and smart manufacturing. *Manufacturing Letters*, 15 (Part B), 60–63. doi:10.1016/j.mfglet.2018.02.011.
27. Aivaliotis, P., Zampetis, A., Michalos, G., & Makris, S. (2017, June 27–30). A machine learning approach for visual recognition of complex parts in robotic manipulation. In *27th International Conference on Flexible Automation and Intelligent Manufacturing (FAIM2017), Modena, Italy*, Vol. 11, pp. 423–430.
28. Vaswani, A., Shazeer, N., Parmar, N., Uszkoreit, J., Jones, L., Gomez, A. N., Kaiser, L., & Polosukhin, I. (2017). Attention is all you need, http://arxiv.org/pdf/1706.03762v5
29. Devlin, J., Chang, M.-W., & Lee, K. (2019). Toutanova, Bert: Pre-training of deep bidirectional transformers for language understanding. In *Proceedings of the 2019 conference of the North American chapter of the association for computational linguistics: Human language technologies*, Vol. 1, pp. 171–4186.
30. Ashton, K. (2009). That 'Internet of Things' Thing. *RFID Journal*, 22(7), 97–114..
31. Knud Lasse Lueth, "State of the IoT. (2018). Number of IoT devices now at 7b – Market accelerating.
32. Statista. (2020). IoT: Number of connected devices worldwide 2012–2025. www.statista.com/statistics/471264/iot-number-of-connected-devices-worldwide/
33. S V Engineering College, Tirupati, India and R. R. B (2018, January). A comprehensive literature review on data analytics in IIoT (Industrial Internet of Things). *HELIX*, 8, 2757–2764.
34. Chhetri, S. R., Faezi, S., Canedo, A., & Faruque, M. A. A. (2019). QUILT: Quality inference from living digital twins in IoT-enabled manufacturing systems. In *Proceedings of the International Conference on Internet of Things Design and Implementation – IoTDI '19, Montreal, Quebec, Canada* (pp. 237–248). ACM Press.
35. Cheng, J., Chen, W., Tao, F., & Lin, C.-L. (2018). Industrial IoT in 5g environment towards smart manufacturing. *Journal of Industrial Information Integration*, 10, 10–19.
36. Karadeniz, A. M., Arif, I., Kanak, A., & Ergun, S. (2019, May). Digital twin of eGastronomic things: A case study for ice cream machines. In *2019 IEEE International Symposium on Circuits and Systems (ISCAS), Sapporo, Japan* (pp. 1–4). IEEE.
37. Sharma, R., & Molineros, J. (1997). Computer vision-based augmented reality for guiding manual assembly. *Presence: Teleoperators & Virtual Environments*, 6(3), 292–317.
38. Billinghurst, M., Clark, A., & Lee, G. (2015). A survey of augmented reality. *Foundations and Trends® in Human–Computer Interaction*, 8(2-3), 73–272.

39. White, G., Cabrera, C., Palade, A., & Clarke, S. (2018). Augmented reality in IoT. In *Conference: The 8th International Workshop on Context-Aware and IoT Services (CIoTS 2018), Hangzhou, China.*
40. Elayan, H., Aloqaily, M., & Guizani, M. (2021). Digital twin for intelligent context-aware IoT healthcare systems. *IEEE Internet Things Journal*, 8(23), 16749–16757.
41. Zhang, J., Li, L., Lin, G., Fang, D., Tai, Y., & Huang, J. (2020). Cyber resilience in healthcare digital twin on lung cancer. *IEEE Access*, 8, 201900–201913.
42. Haleem, A., Javaid, M., Singh, R. P., & Suman, R. (2022). Medical 4.0 technologies for healthcare: Features, capabilities, and applications. *Internet of Things and CyberPhysical Systems, 2022.*
43. Chen, J., Yi, C., Okegbile, S. D., Cai, J., & Shen, X. S. (2023). Networking technologies for enabling human digital twin in personalized healthcare applications: A comprehensive survey. *ArXiv*, abs/2301.03930.
44. Kolekar, S. S., Chen, H., & Kim, K. (2023). Design of precision medicine web-service platform towards health care digital twin. In *2023 Fourteenth International Conference on Ubiquitous and Future Networks (ICUFN)*, 843–848.
45. Ahmed, A., Shoukat, K., Muneeb, M. A., Qasem, D. A. O. A., Shahzad, M. A., Nissa, L. U., ... & Ali, A. (2024). AI and digital twin transforms in the construction of precision medical model: Healthcare management in smart cities. *European Journal of Medical and Health Research*, 2(1), 36–42.
46. Mariam, Z., Niazi, S. K., & Magoola, M. (2024). Unlocking the future of drug development: Generative AI, digital twins, and beyond. *BioMedInformatics*, 4(2), 1441–1456.
47. Ebrahimi, S., Ullah, S. M., Yankson, S., & Ferdowsi, F. (2024). Advancing fault detection and classification through high-fidelity digital twin simulation and AI. In *2024 IEEE Texas Power and Energy Conference (TPEC)*, pp. 1–6.
48. Khan, S., Arslan, T., & Ratnarajah, T. (2022). Digital twin perspective of fourth industrial and healthcare revolution. *IEEE Access*, 10, 25732–25754.
49. Parate, S. S., Bhivgade, A., & Bharati, D. M. (2022). Digital twin technology transforming modern healthcare industry. *International Journal for Research in Applied Science and Engineering Technology.*
50. Song, Y. (2023). The convergence of digital twin technology and personal healthcare. In *2023 26th ACIS International Winter Conference on Software Engineering, Artificial Intelligence, Networking and Parallel/Distributed Computing (SNPD-Winter)*, pp. 1–1.
51. Ullah, H., AbuAli, N. A., & Hayajneh, M. (2023). A digital twin framework for personalized healthcare management services. In *2023 IEEE 9th World Forum on Internet of Things (WF-IoT)*, pp. 1–6.
52. Alsiyabi, N., Kyritsis, M., & Gulliver, S. R. (2021). Investigating the impact of underlying health conditions on privacy concerns of IOT healthcare devices. In *Competitive Advantage in the Digital Economy (CADE 2021)*, 2021, pp. 11–18.

53. Delsi Robinsha, S., & Amutha, B. (2023). IoT revolutionizing healthcare: A survey of smart healthcare system architectures. In *2023 International Conference on Research Methodologies in Knowledge Management, Artificial Intelligence and Telecommunication Engineering (RMKMATE)*, pp. 1–5.
54. Tiase, V. L., Hull, W., McFarland, M. M., Sward, K. A., Del Fiol, G., Staes, C. J., Weir, C. R., & Cummins, M. R. (2019). Patient-generated health data and electronic health record integration: Protocol for a scoping review. *BMJ Open*, 9.
55. Liu, C., Gu, R., Yang, J., Luo, L., Chen, M., Xiong, Y., Huo, Z., Liu, Y., Zhang, K., Gong, J., Wei, L., Lei, Y., Wang, Z., & Sun, Q. (2024). A self-powered dual ratchet angle sensing system for digital twins and smart healthcare. *Advanced Functional Materials*, 34(42), 2405104.
56. Klimo, M., Kvassay, M., & Kvassayová, N. (2023). Digital twin and modelling a 3D human body in healthcare. In *2023 21st International Conference on Emerging eLearning Technologies and Applications (ICETA)*, pp. 307–312.
57. Mihai, S., Yaqoob, M., Hung, D. V., Davis, W., Towakel, P., Raza, M., ... & Nguyen, H. X. (2022). Digital twins: A survey on enabling technologies, challenges, trends and future prospects. *IEEE Communications Surveys & Tutorials*, 24(4), 2255–2291.
58. Sait, J. M., & Sarumathy, S. (2024). Clinical trials in health-care metaverse – A conceptual overview. *Perspectives in Clinical Research*, 16(1), 9–13.
59. Cellina, M., Cè, M., Alì, M., Irmici, G., Ibba, S., Caloro, E., & Papa, S. (2023). Digital twins: The new frontier for personalized medicine?. *Applied Sciences*, 13(13), 7940.
60. Mozumder, M. A., Armand, T. P., Sumon, R. I., Uddin, S. M., Athar, A., & Kim, H. (2023). The metaverse for intelligent healthcare using XAI, blockchain, and immersive technology. In *2023 IEEE International Conference on Metaverse Computing, Networking and Applications (MetaCom)*, pp. 612–616.
61. Akash, S. S., & Ferdous, M. S. (2022). A blockchain based system for healthcare digital twin. *IEEE Access*, 10, 50523–50547.
62. Amofa, S., Xia, Q., Xia, H., Obiri, I. A., Adjei-Arthur, B., Yang, J., & Gao, J. (2024). Blockchain-secure patient digital twin in healthcare using smart contracts. *Plos One*, 19(2), e0286120.
63. Lu, Q., Ye, Z., Fang, Z., Meng, J., Pitt, M., Lin, J., ... & Chen, L. (2021, December). Creating an inter-hospital resilient network for pandemic response based on blockchain and dynamic digital twins. In *2021 Winter Simulation Conference (WSC)* (pp. 1–12). IEEE.
64. Sharma, B., Kaushal, D., Joshi, S., Sharma, M., & Bafila, S. (2023). Transforming healthcare: Exploring the impact and potential of digital twin technology. In *2023 1st DMIHER International Conference on Artificial Intelligence in Education and Industry 4.0 (IDICAIEI)*, Vol. 1, pp. 1–6.
65. Meijer, C., Uh, H. W., & El Bouhaddani, S. (2023). Digital twins in healthcare: Methodological challenges and opportunities. *Journal of Personalized Medicine*, 13(10), 1522.

66. Chu, Y., Li, S., Tang, J., & Wu, H. (2023). The potential of the medical digital twin in diabetes management: A review. *Frontiers in Medicine*, 10, 1178912.
67. Liu, W., Li, B., & Ji, Z. (2023). Internet of Things and digital twin technology-based management system of medical equipment. *Global Clinical Engineering Journal*, 6(1), 46–53.
68. Johnson, Z., & Saikia, M. J. (2024). Digital twins for healthcare using wearables. *Bioengineering*, 11(6), 606.
69. Ghatti, S., Yurish, L. A., Shen, H., Rheuban, K., Enfield, K. B., Facteau, N. R., Engel, G., & Dowdell, K. (2023). Digital twins in healthcare: A survey of current methods. *Archives of Clinical and Biomedical Research*.
70. De Benedictis, A., Mazzocca, N., Somma, A., & Strigaro, C. (2022). Digital twins in healthcare: An architectural proposal and its application in a social distancing case study. *IEEE Journal of Biomedical and Health Informatics*, 27, 5143–5154.
71. Bordukova, M., Makarov, N., Rodriguez-Esteban, R., Schmich, F., & Menden, M. P. (2024). Generative artificial intelligence empowers digital twins in drug discovery and clinical trials. *Expert Opinion on Drug Discovery*, 19(1), 33–42.
72. Aubert, K., Germaneau, A., Rochette, M., Ye, W., Severyns, M., Billot, M., ... & Vendeuvre, T. (2021). Development of digital twins to optimize trauma surgery and postoperative management. A case study focusing on tibial plateau fracture. *Frontiers in Bioengineering and Biotechnology*, 9, 722275.

Chapter 10

Integration of AI and IoT in digital twins for personalized healthcare

D. Jeya Mala, A. Pradeep Reynold, and M. J. Siva Adithya

10.1 INTRODUCTION

Background and driving forces

The prevalence of cardiovascular hazards in society has increased, as a result of changes in lifestyle. The evidence derived from prior research suggests that the dietary element plays a crucial role in determining an individual's overall health, leading to a life free from diseases and promoting good health. Cardiovascular hazards resulting from accidental dietary habits are widely recognized as the prevailing health concern, particularly among adults. Consequently, there is an increasing need to evaluate the efficacy of nutritional supplements in mitigating the onset of such diseases, so promoting the attainment of good health condition. The application of digital twin (DT) technology is regarded as one of the most innovative solutions in the field of manufacturing industry. In the medical field, the utilization of a DT has various applications, including the development of a digital replica of certain human body parts, and the generation of a digital counterpart for drugs or medical devices etc. This research focuses on the utilization of current artificial intelligence (AI) methodologies, namely, genetic artificial intelligence (GenAI) and explainable artificial intelligence (XAI), in conjunction with DT technology to develop a preventative and recommendation system. The aim is to investigate the effects of nutritional supplements on the DT model. The digital model can subsequently serve as a reference model for mitigating cardiovascular risks by providing recommendations for dietary supplements at levels consistent with the requirements set by the World Health Organization. In this work, to evaluate the effects, a machine learning (ML)-model based on XAI will be utilized, incorporating the chi-squared classification method. Through the utilization of this classification methodology, the system possesses the capability to forecast the susceptibility of the ailment, accompanied by a comprehensive rationale elucidating the basis for such determination. The subsequent step in the proposed study involves the implementation of a much promising ML model based on GenAI to identify potential strategies for mitigating the aforementioned issue by suggesting suitable precision nutrition supplements. This recommendation process will

DOI: 10.1201/9781003498117-10

be facilitated by analyzing the influence of key parameters that play a crucial role in maintaining optimal cardiac function. Hence, this research work has expanded the use of DT to the healthcare sector, following its successful implementation in manufacturing and construction industries.

This research primarily focuses on the development of a precision nutrition mechanism utilizing innovative technologies, with the following objectives:

Objectives of this work

- To develop digital replica of the human heart using DT technology.
- To apply XAI based ML model to assess the functioning of the digital replica based on different nutritional supplements parameter values
- To recommend precision nutrition for the prevention of cardio vascular diseases using GenAI-based ML model.

10.1.1 Existing works and research gaps

Zang et al. [1] have presented some examples of generative AI applications in medicine and healthcare. They have discussed some associated issues, such as trust, veracity, clinical safety and reliability, privacy, copyrights, ownership, and opportunities, and AI-driven conversational user interfaces for friendlier human-computer interaction. The Lancet Regional Report 2023 [2] on embracing Generative AI in healthcare, has mentioned that, GenAI marks a technological renaissance with exponential future potential that has surpassed previous technological revolutions brought about by inventions such as the internet, search engines, and smartphones. In contrast to contemporary AI tools, GenAI has the ability to create or generate new original content such as text, images, or even music, thus not just simply mimicking human intelligence, but surpassing it. The Kanbach et al. [3] offered two important contributions from a BMI viewpoint on GenAI. The development of hypotheses based on research into the potential effects of GAI on the company and work environment as industry-wide drivers of BMI and the business model innovation with value creation in domains such as software engineering, healthcare, and financial services in light of Gen AI's possible effects. Saeed and Omlin [4] have performed an extensive meta survey on the application of XAI and its challenges and opportunities. Their review indicated the research directions in this new AI paradigm. Their study also examined the difference between explainability and interpretability. They have provided a development life cycle of XAI based system such as Design, Development and Deployment. They have also examined the trustworthiness of XAI in real time domains implementation. Their study concluded on two major areas: distinction between interpretability and explainability and challenges and research directions on the application of XAI. The Haque et al. [5] have provided a synthesis on XAI literature and the future research directions on using XAI. Their analysis indicated four dimensions of XAI: completeness, accuracy, format and current aspects. Also, they have identified the effects of XAI in applying it for real time domains in terms of usability, fairness, transparency, trust and understand ability. Clement et al. [6] have introduced a novel framework namely XAIR and provided the methods and tools used in implementing XAI. They have also proposed an SDLC model with life cycle phases Requirement analysis, Design, Implementation, Testing and Deployment. Nwakanma et al. [7] have provided a review on the application of XAI in intrusion detection and mitigation techniques using XAI in intelligent connected vehicles. They have identified the characteristics of XAI such as transparency, repeatability and trustworthiness can be applied to provide a safe interconnected intelligent vehicles. They have provided a review on XAI models for intrusion detection and other open research issues found in XAI. Khosravi et al. [8] have explored the role of XAI in education. They have provided a framework with six key aspects in the development of tools used in education. They have analyzed the application of their proposed framework in four AI based educational tools. The Riccordo et al. [9] have examined the application of AI in socially sensitive and safety-critical contexts. They have introduced a local classifier with identification of neighborhood using genetic algorithm. Then they have generated the factual explanations of the decision taken with a set of counterfactuals which can lead to an alternate outcome. Farrow [10] has examined the socio-technical perspective indicates that explicability is a relative term. Consequently, XAIED mediation strategies developed and implemented across education stakeholder communities using language that is not just "explicable" from an expert or technical standpoint, but explainable and interpretable to a range of stakeholders including learners. The discussion considers the impact of XAIED on several educational stakeholder types in light of the transparency of algorithms and the approach taken to explanation. In their research work [11], Wang et al. have applied a mode-agnostic approach to elaborate decisions based on the classification of short length words. Their approach generates the text by applying variationalautoencoders to encode and decode the text. Then an AI based learning technique using decision tree is used to generate the neighbors which are then applied to find the exemplars and counter-exemplars. Yu et al. [12] have identified that the proper nutrition and nutrition supplements help in reducing the cardio-vascular diseases. Their research urges the government and health professionals to focus on cardiovascular diseases and to create a food environment to inculcate healthy food habits to reduce the vulnerabilities associated with heart diseases. Popa et al. [13] have identified DTs as one of the crucial technologies that can be used for health care. They suggested that, when DT is used with Big data analytics, AI and IoT, there are several socio-economic benefits in spite of it has some risks involved. As per their study, this technology has provided several benefits such as prevention and treatment of diseases, patient anonymity and freedom, reduction in cost and equal treatment of individuals etc. Boulos and Zhang [14] have identified the importance of DTs in modern healthcare. They identified that this technology can radically transform the traditional medical records and then accumulating the information to get a new decision to precision medicine in order to provide accurate medicine for public health. They have presented a number of practical solutions using DT and also presented some of the ethical issues associated with it. Sharma et al. [1] have identified the gap in the application of DT in wide range of applications. And so they suggested a reference framework and provided details about best practices of DT and its implementation in the real world scenarios. Harode et al. [15] has applied DT to create a static digital representation of building construction using Building Information Technology (BIM). As the physical model is complex and has limitation in representing the dynamic views of building models, the DT is the right option to achieve it. Using DT one can inspect, monitor, analyze and update the model virtually. Khan et al. [16] has suggested DT as the prominent solution to provide a virtual copy of human organs at the time of Covid 19. By using the detailed model provided by DT, it will be easier to provide personalized solution to each patient. Velazquez et al. [17] have presented cardio twin architecture for Ischemic Heart Disease (IHD) to work on the edge. Their work can classify the cardio-vascular disease conditions in CNN. At the end of their study on "PTB Diagnostic ECG Database," they concluded that using DT on the edge helps in getting the model accuracy of 85.77%accuracy within the time duration of 4.8 sec. Coorey et al. [18] have provided insights on the application of DT in health care to get the advancement in precision cardio-vascular medicine. Using DT, it is better to understand the individual's disease susceptibility and prognosis which thus provides a more personalized treatment instead of having a common solution. Corral-Acero et al. [19] have argued that, the application of DT developed using computationally powerful algorithms and high power systems will help in boosting the capacity of better diagnosis and future treatments can be easily devised based on it. Loh et al. [20] have done an extensive review on the application of AI models from 2011 to 2022. They identified that, even though the AI models exhibit human-like performance, their black box status limits their utility. Lack of trust is the main reason they are rarely used, especially in healthcare. Hence, XAI has been proposed to boost trust in the model's prediction by describing how it is formed, boosting healthcare AI deployment.

Based on the review of existing research works, it is evident that, DTs provide the following advantages in healthcare sector:

- Flawless clinical decisions
- Efficiency
- Scalability
- Efficient healthcare
- Risk reduction in drugs applicability
- Development of high performance medical devices
- Optimized drug dosage etc

10.2 PROPOSED FRAMEWORK

As shown in Figure 10.1, the proposed methodology starts with installing the DT technology and simulates the human heart in a digital manner. The

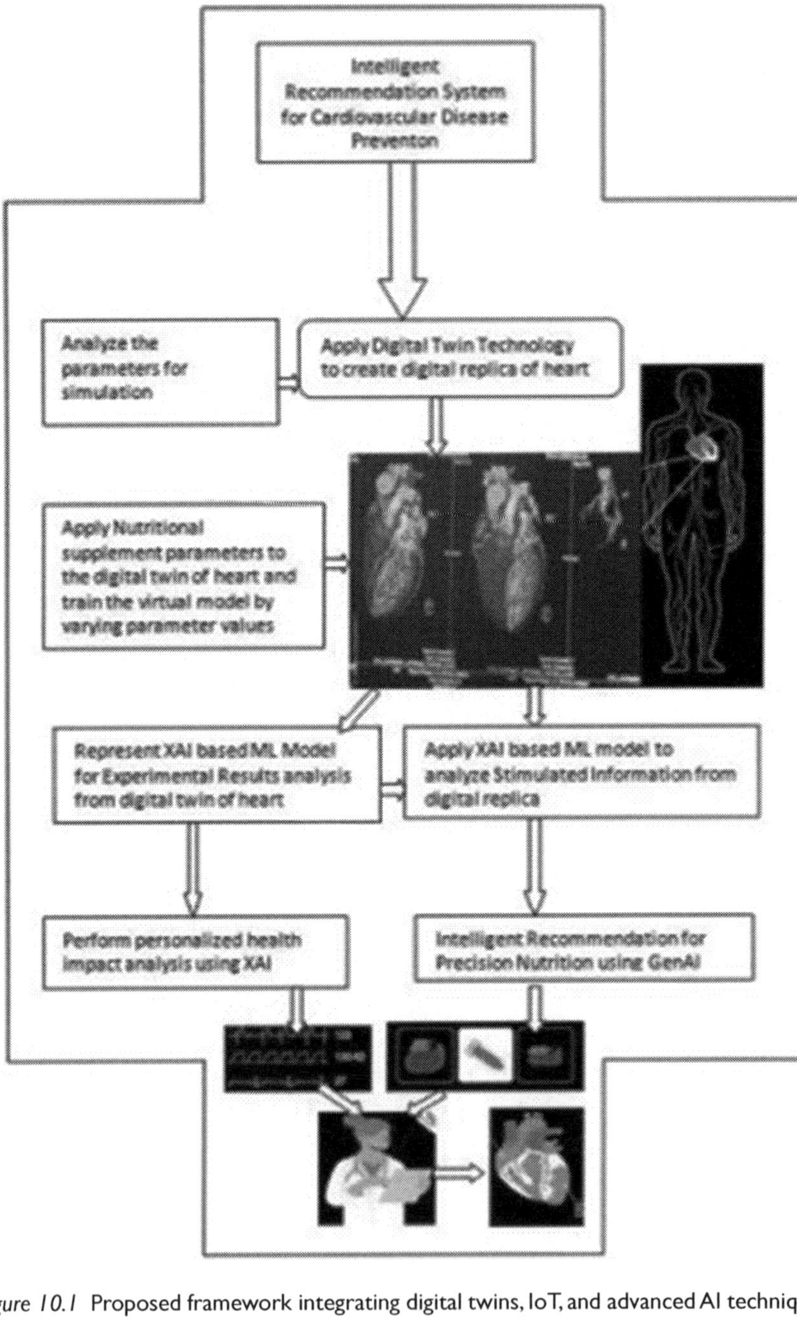

Figure 10.1 Proposed framework integrating digital twins, IoT, and advanced AI techniques.

digital replica of the heart is now taken for experimentation. The experimentation involves the application of the different nutritional parameter values on the digital replica of human heart. To train the model of the human heart, XAI based ML model is going to be applied to detect the pattern of impact and decision making with appropriate explanations. As the nutritional parameters are non-linear but dependent in nature, the proposed ML model is the appropriate choice to analyze the impact of nutritional biomarkers. The application of decision making in XAI based ML model can evaluate the impact of bio-chemical parameters with the actual clinical outcomes and the expected values given as reference values. The XAI based ML model can find the complex relationship between dietary, clinical and cognitive function of the prediction model, it is preferred as one of the best ways for simulation studies. The next task in the proposed work is to apply Gen AI based ML algorithm to get significant outcome using large data set of simulation results derived from the model. The application of GenAI model can identify the impact of significant parameters which are responsible for the proper functioning of the human heart. By using the past and present data of the model, it can produce the high accuracy prediction results

The proposed recommendation system is going to work based on the recommendations given by Belardo et al. [21] and as per WHO (1985). The proposed recommendation system is going to use the recommendation on how the diets should be given for different age groups and different geographical locations.

10.2.1 Chi-squared feature selection

The Chi-Square distribution is a probability distribution that is commonly used in statistical analysis. It is a continuous probability distribution that arises from A random variable, denoted by χ, is said to follow a chi-square distribution if it can be expressed as the summation of squared standard normal variables and is shown in Eq,(10.1).

$$X\,2 = \sum Zi\,2 \tag{10.1}$$

10.3 APPLICATION OF DIGITAL TWINS IN PERSONALIZED HEALTHCARE

For patients with cardiovascular vulnerabilities, the effectiveness of medicines and nutrition supplements need to be analyzed prior on their impact as they can"t be tested directly. The reason behind this complexity is that, each and every individual has their own genomic structure and so, a common medicine or nutrition supplement for all the patients may not be effective. In this kind of scenario, a personalized decision support and recommendation system is the need of the hour. In personalized treatment process, the actual patient will be monitored by giving the nutrition or medicines by means of a complex analysis process. However, it is extremely difficult to assess each and every parameter of a human manually and finding the impact of the nutritional supplements and medicines. Hence, a technique to prepare a virtual copy of the physical entity and assess the impact will be the best solution to be considered. For physical product development, a DT is acting as one such model before going for the actual production. As NASA has employed it for creating virtual replicas of the actual spacecrafts and determine the functionality of each and every part of them before the actual launch, it is now being applied for public health too.

In medical domain, a DT is used for several purposes such as, DT of a human body part, DT of a drug or medical devices etc. In this chapter, the DT technique is going to be applied to create a DT of the human heart and assess the risk factors associated with cardiovascular diseases. To achieve this, the data collected from the digital replica is going to be fed to an ML model which is equipped with XAI to get an explanation on why a particular decision has been taken apart from simple analytical result. Then, based on the analytical result of the simulation study, the system will apply the GenAI-based nutritional supplements recommendation and once again these recommendations will be fed to the DT to assess the impact of such nutrition and medicines and their effectiveness in cardiovascular risks prevention. The application of DT helps in improving the ethical impact of not using animals for testing the drugs or devices or impact of the medicines etc.

The proposed DT technology combines XAI, GenAI, IoT and data analytics to assess the functionality of the human heart and finding out the impact of nutritional supplements in cardiovascular risks prevention. In the proposed work, the DT is going to be designed to maintain a constant link with the physical part that is human heart.

The life cycle data will be collected using DT to improve the functioning of the heart with the application of necessary nutritional supplements into it. Here, the DT is going to provide a simulation environment in which the XAI based rule engine comprising of if-then rules are going to be applied to find the performance of the heart under various parametric values and to provide an explainable decision based on those values.

To assess the impact, an XAI based ML model for classification is going to be applied. By means of this classification, the proposed system will provide decision on the vulnerability status of the disease in future along with the explanation on that particular decision.

Finally, a GenAI-based ML model is going to be applied to recommend and assess the impact of the various nutritional supplements in order to provide a recommender system to suggest the supplements for precision nutrition. As the technology is new and involves high cost, it is rarely being used in healthcare. However, due to the success of DT in manufacturing and construction domains, its application of can be extended to healthcare.

Especially, as this work aims at achieving a precision nutrition mechanism for heart disease prevention, we are proposing to apply it in this chapter.

The extensive literature surveys and field reports provide insight on the need for an innovative method to prevent the cardiovascular diseases. To the best of our knowledge, none of the existing works have applied DT with advanced AI techniques to prevent heart diseases. Hence, this research work is novel and can be a boon to the society on successful implementation.

10.4 APPLICATION OF XAI AND GEN AI IN HEALTHCARE IN DIGITAL TWINS TECHNOLOGY

In this current Gen-Z life style, the occurrence of cardiovascular risks become more common in adults, especially those who are in the lower and upper middle age people. As everyone has their own type of genomic structure, recommending a common medicine or food habits may not help always. In these scenarios, it will be beneficial to go for "personalized nutrition" to those who have risk factors of cardiovascular risks especially due to their food habits. To address this most important critical task of providing personalized solution, it is very important to diagnose each and every individual's heart functioning and the way it reacts to the different diet recommendations.

In order to achieve this, DTs is the boon to healthcare domain in which the technology can be applied to create a digital replica of the actual human heart of each individual when they came for diagnosis. Then, by applying and varying the different nutritional supplements to this digital model virtually, we can get the report of the heart's functioning and based on that, it is easy to recommend the dietary to prevent cardiovascular risks.

As the environmental conditions, gender, age and genetic structure of an individual plays a crucial role in the proper functioning of the human heart, it is of paramount importance to create a digital model and then perform analysis on it. Generally, recommendation of medicine will start only after a disease report is prepared by the physicians. If the recommendation is given well in advance prior to any mishaps happening, it will save millions of human lives from such coronial diseases.

Hence, this proposed work the focus is shifted from recommendation of medicines and dietary advises after the disease to prevention of diseases by providing recommendation at the diagnostics stage itself.

The various factors that are going to be considered are: the physiological, molecular, and behavioral and diet.

Some of the problems associated with the traditional diagnostics methods that may lead to cardiovascular risks are:

(i) The blood pressure (BP) measured using sphygmomanometer will provide the result based on the readings taken in that equipment. However, this measurement normally won't consider age, the time at which the diagnostics is conducted, stress level of the patient, the patient's healthy status that is either he has past disease history or a healthy individual, any drugs is taken just prior to this measurement etc. are not at all taken care [22].

(ii) Only the Doctors based on their next level individual interaction can only finalize whether the patient is prone to cardiovascular risks or not. Otherwise, a mere report will lead to different conclusion on BP based heart disease diagnostics.

(iii) Similarly the other crucial parameters need to be taken into consideration of all these individual specific parameters before coming to the decision making process.

(iv) The traditional diagnostics results are single values only which are independent of each other. To get a conclusion, the physicians need to correlate all these values and have to come to a conclusion.

(v) As human decisions are error-prone, an automated or semi-automated solution to get near accurate results will be the need of the hour. Under all the above stated problems, it is essential to provide a digital version of the human heart with its parameters being updated from time to time based on the current environmental aspects and healthy status of the individuals, will lead to proper diagnostics results and recommendations based on it. The prediction of cardiovascular risks based on molecular and nutritional bio-markers [23] as an enumerated collection of values will yield better predictions than the traditional methods. Hence, this chapter work focuses on developing a novel framework to provide a better recommendation system as personalized nutrition recommender system.

10.5 CASE STUDY AND RESULTS

Here, for the analysis, a dataset from Kaggle is taken which has taken the digital replica of the actual human vital parameters as equivalent daily activities and based on that an emotional analysis is done. This dataset is consist of data collected from various people with different life styles and their behavior and then a systematic analysis of this data is done using ML. Based on that the recommendation system has to provide suggestions on whether that person has cardio vascular risks or not. The data set is available in Ref. [20]. An extraction of data from this dataset is given in Table 10.1.

Figure 10.2 showcases the various levels of entertainment against various timestamps. Figure 10.3 provides insight on which emotion is dominant in the persons based on the data collected. It is observed that, Satisfied has the highest value.

Figures 10.4(a)–(d) analyzed the dominant emotion against the other crucial parameters and it is observed that, the each of these parameters have their crucial impact at different levels on the emotion of a person. Based on the emotional level of a person it will be easier to predict whether that person has any future cardio vascular risks. And based on that the analysts can help the physicians to focus on which attributes are contributing to

Table 10.1 Sample Data

Timestamp	*screennutrition.org/ art-jam*	*Time Investment*	*Total Entertainment (%)*	*Interactive (%)*	*Passive (%)*	*Compulsive (%)*	*Learning and Growth (%)*	*Educational (%)*	*Curiosity Chasing (%)*	*Mindfulness (%)*	*Emotional Intensity*	*Dominant Emotion [Pick]*
2023/09/19 8:05:35 PM MDT	https://medium.com/@rahul.sikder3/how-would-you-grow-spotify-by-20-product-strategy-question-pm-interview-2bdadcdde5e7	300	30		100		69	69		1	3	
2023/09/20 2:48:05 PM MDT	https://medium.com/@jonathan.lethem/be-kind-be-kind-be-kind-da3feb013f00	480	0	0	100	0	90		10	0	3	Satisfying
2023/09/26 2:49:34 PM MDT	https://medium.com/wise-well/mysterious-fats-fuel-disease-more-than-we-knew-new-research-reveals-9c95153912f5	240	50	0	90	0	80	60	50	80	4	Satisfying

(*continued*)

Table 10.1 (Cont.)

Timestamp	*screennutrition.org/ art-jam*	*Time Investment*	*Total Entertainment (%)*	*Interactive (%)*	*Passive (%)*	*Compulsive (%)*	*Learning and Growth (%)*	*Educational (%)*	*Curiosity Chasing (%)*	*Mindfulness (%)*	*Emotional Intensity*	*Dominant Emotion [Pick]*
2023/ 09/26 2:53:01 PM MDT	https://medium. com/@ chrismanhattan/ what-you-need- to-perpare- for-ufos-and- alien-beings- making-contact- 608a67b0142c	360	33	0	90	0	100	100	80	33	2	Sad
2023/ 09/26 2:57:01 PM MDT	https://medium. com/lessons- from-history/ seven- conspiracy- theories-that- turned-out- to-be-true- fdc95e158ca4	480	90	0	90	0	20	0	100	0	5	Satisfying
2023/ 09/26 3:01:56 PM MDT	https://medium. com/wise-well/ finding-your- purpose-is- incredibly- powerful-and- surprisingly- possible- f971e309fd1	480	80	0	90	0	75	75	75	20	3	Satisfying

2023/09/26 3:06:48 PM MDT	www.youtube.com/watch?v=ORdWE_ffirg	420	40	0	90	0	85	70	70	100	5	Joyful
2023/09/26 3:09:30 PM MDT	www.youtube.com/watch?v=1WEAJ-DFkHE	3240	80	0	75	0	75	75	75	25	4	Satisfying
2023/09/26 3:11:14 PM MDT	www.youtube.com/watch?v=hNDgcjVGHIw	720	100	25	50	50	25	25	90	25	5	Exuberant
….												

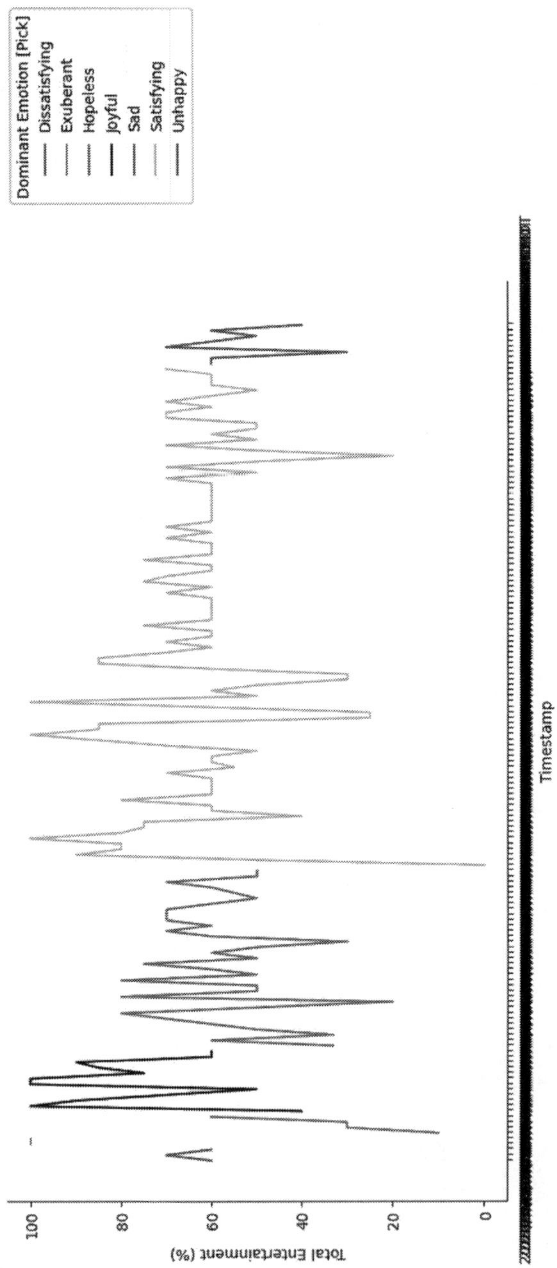

Figure 10.2 Total entertainment vs. timestamp.

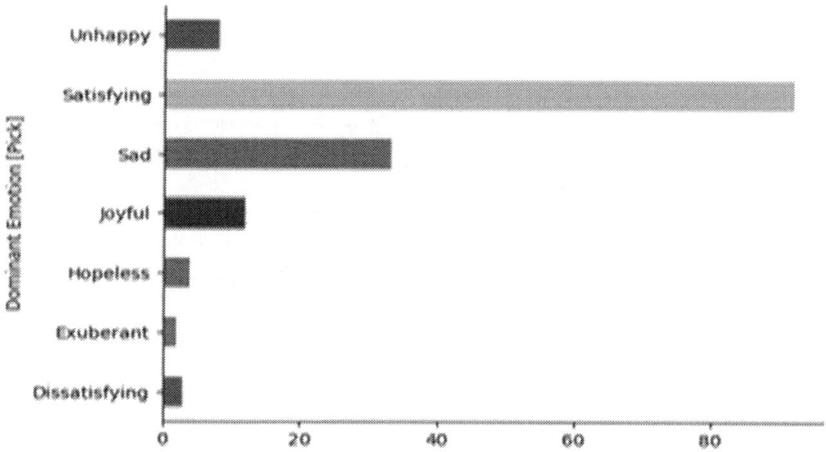

Figure 10.3 Dominant emotion analysis.

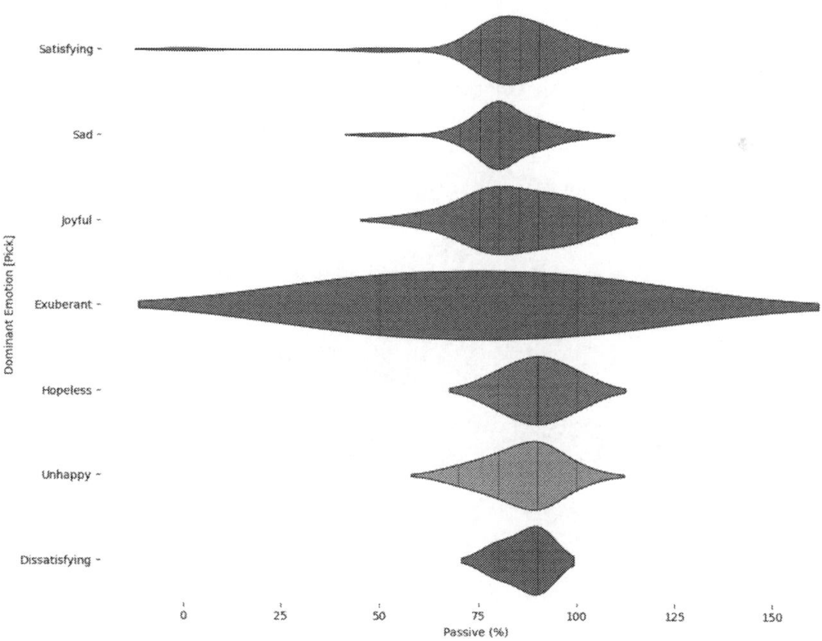

Figure 10.4a Dominant emotion vs. passive percentage.

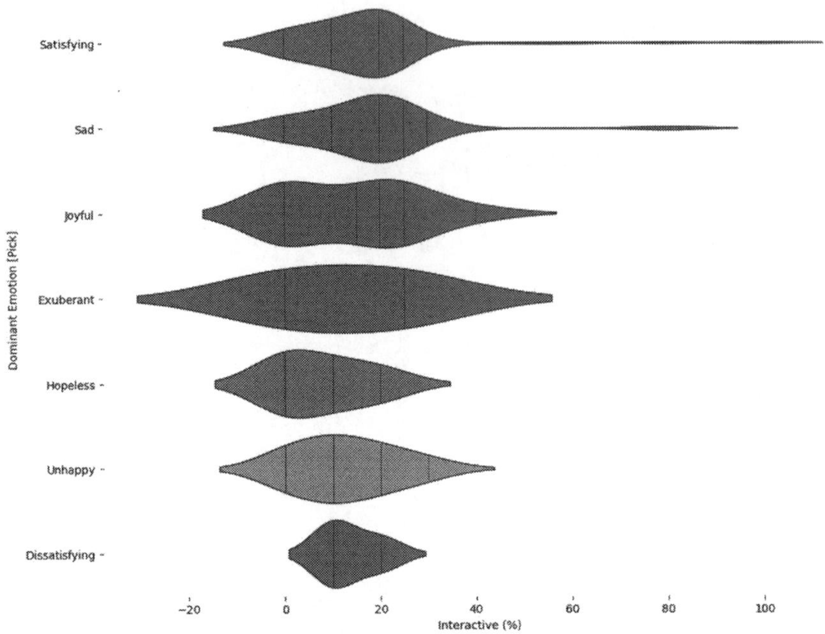

Figure 10.4b Dominant emotion vs. interactive percentage.

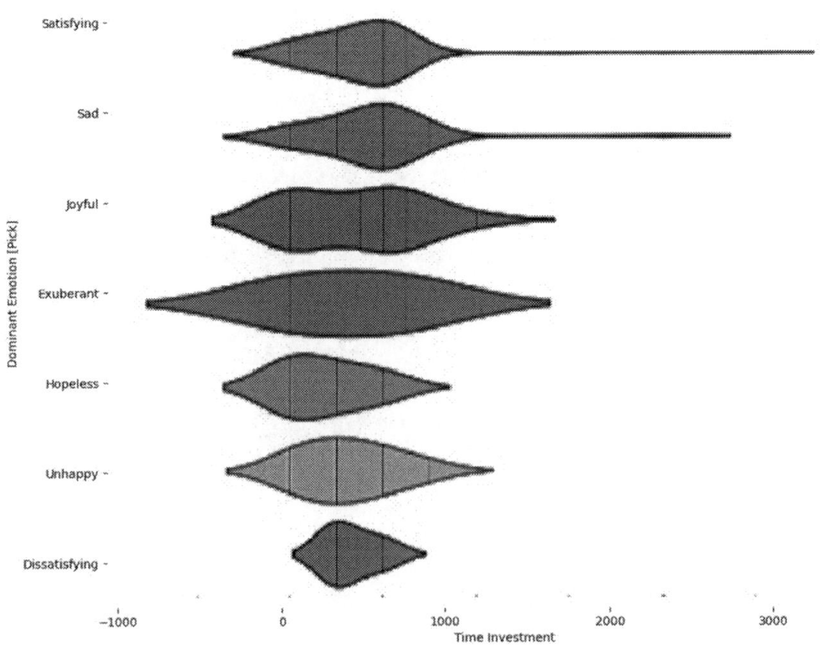

Figure 10.4c Dominant emotion vs. total entertainment percentage.

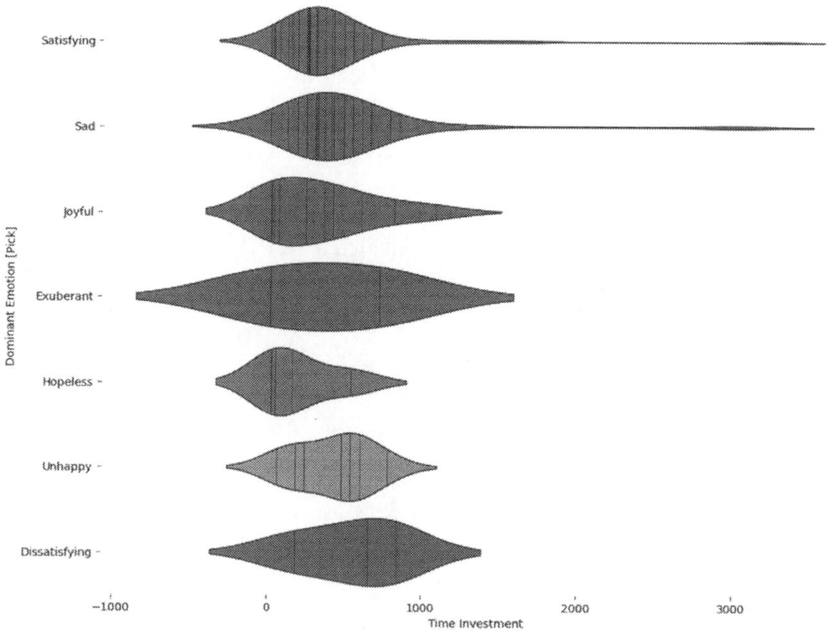

Figure 10.4d Dominant emotion vs. time investment percentage.

reduce the risks. Hence, the proposed work will be a well studied one and can be easily implemented in real-time.

10.6 CONCLUSION

This chapter has provided an insight on how DTs, IoT, and advanced AI techniques could be applied for personalized healthcare. Especially, when it is coming on to cardio-vascular risks, the collection of data using DTs and further analysis using advanced AI techniques will be a real boon to both the patients and medical practioners as it helps in easily analysing the data and coming to a conclusion. Further, the recommendation system can also help in suggesting the proper medications and better counselling if it is based on behavior.

REFERENCES

1. Sharma, A., Kosasih, E., Zhang, J., Brintrup, A., & Calinescu, A. (2022). Digital twins: State of the art theory and practice, challenges, and open research questions. *Journal of Industrial Information Integration*, 30, 100383.

2. Health–Europe, T. L. R. (2023). Embracing generative AI in health care. *The Lancet Regional Health-Europe*, 30.
3. Kanbach, D. K., Heiduk, L., Blueher, G., Schreiter, M., & Lahmann, A. (2024). The GenAI is out of the bottle: Generative artificial intelligence from a business model innovation perspective. *Review of Managerial Science*, 18(4), 1189–1220.
4. Saeed, W., & Omlin, C. (2023). Explainable AI (XAI): A systematic meta-survey of current challenges and future opportunities. *Knowledge-Based Systems*, 263, 110273.
5. Haque, A. B., Islam, A. N., & Mikalef, P. (2023). Explainable Artificial Intelligence (XAI) from a user perspective: A synthesis of prior literature and problematizing avenues for future research. *Technological Forecasting and Social Change*, 186, 122120.
6. Clement, T., Kemmerzell, N., Abdelaal, M., &Amberg, M. (2023). Xair: A systematic metareview of explainable ai (XAI) aligned to the software development process. *Machine Learning and Knowledge Extraction*, 5(1), 78–108.
7. Nwakanma, C. I., Ahakonye, L. A. C., Njoku, J. N., Odirichukwu, J. C., Okolie, S. A., Uzondu, C., ... & Kim, D. S. (2023). Explainable artificial intelligence (xai) for intrusion detection and mitigation in intelligent connected vehicles: A review. *Applied Sciences*, 13(3), 1252.
8. Khosravi, H., Shum, S. B., Chen, G., Conati, C., Tsai, Y. S., Kay, J., & Gašević, D. (2022). Explainable artificial intelligence in education. *Computers and Education: Artificial Intelligence*, 3, 100074.
9. Guidotti, R., Monreale, A., Giannotti, F., Pedreschi, D., Ruggieri, S., &Turini, F. (2019). Factual and counterfactual explanations for black box decision making. *IEEE Intelligent Systems*, 34(6), 14–23.
10. Farrow, R. (2023). The possibilities and limits of XAI in education: A socio-technical perspective. *Learning, Media and Technology*, 48(2), 266–279.
11. Wang, Y., Wang, T. H., Mao, J., Hagenow, M., & Shah, J. (2024). Grounding language plans in demonstrations through counterfactual perturbations. *arXiv* preprint arXiv:2403.17124.
12. Yu, X., Pu, H., & Voss, M. (2024). Overview of anti-inflammatory diets and their promising effects on non-communicable diseases. *British Journal of Nutrition*, 1–21.
13. Popa, E. O., van Hilten, M., Oosterkamp, E., & Bogaardt, M. J. (2021). The use of digital twins in healthcare: Socio-ethical benefits and socio-ethical risks. *Life Sciences, Society and Policy*, 17, 1–25.
14. KamelBoulos, M. N., & Zhang, P. (2021). Digital twins: From personalized medicine to precision public health. *Journal of Personalized Medicine*, 11(8), 745.
15. Sobowale, M., Elghaish, F., & Brooks, T. (2023, November). A systematic review of digital twin as a predictive maintenance approach for existing buildings in the UK. In *23rd International Conference on Construction Applications of Virtual Reality (CONVR 2023)* (pp. 1206–1218).
16. Khan, A., Khan, S. H., Saif, M., Batool, A., Sohail, A., & Waleed Khan, M. (2024). A survey of deep learning techniques for the analysis of COVID-19 and their usability for detecting omicron. *Journal of Experimental & Theoretical Artificial Intelligence*, 36(8), 1779–1821.

17. Martinez-Velazquez, R., Gamez, R., & El Saddik, A. (2019, June). Cardio Twin: A Digital Twin of the human heart running on the edge. In *2019 IEEE international symposium on medical measurements and applications (MeMeA)* (pp. 1–6). IEEE.
18. Coorey, G., Figtree, G. A., Fletcher, D. F., & Redfern, J. (2021). The health digital twin: Advancing precision cardiovascular medicine. *Nature Reviews Cardiology*, 18(12), 803–804. https://doi.org/10.1038/s41569-021-00630-4
19. Corral-Acero, J., Margara, F., Marciniak, M., Rodero, C., Loncaric, F., Feng, Y., Gilbert, A., Fernandes, J. F., Bukhari, H. A., Wajdan, A., Martinez, M. V., Santos, M. S., Shamohammdi, M., Luo, H., Westphal, P., Leeson, P., DiAchille, P., Gurev, V., Mayr, M., Geris, L., ... Lamata, P. (2020). The 'Digital Twin' to enable the vision of precision cardiology. *European Heart Journal*, 41(48), 4556–4564. https://doi.org/10.1093/eurheartj/ehaa159.
20. Loh, H. W., Ooi, C. P., Seoni, S., Barua, P. D., Molinari, F., & Acharya, U. R. (2022). Application of explainable artificial intelligence for healthcare: A systematic review of the last decade (2011–2022). *Computer Methods and Programs in Biomedicine*, 226, 107161.
21. Belardo, D., Michos, E.D., Blankstein, R., Blumenthal, R.S., Ferdinand, K.C., Hall,K., Klatt, K., Natajaran, P., Ostfeld, R.J., Reddy, K. and Rodriguez, R. (2022).Practical, evidence-based approaches to nutritional modifications to reduceatherosclerotic cardiovascular disease: An American society for preventivecardiology clinical practice statement. *American Journal of Preventive Cardiology*, 10, 100323.
22. Sak, J., &Suchodolska, M. (2021). Artificial intelligence in nutrients science research: A review. *Nutrients*, 13(2), 322. https://doi.org/10.3390/nu13020322.
23. Jaffe, A. S., & Miller, W. L. (2018). Meta-analyses and interpretation of troponin values in heart failure. *JACC: Heart Failure*, 6(3), 198–200.

Chapter 11

Global perspectives on digital twin adoption in healthcare

Saurabh Srivastava and Prajna Parimita Dash

11.1 INTRODUCTION

Digital twins (DTs) or digital "look-alikes" comprise a virtual representation of a real-world counterpart: an object, system, or process. It is designed to accurately reflect the real-world counterpart throughout its lifecycle.

Organizations leverage DT technology to remotely troubleshoot equipment, such as spacecraft operating beyond Earth's boundaries. This technology also facilitates the design and testing of new products or systems, such as driving simulators, braking mechanisms, and so on, ensuring they function correctly before actual deployment. Additionally, DTs provide real-time insights into product performance during customer use, enabling continuous monitoring and optimization.

Extending its engineering applications for societal benefits has led to its application in the healthcare industry. DT technology is revolutionizing healthcare by creating virtual replicas of physical entities, such as patients, medical devices, and hospital systems. These DTs enable healthcare providers to simulate, predict, as well as optimize real-world processes, leading to improved patient condition and operational efficiency of medical. In healthcare, DTs model complex biological systems to predict patient outcomes and personalize treatment plans based on individual patient data.

The integration of the Internet of Things (IoT), artificial intelligence (AI), and big data analytics is considered crucial for the development and deployment of DTs in healthcare. These key technologies enable the collection, processing, and analysis of vast amounts of data, providing the foundation for accurate and reliable DTs. As a result, DTs are becoming essential tools for personalized medicine, predictive maintenance, virtual simulations, and continuous patient monitoring in the healthcare industry.

Although the future of DTs in healthcare looks promising, with ongoing research and development aimed at enhancing their capabilities, collaborative efforts among global stakeholders motivate them to overcome current challenges and unlock the full potential of DTs in improving healthcare outcomes.

DOI: 10.1201/9781003498117-11

11.2 EVOLUTION OF DTS

Historically, the US agency NASA is considered the first one to apply the "DT" technology to probe the failure of its Apollo-13 mission in the 1970s [1–2]. Just after two days of the vehicle launch that follows the explosion of one of the oxygen tanks, the NASA flight control team in Houston resolved the issue by simulating and analyzing these conditions on a prototype (physical model) of the Apollo-13 spacecraft and its components [3]. This modeling and testing of various solutions to the problem finally led the engineers and scientists to rectify the issue. The concept of DT dates back to 2005 [4]. In 2014, the term "DT" was formally coined in a white paper by Dr. Grieves [5]. Around the same period, the DT technology set out in the medical domains [6].

Later, his work with J. Vickers demonstrated the application of DTs across the product life cycle in understanding the system behavior [7]. The work emphasized three primary elements of a DT system: (1) a real space containing a physical system or object, (2) a virtual space containing a virtual system of objects, and (3) the data exchange between both spaces.

About10 years after Grieves' definition, NASA researchers outlined in their roadmap—now regarded by aerospace experts as a foundational reference on DTs—that this technology would enhance performance in aviation [8–10].

DTs can be described as virtual machines or computer models that replicate, emulate, or mirror the life of a physical entity. This entity could be an object, a process, a person, or a human-related characteristic. Each DT is connected to its physical counterpart via a unique identifier, which ensures a one-to-one relationship between the DT and its physical twin [11-12].

Presently DT is an active, intelligent, and emerging model that serves as the active mirror to a physical object or process. It replicates the lifecycle of its physical twin to monitor, control, and enhance its operations. The DT continuously forecasts future conditions, such as potential defects, damage, or failures, enabling the simulation and testing of new configurations to proactively carry out maintenance. This process is facilitated by ongoing interaction, communication, and synchronization between the DT, its physical counterpart, and the external environment [13–15].

While DTs have mainly been used in the space industry, they are now finding new applications in three main areas: manufacturing, aviation, and healthcare.

11.3 DTS APPLICATIONS IN HEALTHCARE

Traditionally, in healthcare DTs were mainly employed for predictive maintenance and performance optimization of medical instruments, including aspects like examination speed and energy efficiency. Additionally, DT technology has been used to enhance the management of hospital lifecycles. For instance, GE Healthcare has developed DTs aimed at optimizing hospital management. This major company has long dedicated its predictive analytics platform and AI tools to converting extensive and diverse patient data into actionable insights.

To implement a digital patient twin effectively, four key requirements must be met:

1. Hospitals or healthcare facilities need to have robust digital networking systems in place.
2. Data must be organized and properly annotated.
3. Patients must retain the right to control how their data is used at all times.
4. Medical professionals must be able to access and utilize the information within the digital patient twin in their daily clinical practice.

While the full realization of a digital patient twin in healthcare is still a work in progress, the technology itself is no longer just a concept from science fiction. Advanced AI-driven solutions, which are crucial in this domain, are already in use.

GE Healthcare's real-time predictive system, now operational in the new "command center" at Johns Hopkins Hospital in Baltimore, aims to anticipate patient flow and optimize capacity by using a DT of patient pathways. This system combines prescriptive and predictive analytics along with machine learning, natural language processing, and computer vision to improve decision-making ability. It provides hospital staff with precise and prompt insights, including recommendations for bed assignments, the need for unit support, and predictions of patient surges. Meanwhile, Siemens Healthineers is developing a DT for the human liver [16].

A DT is designed to enhance the operational efficiency and layout of a medical unit facing challenges like rising patient demand, aging infrastructure, or space limitations by rapidly assessing different solutions before implementing the optimal one to improve care delivery. This DT utilizes workflow simulation and 3D computer models to create a dynamic and detailed model that integrates patient pathways, staff scheduling, and movements. Additionally, an offline DT framework is used to evaluate emergency unit performance during major crises, such as earthquakes, tsunamis, or terrorist attacks, as discussed in Ref. [17].

The GE Healthcare command center enumerates DT as "A Digital Twin virtualizes a hospital as a safe environment to test changes in system performance" [18]. According to this healthcare giant, DT has been optimizing several components of the industry, viz., bed configurations [19], surgical block schedule, health system facilities, patient, and the staffing procedure.

In order to enhance its hospital operations, the Johns Hopkins Hospital has already launched the capacity command center [19]. By making a DT of patient pathways, the hospital predicts patient activity and plans capacity according to demand, thus significantly improving patient service, safety, experience, and volume. A few other interesting health application areas of DT include precision cardiology [20], precision oncology [21], and radiotherapy [22]. Ref. [23] introduces a DT platform for the human heart called "Cardio Twin." This system gathers data from various sources, including sensors, medical records, and social networks, and applies different analytical techniques to identify conditions such as ischemic heart disease (IHD) or stroke. Future developments aim to expand the cardio twin platform to enhance disease prevention by mitigating associated risk factors. Another heart-related DT, the "Living Heart" project, is being developed by Dassault Systems [24]. This project features a realistic heart simulation that serves as a technological foundation for education, clinical diagnosis, and disease prevention. It can also assist in designing medical devices and planning treatments for heart conditions like valve stenosis, regurgitation, or prolapse. Additionally, the Virtual Physiological Human (VPH) project, funded by the European Union (EU) [25], seeks to create a comprehensive model of human physiology that spans from the entire body down to the genomic level. This initiative aims to support the development of patient-specific models for personalized and predictive healthcare.

Nicholas Ayache [26] introduced a digital model of a patient's anatomy and physiology that utilizes executable models, with parameters learned from clinical, biological, behavioral, and environmental data. This virtual patient can be employed to better quantify observations, simulate disease progression, and plan interventions to enhance their effectiveness. In a similar context, Ref. [27] describes a DT ecosystem for health and well-being, designed to monitor and assist individuals, especially those with heart conditions like IHD, during emergencies when they are alone. Additionally, Ref. [28] presents CloudDTH, a cloud-based DT framework aimed at elderly healthcare. This system provides real-time monitoring and feedback to manage long-term health and uses machine learning algorithms for rapid crisis prediction. For a broader application, the EU research project MyHealthAvatar [29] is working to develop a digital avatar that represents an individual's health status throughout their life. This avatar integrates diverse health data from clinical, genetic, and sensor sources [30]. Similarly, Ref. [31] proposes an enhancement to SmartFit, a computational framework that utilizes wearable sensors and internet applications. This extension monitors athletic teams, predicts their condition during training, and recommends adjustments to improve performance and health.

11.4 TECHNOLOGICAL ENABLERS

In healthcare, DTs play a crucial role in personalized medicine, diagnostics, and treatment optimization. The key components required for a sound implementation a DT may be summarized as:

1. **Data sources:** Various sensors are employed for a DT. The data from sensors (such as wearable devices, monitors, and imaging equipment) provide real-time information about the physical system. Other data sources may be medical records (including patient history), lab results, and diagnoses. Such relevant data contribute significantly to the DT's accuracy. The insurance records of the patients also contain relevant health information, insurance claims, and treatment history. Besides this, there are other statistically relevant data sets obtained through additional data sources, such as population health data or clinical trials, which enhance the DT's capabilities.
2. **High-quality3D images and animations:** Accurate representation of the physical system relies on detailed 3D models. These models capture anatomical structures, tissue properties, and spatial relationships. Moreover, sophisticated animations help visualize dynamic processes within the DT, such as blood flow, organ function, or disease progression.
3. **Advanced analytics and simulation:** Algorithms analyze data from various sources and simulate interactions within the DT. Real-time decision-making benefits from overlaying the DT with live data.

It must be noted that successful DTs require accurate data integration, robust analytics, and seamless connectivity. The evolving technologies are supporting the practical implementation of DTs through various technological enablers ensuring accurate data integration, computational analysis, and connectivity. One such enabler is the *data integrator.* This key enabler integrates the information through diverse sources which may be a collection of sensors, previous medical records, treatment histories, etc., to formulate a comprehensive representation of the relevant information.

High-quality 3D imaging and animations also require approachable and large-scale data storage and transmission facilities. However, considering an individual patient's real-time monitoring, the significance of IoT devices can't be ruled out. These devices are required for seamless data flow between the physical system and their digital counterparts. Therefore, another category of technological enablers comprises advanced analytics and simulation tools. The joint operation of the above two enablers require another technological enabler to provide seamless connectivity for smooth and hassle-free data-flow operation. Thanks to the power of IoT and edge/cloud computing. Such an enabler also enhances real-time updates while providing predictive capabilities.

11.5 CHALLENGES AND BARRIERS

The implementation of DTs in healthcare faces several challenges and barriers in bridging the gap between different technological enablers. These may be broadly classified into five categories:

1. **Technical challenges:** A critical technical challenge toward a successful DT implementation is *data integration*. It involves the complex integration of diverse data sources (such as sensors, medical records, and insurance records) into a coherent DT. The next complex issue is *model creation*, i.e., dynamic modeling that accurately represents biological systems or patient-specific conditions. This requires sophisticated algorithms and computational resources. Another parameter of concern is *real-time updation*. This ensures real-time synchronization between the physical system and its DT, which is considered essential for effective decision-making.
2. **Regulatory and ethical issues:** The next category comprises privacy concerns and data ownership. Handling sensitive patient data raises privacy and security issues. Compliance with regulations like Health Insurance Portability and Accountability Act (HIPAA) is crucial. Creating and using a DT also requires informed consent, which is again an ethical concern. Further, determining who owns and controls the DT data can be contentious.
3. **Interoperability and standardization:** Different healthcare systems utilize data in various formats. The lack of standardized data formats and interoperability protocols hinders seamless data exchange between different healthcare systems. Moreover, adapting a DT to an existing infrastructure can be challenging.
4. **Clinical adoption and validation:** Demonstrating the clinical utility and safety of DTs requires rigorous validation studies. Another issue is healthcare professionals' acceptance. Convincing healthcare providers to adopt and trust DT technology is vital for an efficient DT ecosystem.
5. **Resource and cost constraints:** Developing and maintaining DTs demand significant resources, including computational power and storage. In other words, this incurs huge infrastructure costs. Further, the expenses shoot more as healthcare professionals need significant pieces of training to effectively use and interpret DT outputs.

11.6 PROSPECTS AND OPPORTUNITIES

Despite the challenges mentioned above, the exciting prospects and opportunities of DTs in healthcare are numerous. Apart from the healthcare workflow optimization, the DTs can be thought to provide significant opportunities in healthcare. These include but are not limited to:

- Personalized treatment and precision medicine
- Early disease detection and prevention
- Virtual clinical trials
- Remote monitoring and telehealth
- Surgical planning and training
- Chronic disease management
- Behavioral health and well-being
- Patient education and empowerment

Apart from the above-mentioned prospects, the emerging DT sector may facilitate research on disease mechanisms, and drug interactions, leading to some novel therapies. The analysis of large-scale DT data will further lead to innovations in the diagnosis process, which is another lucrative measure for the healthcare industry.

11.7 GLOBAL ADOPTION TRENDS

A few insights into the global adoption trends of DT in healthcare are quite promising. The global market is estimated to grow significantly. It is projected to increase from \$1.9 billion in 2024 to an impressive \$33.4 billion by 2035, with a remarkable compound annual growth rate (CAGR) of 30% during this period [32].

Digital health technologies: The adoption of DTs is driven by the increasing use of digital health technologies. These technologies enhance data analytics, simulation capabilities, and personalized medicine.

Data analytics and simulation: Advancements in data analytics and simulation play a crucial role in making DTs more effective and applicable in healthcare.

Personalized medicine: DTs enable personalized treatment approaches, tailoring interventions to individual patients.

Clinical trials acceleration: DTs facilitate faster clinical trials by simulating drug responses and predicting outcomes. This can lead to cost savings in drug design and testing.

Predictive maintenance: DTs empower organizations to implement predictive maintenance strategies, optimize pharmaceutical processes, and enable real-time monitoring.

Seamless data integration: Industry 4.0 technologies have facilitated seamless data integration, allowing the development of virtual replicas of physical assets and processes [32, 33].

Nearly 90% of healthcare executives consider DTs essential for collaboration between different systemic units within their organizations. Over 65%

of healthcare executives anticipate increased investment from pharmaceutical players in this domain over the next three years [33].

11.8 CONCLUSION

The exploration of DTs within the healthcare sector reveals a transformative technology with the potential to revolutionize how we approach patient care, medical device management, and healthcare operations. DTs have evolved into sophisticated tools that provide real-time, data-driven insights, enabling healthcare providers to simulate, predict, and optimize processes with unprecedented precision.

Throughout this chapter, we have examined the evolution of DTs from their inception to their growing adoption in healthcare. The integration of key technological enablers such as the IoT, AI, and big data analytics has been crucial in harnessing the full potential of DTs, allowing for more personalized and predictive healthcare solutions. The ability of DTs to create accurate virtual replicas of patients, devices, and systems opens up new avenues for innovation, particularly in the realms of personalized medicine, early disease detection, and virtual clinical trials.

However, as promising as DTs are, their implementation is not without significant challenges. Technical hurdles, such as data integration and real-time updating, regulatory and ethical considerations surrounding patient data privacy, and the need for interoperability across different healthcare systems all pose barriers that must be addressed. Moreover, the resource demands for developing and maintaining DTs, along with the necessity for rigorous clinical validation, highlight the complexities of integrating this technology into mainstream healthcare practice.

Despite these challenges, the future of DTs in healthcare appears bright. With continued advancements in enabling technologies and increased collaboration among global stakeholders, many of the current barriers can be overcome. The projected market growth and rising investment in DT technology further underscore its potential to become an integral component of modern healthcare. As DTs continue to mature and evolve, they are set to play a pivotal role in enhancing patient outcomes, optimizing healthcare delivery, and driving the next wave of innovation in the medical field.

In conclusion, while the journey to fully realizing the benefits of DTs in healthcare is still ongoing, the foundation has been laid for a future where DTs are central to a more efficient, personalized, and predictive healthcare ecosystem.

REFERENCES

1. Williams, D. R. (2021). [Online]. Available: https://nssdc.gsfc.nasa.gov/planetary/lunar/ap13acc.html.

2. Allen, B. D. (2021). Digital Twins and Living Models at NASA. [Online]. Available: https://ntrs.nasa.gov/api/citations/20210023699/downloads/ASME%20Digital%20Twin%20Summit%20Keynote_final.pdf. [Accessed August 1, 2024].
3. Barricelli, B. R., Casiraghi, E., & Fogli, D. (2019). A Survey on Digital Twin: Definitions, Characteristics, Applications, and Design Implications. *IEEE Access*, 7, 167653–167671.
4. Grieves, M. W. (2005). Product Lifecycle Management: The New Paradigm for Enterprises. *International Journal of Product Development*, 2(1–2), 71–84.
5. Grieves, M. (2014). Digital Twin: Manufacturing Excellence through Virtual Factory Replication. White paper, 1, 1–7.
6. Bavo, A. M., Wilkins, B. T., Garot, P., De Bock, S., Saw, J., Søndergaard, L., Backer, O. D., & Iannaccone, F. (2020). Validation of a Computational Model Aiming to Optimize Preprocedural Planning in Percutaneous Left Atrial Appendage Closure. *Journal of Cardiovascular Computed Tomography*, 14(2), 149–154.
7. Grieves, M., & Vickers, J. (2017). Digital Twin: Mitigating Unpredictable, Undesirable Emergent Behavior in Complex Systems. In J. Kahlen, S. Flumerfelt, & A. Alves (Eds.), *Transdisciplinary Perspectives on Complex Systems* (pp. 85–113). Springer.
8. Shafto, M., Conroy, M., Doyle, R., Glaessgen, E., Kemp, C., LeMoigne, J., & Wang, L. (2010). *DRAFT Modeling, Simulation, Information Technology & Processing Roadmap Technology Area 11*. National Aeronautics and Space Administration.
9. Glaessgen, E. H., & Stargel, D. (2012). The Digital Twin Paradigm for Future NASA and U.S. Air Force Vehicles. In *53rd AIAA/ASME/ASCE/AHS/ASC Structures, Structural Dynamics and Materials Conference 20th AIAA/ASME/AHS Adaptive Structures Conference 14th AIAA, Honolulu, Hawaii, 1818*.
10. Tuegel, E. J., Ingraffea, A. R., Eason, T. G., & Spottswood, S. M. (2011). Reengineering Aircraft Structural Life Prediction Using a Digital Twin. *International Journal of Aerospace Engineering*, 2011(1), 1–14.
11. Ríos, J., Hernández, J. C., Oliva, M., & Mas, F. (n.d.). Product Avatar as Digital Counterpart of a Physical Individual Product: Literature Review and Implications in an Aircraft. In R. Curran, N. Wognum, M. Borsato, J. Stjepandić, & W. J. C. Verhagen (Eds.), *Transdisciplinary Lifecycle Analysis of Systems* (pp. 657–666). IOS Press.
12. Kiritsis, D. (2011). Closed-Loop PLM for Intelligent Products in the Era of the Internet of Things. *Computer-Aided Design*, 43(5), 479–501.
13. Kritzinger, W., Karner, M., Traar, G., Henjes, J., & Sihn, W. (2018). Digital Twin in Manufacturing: A Categorical Literature Review and Classification. *IFAC-PapersOnLine*, 51(11), 1016–1022.
14. Boschert, S., & Rosen, R. (2016). Digital Twin—The Simulation Aspect. In P. Hehenberger & D. Bradley (Eds.), *Mechatronic Futures* (pp. 59–74). Springer. https://doi.org/10.1007/978-3-319-32156-1_5
15. Negri, E., Fumagalli, L., & Macchi, M. (2017). A Review of the Roles of Digital Twin in CPS-Based Production Systems. *Procedia Manufacturing*, 11, 939–948.

16. Albrecht, R. (2024). Digital Twin: Modeling the Human Liver. *Siemens Healthineers*. [Online]. Available: www.siemens-healthineers.com/perspectives/modeling-the-human-liver. [Accessed August 1, 2024].
17. Karakra, A., Lamine, E., Fontanili, F., & Lamothe, J. (2020). HospiT'Win: A Digital Twin Framework for Patients' Pathways Real-Time Monitoring and Hospital Organizational Resilience Capacity Rnhancement. In *9th International Workshop on Innovative Simulation for Health Care, IWISH, 2020*, pp. 62–71.
18. GE Healthcare. (2024). Digital Twin. [Online]. Available: www.gehccommandcenter.com/digital-twin. [Accessed August 1, 2024].
19. Office of Capacity Management. (2024). Emergency Medicine. John Hopkins Medicine. [Online]. Available: www.hopkinsmedicine.org/emergency-medicine/c3. [Accessed August 1, 2024].
20. Santos, L. S. A., Sodre, L. C., Valle, R. S., Silva, B. A., Abi-chacra, E. V., Silva, L. M., ... & Branquinha, M. H. (2012). Antimicrobial Action of Chelating Agents: Repercussions on the Microorganism Development, Virulence and Pathogenesis. *Current Medicinal Chemistry*, 19(17), 2715–2737.
21. Wise, H. C., & Solit, D. B. (2019). Precision Oncology: Three Small Steps Forward. *Cancer Cell*, 35(6), 825–826.
22. Lou, B., Doken, S., Zhuang, T., Wingerter, D., Gidwani, M., Mistry, N., ... & Abazeed, M. E. (2019). An Image-Based Deep Learning Framework for Individualising Radiotherapy Dose: A Retrospective Analysis of Outcome Prediction. *The Lancet Digital Health*, 1(3), e136–e147.
23. Martinez-Velazquez, R., Gamez, R., & Saddik, A. E. (2019). Cardio Twin: A Digital Twin of the Human Heart Running on the Edge. In *2019 IEEE International Symposium on Medical Measurements and Applications (MeMeA), Istanbul, Turkey*, pp. 1–6.
24. Dassault Systèmes. (2024). The Living Heart Project. [Online]. Available: www.3ds.com/products-services/simulia/solutions/life-sciences-healthcare/the-living-heart-project/. [Accessed August 1, 2024].
25. Viceconti, M., Clapworthy, G., & Jan, S. V. S. (2008). The Virtual Physiological Human – A European Initiative for In Silico Human Modelling. *Journal of Physiological Sciences*, 58(7), 441–446.
26. Ayache, N. (2019). AI and Healthcare: Towards a Digital Twin. In *5th International Symposium on Multidisciplinary Computational Anatomy, Fukuoka, Japan*.
27. Ferdousi, R., Laamarti, F., Hossain, M. A., Yang, C., & Saddik, A. E. (2022). Digital Twins for Well-Being: An Overview [Version 2; Peer Review: 1 Approved, 1 Not Approved]. *Digital Twin*, 1, 7.
28. Liu, Y., Zhou, L., Ren, L., Wang, F., Liu, R., Pang, Z., & Deen, M. J. (2019). A Novel Cloud-Based Framework for the Elderly Healthcare Services Using Digital Twin. *IEEE Access*, 7, 49088–49101.
29. Parvinzamir, F., Zhao, Y., Deng, Z., Zha, X., Ersotelos, N., Dong, F., Liu, E., & Clapworthy, G. (2015). MyHealthAvatar: A Case Study of Web-Based Interactive Visual Analytics of Lifestyle Data. In *2015 IEEE International Conference on Computer and Information Technology; Ubiquitous Computing and Communications; Dependable, Autonomic and Secure Computing; Pervasive Intelligence and Computing, Liverpool, UK*.

30. Kondylakis, H., Flouris, G., Fundulaki, I., Papakonstantinou, V., & Tsiknakis, M. (2015). Flexible Access to Patient Data through e-Consent. In *Proceedings of the 5th EAI international conference on wireless mobile communication and healthcare, London*, pp. 263–266.
31. Barricelli, B. R., Casiraghi, E., Gliozzo, J., Petrini, A., & Valtolina, S. (2020). Human Digital Twin for Fitness Management. *IEEE Access*, 8, 26637–26664.
32. Research and Markets. (2024). Digital Twins in Healthcare Market, Industry Trends and Global Forecasts, till 2035 – Distribution by Therapeutic Area, Type of Digital Twin, Areas of Application, End Users and Key Geographical Regions. [Online]. Available: www.researchandmarkets.com/report/healthcare-digital-twins. [Accessed August 6, 2024].
33. Research and Markets. (2024). Digital Twins in Healthcare Global Market Report 2024. [Online]. Available: www.researchandmarkets.com/reports/5953352/digital-twins-in-healthcare-global-market-report. [Accessed August 5, 2024].

Index

FSC
www.fsc.org
MIX
Papier | Fördert
gute Waldnutzung
FSC® C083411

Kolibri 360 GmbH
Ferdinand-Jühlke-Straße 7
99095 Erfurt, Deutschland
produktsicherheit@kolibri360.de

Quantum Efficiency in Complex Systems, Part I: Biomolecular systems

SEMICONDUCTORS
AND SEMIMETALS

Volume 83

EICKE R. WEBER

Freiburg, Germany

MICHAEL THORWART

Hamburg, Germany

ULI WÜRFEL

Freiburg, Germany

ELSEVIER

AMSTERDAM • BOSTON • HEIDELBERG • LONDON
NEW YORK • OXFORD • PARIS • SAN DIEGO
SAN FRANCISCO • SINGAPORE • SYDNEY • TOKYO
Academic Press is an imprint of Elsevier

Academic Press is an imprint of Elsevier
525 B Street, Suite 1900, San Diego, CA 92101-4495, USA
30 Corporate Drive, Suite 400, Burlington, MA 01803, USA
32 Jamestown Road, London NW1 7BY, UK

First edition 2010

Copyright © 2010 Elsevier Inc. All rights reserved.

No part of this publication may be reproduced, stored in a retrieval system or transmitted in any form or by any means electronic, mechanical, photocopying, recording or otherwise without the prior written permission of the publisher.

Permissions may be sought directly from Elsevier's Science & Technology Rights Department in Oxford, UK: phone (+44) (0) 1865 843830; fax (+44) (0) 1865 853333; email: permissions@elsevier.com. Alternatively you can submit your request online by visiting the Elsevier web site at http://elsevier.com/locate/permissions, and selecting *Obtaining permission to use Elsevier material.*

Notice
No responsibility is assumed by the publisher for any injury and/or damage to persons or property as a matter of products liability, negligence or otherwise, or from any use or operation of any methods, products, instructions or ideas contained in the material herein. Because of rapid advances in the medical sciences, in particular, independent verification of diagnoses and drug dosages should be made.

ISBN: 978-0-12-375042-6
ISSN: 0080-8784

For information on all Academic Press publications visit our web site at *elsevierdirect.com*

Printed and bound by CPI Group (UK) Ltd, Croydon, CR0 4YY

Transferred to Digital Print 2011

Working together to grow libraries in developing countries

www.elsevier.com | www.bookaid.org | www.sabre.org

ELSEVIER BOOK AID International Sabre Foundation

CONTENTS

FOREWORD

Condensed matter physics is rapidly developing, in recent years, to provide the basis for a solid fundamental understanding of the behavior of electric carriers in ever more complex structures.

This development is fueled, on the one side, by stunning progress in our understanding of the fundamental physical processes: nonequilibrium statistics, quantum mechanics of open systems, quantum chaos, quantum information science, experimental quantum optics, surface physics, photonics, and computational physics have matured to a level that, today, allows us to do the first steps toward a *control* of complex systems, in the classical as well as in the quantum realm. Condensed matter physics is no more restricted to the solid state but is, nowadays, discussed and realized in prima facie very diverse physical settings, from atomic matter waves over interacting Rydberg atoms to clusters and photonic crystals. With an unprecedented control on the microscopic constituents of matter, nowadays, we are able to isolate single features of solid-state transport phenomena in dedicated experiments and to scrutinize their robustness when embedded in ever more complex environments. Powerful computational methods together with a much deeper analytical understanding of the mathematical structure of many body quantum mechanics permit quantitative treatments at a level of complexity far beyond what was considered to be achievable only few decades ago.

On the other side, the technological needs of modern, highly developed societies on a global scale define unprecedented challenges, notably in the energy sector. These will only be met if we succeed to come up with novel technological solutions, which qualitatively enhance our energy efficiency. The novel devices that will emerge from such a technological revolution ought to be available at lower cost, yet with qualitatively improved performance. They need to be robust and transportable. The fundamental insights expected from the above research areas, therefore, need to be implemented with the help of affordable, hitherto unknown, novel (solid state) materials. The invention of such materials itself will require a detailed understanding of their microscopic structure, and thus hinges once again on our progresses on the fundamental science side.

Although such challenge is enormous, it is also intellectually highly rewarding and attractive as it fosters the confluence of widely diverse scientific disciplines, which would otherwise rarely make contact: quantum physics meets chemistry, engineering, and material science.

A case in point is the field of organic electronics and of electronic and energy transfer processes in biological systems. New and suprising experimental data abound, which suggest that quantum mechanics might play a much more prominent role in such processes at room temperature. Already today we can expect that the insight we gain from the study of these highly structured, multihierarchical, nonequilibrium systems can be utilizied for new kinds of electronic switching and computing, or for the harvesting of energy from the sun in the form of photovoltaics – to name just a few of potentially highly relevant applications.

Yet, we have, so far, little understanding to which degree quantum phenomena such as many-body coherences and entanglement play a role in determining the electronic and optical properties of such complex structures. Neither do we understand under which conditions quantum coherence can persist in such, in general, widely open systems, and what defines the relevant timescales, nor do we have a general understanding of the dynamical manifestations thereof. The specific research area of organic electronics and of biological charge and energy-transfer units provides, thus, a nucleus for the truly interdisciplinary research effort, which will be needed to face the above challenges ahead.

The two parts of this volume will present a unique collection of contributions from leading scientists daring to venture into this, rather, new field. Most of the chapter authors participated in a workshop on the topic, "Quantum Efficiency – From Biology to Materilas Science" in the series of black-forest workshops, sponsored by the Freiburg Institute of Advanced Studies FRIAS, and jointly organised together with the Institute of Physics of the Albert-Ludwigs University of Freiburg, in the Fall of 2009.

It is expected that this volume will stimulate further work in this field, with the objective to, ultimately, use the fundamental insights that will be gained to guide the development of more efficient opto-electronic and light-harvesting devices, at the lowest possible cost.

Eicke R. Weber
Freiburg, September 2010

LIST OF CONTRIBUTORS

Eicke R. Weber, Director Fraunhofer-Institut für Solare Energiesysteme ISE Sprecher, Allianz Energie der Fraunhofergesellschaft Heidenhofstr. 2, 79110 Freiburg, Germany. (Foreword)

Andreas Buchleitner, Department for Quantum Optics and Statistics, Institute of Physics, Albert Ludwigs University of Freiburg, Hermann-Herder-Str. 3, D-79104 Freiburg, email: a.buchleitner@physik.uni-freiburg.de. (Ch1)

Florian Mintert, Department for Quantum Optics and Statistics, Institute of Physics, Albert Ludwigs University of Freiburg, Hermann-Herder-Str. 3, D-79104 Freiburg, email: florian.mintert@physik.uni-freiburg.de. (Ch1)

Jürgen Köhler, Experimental Physics IV, and Bayreuth Institute of Macromolecular Research (BIMF), University of Bayreuth, 95440 Bayreuth, Germany, email: juergen.koehler@uni-bayreuth.de. (Ch3)

Michael Thorwart, I. Institut für Theoretische Physik, Universität Hamburg, Jungiusstraße 9, 20355 Hamburg, Germany, email: michael.thorwart@physik.uni-hamburg.de. (Ch2)

Peter Nalbach, School of Soft Matter Research, Freiburg Institute for Advanced Studies (FRIAS), Albert-Ludwigs-Universität Freiburg, Albertstraße, 19, 79104 Freiburg, Germany.
I. Institut für Theoretische Physik, Universität Hamburg, Jungiusstraße 9, 20355 Hamburg, Germany, email: peter.nalbach@physik.uni-hamburg.de. (Ch2)

Richard J. Cogdell, Experimental Physics IV, and Bayreuth Institute of Macromolecular Research (BIMF), University of Bayreuth, 95440 Bayreuth, Germany. (Ch3)

Torsten Scholak, Department for Quantum Optics and Statistics, Institute of Physics, Albert Ludwigs University of Freiburg, Hermann-Herder-Str. 3, D-79104 Freiburg, email: torsten.scholak@physik.uni-freiburg.de. (Ch1)

Thomas Wellens, Department for Quantum Optics and Statistics, Institute of Physics, Albert Ludwigs University of Freiburg, Hermann-Herder-Str. 3, D-79104 Freiburg, email: thomas.wellens@physik.uni-freiburg.de. (Ch1)

CHAPTER 1

Transport and Entanglement

T. Scholak, F. Mintert, T. Wellens, and **A. Buchleitner**

Contents

Transport phenomena are all around us, from microscopic to macroscopic scales, and they mediate fundamental transfer processes of matter, charge, or energy. Much of present day science and technology ultimately relies on transport processes, from radiation transfer in the atmosphere, with its very tangible impact on climatic conditions, over the long distance transfer of electrical energy, controlled chemical reactions in large molecules, signal processing in biological tissue, to charge transfer in semiconductor devices – be it detectors of high-energy or low-energy particles or photons,

Semiconductors and Semimetals, Volume 83
ISSN 0080-8784, DOI: 10.1016/B978-0-12-375042-6.00001-8

© 2010 Elsevier Inc.
All rights reserved.

efficient light sources like LEDs, or photovoltaic solar cells – random lasers, and even quantum cryptography and computation. Irrespective of the actual scale, all practical applications here listed, and equally so all the underlying, paradigmatic model systems bear the common feature of some sort of complexity, in the sense that transport is mediated by many more than just one degree of freedom, and that these different degrees of freedom are only partially controlled and garnish the dynamics with different characteristic length and timescales. The unavoidable lack of control is summarized as "disorder" or "noise" inflicted on the transport process of interest – which occurs in the "system's" degrees of freedom – by some noisy environment.

Complexity is ambivalent in nature, because it creates novel and unexpected patterns that emerge, e.g., as, often very robust, collective modes, but can also induce instabilities and sudden phase transitions. Hence, disorder, noise, and other typical traits of complex systems can manifest as a nuisance as well as a virtue, on macroscopic, as well as on microscopic scales (Anderson, 1958; Buchleitner and Hornberger, 2002; Gammaitoni *et al.*, 1998; Gutzwiller, 1990; Haake, 1991; Wellens *et al.*, 2004). When it comes to technological and engineering applications, however, disorder and noise are widely considered as purely detrimental, and the art of engineering, thus, largely consists in screening them out. This is ever more true on the microscopic level and in the context of quantum engineering – the quantum computer being a prime example: here, disorder and noise are conceived as the cause of decoherence, i.e., of the fading away of quantum interference effects – which are the very source of its formidable potential efficiency as compared with classical supercomputing devices. In turn, when disorder and noise cannot be screened away, the widespread opinion is that quantum coherence effects are bound to faint on the associated length and timescales. Biological systems, large macromolecular structures, and equally so multilayered semiconductor structures as used in detector, LED, and solar cell technology – which often operate at ambient temperatures – apparently fall, precisely, in this latter category.

It must be noted, however, that much of this intuitive judgement on the sustainability of quantum coherence at high temperatures, and, possibly, on large scales, neglects the potential role of residual symmetries and implicitly assumes thermodynamic equilibrium. Weak localization (Bergmann, 1958; van Albada and Lagendijk, 1985; Wellens and Grémaud, 2009; Wolf and Maret, 1985) and maser and laser theory (Briegel *et al.*, 1994; Cai *et al.*, 1994; Haken, 1994) provide highly relevant examples for coherence effects that prevail in the presence of disorder and noise – because of time-reversal symmetry in the first case, and because of nonequilibrium statistical effects in the latter. Because biological systems are off-equilibrium by their very definition, and so are any technological devices that exhibit time-dependent transport; it is therefore much less clear-cut a case that quantum coherence cannot persist, at least on transient, yet exploitable timescales, even in such complex systems. Under this perspective, the actual challenge rather is to identify the relevant degrees of freedom which potentially sustain coherence, the associated timescales, and the specific or potential functional role of coherence. Once again, this challenge is highly nontrivial as a result of the abundance and intricate coupling of a complex system's many degrees of freedom.

In comparison to engineers, biological evolution has had ample time to test the potential of quantum coherence for its specific purpose to improve a species' adaption to its environment. Indeed, recent experimental results (Cheng and Fleming, 2009; Collini *et al.*, 2010; Engel *et al.*, 2007; Lee *et al.*, 2007; Panitchayangkoon *et al.*, 2010) on the photosynthetic light-harvesting complexes used, e.g., by bacteria or higher plants (Blankenship, 2001; van Amerongen *et al.*, 2000), provide unambiguous evidence of a crucial role of quantum coherence for the stunning efficiency of excitation transfer on the underlying macromolecular level. These experiments raise novel and highly intriguing questions, e.g., on the physical origin of the surprisingly long coherence times and lengths, and on the mechanisms that, in the presence of that coherence, mediate the efficient transport. Convincing answers to these questions have the potential to very fundamentally alter our understanding of the role of quantum mechanics for the physical reality around us – as we perceive it, *and as we shape it*.

In our present contribution, we provide the skeleton of a modern quantum mechanical transport theory for molecular samples such as the FMO light-harvesting complex (Blankenship, 2001) often investigated in the above-mentioned experiments. We do not strive here for the quantitatively accurate modeling of a specific biological functional unit, though, but rather for identifying the fundamental features of coherent quantum transport on multiply connected, finite and disordered structures, together with the relevant timescales, which need to be compared with typical, environment-induced decay rates. Given the variability of biological samples and the remaining experimental uncertainties, e.g., on relevant coupling constants, as well as the astonishing ability of evolution to tune its basic constituents for better performance in variable environmental conditions, our approach is statistical from the very outset. This allows us to identify rare molecular configurations that exploit quantum coherence for better excitation transfer, to assess their statistical weight as well as their robustness, and to statistically correlate multisite coherence properties with transfer efficiencies. Indeed, we will show that strong multisite coherence and entanglement are an essential, necessary prerequisite for efficient transport.

We will start out, in Section 1, by a short recollection of the essential ingredients of quantum transport in disordered systems, before we introduce measures of quantum coherence and entanglement in multisite systems in Section 2. Section 3 will then specialize on excitation transport in FMO-like structures – under strictly coherent conditions as well as in presence of a dephasing environment. Section 4 concludes the article.

1. COHERENT TRANSPORT IN DISORDERED SYSTEMS

To set the stage, we will first introduce a general model Hamiltonian for quantum transport in disordered systems. Then, we will focus on the question whether quantum interference acts constructively or destructively on the transport efficiency. As we will see, partial – or even complete – suppression of transport is expected after averaging over the disorder. However, quantum coherence typically leads to large fluctuations, thus admitting more efficient transport for certain realizations of the disorder.

1.1. Model Hamiltonian

Although most systems in which energy transport occurs, such as solar cells or light-harvesting complexes, are typically composed of a large number of microscopic constituents, they can often be effectively described in terms of relatively few relevant degrees of freedom: for example, in a light-harvesting complex, each molecule is reduced to its ground state and one exited state, so that the entire collection of complex macro-molecules is described in terms of a few coupled two-level systems; similarly, considering transport of excitations in a gas of cold Rydberg atoms (Akulin *et al.*, 1999; Anderson *et al.*, 1998; Carroll *et al.*, 2006), each of the atoms can often be reduced to those two atomic levels whose transition frequency is closest to a given frequency. A typical model Hamiltonian is then of the form:

$$H = \sum_i \frac{\epsilon_i}{2}\sigma_z^{(i)} + \sum_{i\neq j} V_{ji}\sigma_+^{(j)}\sigma_-^{(i)}, \tag{1.1}$$

where the Pauli matrix $\sigma_z^{(i)}$ describes the ground and excited state of site i, with excitation energy ϵ_i. The operator $\sigma_+^{(j)}\sigma_-^{(i)}$ describes the transfer of an excitation from site i to site j with corresponding coupling strength $V_{ji} = V_{ij}^*$.

According to Eq. (1.1), the total number of excitations $\sum_i \sigma_+^{(i)}\sigma_-^{(i)}$ is conserved, which is characteristic for near-resonant exchange processes.

Starting initially with a single excitation, we can, therefore, reduce the exponentially large Hilbert space to the subspace containing only a single excitation. The corresponding Hamiltonian then reads as follows:

$$H = \sum_{i} \epsilon_i |i\rangle\langle i| + \sum_{i \neq j} V_{ji} |j\rangle\langle i|, \tag{1.2}$$

where $|i\rangle$ denotes the state where the excitation is located at site i. Hamiltonians of the form given in Eq. (1.2) are also frequently used to describe electronic transport. In this case, $|i\rangle$ describes a state where the electron is localized inside the attractive potential formed by the corresponding atom, with the individual atoms arranged in a (more or less) periodic lattice. Only a single bound state (usually the ground state) is taken into account for each atom (tight-binding approximation). The coupling V_{ji} then arises from the overlap between the wavefunctions corresponding to different localized states $|i\rangle$ and $|j\rangle$. Usually, this gives rise to coupling only between neighboring atoms, with constant $V_{ji} = V$.

Finally, Eq. (1.2) with constant nearest-neighbor couplings can also be regarded as a discretized version of a wave equation, provided the distance between neighboring sites is smaller than the wavelength. Then, the nondiagonal coupling term in Eq. (1.2) represents the Laplace operator occuring, e.g., in the Helmholtz equation for electromagnetic waves, or in the kinetic energy for a quantum particle, whereas the diagonal terms ϵ_i correspond to a spatially varying potential. Indeed, the interference phenomena of coherent transport discussed in this section apply equally well to transport of waves as to the discrete model given by Eq. (1.2).

In many cases, however, the Hamiltonian of the system is not precisely known. In the case of a periodic system, this may be due to the presence of impurities at random, unknown lattice sites; or, in the case of a finite complex (Adolphs and Renger, 2006), this may be because of its complicated spatial structure that can be resolved, e.g., by X-ray scattering only with limited accuracy. This imperfect knowledge is accounted for by introducing *disorder* into the model. In this case, the matrix elements of the Hamiltonian are treated as stochastic variables following a certain statistical distribution, which depends on the model under consideration. In many cases, the randomness only affects either the ϵ_i's or the V_{ji}'s (diagonal or off-diagonal disorder). For example, dipolar coupling between identical atoms (i.e., $\epsilon_i = \text{const}$) placed at random positions $\mathbf{r_i}$ gives rise to off-diagonal disorder because V_{ji} is then proportional to $|\mathbf{r_i} - \mathbf{r_j}|^{-3}$.

1.2. Path amplitudes

In the following, we will be interested in the *transfer probability* to find the excitation at a particular output site j after it has been injected at the input site i:

$$p_j(t) = |a_j(t)|^2, \text{ with } a_j(t) = \langle j|\mathcal{U}(t)|i\rangle, \tag{1.3}$$

under the assumption of purely coherent dynamics, i.e., $\mathcal{U}(t) = \exp(-iHt/\hbar)$. In terms of the Green's function of the Hamiltonian (1.2):

$$G_{ji}(z) = \left\langle j \left| \frac{1}{z-H} \right| i \right\rangle, \tag{1.4}$$

the amplitude a_j can be expressed as follows (for $t > 0$):

$$a_j(t) = \frac{1}{2\pi i} \int_{\mathcal{C}} \mathrm{d}z\, \mathrm{e}^{-izt/\hbar} G_{ji}(z), \tag{1.5}$$

where the contour $\mathcal{C}$ runs above the real axis from $-\infty + i\epsilon$ to $+\infty + i\epsilon$, $\epsilon > 0$. The Green's function, in turn, can be expanded in powers of the coupling elements:

$$G_{ji}(z) = \delta_{ij}\frac{1}{z-\epsilon_i} + (1-\delta_{ij})\frac{1}{z-\epsilon_j}V_{ji}\frac{1}{z-\epsilon_i} + \frac{1}{z-\epsilon_j}\sum_{k\neq i,j} V_{jk}\frac{1}{z-\epsilon_k}V_{ki}\frac{1}{z-\epsilon_i}$$
$$+ \frac{1}{z-\epsilon_j}\sum_{k\neq j} V_{jk}\frac{1}{z-\epsilon_k}\sum_{l\neq k,i} V_{kl}\frac{1}{z-\epsilon_l}V_{li}\frac{1}{z-\epsilon_i} + \cdots. \tag{1.6}$$

Each term in the above expansion defines an amplitude for a certain path connecting the input with the output sites through certain intermediate sites $l, k, \ldots$. Two examples are shown in Fig. 1.1. By means of Eqs. (1.5) and (1.6), the transfer amplitude $a_j(t)$ results as the sum over all possible path amplitudes:

$$a_j(t) = \sum_{\gamma} a_j^{(\gamma)}(t), \tag{1.7}$$

where the index γ labels the paths. The corresponding transfer probability reads as follows:

$$p_j(t) = \sum_{\gamma,\gamma'} a_j^{(\gamma)} \left(a_j^{(\gamma')}\right)^* = \sum_{\gamma} \left|a_j^{(\gamma)}\right|^2 + \sum_{\gamma\neq\gamma'} a_j^{(\gamma)} \left(a_j^{(\gamma')}\right)^*. \tag{1.8}$$

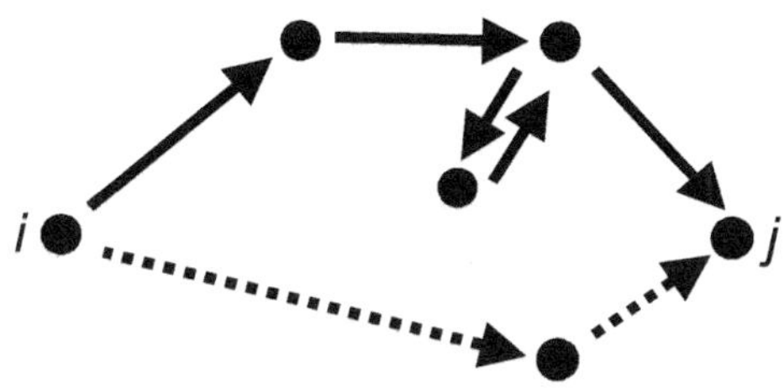

FIGURE 1.1 Examples for two different paths (solid and dashed arrows, respectively) connecting the input and output sites i and j. The transfer amplitude a_j results as a coherent sum over all possible path amplitudes.

The first term on the right-hand side of Eq. (1.8) represents the sum of the probabilities of each single path[1]. This describes a classical transport process, e.g., random walk or diffusion, which is characterized in terms of transition probabilities where the phase factors of the amplitudes do not matter. If only this term were present, the excitation would reach, at sufficiently long times, every site which is connected to the input site through some arbitrary path. However, coherent effects – arising from interference between amplitudes corresponding to different paths γ and γ' – are described by the second term in Eq. (1.8).

In general, this second term can be either positive or negative, i.e., amount to enhancement of transport through constructive interference, or decrease of transport through destructive interference. However, because the path amplitudes $a_j^{(\gamma)}$ acquire a random phase depending on the realization of the disorder, one could expect the interference terms in Eq. (1.8) to vanish on average, and thus no traces of coherent transport to survive the disorder average. Indeed, this happens in some cases, but, as further discussed in Section 1.3, in other cases coherent effects *do* survive and may even completely change the character of transport as compared with the classical case.

1.3. Weak localization

In the following scenario, it is quite easy to see that not all interference terms are cancelled by the disorder average: to demonstrate this, let us assume that the output and input sites are equal, $i = j$, and that the Hamiltonian fulfills the property of time-reversal invariance. For Eq. (1.2), this is

[1]In the simple form presented here, the path probabilities represented by the diagonal terms in Eq. (1.8) are not necessarily normalized to 1 when summing over all output sites. For this purpose, one would have to consider a more elaborate version of the diagrammatic expansion, where the on-site energies ϵ_i are replaced by self-energies, which, in turn, are given by the diagonal elements $\overline{G_{ii}(z)}$ of the disorder-averaged Green's function (Abou-Chacra *et al.*, 1973; Feenberg, 1948). This, however, does not change the arguments presented here.

the case if the coupling matrix elements V_{kl} are real, such that $V_{kl} = V_{lk}^* = V_{lk}$. By virtue of Eqs. (1.5) and (1.6), the amplitude for a single path p reads

$$a_i^{(\gamma)}(t) = \frac{1}{2\pi i} \int_C \mathrm{d}z\, \mathrm{e}^{-izt/\hbar} \frac{1}{z - \epsilon_i} V_{ik} \frac{1}{z - \epsilon_k} \cdots V_{mi} \frac{1}{z - \epsilon_i}, \tag{1.9}$$

where the indices $m \ldots k$ label all intermediate sites. For the reversed path $\widetilde{\gamma}$, where the particle passes through the same intermediate sites as in the path γ, but in opposite order (see Fig. 1.2), Eq. (1.9) yields exactly the same amplitude as for γ, i.e., $a_i^{(\gamma)} = a_i^{(\widetilde{\gamma})}$. Therefore, the interference term $a_i^{(\gamma)} \left(a_i^{(\widetilde{\gamma})}\right)^* = \left|a_i^{(\gamma)}\right|^2$ is always positive – for each realization of the disorder, even if the phase of $a_i^{(\gamma)}$ is completely random! – and hence remains positive after the disorder average. Even if all other interference terms vanish, this increases, on average, the *return probability* p_i (defined in the same way as the transfer probability, but for $i = j$) by a factor of two:

$$\overline{p_i} = \sum_\gamma \overline{|a_i^{(\gamma)}|^2} + \sum_\gamma \overline{a_i^{(\gamma)} \left(a_i^{(\widetilde{\gamma})}\right)^*} = 2 \sum_\gamma \overline{|a_i^{(\gamma)}|^2}. \tag{1.10}$$

Here, and in the following, the disorder average is denoted by $\overline{(\ldots)}$. To be precise, we note that the factor of two in Eq. (1.10) is only reached if all relevant paths γ, which contribute to $\overline{p_i}$, pass through at least two intermediate sites – otherwise, there exists no reversed path $\widetilde{\gamma} \neq \gamma$. Therefore, the enhancement factor is, in general, smaller than two. The enhancement of the average return probability described by Eq. (1.10) is also known as *coherent backscattering*. It has been observed, e.g., by scattering light on diffusive samples (Chanelière *et al.*, 2004; Kuga and Ishimaru, 1984; van Albada and Lagendijk, 1985; Wolf and Maret, 1985).

Remember, however, that we have originally been interested in the situation where the output site is different from the input site. What about

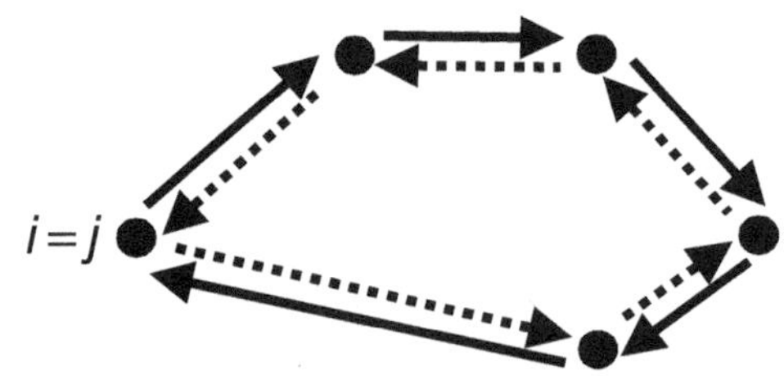

FIGURE 1.2 In the presence of time-reversal symmetry, the amplitudes of the two reversed paths γ and $\widetilde{\gamma}$ (solid and dashed arrows, respectively) are the same – for each realization of the disorder! The interference between these amplitudes increases the average return probability by a factor of two.

the impact of quantum interference in this case? Because the total norm is conserved, an increase of the return probability must necessarily go along with a reduction of transport toward other sites. If the return probability – and therefore also its increase by at most a factor of two – is small, the corresponding decrease of the transfer probability at other sites is also small. This is, therefore, called *weak localization* (Bergmann, 1958). Although it does not change the character of diffusive classical transport qualitatively, it amounts to a small correction corresponding to a reduction of the diffusion constant as compared with the classical prediction. Even if this effect is small, it can be experimentally measured by taking advantage of its dependence on the time-reversal symmetry. In the case of electronic transport, for example, this symmetry can be broken by applying magnetic fields, thereby switching off the weak localization effect. Correspondingly, the conductivity of electrons in disordered metals is larger in the presence of magnetic fields than without – even if the fields are so small that the classical electronic motion remains unaffected (Bergmann, 1958).

1.4. Anderson localization

As discussed earlier, constructive interference between time-reversed path amplitudes at the initial site necessarily implies destructive interference at other sites. Thereby, transport toward other sites is – on average – *reduced* by quantum interference. How strongly the transport is reduced is determined mainly by the value of the return probability. The latter, in turn, crucially depends on the dimensionality of the system. Considering classical random walks on discrete lattices, e.g., the particle comes back to its initial position *with certainty* (if one waits long enough) in the one- and two-dimensional lattices, whereas, in three dimensions, it *never* returns (at long times) (Pólya, 1921). Correspondingly, the impact of quantum interference is, in general, stronger for lower dimensions.

Indeed, it has been found that quantum interference may not only reduce, but also completely suppress the classically diffusive transport. In this case, the particle remains, even in the limit of long times, *exponentially localized* around the initial site. In other words, the transfer probability decays exponentially with increasing distance from the initial site, where the inverse exponent defines the *localization length*. This has to be contrasted with the classical prediction according to which the particle would continue propagating toward more and more distant sites. This suppression of transport resulting from destructive quantum interference in the presence of disorder is known as *Anderson localization* (Anderson, 1958). It was demonstrated originally for the *Anderson model* (Anderson, 1958), defined by Eq. (1.2) with constant nearest-neighbor coupling V and random on-site energies ϵ_i, which are independently and uniformly distributed in some interval $[-W/2, W/2]$. Thus, W is a measure for the strength of the disorder in the Anderson model.

In accordance with the dimensionality argument given earlier, it has been found that, in one and two dimensions, all eigenstates of the Anderson model are exponentially localized, even for arbitrarily weak disorder! Because only those eigenstates that overlap with the initial site get populated, the particle remains localized in the vicinity of the initial site. In 1D, the localization length for small disorder (and states with small energy $E \ll V$) is given by $\xi = 96V^2/W^2$ (Kramer and MacKinnon, 1993). In 2D, ξ depends exponentially on V^2/W^2 (Sheng, 2006), such that the localization length may become extremely large (MacKinnon and Kramer, 1982). If the localization length (strictly defined through one single number only for an infinite system) is larger than the system size, localization does not manifest in the dynamics, and the particle propagates diffusively over the whole system.

In 3D, there exists a phase transition: only if the disorder strength is larger than a certain critical value ($W_c \simeq 16V$; Vollhardt and Wölfle, 1992), all eigenstates are localized, and thus transport is completely suppressed. For disorder strengths smaller than the critical value, those eigenstates with energies inside a certain window (approximately given by $|E| < 6V$; Vollhardt and Wölfle, 1992) – are extended over the entire system, whereas the remaining eigenstates (outside this window) are still localized. The existence of at least a few extended eigenstates then allows the particle to propagate over the whole sample. If the disorder strength is well below the critical value, almost all eigenstates are extended. This is the regime of weak localization (see Section 1.3), where the transport is essentially classical, and quantum interference only leads to a slight reduction of the diffusion constant.

The characteristics of Anderson localization described earlier (localization in 1D and 2D, phase transition in 3D) are qualitatively valid also for other models apart from the Anderson model, for example, for off-diagonal instead of diagonal disorder (Soukoulis and Economou, 1981; Xiong and Evangelou, 2001), or in driven chaotic systems (e.g., the kicked rotor (Casati *et al.*, 1979; Zhang *et al.*, 2004) or the driven hydrogen atom (Casati *et al.*, 1979; Krug and Buchleitner, 2005; Maeda and Gallagher, 2004)), which can be mapped onto the Anderson model (Fishman *et al.*, 1982; Lemarié *et al.*, 2010). An exception is the case of long-range interactions, where the coupling strength $V_{ji} \propto |\mathbf{r_i} - \mathbf{r_j}|^{-\alpha}$ depends algebraically, with exponent $-\alpha$, on the randomly distributed positions $\mathbf{r_i}$ of the individual sites. It has been found (Cizeau and Bouchaud, 1994) that the localization properties are then determined by the parameter $\mu = d/\alpha$, where d denotes the dimension of the system. Anderson localization, i.e., exponential localization of all eigenstates, occurs for $\mu \to 0$. Hence, as expected, low dimensions and short-range interactions (i.e., large α) favor the occurrence of Anderson localization. However, only extended states are present for $\mu > 2$, whereas the regime $0 < \mu \leq 2$ gives rise to algebraically localized states. The physically relevant case of dipolar coupling, i.e., $\alpha = 3$, in three dimensions, $d = 3$ – which we will consider in Section 3 – corresponds to $\mu = 1$, i.e., algebraic localization. The particle then reaches arbitrarily distant sites, but slower than for any diffusive process.

In the case of wave propagation in random potentials, the parameters determining the occurrence of Anderson localization are the wavelength $\lambda = 2\pi/k$ and the *mean free path* ℓ (i.e., the distance the wave travels before being scattered). According to the Ioffe–Regel-criterion (Ioffe and Regel, 1960), Anderson localization in 3D is expected for $k\ell \lesssim 1$, whereas $k\ell \gg 1$ gives rise to diffusive transport and weak localization.

Although, as the earlier discussion shows, Anderson localization appears to be a universal phenomenon of coherent transport in the presence of disorder, it is interesting to note that a simple intuitive understanding of this effect is still lacking. Why do the path amplitudes interfere *perfectly* destructively for distances much larger than the localization length? In contrast to the weak localization effect, which admits a clear interpretation in terms of time-reversed paths (see Fig. 1.2), a perturbative description of Anderson localization in terms of interfering path amplitudes is much more complicated, if not impossible. Nevertheless, there exists a self-consistent theory (Vollhardt and Wölfle, 1980), which explains Anderson localization as an extreme case of weak localization. It successfully describes many aspects of the Anderson localization phenomenon, e.g., the existence of a phase transition from the diffusive to the localized regime in 3D, even though it does not reproduce the numerically obtained critical exponents of the phase transition (Schreiber and Grussbach, 1996).

1.5. Fluctuations

As we have seen in the earlier sections, quantum interference reduces transport *on average*, leading to a partial or even complete suppression of diffusion. This does not exclude, however, the possibility that, *for some realizations of the disorder*, the transfer probability may also be enhanced by quantum interference. To identify such exceptional situations, one has to look at the *fluctuations* of the transfer probability under variation of the disorder realization.

At least to our knowledge, the fluctuations of the time-dependent transfer probability in a closed, discrete system as defined by Eqs. (1.2) and (1.3) have not yet been studied intensively (see, however, Casati *et al.*, 1990; Krug *et al.*, 2003). Much more is known about the fluctuations of *conductance*, which is defined for an open system with a large number N of input and output channels (Landauer, 1957):

$$g = \sum_{i,j=1}^{N} |t_{ji}|^2, \tag{1.11}$$

with t_{ji} the transmission amplitude from the input channel i to the output channel j. According to Eq. (1.11), the dimensionless conductance g is normalized such that the maximum value of g – reached in the case of perfect transmission – equals N. Roughly speaking, the weak localization regime then corresponds to $g \gg 1$, whereas Anderson localization amounts to a small conductance that decreases exponentially with the system size.

In the weak localization regime, g can be shown to exhibit Gaussian statistics (Pichard *et al.*, 1990). Remarkably, the variance $\overline{\delta g^2}$ of these fluctuations turns out to be a constant of the order of 1, depending on the symmetry class (absence or presence of time-reversal symmetry), but independent of the number N of channels, the length of the sample or of microscopic details such as the mean free path! They are therefore called *universal conductance fluctuations* (Al'tshuler, 1985; Imry, 1986; Lee and Stone, 1985). Moreover, the individual transmission intensities then fulfill: $\overline{|t_{ji}|^4} = 2\left(\overline{|t_{ji}|^2}\right)^2$, i.e., their fluctuations are of the same order as their mean values. This property also applies, e.g., to the intensity distribution of light reflected from a disordered sample (Wolf *et al.*, 1988), as well as to the transfer probability defined earlier, see Eq. (1.8). This can easily be seen as follows:

$$\overline{p_j(t)^2} = \sum_{\gamma_1,\gamma_2,\gamma_3,\gamma_4} \overline{a_j^{(\gamma_1)} a_j^{(\gamma_2)} \left(a_j^{(\gamma_3)} a_j^{(\gamma_4)}\right)^*} \tag{1.12}$$

$$\simeq 2 \sum_{\gamma_1} \overline{|a_j^{(\gamma_1)}|^2} \sum_{\gamma_2} \overline{|a_j^{(\gamma_2)}|^2} = 2\left(\overline{p_j(t)}\right)^2. \tag{1.13}$$

In the weak localization regime (and for $i \neq j$), one assumes that interference between different paths can be neglected. Hence, the average in Eq. (1.12) only survives if either $\gamma_3 = \gamma_1, \gamma_4 = \gamma_2$ or $\gamma_3 = \gamma_2, \gamma_4 = \gamma_1$, giving rise to the factor 2 in Eq. (1.13).

However, in the localized regime, it has been found that the fluctuations of $\ln(g)$ – but not of g itself! – are described by a Gaussian normal distribution (Abrikosov, 1981; Kumar, 1985; Pichard *et al.*, 1990), at least for quasi-1D sample geometries, and approximately also in 2D and 3D (Muttalib *et al.*, 2005). The wings of this distribution, therefore, correspond to values of g, which are exponentially larger than its mean value. One may therefore ask if it is possible to find certain realizations of the disorder where quantum interference influences the conductance in a constructive way. This appears to be especially plausible in the case of finite, not too large sample sizes, where the mean value of g is not yet exponentially suppressed. We will come back to this question in Section 3.

2. MANY-BODY COHERENCE AND ENTANGLEMENT

As we have seen in the earlier section, phase coherence between different path alternatives plays a crucial role for the propagation of a single excitation injected into a quantum mechanical many-body system. In this section, we will discuss, once again from a rather general point of view, the notions of coherence and of entanglement in a quantum many-body system, and define tools for the quantitative characterization thereof.

2.1. Basic concepts

2.1.1. Single-particle coherence

In order to elucidate the general notion of coherence, let us start out with the well-known double-slit for a single particle. Here, the wave function

$$\Psi(\vec{x}) = \alpha\Psi_{\mathrm{L}}(\vec{x}) + \beta\Psi_{\mathrm{R}}(\vec{x}) \tag{2.14}$$

consists of a coherent superposition of one wave function $\Psi_{\mathrm{L}}(\vec{x})$ describing the passage through the left slit, and another wave function $\Psi_{\mathrm{R}}(\vec{x})$ describing the passage through the right slit. The interference fringes that give evidence of phase coherence result from the cross terms $\Psi_{\mathrm{L}}^*(\vec{x})\Psi_{\mathrm{R}}(\vec{x})$ and $\Psi_{\mathrm{R}}^*(\vec{x})\Psi_{\mathrm{L}}(\vec{x})$ in the particle density $|\Psi(\vec{x})|^2$.

In order to describe situations in which the interaction with an environment or the average over disorder – as discussed in Section 1 – leads to imperfect phase coherence, we change to the density matrix picture. The diagonal elements $\varrho(\vec{x},\vec{x})$ of the density matrix ϱ give the probability density to find the particle at position $\vec{x}$, whereas the nondiagonal elements

$$\varrho(\vec{x},\vec{x}'),\ (\vec{x} \neq \vec{x}') \tag{2.15}$$

characterize the coherence properties. In the case of perfect coherence, the particle is described by a wave function $\Psi(\vec{x})$, which, in turn, defines the density matrix $\varrho(\vec{x},\vec{x}') = \Psi(\vec{x})\Psi^*(\vec{x}')$. Consequently, its matrix elements fulfill

$$|\varrho(\vec{x},\vec{x}')| = \sqrt{\varrho(\vec{x},\vec{x})\varrho(\vec{x}',\vec{x}')}, \tag{2.16}$$

and the particle has maximal *degree of coherence* between $\vec{x}$ and $\vec{x}'$. Generally, the degree of coherence is quantified as $g_1(\vec{x},\vec{x}') = |\varrho(\vec{x},\vec{x}')|/\sqrt{\varrho(\vec{x},\vec{x})\varrho(\vec{x}',\vec{x}')} \leq 1$. Note that, by definition, $g_1(\vec{x},\vec{x}) = 1$ for the diagonal elements. However, the nondiagonal elements $g_1(\vec{x},\vec{x}')$ typically decay with increasing distance between $\vec{x}$ and $\vec{x}'$. The length scale of this decay then defines the *coherence length*. For example, in the case of an exponential decay

$$|\varrho(\vec{x},\vec{x}')| = \sqrt{\varrho(\vec{x},\vec{x})\varrho(\vec{x}',\vec{x}')}e^{-\frac{|\vec{x}-\vec{x}'|}{x_0}}, \tag{2.17}$$

the coherence length is x_0. For perfect coherence, the coherence length is infinite, or, in other words: $g_1(\vec{x},\vec{x}') = 1$ for all $\vec{x}$ and $\vec{x}'$.

Applying this concept to an arbitrary two-state system, described in terms of its energy ground state $|g\rangle$ and an excited state $|e\rangle$, coherences of such a single-particle system are identified with the nondiagonal elements ϱ_{ge} and $\varrho_{eg} = \varrho_{ge}^*$ of its density matrix:

$$\varrho = \begin{bmatrix} \varrho_{ee} & \varrho_{ge} \\ \varrho_{ge}^* & \varrho_{gg} \end{bmatrix}. \tag{2.18}$$

The diagonal elements $\varrho_{gg} = \langle g|\varrho|g\rangle$ and $\varrho_{ee} = \langle e|\varrho|e\rangle$ give the probability for the particle to reside in its ground state $|g\rangle$ or in its excited state $|e\rangle$, and $\sqrt{\varrho_{gg}\varrho_{ee}}$ is the maximum value of the modulus $|\varrho_{eg}|$ for any valid density matrix ϱ (which has non-negative eigenvalues).

Similarly to the above, the nondiagonal elements define the degree of coherence as $g_1 = |\varrho_{ge}|/\sqrt{\varrho_{ee}\varrho_{gg}} \leq 1$. If $g_1 = 1$, the system is in a pure state with perfect phase coherence between the ground state and the excited state. The degree of coherence is related to the linear entropy,

$$1 - \mathrm{Tr}\varrho^2 = 2\varrho_{ee}\varrho_{gg}(1 - g_1^2), \tag{2.19}$$

of ρ, which vanishes for pure states. As compared with g_1, the linear entropy has the advantage that it provides a basis-independent definition of single-body coherence, i.e., it remains constant under arbitrary unitary transformations of the two-level system.

2.1.2. Two-body coherence and entanglement

Imagine a two-site system with a single excitation spread coherently over both sites:

$$|\Psi\rangle = \alpha|eg\rangle + \beta|ge\rangle, \tag{2.20}$$

Determining the reduced density matrices for the individual sites, see Eq. (2.31) below, we find only diagonal elements: $\rho_1 = \begin{bmatrix} |\alpha|^2 & 0 \\ 0 & |\beta|^2 \end{bmatrix}$ and $\rho_2 = \begin{bmatrix} |\beta|^2 & 0 \\ 0 & \alpha|^2 \end{bmatrix}$, i.e., the single-body coherences of $|\Psi\rangle$ vanish! Nevertheless, this state exhibits two-body coherence, because interference phenomena can be observed in collective observables of both sites. Similarly to the single-body coherence defined earlier, it seems natural to identify such two-body coherence through the nondiagonal elements of the density matrix

$$\varrho_\Psi = |\Psi\rangle\langle\Psi| = \begin{bmatrix} 0 & 0 & 0 & 0 \\ 0 & |\beta|^2 & \beta\alpha^* & 0 \\ 0 & \beta^*\alpha & |\alpha|^2 & 0 \\ 0 & 0 & 0 & 0 \end{bmatrix}. \tag{2.21}$$

The finite elements $\langle eg|\varrho_\Psi|ge\rangle = \alpha\beta^*$ and $\langle ge|\varrho_\Psi|eg\rangle = \beta\alpha^*$ apparently give evidence of the two-body coherence. However, the mere presence of some nondiagonal elements is not yet a sufficient indicator for two-body coherence. This is demonstrated by the following counter-example:

$$|\Phi\rangle = (\alpha_1|g\rangle + \beta_1|e\rangle) \otimes (\alpha_2|g\rangle + \beta_2|e\rangle). \tag{2.22}$$

Here, each site is in a coherent superposition of the ground and the excited state. The coherence can be verified through interference measurements on the individual sites, but there is no two-body coherence. Nevertheless, the corresponding density matrix reads as follows:

$$\varrho_\Phi = \begin{bmatrix} |\beta_1|^2 & |\beta_2|^2 & |\beta_1|^2 & \alpha_2\beta_2^* & \alpha_1\beta_1^* & |\beta_2|^2 & \alpha_1\beta_1^* & \alpha_2\beta_2^* \\ |\beta_1|^2 & \alpha_2^*\beta_2 & |\beta_1|^2 & |\alpha_2|^2 & \alpha_1\beta_1^* & \alpha_2^*\beta_2 & \alpha_1\beta_1^* & |\alpha_2|^2 \\ \alpha_1^*\beta_1 & |\beta_2|^2 & \alpha_1^*\beta_1 & \alpha_2\beta_2^* & |\alpha_1|^2 & |\beta_2|^2 & |\alpha_1|^2 & \alpha_2\beta_2^* \\ \alpha_1^*\beta_1 & \alpha_2^*\beta_2 & \alpha_1^*\beta_1 & |\alpha_2|^2 & |\alpha_1|^2 & \alpha_2^*\beta_2 & |\alpha_1|^2 & |\alpha_2|^2 \end{bmatrix}. \tag{2.23}$$

Also here, the matrix elements $\langle eg|\varrho|ge\rangle = \alpha_1\beta_1^*\alpha_2^*\beta_2$ and $\langle ge|\varrho|eg\rangle = \alpha_1^*\beta_1\alpha_2\beta_2^*$, associated with the coherence between the state with a single excitation on the first site and the state with a single excitation on the second site, are finite. Hence, the fact that these matrix elements are different from zero is not yet sufficient in order to distinguish two-body coherence from single-body coherence. Instead, it turns out that two-body coherence is associated with the occurrence of *entanglement* between the two sites.

To fix terminology, we define a pure state $|\Psi\rangle$ (of two distinguishable particles as opposed to entanglement of indistinguishable particles;

Eckert *et al.*, 2002; Ghirardi and Marinatto, 2004; Schliemann *et al.*, 2001; Zanardi, 2002) to be entangled if it cannot be described as a simple product of single-body states:

$$|\Psi\rangle \neq |\Phi_1\rangle \otimes |\Phi_2\rangle. \tag{2.24}$$

Otherwise, it is called *separable*. Entangled states carry coherence that cannot be understood, or experimentally verified, in terms of single-particle properties alone. Conversely, all coherence properties of separable states can be described completely in terms of the individual subsystems.

2.1.3. Many-body entanglement

This concept can be generalized straightforwardly to systems with more than two sites: a pure state of an N-body system is considered n-body entangled, if it cannot be written as a product of states of less than n sites. Similarly to the earlier characterization of two-body coherence in terms of entanglement, n-body entanglement of a state implies that its coherence properties can be completely characterized only in terms of collective observables of n subsystems.

2.1.4. Imperfect phase coherence: mixed states

In the case of mixed states, the characterization of entanglement turns out to be more involved. First, any mixed quantum state can be represented as a statistical mixture of pure states:

$$\varrho = \sum_i p_i |\Psi_i\rangle\langle\Psi_i|, \tag{2.25}$$

with probabilities p_i, i.e., $p_i \geq 0$ and $\sum_i p_i = 1$. Unfortunately, however, there are many different statistical ensembles of pure states that give rise to the same density matrix, i.e., that describe the same physical situation (Hughston *et al.*, 1993; Schrödinger, 1936). For example, an ensemble of pure states each corresponding to a particle that passes a double slit in a coherent superposition of both path alternatives $|\mathrm{L}\rangle$ and $|\mathrm{R}\rangle$ (for left and right)

$$|\psi_i\rangle = \frac{1}{\sqrt{2}}(|\mathrm{L}\rangle + \mathrm{e}^{i\varphi_i}|\mathrm{R}\rangle), \tag{2.26}$$

but with different relative phases φ_i, gives rise to exactly the same density matrix as an ensemble in which half of the particles take the left slit and the other half take the right slit:

$$\begin{aligned} \varrho &= \frac{1}{2}\sum_i p_i \left(|\mathrm{L}\rangle\langle\mathrm{L}| + |\mathrm{R}\rangle\langle\mathrm{R}| + \mathrm{e}^{i\varphi_i}|\mathrm{R}\rangle\langle\mathrm{L}| + \mathrm{e}^{-i\varphi_i}|\mathrm{L}\rangle\langle\mathrm{R}|\right) \\ &= \frac{1}{2}|\mathrm{L}\rangle\langle\mathrm{L}| + \frac{1}{2}|\mathrm{R}\rangle\langle\mathrm{R}|, \end{aligned} \tag{2.27}$$

for many possible different choices of probabilities p_i and corresponding phases φ_i.

Similarly as above, where the inspection of a single nondiagonal matrix element was not sufficient to identify many-body coherences inscribed into a pure state, the inspection of a single valid ensemble here does not provide sufficient information to infer the entanglement properties of the mixed state it represents.

Instead, a mixed quantum state is defined to be entangled, i.e., to carry many-body coherence, if it cannot be described by a statistical ensemble of pure states which each exhibit only single-body coherence (Werner, 1989). It can be shown (Werner, 1989) that only states that fulfill this criterion display quantum mechanical nonlocal behavior in the sense of Einstein, Podolsky and Rosen (Bell, 1965; Einstein *et al.*, 1935).

This concept now translates directly to n-body entanglement in an N-body system: a mixed state is n-body entangled if it cannot be described by an ensemble of pure states without any n-body entangled contribution. In the case of a four-body system, e.g., a mixed state ϱ that can be described like in Eq. (2.25) as a statistical mixture of the following pure states:

$$|\Psi_1\rangle = |\chi^{(1)}\rangle_{12} \otimes |\varphi^{(1)}\rangle_3 \otimes |\kappa^{(1)}\rangle_4, \tag{2.28}$$

$$|\Psi_2\rangle = |\varphi^{(2)}\rangle_1 \otimes |\chi^{(2)}\rangle_{23} \otimes |\kappa^{(2)}\rangle_4, \tag{2.29}$$

$$|\Psi_3\rangle = |\varphi^{(3)}\rangle_1 \otimes |\kappa^{(3)}\rangle_2 \otimes |\chi^{(3)}\rangle_{34}, \tag{2.30}$$

with two-body entangled components $|\chi^{(i)}\rangle_{nm}$ ($i = 1, 2, 3$) of sites n and m, does not carry any three-body or four-body entanglement, even if the entire many-body state can *not* be broken up into two parts that are not entangled with each other. An analogous situation is sketched in Fig. 1.3, for the case of a 10-body state.

2.2. Tools to characterize entanglement

2.2.1. Two-body entanglement of pure states

The most elementary problem in the theory of entangled states is to decide whether a pure state $|\Psi\rangle$ of a two-body system is of the form of Eq. (2.24), or

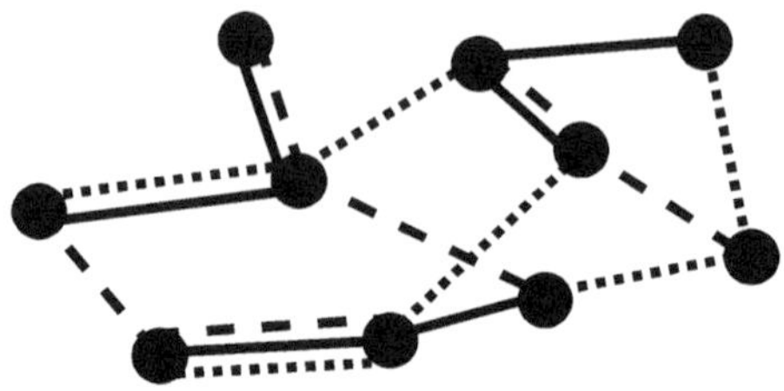

FIGURE 1.3 Three-body entanglement in a 10-body system. The 10-body density matrix ρ is defined as a statistical mixture of three states $|\Psi_1\rangle$, $|\Psi_2\rangle$, and $|\Psi_3\rangle$ (solid, dotted, and dashed lines, respectively), see Eq. (2.25). The individual lines denote the presence of entanglement between the respective sites in the states $|\Psi_i\rangle$. Note that each state $|\Psi_1\rangle$, $|\Psi_2\rangle$, and $|\Psi_3\rangle$ exhibits entanglement between at most three sites. Therefore, even if the entire 10-body state cannot be broken up into two distinct parts, it is not 10-body entangled, but only 3-body entangled.

not, i.e., if it is separable or entangled. This question has a straightforward answer, that can be found with the help of the reduced density matrix of either one of the two subsystems

$$\varrho_1 = \mathrm{Tr}_2|\Psi\rangle\langle\Psi|,\ \varrho_2 = \mathrm{Tr}_1|\Psi\rangle\langle\Psi|, \tag{2.31}$$

where Tr_1 and Tr_2 denote the partial trace over the first and the second subsystem. If $|\Psi\rangle$ is of product form as in Eq. (2.24), then both reduced density matrices are pure, i.e., both of them have exactly one nonvanishing eigenvalue, or, equivalently, the v. Neumann entropy $-\mathrm{Tr}\varrho_i \ln \varrho_i$ and the linear entropy $1 - \mathrm{Tr}\varrho_i^2 = 1$ $(i = 1, 2)$ vanish; in turn, if $|\Psi\rangle$ is not of product form, then both reduced density matrices are mixed, i.e., they have finite entropy. Because of its simplicity, this criterion is also often applied to systems with more than two units. Then, the system is divided into two parts, each of which can consist of several units. Furthermore, if a reduced density matrix is mixed, the value of its entropy provides a quantification of the degree of entanglement of the state $|\Psi\rangle$ (Vidal, 2000).

2.2.2. Many-body entanglement of pure states

This concept can be generalized to quantities that describe the entanglement of pure states of N-particle systems. To find such quantities – that are positive if and only if at least n sites, with $1 < n \leq N$, are entangled with each other – let us first rewrite the linear entropy of the reduced density matrix ρ_1, see Eq. (2.31), more explicitly:

$$1 - \mathrm{Tr}\varrho_1^2 = \sum_{i_1 i_2 j_1 j_2} \Psi^*_{i_1 j_1} \Psi^*_{i_2 j_2} (\Psi_{i_1 j_1} \Psi_{i_2 j_2} - \Psi_{i_1 j_2} \Psi_{i_2 j_1}). \tag{2.32}$$

The two terms in the bracket are distinguished from each other only by a permutation of indices. For a separable state $\Psi_{ij} = \varphi_i \phi_j$, this permutation is irrelevant because $\varphi_{i_1}\phi_{j_2}\varphi_{i_2}\phi_{j_1} = \varphi_{i_1}\phi_{j_1}\varphi_{i_2}\phi_{j_2}$, and the two terms in the bracket cancel each other.

Bearing this in mind, we can now consider states of three subsystems, and construct the function

$$\tau_3 = \left(\sum_{\alpha_1,\alpha_2,\alpha_3=0}^{2} \sum_{i_1\ldots k_3=1}^{d} e^{\frac{2\pi i}{3}(\alpha_1+\alpha_2+\alpha_3)} \Psi^*_{i_1 j_1 k_1} \Psi^*_{i_2 j_2 k_2} \Psi^*_{i_3 j_3 k_3} \Psi_{\vec{x}_1(\vec{\alpha})} \Psi_{\vec{x}_2(\vec{\alpha})} \Psi_{\vec{x}_3(\vec{\alpha})} \right)^{\frac{1}{3}}, \tag{2.33}$$

where d denotes the dimension of the single particle Hilbert spaces, and

$$\vec{x}_q(\alpha) = \left[(\Pi^{\alpha_1}\vec{i})_q,\ (\Pi^{\alpha_2}\vec{j})_q,\ (\Pi^{\alpha_3}\vec{p})_q \right], \quad (q = 1, 2, 3), \tag{2.34}$$

where Π is the cyclic permutation. It maps a vector $\vec{i}$ of indices i_1, i_2, i_3 onto the vector with cyclically permuted indices, i.e., $\Pi[i_1, i_2, i_3] = [i_2, i_3, i_1]$. One can easily check that τ_3 vanishes if one subsystem is not entangled with the other two. For example, if the first subsystem factorizes off, i.e., if $\Psi_{ijp} = \phi_i \Phi_{jq}$, then τ_3 factorizes into

$$\left(\sum_{\alpha=0}^{2} \sum_{i_1 i_2 i_3=1}^{d} e^{\frac{2\pi i}{3}\alpha} \phi^*_{i_1} \phi^*_{i_2} \phi^*_{i_3} \underbrace{\phi_{(\Pi^\alpha \vec{i})_1} \phi_{(\Pi^\alpha \vec{i})_2} \phi_{(\Pi^\alpha \vec{i})_3}}_{\text{independent of } \alpha} \right)^{\frac{1}{3}} \tag{2.35}$$

and a term that depends only on the second and third subsystem. Because the product of the last three terms in Eq. (2.35) is independent of α, the summation over this index reduces to $\sum_{\alpha=1}^{3} e^{\frac{2\pi i}{3}\alpha} = 0$, so that τ_3 vanishes.

If we want a quantity that is positive already if two components of a three-body system are entangled with each other, we can construct, very similarly to Eq. (2.33):

$$\tau_2 = \left(\sum_{\alpha_1,\alpha_2,\alpha_3=0}^{1} \sum_{i_1\ldots k_2=1}^{d} (i^{\alpha_1+\alpha_2} + i^{\alpha_1+\alpha_3} + i^{\alpha_2+\alpha_3}) \times \Psi^*_{i_1 j_1 k_1} \Psi^*_{i_2 j_2 k_2} \Psi_{\vec{x}_1(\vec{\alpha})} \Psi_{\vec{x}_2(\vec{\alpha})} \right)^{\frac{1}{2}}, \tag{2.36}$$

with $\Pi[i_1, i_2] = [i_2, i_1]$, and $\vec{x}_i(\vec{\alpha})$ $(i = 1, 2)$ defined analogously to Eq. (2.34). Similarly, one can construct for an N-body system a hierarchy τ_n $(n = 2 \ldots N)$ of entanglement quantifiers. A systematic construction of these quantities can be found in Appendix A.

As discussed in Section 1, one often encounters the situation where there is only one single excitation present in the system, see Eq. (1.2). This will also be the case in Section 3, where we will apply the τ_n to characterize the many-body coherence that is established during energy transport across a molecular network. In this case, all the quantities τ_n can be expressed in terms of the moments

$$M_n = \sum_{i=1}^{N} |\langle i|\Psi\rangle|^{2n} \tag{2.37}$$

of the excitation's spatial distribution over the sites i, like

$$\tau_2 = \sqrt{\tfrac{1}{1-1/N}(1 - M_2)}, \tag{2.38}$$

$$\tau_3 = \sqrt[3]{\tfrac{1}{1-3/N+2/N^2}\,(1 - 3M_2 + 2M_3)}, \tag{2.39}$$

where $|i\rangle$ denotes the state with the excitation located at one specific site i. Higher order terms are given in Appendix A, in Eqs. (A.10) and (A.11). All τ_n are normalized to the value one – which indicates that the excitation is maximally delocalized over the entire system, i.e., $|\langle i|\Psi\rangle|^2 = 1/N$ and, consequently, $M_n = 1/N^{n-1}$.

2.2.3. Bell inequalities

Although the quantities described in Sections 2.2.1 and 2.2.2 above are sufficient for a formal description of pure-state entanglement, one might wish, from a more physical viewpoint, to assess entanglement directly, by measuring specific observables. Furthermore, the entanglement criterion thereby obtained should not rely on the fact that the state is pure, what is hardly ever the case in a real laboratory experiment.

Such a description of entanglement is possible using the Bell inequalities (Bell, 1965; Clauser *et al.*, 1969; Greenberger *et al.*, 1990). In general, a Bell inequality describes bounds on the statistical correlations between measurement results on individual subsystems. It is expressed in terms of expectation values of local observables $A_i^{(j)}$, where the index 'i' labels the different observables and the index 'j' denotes the subsystem with which the observable is associated. The most elementary Bell inequality is defined for two subsystems with two observables in each subsystem. Each observable, in turn, adopts two possible values -1 and 1. For example, the value -1 may correspond to no excitation on the respective site, whereas 1 is obtained if the site carries an excitation. For this setting, the

Bell inequality reads as follows :

$$\langle A_1^{(1)}A_1^{(2)} + A_1^{(1)}A_2^{(2)} + A_2^{(1)}A_1^{(2)} - A_2^{(1)}A_2^{(2)}\rangle \leq 2. \tag{2.40}$$

It applies to any model that attempts to describe the four observables $A_1^{(1)}$, $A_2^{(1)}$, $A_1^{(2)}$, and $A_2^{(2)}$ as classical random variables. In quantum mechanics, however, values up to $2\sqrt{2}$ can be reached. Simply by measuring two different (noncommuting) observables on both sites, one can thus verify that the correlations between these two sites are of quantum mechanical origin, and thus display two-body coherence. In a similar fashion, also inequalities for more sites can be defined (Greenberger *et al.*, 1990; Werner and Wolf, 2001; Żukowski and Brukner, 2002). A disadvantage of Bell inequalities is that there are entangled states that cannot be detected by any Bell inequality (Werner, 1989).

2.2.4. Entanglement witnesses

This is different for so-called entanglement witnesses (Horodecki *et al.*, 1996), for which it is rigorously proven that there exists one for any entangled state. This is the main reason why witnesses are often preferred to Bell inequalities. However, witnesses do not provide as clear an interpretation as the Bell inequalities. An entanglement witness is an observable, i.e., a Hermitean operator W that has non-negative expectation values with respect to all separable pure states:

$$\langle \Phi_s | W | \Phi_s \rangle \geq 0. \tag{2.41}$$

Therefore, if one obtains a negative expectation value:

$$\text{Tr}\, \varrho W < 0 \tag{2.42}$$

for some state ϱ, then this proves that the state cannot be expressed as a statistical mixture of product states, i.e., that the state is entangled, and thus bears two-body coherence. This concept can be generalized straightforwardly to many-body systems with any degree of entanglement: if a witness is constructed such that its expectation values are non-negative for all pure states that do not carry entanglement between at least n units, then a negative expectation value indicates proper n-body entanglement (Gühne and Toth, 2009).

Both Bell inequalities and entanglement witnesses are defined in terms of quantum mechanical observables, i.e., they define an experimental prescription of how to verify entanglement in a laboratory experiment.

However, each of these tools has to be tailored specifically for the state in question. This means that, first, one has to know the state in advance, in order to define the appropriate tool, and, second, that the experimental flexibility to implement measurements of the desired observables is required.

Recent attempts, therefore, develop nonlinear generalizations of these tools, in the desire to detect a larger class of entangled states (Gühne and Seevinck, 2010; Huber *et al.*, 2010; Salles *et al.*, 2010). However, the necessary adjustment of witnesses or Bell inequalities to the state under scrutiny can, thereby, be alleviated only to some extent. In particular, the observation of any nontrivial dynamical evolution, which realizes a continuous family of distinct quantum states at different times, would require the continuous parametrization of these tools (and the experimental implementation thereof), with potentially considerable overhead.

2.2.5. Convex roofs: from pure to mixed states

The approach that we will pursue in Section 3.4 below relies on the so-called convex roof (Bennett *et al.*, 1996; Uhlmann, 1998) construction. This mathematical tool defines a generalization of any function that can characterize entanglement properties of pure states to the regime of mixed states. Although it seems to be a very formal tool at first sight, it allows us to gain rather good insight into the many-body coherence properties that we are here interested in.

Suppose we have a function that is sensitive to entanglement properties of a certain type – like τ_n above, that is positive only if a state bears n-body entanglement. Then, we can apply this function to any pure state in the decomposition Eq. (2.25). As we have seen earlier, however, the inspection of only one single pure-state ensemble that represents a mixed state ϱ can lead to an erroneous conclusion on the entanglement properties of ϱ. Rather than taking the average of our pure-state entanglement function over an arbitrary pure-state decomposition, we therefore need to find the ensemble that minimizes this average:

$$\tau(\varrho) = \min \sum_i p_i \tau(\Psi_i). \tag{2.43}$$

The minimization is to be performed over all pure-state ensembles that represent the state ϱ, as in Eq. (2.25).

Although this definition formally provides a reliable characterization of any kind of many-body coherence inscribed into an arbitrary many-body mixed state, the numerical effort to solve Eq. (2.43) actually limits its practical use very significantly, as one proceeds to larger particle numbers and/or subsystem dimensions. Indeed, only for two two-level systems can Eq. (2.43) be evaluated algebraically (Wootters, 1998). However, there exist various approximations to the convex roof (Breuer, 2006; Chen *et al.*, 2005a,b; Gao and Fei, 2008; Gao *et al.*, 2006; Li *et al.*, 2009; Mintert and Buchleitner, 2005, 2007; Mintert *et al.*, 2004, 2005), which can be calculated efficiently, even for larger systems, and therefore provide a viable tool for the investigation of many-body coherence properties. In Section 3.4. below we will use the lower bound defined in Mintert and Buchleitner (2005) and Mintert *et al.* (2005) to estimate τ_2 for mixed quantum states.

3. FAST AND EFFICIENT TRANSPORT IN MOLECULAR NETWORKS

With the appropriate tools to characterize many-site entanglement at hand, we are now set to relate transport and entanglement properties. For this purpose, we choose a model system consisting of a small number of molecules that are placed at random positions, and are coupled to each other by dipole–dipole interactions. We are particularly interested in the transfer efficiency between two predefined molecular sites within a finite-time window. First, we focus on the question raised in Section 1: can we identify conditions under which transport is enhanced by constructive quantum interference? After giving a positive answer, we will correlate transfer efficiency and multisite entanglement.

3.1. Model and definition of the transfer efficiency

To model coherent transport of a single excitation across a sample of molecular sites, we consider the Hamiltonian (1.2). Under the assumption that all molecules be identical, we can adjust the energy scale such that $\epsilon_i = 0$, at all sites. For resonant and isotropic dipole interaction between the molecules, the coupling matrix elements read $V_{ji} = \alpha/|\mathbf{r_i} - \mathbf{r_j}|^3$, with real α, which also implies time-reversal invariance (see Section 1).

Note that, by choosing this model Hamiltonian, we do not aim at the accurate modeling of a specific system – like a certain light-harvesting complex (Cheng and Fleming, 2009; F. M. *et al.*, 2007) or a specific solar cell architecture, but rather target general principles that characterize energy transport in finite, disordered systems. In the same vein, we use a statistical approach – that allows us to assess the variations of the transport properties of a given realization under variations of its specific conformation. The statistical ensemble is here generated by randomization of the individual molecular positions $\mathbf{r_i}$.

In the following, we quantify the transport efficiency by the probability that an excitation injected at the "in"-site is found at some later time at the "out"-site. We place these two sites at the poles of a sphere, whereas

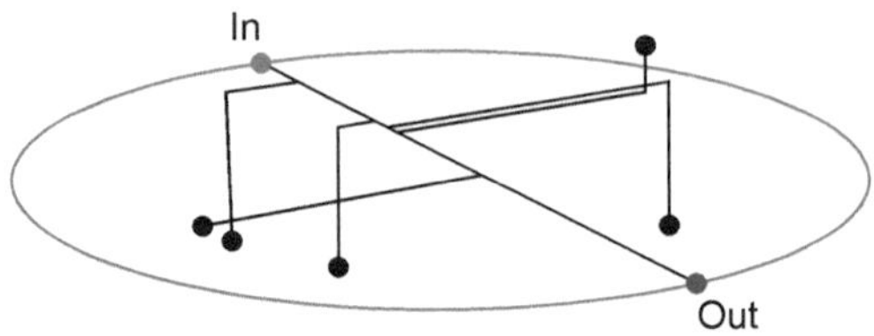

FIGURE 1.4 Typical random configuration of $N = 7$ molecular sites within a sphere with the "in"- and "out"-sites at its poles. Straight lines guide the eye to locate the molecules' positions in three-dimensional space.

all other sites' positions are randomly chosen from a uniform probability distribution, inside this sphere. A typical configuration thus obtained is depicted in Fig. 1.4.

Given the high efficiency of energy transfer in light-harvesting complexes mentioned in the introduction, we now wish to determine the conditions under which an excitation can travel from "in" to the "out" *deterministically and fast*. We define "fast" with respect to the natural timescale given by the direct coupling $V_{\mathrm{out,in}}$ between "in" and "out." If only these two molecules were present, the excitation transfer would require the time $\pi\hbar/(2V_{\mathrm{out,in}})$. Because the role of the intermediate molecules is to aid the transport, we choose a significantly shorter timescale for the excitation transfer to occur. Although the exact choice of this time window is immaterial for our subsequent findings, we fix $\mathcal{T} = \pi\hbar/(20V_{\mathrm{out,in}})$ for specificity, i.e., 1/10 of the above fundamental scale.

For each realization of the molecular network, as in Fig. 1.4, we numerically determine the transfer probability $p_{\mathrm{out}}(t) = |\langle \mathrm{out}|\psi(t)\rangle|^2$, with $|\psi(t)\rangle = \exp(-iHt/\hbar)|\mathrm{in}\rangle$, see Eq. (1.3). The transfer efficiency is then defined as the maximum value of $p_{\mathrm{out}}(t)$ within the interval $\mathcal{T}$,

$$p_{\mathrm{out}}^{(\mathcal{T})} = \max_{t\in[0,\mathcal{T}]} p_{\mathrm{out}}(t). \tag{3.44}$$

Alternatively, one may also consider the time-averaged transfer probability $\langle p_{\mathrm{out}}\rangle_{\mathcal{T}} = \int_0^{\mathcal{T}} dt\, p_{\mathrm{out}}(t)/\mathcal{T}$. We verified that these two quantities are directly related to each other in our present scenario, i.e., high values of $p_{\mathrm{out}}^{(\mathcal{T})}$ imply high values of $\langle p_{\mathrm{out}}\rangle_{\mathcal{T}}$, and vice versa. This is because of the fact that extremely narrow peaks of $p_{\mathrm{out}}(t)$ (i.e., much narrower than $\mathcal{T}$) do not occur because the total duration $\mathcal{T}$ already represents a short timescale for the Hamiltonians here under consideration.

As an example, Fig. 1.5 displays $p_{\mathrm{out}}(t)$ (dashed line) for the configuration shown in Fig. 1.4. The corresponding transfer efficiency for this configuration turns out to be rather low: $p_{\mathrm{out}}^{(\mathcal{T})} = 4.8\%$. Repeating this analysis for 500 different random configurations of $N = 7$ molecules, we find the distribution of transfer efficiencies shown in Fig. 1.6: most configurations achieve only low efficiencies (less than 5%), similar to the typical example of Fig. 1.5. In rare cases, however, also high values of $p_{\text{out}}^{(\mathcal{T})}$ occur: the best configuration among the ones shown in Fig. 1.6 reaches an efficiency of almost 95%! Analyzing a larger ensemble (10^8 configurations), we find that roughly one out of 2×10^5 configurations exhibits an efficiency larger than 90%.

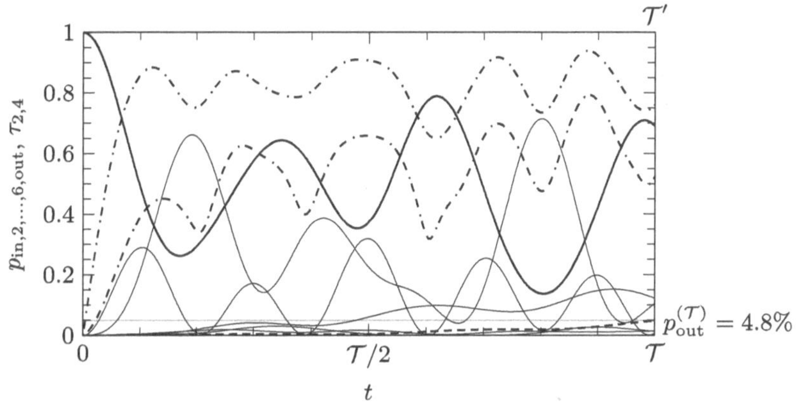

FIGURE 1.5 Time evolution of the on-site probabilities $|\langle i|\psi(t)\rangle|^2$ generated by the Hamiltonian as defined by the configuration shown in Fig. 1.4: output site (dashed line), input site (thick solid line), and intermediate sites (thin solid lines). The maximum of $|\langle \text{out}|\psi(t)\rangle|^2$, for $t \leq \mathcal{T}$, defines the transfer efficiency $p_{\text{out}}^{(\mathcal{T})}$. The dash-dotted and dash-dash-dotted lines display the time evolution of bi- and quadri-partite entanglement, τ_2 and τ_4, within the sample, respectively.

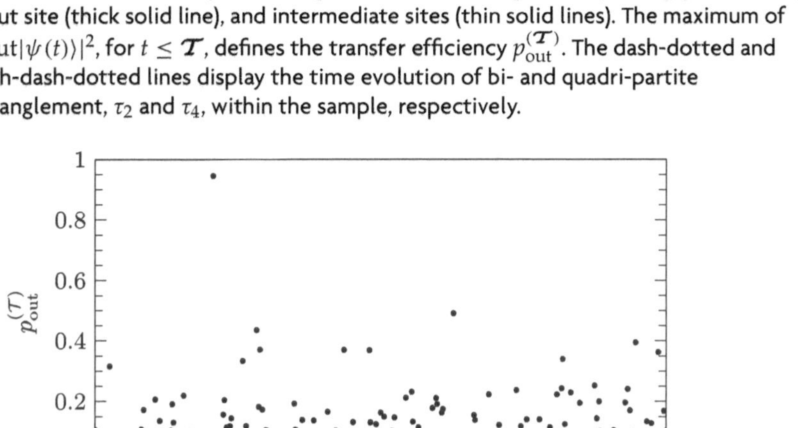

FIGURE 1.6 Transfer efficiencies for an ensemble of 500 different random configurations of $N = 7$ molecules. The majority of configurations exhibit rather low efficiencies (< 5%), also larger values up to almost 95% can be reached, in rare cases.

3.2. Optimal configurations

Let us now focus our attention to those particular configurations that reach high-transfer efficiencies: beyond the random search above in Section 3.1, we can optimize the transfer efficiency by means of an evolutionary algorithm (Auger and Hansen, 2005). In doing so, we indeed find certain *optimal configurations* – as the one shown in Fig. 1.7 – which reach the maximum transfer efficiency $p_{\text{out}}^{(\mathcal{T})} = 1$!

In order to determine general conditions for perfect transfer, let us first expand the states with the excitation at the input or output site, in the energy eigenstates of the random Hamiltonian:

$$|\text{in}\rangle = \sum_k a_k |E_k\rangle, \text{ and } |\text{out}\rangle = \sum_k b_k |E_k\rangle. \tag{3.45}$$

Because $H|E_k\rangle = E_k|E_k\rangle$, and $\sum_k |a_k|^2 = \sum_k |b_k|^2 = 1$, the coherent transfer probability reads

$$p_{\text{out}}(t) = \left| \sum_k a_k^* b_k e^{-iE_k t/\hbar} \right|^2. \tag{3.46}$$

From this, we can derive the following inequalities:

$$p_{\text{out}}(t) \le \left(\sum_k |a_k b_k| \right)^2 \le \left(\sum_k |a_k|^2 \right) \left(\sum_l |b_l|^2 \right) = 1, \tag{3.47}$$

and check under what conditions equality, i.e., $p_{\text{out}}(t) = 1$, is reached. For the second inequality (Cauchy-Schwarz) in Eq. (3.47), this is the case if and only if $|a_k| = |b_k|$ for all k, i.e., if all eigenstates $|E_k\rangle$ exhibit the same

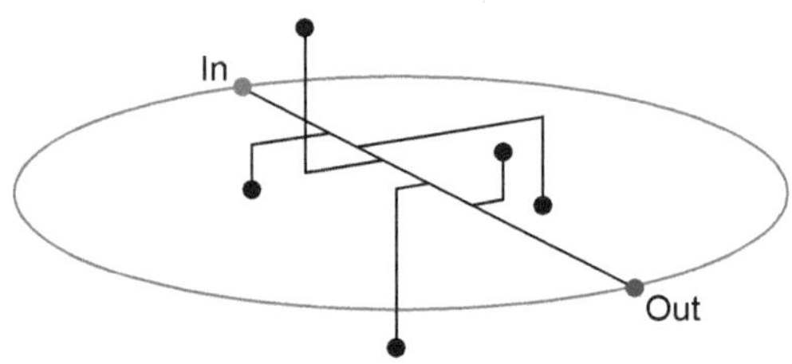

FIGURE 1.7 Optimal configuration of $N = 7$ molecules offering fast and complete transport from input to output.

overlap with the input as with the output site. This condition is always fulfilled for a Hamiltonian that satisfies the symmetry property $PHP = H$, with $P = P^\dagger$, $|\text{out}\rangle = P|\text{in}\rangle$, and $|\text{in}\rangle = P|\text{out}\rangle$ – however, it is only sufficient but not necessary for $|a_k| = |b_k|$ to hold.

In addition to the requirement $|a_k| = |b_k|$, perfect transfer is achieved only if the phases ϕ_k defined by $a_k^* b_k e^{-iE_k t/\hbar} = |a_k b_k| e^{i\phi_k}$ are identical for each eigenstate k with $|a_k| = |b_k| > 0$. If many eigenstates with $|a_k| = |b_k| > 0$ generate the dynamics, this condition is, in general, only met after extremely long times (Hemmer *et al.*, 1958) – unless the eigenfrequencies $E_j/\hbar$ are properly adjusted.

That such optimal adjustment does not imply strong symmetry properties of the Hamiltonian is spelled out by Fig. 1.7, which shows one of the optimal configurations singled out by the evolutionary algorithm – the corresponding time evolution is depicted in Fig. 1.8. Note that the molecular arrangement is asymmetric and nonperiodic, hence far from trivial (e.g., lattice-like or collinear) structures. We have also tested the robustness of such optimal configurations, and verified that they remain close to optimal under small variations of the positions of the individual molecules. This property enables the evolutionary algorithm to find optimal configurations quite efficiently.

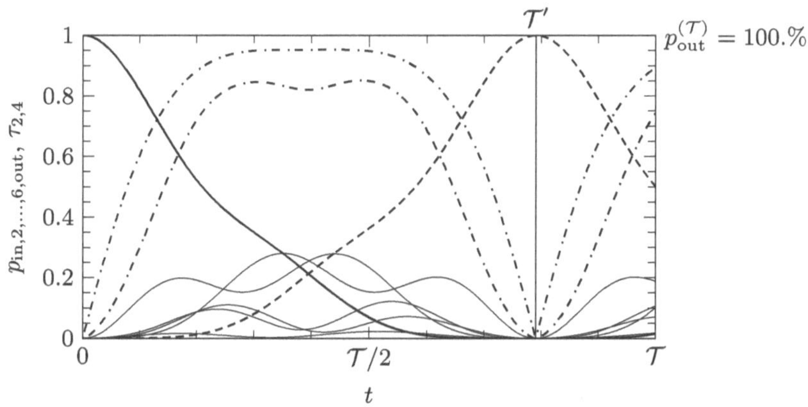

FIGURE 1.8 Time evolution of the on-site probabilities $|\langle i|\psi(t)\rangle|^2$ generated by the Hamiltonian that is defined by the optimal configuration shown in Fig. 1.7: output site (dashed line), input site (thick solid line), and intermediate sites (thin solid lines). Perfect transfer $p_{\text{out}}(t) = 1$ is achieved at a time $\mathcal{T}' < \mathcal{T}$. The dash-dotted and dash-dash-dotted lines display the time evolution of bipartite and quadripartite entanglement, τ_2 and τ_4, respectively. Note the perfect vanishing of both entanglement quantifiers at the instant of perfect transfer because the latter prevents any nonvanishing amplitudes on other sites than the output site.

3.3. Impact of decoherence

Given the exceptionally large transfer efficiencies found earlier for optimal molecular configurations, we still need to ponder this constructive quantum interference effect against the unavoidable and – particularly in the biological functional units that largely motivate our present study – ubiquitous presence of ambient noise. All experimental data that by now unambiguously demonstrate multisite coherences also show that these coherences only survive on finite timescales, and faint for longer times. Hence, if we want to argue that quantum effects are instrumental for the remarkable efficiency of light-harvesting units like the FMO, the "quantum gain" with respect to a classical transport process must stem from those transient timescales over which quantum coherence prevails (Cheng and Fleming, 2009; Kühn *et al.*, 2002). We thus need to assess the impact of noise on the coherent transfer efficiencies observed earlier, on timescales of the order of $\mathcal{T}$.

For this purpose, we locally couple the molecular sites to a dephasing environment. The time evolution of the density matrix can then be modeled by the following master equation (Carmichael, 1999):

$$\dot{\varrho}_{ij} = -\frac{i}{\hbar}[H, \varrho]_{ij} + \Gamma(\delta_{ij} - 1)\rho_{ij}, \tag{3.48}$$

which enforces the decay of the phase coherences ρ_{ij}, $i \neq j$ with rate Γ. Figure 1.9 shows the transfer efficiencies that are obtained for the very same ensemble of 500 configurations as used to generate Fig. 1.6, now with nonvanishing dephasing at a rate $\Gamma = 1/(10\mathcal{T})$. We see that all those configurations that exhibit efficient transport in the absence of dephasing actually do maintain this characteristic property - albeit on a reduced level (indicated by the open circles). On the other hand, some configurations with low-transfer efficiencies slightly profit from dephasing, as indicated in the figure by the filled circles. However, noise does – by far – not suffice to render the blocking configurations more efficient than those which mediate transport by constructive quantum interference. This clearly demonstrates that the efficiency of energy harvesting is brought about by optimal molecular configurations (as the one depicted in Fig. 1.7) that give rise to constructive multipath interference on transmission.

Noise can, at best, restore the classical transport process, and this only on sufficiently long timescales (Bluemel *et al.*, 1991; Zhang *et al.*, 2004). This is also confirmed when comparing the average transfer efficiency over a large ensemble of molecular configurations, in the absence and in the presence of dephasing, for different timescales: On the above, short timescale, the average transport efficiency is larger in the absence of dephasing

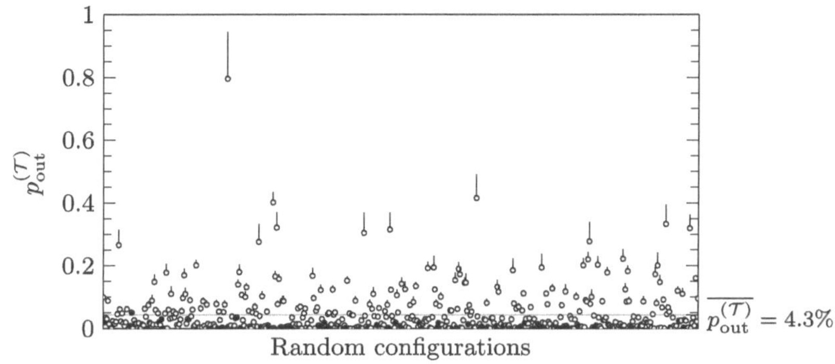

FIGURE 1.9 Transfer efficiencies for the same 500 random configurations as in Fig. 1.6, but with dephasing rate $\Gamma = 1/(10\mathcal{T})$. The bars with filled or open circles, respectively, indicate losses or gains with respect to the decoherence-free dynamics. High coherent transfer efficiencies are always reduced by dephasing, though prevail over the only slightly improved transfer efficiencies mediated by blocking molecular conformations in the presence of noise. This proves that the enhancement of transfer efficiency is because of quantum interference rather than of noise, on the transient timescales where coherence can be experimentally detected.

($\overline{p_{out}^{(\mathcal{T})}} = 4.9\%$) than in its presence ($\overline{p_{out}^{(\mathcal{T})}} = 4.3\%$), and equally so the time-integrated average transfer probability $\overline{\langle p_{out}\rangle_{\mathcal{T}}}$ (see the discussion after Eq. (3.44)), which drops from 1.8% to 1.7%. At first sight, this seems to contradict Section 1 , where we stated that quantum interference on average reduces transport. Suppressing these interferences by noise should, therefore, increase the average transport efficiency. Remember, however, that coherent backscattering – which, as discussed in Section 1.3, is responsible for reducing the transport efficiency in the absence of noise – affects only those path amplitudes that return to the initial site after passing through at least two intermediate sites, see the discussion after Eq. (1.10) – and this takes a certain time! Therefore, only after that time can we expect that the suppression of quantum interference improves the transport efficiency. Indeed, increasing our time window by a factor of 10, we find $\overline{\langle p_{out}\rangle_{\mathcal{T}}} = 5.0\%$ without dephasing to be smaller than $\overline{\langle p_{out}\rangle_{\mathcal{T}}} = 6.2\%$ with dephasing. Hence, for long times and nonoptimized configurations, dephasing enhances the transfer efficiency (Plenio and Huelga, 2008; Rebentrost *et al.*, 2009), as to be expected.

3.4. Transport and entanglement

As advocated earlier in Section 2, the theory of many-body entanglement can provide us with good insight in the many-body coherence that is dynamically generated during a transport process (Asadian *et al.*, 2010;

Sarovar *et al.*, 2010; Thorwart *et al.*, 2009). Therefore, let us now address the question whether exceptional multisite entanglement properties characterize those configurations that show particularly good transport properties.

For this purpose, we examine the entanglement quantifiers τ_n introduced in Section 2.2.2 and Appendix A. As discussed there, $\tau_n = 1$ for each $n \leq N$, provided the excitation is equally distributed among all N sites, whereas $\tau_n = 0$ if the excitation is localized on less than n sites. For the optimal configuration depicted in Fig. 1.7, the time evolution of the bipartite and quadripartite entanglement τ_2 and τ_4 is presented in Fig. 1.8 (dash-dotted and dash-dash-dotted lines). We see that both, τ_2 and τ_4, reach large values in the interval $0 < t < \mathcal{T}'$, where $\mathcal{T}'$ denotes the time where the maximum transfer probability is reached. This implies that the excitation is spread among at least four sites, which can also be deduced by analyzing the individual on-site probabilities (dashed and solid lines in Fig. 1.8). In turn, because excitation transfer is perfect for this specific molecular conformation, entanglement must – and does – vanish when the exciton reaches the output site. Only when no other than the output site has finite amplitude can the output population reach its ideal value one. This is in stark contrast to the excitation and entanglement dynamics on typical configurations, as illustrated in Fig. 1.5: there, bipartite and quadripartite entanglement never vanish during the entire time interval $\mathcal{T}$. The latter immediately implies that the excitation cannot be delivered deterministically at the target site.

To correlate transfer efficiency and multisite entanglement, we quantify the dynamically generated entanglement by its maximum value during the transfer interval $[0, \mathcal{T}']$ – much as the transfer efficiency itself, see Eq. (3.44):

$$\tau_n^{(\mathcal{T}')} = \max_{t \in [0, \mathcal{T}']} \tau_n(t). \tag{3.49}$$

Figure 1.10 displays, for $N = 7$ sites and strictly coherent dynamics, $\Gamma = 0$, the conditional probability distribution of the transfer efficiency, at fixed values of the bipartite entanglement $\tau_2^{(\mathcal{T}')}$, see Eq. (2.38). We can clearly identify a sharp edge that defines a minimum amount of entanglement necessary to reach high transport efficiencies. For lower transfer efficiencies, the distribution exhibits a kink at $\tau_2^{(\mathcal{T}')} = \sqrt{7/12} \simeq 0.76$. This corresponds to maximal entanglement between exactly two of $N = 7$ sites. Here, transport is inhibited because the excitation may be trapped in a singlet state between "in" and another site that is accidentally placed very close.

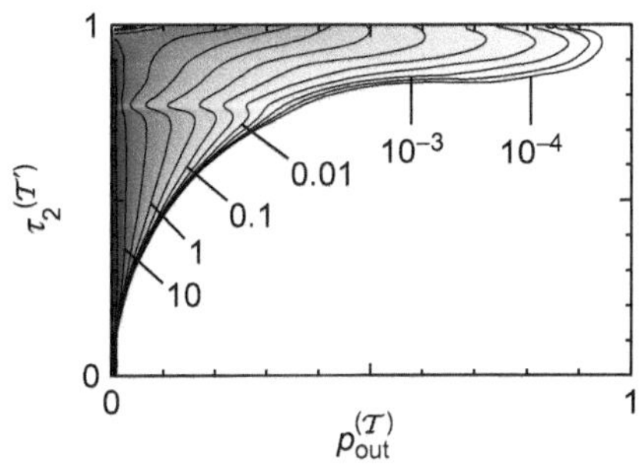

FIGURE 1.10 Probability distribution $P\left(p_{\text{out}}^{(\mathcal{T})} \middle| \tau_2^{(\mathcal{T}')}\right)$ of the transfer efficiency conditioned on bipartite entanglement τ_2, for $N = 7$ sites and strictly coherent dynamics, $\Gamma = 0$: Efficient excitation transfer requires strong bipartite entanglement.

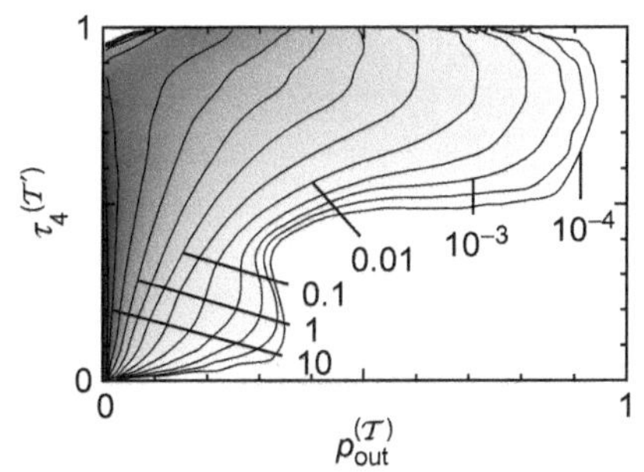

FIGURE 1.11 Conditional probability distribution of the transfer efficiency as in Fig. 1.10, but now conditioned on quadripartite entanglement $\tau_4^{(\mathcal{T}')}$. The persistence of the correlation also for this larger number of sites shows that the excitation must be spread among at least four sites, to enable optimal transfer efficiencies. However, moderate transfer efficiencies require the entanglement of fewer sites, as evident from a comparison with Fig. 1.10.

Such strong correlation between transfer efficiency and entanglement still persists in the case of quadripartite entanglement $\tau_4^{(\mathcal{T}')}$ defined by Eq. (A.10), as apparent from Fig. 1.11: again, high transfer efficiencies require strong entanglement – e.g., $p_{\text{out}}^{(\mathcal{T})} > 0.5$ implies $\tau_4^{(\mathcal{T}')} > 0.5$. The correlation between transport efficiency and τ_4, however, is less pronounced than in the case of τ_2. This is not surprising, because entanglement between at least four sites implies that the excitation is delocalized over more than half of the entire molecular sample, and efficient transfer requires strong refocussing of the excitation on the output site. Furthermore, in contrast

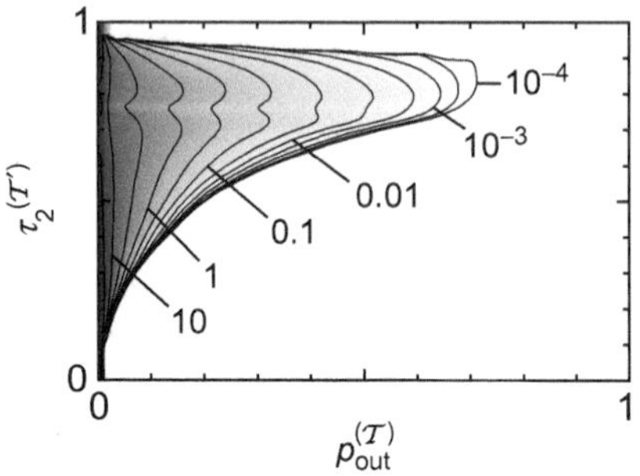

FIGURE 1.12 Same as Fig. 1.10, in the presence of dephasing, with rate $\Gamma = 1/(5\mathcal{T})$. As expected, dephasing reduces both the bi-partite entanglement and the transfer efficiency as compared to Fig. 1.10, see also Fig. 1.9. Notwithstanding, the strong correlation between transfer efficiency and entanglement persists.

to Fig. 1.10, moderate values of the transfer efficiency, i.e., $p_{\text{out}}^{(\mathcal{T})} > 0.1$, can already be reached at very low $\tau_4^{(\mathcal{T}')}$, i.e., can be mediated by entanglement between only two or three sites. Some – although not maximal – entanglement between at least four sites is, however, strictly necessary to achieve high transfer efficiencies.

Finally, to gauge the robustness of the observed correlation under decoherence, Fig. 1.12 shows the conditional probability density $P\left(p_{\text{out}}^{(\mathcal{T})} \middle| \tau_2^{(\mathcal{T}')}\right)$, in the presence of dephasing with rate $\Gamma = 1/(5\mathcal{T})$. To estimate the bipartite entanglement built up under these conditions, in unavoidably mixed states, we use the lower bound (Mintert *et al.* 2004, Mintert and Buchleitner 2005)) mentioned in Section 2.2.5. In comparison with Fig. 1.10, we see that the maximally achieved transfer efficiency is reduced by dephasing, as already observed in Fig. 1.9, and so is the entanglement. However, the strong correlation between transfer efficiency and entanglement persists.

4. CONCLUSIONS

Our earlier statistical treatment of excitation transport across a molecular network mimicking the FMO light-harvesting complex clearly shows the potential of quantum coherence to *enhance* transport, on transient timescales. The thus-achieved transfer probability can reach 100% – a value unachievable by classically diffusive, unbiased transport. Furthermore, because such quantum transfer is brought about by constructive multipath interference along intermediate sites of the molecular complex, coherent quantum transport is certainly *faster* than classically diffusive transport, for comparable inter-site coupling strengths. Taking both transfer probability and transfer time together, coherence thus defines levels of quantum efficiency unreached by a classical transport process on the same network.

Inasmuch as quantum coherence is often assumed in related literature to enforce strictly destructive interference on transmission, and hence to induce Anderson localization, our results presented here invalidate this fundamental hypothesis, as well as its immediate consequence that coherence has to be disrupted by noise to unlock the transport: as well known, the conductance across a disordered sample is determined by the ratio of localization length to sample length, and is hence exponentially suppressed only in the thermodynamic limit of infinite samples. For finite sample lengths, the transport is characterized by extremely strong fluctuations under variations of the potential, giving rise to the effects here observed (Abrikosov, 1981; Casati *et al.*, 1990; Krug *et al.*, 2003; Kumar, 1985; Pichard *et al.*, 1990).

We have also seen that the constructive interference mediated by optimal molecular conformations is robust against small perturbations – as indirectly also spelled out by the rapid convergence of the genetic algorithm used to identify such configurations. Because we are here dealing with a multipath interference phenomenon, this appears surprising on a first glance: a slight perturbation of a symmetric double well potential immediately suppresses the tunnel current, and a small perturbation of an infinite, perfectly periodic one-dimensional potential localizes the initially extended eigenstates. However, note that the optimal configurations we find are truly three dimensional in nature, and so are the transporting wave functions, as spelled out by our statistical correlation of transfer efficiency and multisite entanglement. This indicates that three-dimensional delocalization of the wave function as quantified by our multisite entanglement quantifiers implies a certain rigidity of the constructive interference condition against perturbations, an important feature which will be subject of future research.

Finally, the experimental results motivating this study, as well as our present results themselves suggest that quantum coherence holds the potential to steer quantum transport efficiencies in engineered devices as abundant in semiconductor technology. Although, on a microscopic level, these often need much more refined model Hamiltonians, their essential structure only requires interfaces and interactions as additional structural elements, which, however, nowadays do not prevent any more an efficient microscopic modeling. The real challenge for theory, experiment and engineering will be to describe and design multihierarchical structures with the stunning structural versatility of life matter. To implement such multiscale features in our theoretical understanding of complex, open quantum systems, and in our experimental tools to characterize and design them, opens a completely new field of research with fascinating perspectives.

APPENDIX

A. Tangles

We briefly review the underlying framework for the separability criteria τ_n, Eqs. (2.36) and (2.33), and define them for systems with an arbitrary number N of subsystems, and for an arbitrary degree of separability n. As it can be seen in Eqs. (2.36) and (2.33), the τ_n are not of the form of a regular expectation value, but they are n-linear both in Ψ and in Ψ^*. Formally, such expressions can be constructed as expectation values of suitably chosen operators with respect to a n-fold tensor product of the state $|\Psi\rangle$ with itself. That is, for any value of n, τ_n reads

$$\tau_n = \sqrt[n]{\langle\Psi|^{\otimes n}\boldsymbol{\mathcal{A}}_n|\Psi\rangle^{\otimes n}}. \tag{A.1}$$

Using an n-fold tensor product of a state implies that – on the formal level – we are considering the n-fold tensor product of the N-body Hilbert space. The central building block that enters the operator $\boldsymbol{\mathcal{A}}_n$ is the cyclic permutation on the n-fold product of a single-subsystem Hilbert space. It is defined through its action

$$\Pi_n|\phi_1\rangle \otimes |\phi_2\rangle \otimes \cdots \otimes |\phi_n\rangle = |\phi_2\rangle \otimes |\phi_3\rangle \otimes \cdots \otimes |\phi_n\rangle \otimes |\phi_1\rangle \tag{A.2}$$

on a tensor product of n arbitrary single-subsystem states $|\phi_i\rangle$, and has eigenvalues $\lambda_j = \mathrm{e}^{-\frac{2\pi i}{n}j}$ $(j = 0, \ldots, n-1)$. The projector

$$\boldsymbol{\mathcal{P}}_n = \frac{1}{n}\sum_{j=1}^{n} \mathrm{e}^{-\frac{2\pi i}{n}j}\,(\Pi_n)^j \tag{A.3}$$

projects on eigenstates of Π_n with eigenvalue $\mathrm{e}^{\frac{2\pi i}{n}}$, whereas

$$\boldsymbol{\mathcal{S}}_n = \frac{1}{n}\sum_{j=1}^{n} (\Pi_n)^j \tag{A.4}$$

projects onto symmetric states, i.e., eigenstates of Π_n with eigenvalue 1.

For the moment, we take $n = N$ and define in terms of these projectors

$$\mathcal{A}_N = \mathcal{P}_N^{(1)} \otimes \mathcal{P}_N^{(2)} \otimes \cdots \otimes \mathcal{P}_N^{(N)}, \tag{A.5}$$

where the index i in $\mathcal{P}_N^{(i)}$ denotes the subsystem, upon whose N-fold version $\mathcal{P}_N^{(i)}$ acts on. To see that the expectation value

$$\langle\Psi|^{\otimes N}\mathcal{A}_N|\Psi\rangle^{\otimes N} \tag{A.6}$$

is positive only if the state $|\Psi\rangle$ contains entanglement shared between all the N subsystems, let us consider a biseparable state $|\Psi_{\text{BS}}\rangle$ that factorizes into two terms, i.e., $|\Psi_{\text{BS}}\rangle = |\psi_1\rangle \otimes |\psi_2\rangle$ such that $|\psi_1\rangle$ includes the subsystems i_1 to i_k and $|\psi_2\rangle$ includes the subsystems i_{k+1} to i_m. The n-fold state $|\Psi_{\text{BS}}\rangle^{\otimes N}$ is invariant – that is, in particular, symmetric – under the simultaneous application of all cyclic permutations on all N–tupled subsystems associated with the state $|\psi_1\rangle$:

$$\Pi^{(i_1 \ldots i_k)} = \Pi_N^{(i_1)} \otimes \Pi_N^{(i_2)} \otimes \cdots \otimes \Pi_N^{(i_k)}. \tag{A.7}$$

(or similarly for $|\psi_2\rangle$). However, the operator

$$\mathcal{P}_N^{(i_1)} \otimes \mathcal{P}_N^{(i_2)} \otimes \cdots \otimes \mathcal{P}_N^{(i_k)} \tag{A.8}$$

projects onto eigenstates with eigenvalue $e^{2\pi i \frac{k}{N}}$ of the simultaneous cyclic permutation $\Pi^{(i_1 \ldots i_k)}$. Because vectors with different permutation symmetry are orthogonal to each other, the N-fold state $|\psi_1\rangle^{\otimes N}$ lies in the null-space of $\Pi^{(i_1 \ldots i_k)}$, and therefore, the expectation value $\langle\psi_1|^{\otimes N}\Pi^{(i_1 \ldots i_k)}|\psi_1\rangle^{\otimes N}$ vanishes. In turn, the expectation value $\langle\Psi|^{\otimes N}\mathcal{A}_N|\Psi\rangle^{\otimes N}$ can be positive only if the state $|\Psi\rangle$ is genuinely multipartite entangled.

Using exactly the same reasoning, we can now also construct the τ_n for $n < N$, that are positive only if the state is at least n-partite entangled. For this purpose, let us consider the operator

$$\mathcal{P}_n^{(1)} \otimes \mathcal{P}_n^{(2)} \otimes \cdots \otimes \mathcal{P}_n^{(n)} \otimes \mathcal{S}_n^{(n+1)} \otimes \cdots \otimes \mathcal{S}_n^{(N)} \tag{A.9}$$

on n replica of $\mathcal{H}$, i.e., on $\mathcal{H}^{\otimes n}$. Expectation values $\langle\Psi|^{\otimes n}\mathcal{P}_n^{(1)} \otimes \mathcal{P}_n^{(2)} \otimes \cdots \otimes \mathcal{P}_n^{(r)} \otimes \mathcal{S}_n^{(n+1)} \otimes \cdots \otimes \mathcal{S}_n^{(N)}|\Psi\rangle^{\otimes n}$ are positive only if at least the first r subsystems are entangled with each other. Symmetrizing Eq. (A.9) with respect to all subsystems, one ends up with the operator $\mathcal{A}_n$ whose expectation values with respect to the n-fold tensor product of a quantum state $|\Psi\rangle$ is positive if at least n subsystems are entangled with each other,

If there is a single excitation only, the functions τ_4 and τ_5 read

$$\tau_4 = \sqrt[4]{\frac{1 - 6M_2 + 8M_3 + 3M_2^2 - 6M_4}{1 - 6/N + 11/N^2 - 6/N^3}}, \tag{A.10}$$

$$\tau_5 = \sqrt[5]{\frac{1 - 10M_2 + 20M_3 + 15M_2^2 - 30M_4 - 20M_2M_3 + 24M_5}{1 - 10/N + 35/N^2 - 50/N^3 + 24/N^4}}, \tag{A.11}$$

with M_n defined in Eq. (2.37), and the τ_n are normalized to a maximum value of unity.

REFERENCES

Abou-Chacra, R., Anderson, P. W., and Thouless, D. J. (1973). *J. Phys. C.* **6**, 1734.

Abrikosov, A. A. (1981). *Solid State Commun.* **37**, 991.

Adolphs, J., and Renger, T. (2006). *Biophys. J.* **91**, 2778.

Akulin, V. M., de Tomasi, F., Mourachko, I., and Pillet, P. (1999). *Physica D: Nonl. Phen.* **131**, 125.

Al'tshuler, B. L. (1985). *JETP Lett.* **41**, 648.

Anderson, P. W. (1958). *Phys. Rev.* **109**, 1492.

Anderson, W. R., Veale, J. R., and Gallagher, T. F. (1998). *Phys. Rev. Lett.* **80**, 249.

Asadian, A., Tiersch, M., Guerreschi, G. G., Cai, J., Popescu, S., and Briegel, H. J. (2010). *N. J. Phys.* **12**, 075019.

Auger, A., and Hansen, N. (2005). *The 2005 IEEE Congr. Evol. Comput. (CEC05)* **2**, 1769.

Bell, J. S. (1965). *Physics* **1**, 195.

Bennett, C. H., DiVincenzo, D. P., Smolin, J. A., and Wootters, W. K. (1996). *Phys. Rev. A* **54**, 3824.

Bergmann, G. (1958). *Phys. Rep.* **109**, 1492.

Blankenship, R. E. (2001). "Molecular Mechanisms of Photosynthesis." Blackwell Publishing Limited.

Blümel, R., Buchleitner, A., Graham, R., Sirko, L., Smilansky, U., and Walther, H. (1991). *Phys. Rev. A* **44**, 4521.

Breuer, H.-P. (2006). *J. Phys. A* **39**, 11847.

Briegel, H.-J., Englert, B.-G., Sterpi, N., and Walther, H. (1994). *Phys. Rev. A* **49**, 2962.

Buchleitner, A., and Hornberger, K., eds. (2002). "Coherent Evolution in Noisy Environments." Springer, Berlin.

Cai, J., Popescu, S., and Briegel, H.-J. (2010). *Phys. Rev. E* **82**, 021921.

Carmichael, H. (1999). "Quantum Statistical Methods in Quantum Optics - Master Equations and Fokker-Planck Equations." Springer, Berlin.

Carroll, T. J., Sunder, S., and Noel, M. W. (2006). *Phys. Rev. A* **73**, 032725.

Casati, G., Chirikov, B. V., Ford, J., and Izrailev, F. M. (1979). "Stochastic Behaviour in Classical and Quantum Hamiltonian Systems", in Lecture Notes in Physics, edited by Casati, G., and Ford, J., vol. 93. Springer, Berlin, 334–352.

Casati, G., Guarneri, I., and Shepelyansky, D. (1990). *Physica A* **163**, 205.

Chanelière, T., Wilkowski, D., Bidel, Y., Kaiser, R., and Miniatura, C. (2004). *Phys. Rev. E* **70**, 036602.

Chen, K., Albeverio, S., and Fei, S.-M. (2005a). *Phys. Rev. Lett.* **95**, 210501.
Chen, K., Albeverio, S., and Fei, S.-M. (2005b). *Phys. Rev. Lett.* **95**, 040504.
Cheng, Y.-C., and Fleming, G. R. (2009). *Annu. Rev. Phys. Chem.* **60**, 241.
Cizeau, P., and Bouchaud, J. P. (1994). *Phys. Rev. E* **50**, 1810.
Clauser, J. F., Horne, M. A., Shimony, A., and Holt, R. A. (1969). *Phys. Rev. Lett.* **23**, 880.
Collini, E., Wong, C. Y., Wilk, K. E., Curmi, P. M. G., Brumer, P., and Scholes, G. D. (2010). *Nature* **463**, 644.
Eckert, K., Schliemann, J., Bruß, D., and Lewenstein, M. (2002). *Ann. Phys.* **299**, 88.
Einstein, A., Podolsky, B., and Rosen, N. (1935). *Phys. Rev.* **47**, 777.
Engel, G., Calhoun, T., Read, E., Ahn, T.-K., Mancal, T., Cheng, Y.-C., Blankenship, R., and Fleming, G. (2007). *Nature* **446**, 782.
Feenberg, E. (1948). *Phys. Rev.* **74**, 206.
Fishman, S., Grempel, D. R., and Prange, R. E. (1982). *Phys. Rev. Lett.* **49**, 509.
Gammaitoni, L., Hänggi, P., Jung, P., and Marchesoni, F. (1998). *Rev. Mod. Phys.* **70**, 223.
Gao, X., and Fei, S. (2008). *Eur. Phys. J. Spec. Top.* **159**, 71.
Gao, X.-H., Fei, S.-M., and Wu, K. (2006). *Phys. Rev. A* **74**, 050303.
Ghirardi, G., and Marinatto, L. (2004). *Phys. Rev. A* **70**, 012109.
Greenberger, D. M., Horne, M. A., Shimony, A., and Zeilinger, A. (1990). *Am. J. Phys.* **58**, 1131.
Gühne, O., and Toth, G. (2009). *Phys. Rep.* **474**, 1, arxiv:0811.2803.
Gühne, O., and Seevinck, M. (2010). *New J. Phys.* **12**, 053002.
Gutzwiller, M. (1990). "Chaos in Classical and Quantum Mechanics." Springer, Berlin.
Haake, F. (1991). "Quantum Signatures of Chaos." Springer, Berlin.
Haken, H. (1994). "Hermann Haken." Springer, Berlin.
Hemmer, P. C., Maximon, L. C., and Wergeland, H. (1958). *Phys. Rev.* **111**, 689.
Horodecki, M., Horodecki, P., and Horodecki, R. (1996). *Phys. Lett. A* **223**, 1.
Huber, M., Mintert, F., Gabriel, A., and Hiesmayr, B. C. (2010). *Phys. Rev. Lett.* **104**, 210501.
Hughston, L. P., Jozsa, R., and Wootters, W. K. (1993). *Phys. Lett. A* **183**, 14.
Imry, Y. (1986). *Europhys. Lett.* **1**, 249.
Ioffe, A. F., and Regel, A. R. (1960). *Progr. Semicond.* **4**, 237.
Kramer, B., and MacKinnon, A. (1993). *Rep. Progr. Phys.* **56**, 1469.
Krug, A., and Buchleitner, A. (2005). *Phys. Rev. A* **72**, 061402.
Krug, A., Wimberger, S., and Buchleitner, A. (2003). *Eur. Phys. J. D* **26**, 21.
Kuga, Y., and Ishimaru, A. (1984). *J. Opt. Soc. Am. A* **1**, 831.
Kühn, O., Sundström, V., and Pullerits, T. (2002). *Chem. Phys.* **275**, 15 .
Kumar, N. (1985). *Phys. Rev. B* **31**, 5513.
Landauer, R. (1957). *IBM J. Res. Develop.* **1**, 233.
Lee, H., Cheng, Y.-C., and Fleming, G. R. (2007). *Science* **316**, 1462.
Lee, P. A., and Stone, A. D. (1985). *Phys. Rev. Lett.* **55**, 1622.
Lemarié, G., Lignier, H., Delande, D., Szriftgiser, P., and Garreau, J. C. (2010). *Phys. Rev. Lett.* **105**, 090601.
Li, M., Fei, S.-M., and Wang, Z.-X. (2009). *J. Phys. A* **42**, 145303.
MacKinnon, A., and Kramer, B. (1982). *Phys. Rev. Lett.* **49**, 695.
Maeda, H., and Gallagher, T. F. (2004). *Phys. Rev. Lett.* **93**, 193002.
Mintert, F., and Buchleitner, A. (2005). *Phys. Rev. A* **72**, 012336.
Mintert, F., and Buchleitner, A. (2007). *Phys. Rev. Lett.* **98**, 140505.
Mintert, F., Kuś, M., and Buchleitner, A. (2004). *Phys. Rev. Lett.* **92**, 167902.
Mintert, F., Kuś, M., and Buchleitner, A. (2005). *Phys. Rev. Lett.* **95**, 260502.
Mü, F., Madjet, M. E.-A., Adolphs, J., Abdurahman, A., Rabenstein, B., Ishikita, H., Knapp, E.-W., and Renger, T. (2007). *Proc. Nat. Acad. Sci.* **104**, 16862.
Muttalib, K. A., Markos, P., and Wölfle, P. (2005). *Phys. Rev. B* **72**, 125317.

Panitchayangkoon, G., Hayes, D., Fransted, K. A., Caram, J. R., Harel, E., Wen, J., Blankenship, R. E., and Engel, G. S. (2010). *Proc. Nat. Acad. Sci.* **107**, 12766.
Pichard, J. L., Zanon, N., Imry, Y., and Stone, A. D. (1990). *J. Phys. France* **51**, 587.
Plenio, M. B., and Huelga, S. F. (2008). *N. J. Phys.* **10**, 113019.
Pólya, G. (1921). *Mathematische Annalen* **84**, 149.
Rebentrost, P., Mohseni, M., Kassal, I., Lloyd, S., and Aspuru-Guzik, A. (2009). *New J. Phys.* **11**, 033003.
Salles, A., Cavalcanti, D., Acín, A. Pérez-García, D., and Wolf, M. M. (2010). *Quant. Inf. Comp.* **10**, 703.
Sarovar, M., Ishizaki, A., Fleming, G. R., and Whaley, K. B. (2010). *Nat. Phys.* **6**, 462.
Schliemann, J., Cirac, J. I., Kuś, M., Lewenstein, M., and Loss, D. (2001). *Phys. Rev. A* **64**, 022303.
Schreiber, M., and Grussbach, H. (1996). *Phys. Rev. Lett.* **76**, 1687.
Schrödinger, E. (1936). *Proc. Cambridge Philos. Soc.* **32**, 446.
Sheng, P. (2006). "Introduction to Wave Scattering, Localization and Mesoscopic Phenomena." Springer, Berlin.
Soukoulis, C. M., and Economou, E. N. (1981). *Phys. Rev. B* **24**, 5698.
Thorwart, M., Eckel, J., Reina, J., Nalbach, P., and Weiss, S. (2009). *Chem. Phys. Lett.* **478**, 234.
Uhlmann, A. (1998). *Open Sys. & Inf. Dyn.* **5**, 209.
van Albada, M. P., and Lagendijk, A. (1985). *Phys. Rev. Lett.* **55**, 2692.
van Amerongen, H., van Grondelle, R., and Valkunas, L. (2000). "Photosynthetic Excitons." World Scientific Books, Singapore.
Vidal, G. (2000). *J. Mod. Opt.* **47**, 355.
Vollhardt, D., and Wölfle, P. (1980). *Phys. Rev. B* **22**, 4666.
Vollhardt, D., and Wölfle, P. (1992). in "Electronic Phase Transitions," edited by Hanke, W., and Kopaev, Y. North-Holland, Amsterdam, 1–78.
Wellens, T., Shatokhin, V., and Buchleitner, A. (2004). *Rep. Progr. Phys.* **67**, 45.
Wellens, T., and Grémaud, B. (2009). *Phys. Rev. A* **80**, 063827.
Werner, R. F. (1989). *Phys. Rev. A* **40**, 4277.
Werner, R. F., and Wolf, M. M. (2001). *Phys. Rev. A* **64**, 032112.
Wolf, P.-E., and Maret, G. (1985). *Phys. Rev. Lett.* **55**, 2696.
Wolf, P. E., Maret, G., Akkermans, E., and Maynard, R. (1988). *J. Phys. (France)* **49**, 63.
Wootters, W. K. (1998). *Phys. Rev. Lett.* **80**, 2245.
Xiong, S.-J., and Evangelou, S. N. (2001). *Phys. Rev. B* **64**, 113107.
Zanardi, P. (2002). *Phys. Rev. A* **65**, 042101.
Zhang, C., Liu, J., Raizen, M. G., and Niu, Q. (2004). *Phys. Rev. Lett.* **92**, 054101.
Żukowski, M., and Brukner, C. (2002). *Phys. Rev. Lett.* **88**, 210401.

CHAPTER 2

Quantum Coherence and Entanglement in Photosynthetic Light-Harvesting Complexes

P. Nalbach[*,†] and **M. Thorwart**[†]

Contents

[*] School of Soft Matter Research, Freiburg Institute for Advanced Studies (FRIAS), Albert-Ludwigs-Universität Freiburg, Albertstrasse 19, 79104 Freiburg, Germany

[†] I. Institut für Theoretische Physik, Universität Hamburg, Jungiusstrasse 9, 20355 Hamburg, Germany

Semiconductors and Semimetals, Volume 83
ISSN 0080-8784, DOI: 10.1016/B978-0-12-375042-6.00002-X

© 2010 Elsevier Inc.
All rights reserved.

1. EXCITONIC ENERGY TRANSFER IN PHOTOSYNTHETIC LIGHT-HARVESTING COMPLEXES

The energy source of essentially all living creatures on earth can be traced back to the sun, and it is harvested by photosynthesis. The photosynthetic conversion of physical energy of sunlight into its chemical form suitable for cellular processes involves many physical and chemical mechanisms (Blankenship, 2002; van Amerongen *et al.*, 2000). Photosynthesis starts with the absorption of a photon by a light-harvesting pigment forming an exciton, followed by the transfer of the exciton to the reaction center, where charge separation is initiated. The separated charges are used to drive chemical reactions that allow to store energy chemically for later use. Our focus lies in the transfer process of the excitation energy after absorption of a photon until it reaches the reaction center. Surprisingly, at low light intensities, the quantum efficiency of this transfer process is near unity. At higher light intensities, protection processes down regulate the efficiency to protect the reaction center and biological functions further down the process chain from damage.

Most of the world's chlorophyll, about 50%, is found in the light-harvesting biomolecular complex LHC-II of green plants. Plants, generally, exhibit two distinctive photosynthetic functional molecular complexes: PS-I and PS-II. The light-harvesting complex LHC-II is one of various antennae for the PS-II system. Experimentally, it is rather easy to separate LHC-II from the photosynthetic complex which allows detailed studies. Accordingly, it is one of the few light-harvesting complexes for which detailed structural data are available. It is known that LHC-II is a trimer where each subunit consists of 12 chlorophyll molecules, the pigments or chromophores which are excited by absorbing photons from the sunlight. The photosynthetic apparatus in plants is typically rather complicated because plants are evolutionary – already far evolved. Photosynthesis, however, was already used very early in evolution by bacteria, and this simpler photosynthetic apparatus can still be found in certain bacteria species, like green sulfur or purple bacteria. Experimentally, these bacterial systems are advantageous because their photosynthetic apparatus can be chemically fragmented into their functional subunits which allows detailed structural and spectroscopic investigations.

Purple bacteria exhibit two light-harvesting complexes, the smaller LH2 complex with 27 chromophores, which form two rings with 9 and 18 chromophores, respectively. The larger complex, LH1-RC, exhibits a single ring with 32 chromophores and the reaction center in its center. On average, about 10 LH2 rings surround an LH1-RC system.[1] In green sulfur bacteria such as the *Chlorobaculum tepidum*, the antennae form a larger conglomerate but they are connected to the reaction center exclusively by the small Fenna–Matthews–Olson (FMO) complex, a trimer of which each monomer contains seven chromophores (Fenna and Matthews, 1975; Li *et al.*, 1997; Milder *et al.*, 2010; van Groendelle and Novoderezhkin, 2006). Its purpose is purely to conduct the excitonic energy from the antennae to the reaction center. The FMO is probably one of the best characterized and investigated light-harvesting complexes. Its optical properties are nicely reviewed in a recent study (Milder *et al.*, 2010).

After absorbing a photon and formation of an exciton, the energy is transferred toward the reaction center. In purple bacteria, for example, the original absorption is thought to be mainly in the outer ring of chromophores of the LH2 ring-complex. Transfer from the outer to the inner ring happens in less than 1 ps. From there, the energy is transported through other LH2 rings to an LH1 ring and subsequently to the reaction center, which occurs in vivo on a timescale of 5–50 ps. These transfer processes are thus very fast in comparison with the decay of an excited chromophore (with subsequent reemission of a photon) with a lifetime of about 1.1 ns measured for a chromophore of an outer ring of LH2.

These timescales reflect the extraordinary quantum efficiency of the excitonic energy transfer in photosynthesis. However, it is still unclear why transfer is so much faster than the direct decay of excitons. An understanding of this question might be gained from the design principles of photosynthetic complexes. It would allow to exploit the near-unity efficiency of energy transfer for artificially designed light-harvesting complexes. Especially organic solar cells might benefit because one of their main obstacles toward an increased efficiency comes from very high exciton losses during transport after their formation but before charge separation.

1.1. Transport – incoherent hopping

Pigments or chromophores have electronic excitations with discrete frequencies in the range of visible light. Photons accordingly excite

[1]For a more detailed discussion of the light-harvesting complexes of purple bacteria we refer to the contribution by R. J. Cogdell and J. Köhler in this book.

electrons of the chromophore i from a ground state $|g_i\rangle$ to an excited state $|e_i\rangle$. Multiple simultaneous excitations can safely be neglected because the typical photon flux in the visible range on a sunny day is about 10^{21} photons/m^2. With a cross section of about 1 Å^2, an individual chromophore absorbs about 10 photons per second. With transfer times on the order of 50 ps, simultaneous multiple excitations are extremely unlikely in nature. In contrast, under experimental laser illumination, however, multiple excitations are likely. Restricting our considerations to the electronic ground and excited state, we obtain the Hamiltonian

$$H_{\mathrm{ch},i} = E_{g,i}|g_i\rangle\langle g_i| + E_{e,i}|e_i\rangle\langle e_i|. \tag{2.1}$$

with the ground (excited) state energy $E_{g,i}$ ($E_{e,i}$).

The estimation about multiple excitations holds as well for complexes of chromophores through which the excitation energy shall be transported to reach the reaction center. Accordingly, we can focus on the *single excitation subspace* spanned by states $|i\rangle$, which denotes a state with chromophore i in its excited state and all other chromophores in the complex in their ground states. Naturally, different chromophores i have different excitation or site energies E_i, and the site-energy Hamiltonian is given as

$$H_{\mathrm{ch}} = \sum_i E_i|i\rangle\langle i|. \tag{2.2}$$

Each chromophore is embedded within a protein, which protects it from its immediate environment, namely polar solvent (mainly water). The chromophore, as a chemical complex, has a characteristic vibration spectrum and by coupling to the embedding protein enlarges its vibration spectrum, accordingly. Naturally, the electronic excitations couple to the vibrational spectrum of the molecule. Furthermore, fluctuations of the surrounding solvent, or due to other close-by proteins, disturb the electronic excitation of the chromophore. Assuming that the complex is stable in its ground and excited state, we can describe all vibrational degrees of freedom in a lowest order approximation by harmonic fluctuations with the Hamiltonian

$$H_{ev,i} = \frac{1}{2}\sum_\kappa \left(p_{j,\kappa}^2 + \omega_{j,\kappa}^2 q_{j,\kappa}^2\right) + |e_i\rangle\langle e_i| \sum_\kappa \nu_\kappa^{(j)} q_{j,\kappa} \tag{2.3}$$

with momenta $p_{i,\kappa}$, displacement $q_{i,\kappa}$, frequency $\omega_{i,\kappa}$, and coupling $\nu_\kappa^{(i)}$ for chromophore i and index κ running over all fluctuation modes. We have, thereby, defined the fluctuations around the positions of the atoms in their electronic ground state.

We have furthermore neglected fluctuations, which generate transitions between the electronic ground and excited state because there are no vibrations in resonance with the optical electronic transition and thus these fluctuations have little effect (Weiss, 2008). The linewidth of the optical absorption is determined by the fluctuations of the transition energy, which we consider in the following. A more detailed discussion of the environmental fluctuation spectrum will be given in Section 2.3. Restricting our consideration as before to the *single excitation subspace*, the Hamiltonian describing the coupling to the environments becomes

$$H_{ev} = \frac{1}{2}\sum_{i}\sum_{\kappa}\left(p_{j,\kappa}^2 + \omega_{j,\kappa}^2 q_{j,\kappa}^2\right) + \sum_{i} |i\rangle\langle i| \sum_{\kappa} \nu_{\kappa}^{(j)} q_{j,\kappa}. \tag{2.4}$$

Excitation of a chromophore also modifies its dipole moment, and this changing dipole allows the chromophores to interact with each other. Thus, Coulomb dipole–dipole coupling, V_{ij}, allows for a transfer of excitation (without electron transfer) from chromophore i to j resulting in a interchromophore coupling Hamiltonian

$$H_{\text{ch–ch}} = \sum_{i,j} V_{ij}\left\{|i\rangle\langle j| + |j\rangle\langle i|\right\}. \tag{2.5}$$

The theoretical formulation for energy transfer through the dipole–dipole coupling, which is nowadays widely applied to photosynthetic systems was provided by Theodor Förster in the 1940s (Förster, 1948). It holds for the case when the chromophores are spatially rather distant and thus weakly coupled and the environmental fluctuations, in contrast, are rather strong. Formally, Förster's treatment also holds when the chromophores are very close and thus strongly coupled by coherent exciton motion (Knox and Gülen, 1993). Förster solved the dynamical problem of the total Hamiltonian $H = H_{\text{ch}} + H_{\text{ch–ch}} + H_{ev}$ by treating the electronic coupling $H_{\text{ch–ch}}$ perturbatively up to second order which results in energy transfer by incoherent hopping between the chromophores.

The Förster approach results in incoherent hopping by construction, but, at the same time, this behavior fits expectations. Temperature and associated thermal fluctuations are by themselves not necessarily enough to overdamp the microscopic quantum dynamics because electronic couplings up to $100/\text{cm}^{-1} \simeq 150\ \text{K}/k_{\text{B}}$ are found in the FMO complex. Room temperature, thus, only exceeds the electronic coupling scale by a factor of two, which is generally not enough to overdamp dynamics (Leggett *et al.*, 1987; Weiss, 2008). From analyzing absorption linewidths, however, it is known that the coupling of the environmental fluctuations to the chromophores is rather strong or, in other words, the reorganization energy is of the order of the electronic coupling itself. Under the commonly used Markov assumption, i.e., when the reorganization of the environment itself is faster (or, in other words, the correlation function of the environmental fluctuations decays faster) than the electronic transitions, such a strong coupling to the environment is sufficient to overdamp the dynamics (Leggett *et al.*, 1987; Weiss, 2008). Nevertheless, it is a longstanding question (Reineker, 1982) whether the transfer of excitonic energy can also have quantum coherent features.

1.2. Signatures of quantum coherence

Recent experiments performed by ultrafast optical spectroscopy (Engel *et al.*, 2007; Lee *et al.*, 2007) have revealed long-lasting beating signals in a two-dimensional Fourier transform electronic spectrum (Brixner *et al.*, 2005) recorded from green sulfur bacteria such as *Chlorobium tepidum*. This behavior cannot be explained within an incoherent hopping model. The observed (Engel *et al.*, 2007) long-lived excitonic coherence lasted up to several hundred femtoseconds and thus to timescales comparable with that of the energy transfer. These experiments have been performed at low temperature $T = 77$ K and clearly suggest that the exciton moves coherently through the FMO complex rather than by incoherent hopping.

Similarly, Lee *et al.* (2007) found coherent beating signals at low temperatures in a two-color electronic coherence photon echo experiment. It directly probed electronic coherences by mixing of the bacteriopheophytin and accessory bacteriochlorophyll excited states in the reaction center of the purple bacterium *Rhodobacter sphaeroides*. These measurements were performed at 77 K and at 180 K. The coherence beatings in these measurements were explained by the authors (Cheng and Fleming, 2009) by a strong correlation between protein-induced fluctuations in the transition energies of neighboring chromophores, leading to the conclusion that protein-correlated environments, in fact, preserve and support electronic coherence in photosynthetic complexes.

By introducing an angle-resolved coherent optical wave mixing technique, the quantum beating signals between coherently coupled electronic transitions in the light-harvesting complex of purple bacteria could directly be observed (Mercer *et al.*, 2009). Recently, an ultrafast polarization experiment (Collini and Scholes, 2009) has revealed quantum coherent intrachain (but not interchain) electronic energy transfer in conjugated polymers with different chain conformations as model multichromophoric systems at room temperature. The data suggest that chemical donor–acceptor bonds help to correlate dephasing perturbations. Also in the light-harvesting proteins of cryptophyte marine algae, quantum coherent couplings have been identified by exceptionally long-lasting excitation oscillations even at ambient temperature (Collini *et al.*, 2010). Very recent experiments have confirmed the quantum coherent beating signals even in the FMO complex at physiological temperatures (Panitchayangkoon *et al.*, 2010).

1.3. Perspectives by quantum dynamics

For a short introduction into the various aspects of quantum coherence and its role in photosynthesis, we refer to the review of Scholes (Scholes, 2010). Since the first observation of quantum coherent dynamics in light-harvesting complexes, many investigations have tried to clarify the role of quantum coherence for the functionality and the near-unity quantum efficiency of energy transfer. The idea is that incoherent hopping leading to a Markovian random walk of localized excitonic states between the nodes of the network of chromophores will be very slow on large networks. Quantum information theory deals with similar problems and has revealed that quantum coherence can considerably shorten transfer times in random walks (Caruso *et al.*, 2009, 2010; Chin *et al.*, 2009; Mohseni *et al.*, 2008; Plenio and Huelga, 2008; Rebentrost *et al.*, 2009a,b,c; Rivas *et al.*, 2009; Scholak *et al.*, 2009). At the same time, the role of the specific ring structures of LH2 was discussed as favoring stability (Fassioli *et al.*, 2009, 2010; Olaya-Castro *et al.*, 2008). The combination of optimized exciton trapping (Cao and Silbey, 2009) with powerful quantum coherent adaptive control schemes (Herek *et al.*, 2002; Savolainen *et al.*, 2008; Wohlleben *et al.*, 2005) could, in addition, allow to exploit quantum effects to direct from outside the outcome of photochemical processes. Effects beyond the lowest-order Förster treatment, such as the failure of the point-dipole approximation and the ensuing solvent screening and the sharing of common bath modes have been considered, recently, in a generalized Förster theory (Beljonne *et al.*, 2009).

As central question, we address why quantum coherence in excitonic energy transfer survives for several hundred femtoseconds under physiological conditions (room temperature and embedded in wet and disordered biological environments).

2. BATH-SUSTAINED QUANTUM COHERENCE IN A SINGLE EXCITON PAIR

Photosynthetic energy-transfer processes in light-harvesting complexes are often discussed theoretically in simplified low-dimensional models describing a few individual chromophores, which mutually interact by dipolar couplings and which are exposed to the fluctuations of the polar solvent molecules and the protein host (Blankenship, 2002; Gilmore and McKenzie, 2005, 2006, 2008; Leggett *et al.*, 1987; van Amerongen *et al.*, 2000; Weiss, 2008). Two limiting cases are commonly considered: (i) When the dipole coupling between the chromophores is weak in comparison with the coupling of the chromophore to environmental fluctuations, the excitons are considered to be localized at the chromophore sites. The weak electronic coupling can then be treated perturbatively, resulting in an incoherent hopping dynamics described by the standard Förster theory (Förster, 1948, 1965; May and Kühn, 2004). (ii) In the opposite limit of weak coupling to the environmental fluctuations, standard perturbative quantum master equations are used (Caruso *et al.*, 2009, 2010; Chin *et al.*, 2009; Fassioli *et al.*, 2009, 2010; Mohseni *et al.*, 2008; Olaya-Castro *et al.*, 2008; Plenio and Huelga, 2008; Rebentrost *et al.*, 2009a,b,c; Rivas *et al.*, 2009), resulting in a damped coherent dynamics for the exciton transfer. They are based on Markovian approximation, which renders the time evolution memoryless and, thus, allows for a straightforward numerical solution. Such master equations are appropriate in the case of a clear separation of timescales, i.e., when the timescale of environmental fluctuations is much smaller than the timescale on which the system dynamics evolves. Formally, this is captured by the requirement that the bath reorganization energy (Weiss, 2008) is much larger than the typical system energy. It is important to realize that this condition is typically not fulfilled for the energy transfer dynamics in biomolecular light-harvesting complexes in a protein-solvent environment (Gilmore and McKenzie, 2005, 2006, 2008; Urboniene *et al.*, 2007). Here, in addition to the rather slow polarization fluctuations of the polar solvent molecules, the protein cage acts also as a frequency filter which particularly shapes the frequency distribution of the environmental modes. A structured environment, in general, induces strong non-Markovian effects (Weiss, 2008), which cannot be captured by Bloch–Redfield–like time-local master equations. Similar effects are known for electronic spin qubits in semiconductor quantum dots (Thorwart *et al.*, 2005) and in donor-based charge qubit crystal systems (Eckel *et al.*, 2006).

2.1. Model for a single chromophore pair

In a first approach to the full excitonic energy-transfer dynamics, we address the simplest model which is a donor–acceptor pair of two chromophores. As initiation, the donor is excited by absorbing a photon, which we use as initial state. The electronic coupling to the acceptor then causes exciton energy transfer, which is described by the standard Hamiltonian

$$H_{\rm da} = V_{\rm da}\left\{|d\rangle\langle a| + |a\rangle\langle d|\right\} + \epsilon_{\rm d}|d\rangle\langle d| + \epsilon_{\rm a}|a\rangle\langle a| + \sum_{j=a/d} H_{ev,j}. \tag{2.6}$$

The state $|d\rangle$ ($|a\rangle$) denotes the exciton to be at the donor (acceptor), $V_{\rm da}$ is the respective electronic coupling between donor and acceptor and $\epsilon_{\rm d}$ ($\epsilon_{\rm a}$) is the excited electronic energy of the donor (acceptor), respectively. The part, $H_{ev,j}$ (see Eq. (2.3)) describes the coupling of the exciton to environmental Gaussian fluctuations.

In a first approach (see Appendix A for further details), we further simplify our donor–acceptor system to a single spin-boson model with the Pauli matrices $\sigma_z = |a\rangle\langle a| - |d\rangle\langle d|$ and $\sigma_x = |a\rangle\langle d| + |d\rangle\langle a|$:

$$H_{\mathrm{da}} = \frac{\Delta}{2}\sigma_x + \hbar\sigma_z \sum_{\kappa} \lambda_\kappa (b_\kappa^\dagger + b_\kappa) + \sum_{\kappa} \hbar\omega_\kappa b_\kappa^\dagger b_\kappa, \tag{2.7}$$

where we, furthermore, focus on equal chromophores $\epsilon = \epsilon_d - \epsilon_a$, set $\Delta = 2V_{da}$, and where b_κ are bosonic bath operators with couplings λ_κ. A single bosonic bath coupled through σ_z to the donor–acceptor pair assumes fully anticorrelated environmental fluctuations at the chromophore sites. We will discuss spatial correlations in the environmental fluctuations in more detail in Chapter 4. In general, such correlations only quantitatively modify the dynamics for a single donor–acceptor system.

In order to determine the influence of the environmental fluctuations on the dynamics, their spectral density (Weiss, 2008) has to be specified. It can be determined within the standard modelling of solvation (Gilmore and McKenzie, 2008) or is assumed phenomenologically and justified by successfully describing experiments (Ishizaki and Fleming, 2009a; Read *et al.*, 2008; Thorwart *et al.*, 2009; Zhang *et al.*, 1998; Zigmantas *et al.*, 2006). We discuss the spectral density in more detail in the following Section 2.3. To be specific, we use an Ohmic form,

$$G(\omega) = 2\pi\alpha\omega e^{-\omega/\omega_c} \tag{2.8}$$

with an exponential high-frequency cutoff ω_c. The dimensionless damping constant α of the protein-solvent can be related to the parameters of a dielectric continuum model within standard theory of solvation (Gilmore and McKenzie, 2008). One finds for the order of magnitude of $\alpha \sim 0.01 - 0.1$ (Gilmore and McKenzie, 2006, 2008). The timescale for the bath dynamics given by ω_c^{-1} is related to the reorganization energy $E_r \sim 2\alpha\hbar\omega_c$. If $\Delta \ll \omega_c$ and $\alpha \ll 1$, the bath evolves fast compared with the system and loses its memory quickly, rendering a Markovian approximation and the standard Bloch–Redfield treatment (May and Kühn, 2004) suitable. That is the usual situation encountered in many physical systems, e.g., quantum optics, ion traps, quantum dots, and superconducting devices (Makhlin *et al.*, 2001). It is qualitatively different for the excitons in the biomolecular environment where $\hbar\omega_c$ is typically of the order of $\sim 2 - 8$ meV, while the Förster coupling constants can range from $\hbar\Delta \sim 0.2 - 100$ meV (Gilmore and McKenzie, 2006, 2008). Hence, the bath generically responds slower than the dynamics of the excitons evolves, and non-Markovian effects become dominant. The case of very strongly damped two-state system with $\alpha > 1$ shows coherent oscillations for $\Delta \gtrsim \omega_c$ which was shown using quantum Monte Carlo simulations (Egger and

Mak, 1994; Mühlbacher and Egger, 2003) and by applying the numerical renormalization group (Bulla *et al.*, 2005).

2.2. Population dynamics of a single chromophore pair

Using the numerically exact real-time quasi-adiabatic propagator path integral (QUAPI) (Makri and Makarov 1995a,b; Makri *et al.* 1996; Nalbach and Thorwart 2009; Thorwart *et al.* 2000, 1998 see Appendix B for details), we calculate the population difference $P(t) = \langle \sigma_z \rangle_t$ (Weiss, 2008) for the single donor–acceptor pair. We choose $P(0) = 1$, fixing the donor initially in its excited state. Figure 2.1 shows the results for $\alpha = 0.1$ as typical for photosynthetic systems (Adolphs and Renger, 2006; Cho *et al.*, 2005; Gilmore and McKenzie, 2006). $P(t)$ decays with time in an oscillatory way. The decay occurs faster for large ω_c, whereas for small ω_c, the slow bath sustains more coherent oscillations. In general, for smaller ω_c, the spectral weight of the bath modes around the system frequency Δ is suppressed and the decohering influence is reduced, yielding prolonged coherence. In fact, choosing $\alpha = 0.1, \omega_c = 0.1\Delta$ (consistent with Engel *et al.* (2007)), we find a coherence time of 1 ps that agrees well with the measured value of at least 660 fs (Engel *et al.*, 2007), given the complexity of the experimental setup and the simplicity of our model. We should clearly point out that a comparison with Born–Markov results (Weiss, 2008) for $P(t)$ strongly fails in the range of small ω_c. We will discuss this point in more detail in the Appendix B.

2.3. Environmental fluctuation spectra

The environmental fluctuations for chromophores in light-harvesting complexes are, generally, formed by two distinct contributions namely the

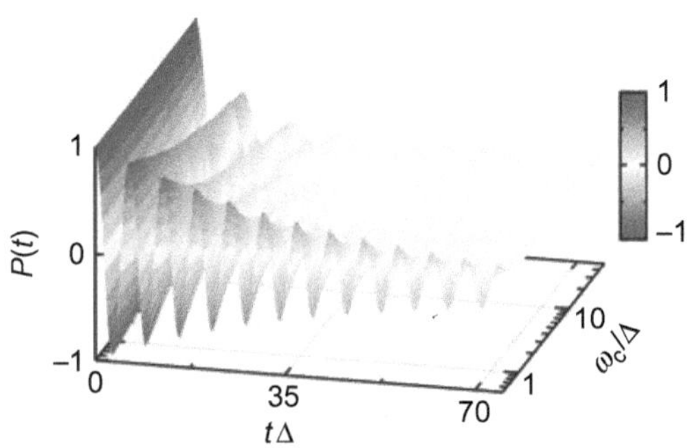

FIGURE 2.1 Population difference $P(t)$ for a single chromophore pair and full cross-over from a Markovian to a non-Markovian bath. Parameters are $k_B T = 0.1\hbar\Delta$, and $\alpha = 0.1$.

vibrational spectrum of the protein host in which they are embedded and the polarization fluctuations of the polar solvent itself. Typically, this is mainly water, in which the proteins themselves are emersed. Two approaches are commonly used to obtain the spectra.

By using Onsager's approach to describe the solvent as polarizable continuum and by calculating the back reaction of the polarization of the environment onto the dipolar quantum system, the spectral function becomes a sum of various Debye spectra (Gilmore and McKenzie, 2005, 2006, 2008), which under typical conditions reduces to an Ohmic spectral density with a Debye-like cutoff leading to

$$G(\omega) := \sum_{\kappa} |\lambda_\kappa|^2 \delta(\omega - \omega_\kappa) = 2\lambda \frac{\omega\omega_c}{\omega_c^2 + \omega^2} \tag{2.9}$$

with the reorganization energy λ and the timescale of environmental relaxation ω_c^{-1}. The Debye spectral density has been successfully used for theoretical analyses of experimental results (Ishizaki and Fleming, 2009a; Read *et al.*, 2008; Zhang *et al.*, 1998; Zigmantas *et al.*, 2006), i.e., in the discussion of absorption linewidth experiments. Super-Ohmic spectral functions were also used (Adolphs and Renger, 2006) but they generically lead to weak-damping dynamics. Here, we focus solely on Ohmic spectra.

Continuum models of the environment only capture the continuous part of the environmental spectrum. The embedding protein, even though large molecular complexes, are still finite with discrete vibrational spectra. At least at high frequencies, the spectra typically have pronounced localized modes, which are totally neglected when using Eq. (2.9). As long as the discrete vibrational excitation energies are far away from the energy scale of the electronic coupling, they will not strongly influence the energy-transfer dynamics. In the opposite case, these vibrations cannot be described within a system-bath approach, and their full quantum dynamics must be taken into account. In this case, the coherent vibrations become part of the system. This situation is encountered in the case of *vibrational coherences*. Thus, we implicitly assume that all discrete vibrational excitation energies are not in resonance with the electronic coupling energies.

Nevertheless, this discussion shows that the high-frequency tail of the environmental spectral density is neither experimentally nor theoretically fully controlled, although its specific form quantitatively modifies theoretically results. Earlier, we used an exponentially cutoff Ohmic spectrum, Eq. (2.8), which in the field of open quantum dynamics (Leggett *et al.*, 1987; Nalbach and Thorwart, 2009) is more popular.

2.4. Conclusion for a single chromophore pair

So far, we have reached an understanding how quantum coherence in the excitonic energy transfer can live for up to several hundred femtoseconds despite the strong coupling to high-temperature environmental fluctuations. Studying a simple donor–acceptor pair system shows that environmental fluctuations as typical in light-harvesting complexes are *slower* than the excitonic transfer dynamics and, thus, cannot destroy quantum coherence substantially which allows the coherence to live on timescales comparable to the total transfer time. Thus, we argue that long-lived quantum coherence in excitonic energy transfer in light-harvesting complexes is a result of the fluctuation spectra, which the chromophores feel. These spectra are tuned by the protein cage in which the chromophores are embedded, and it is conceivable that evolution trimmed the spectra in order to allow for quantum coherence in order to promote transfer efficiency.

3. BATH-SUSTAINED QUANTUM ENTANGLEMENT OF TWO CHROMOPHORE PAIRS

The first observation of quantum coherent dynamics in light-harvesting complexes (Engel *et al.*, 2007) revived earlier speculations that the near-unity quantum efficiency of energy transfer might be a result of the quantum speed-up of the search of an exciton for its most efficient way to the reaction center. They are supported by similar findings for a quantum random walk on a network of several nodes. Many investigations have tried to clarify the role of quantum coherence for the superior quantum efficiency (Caruso *et al.*, 2009, 2010; Chin *et al.*, 2009; Mohseni *et al.*, 2008; Plenio and Huelga, 2008; Rebentrost *et al.*, 2009a,b,c; Rivas *et al.*, 2009; Scholak *et al.*, 2009), but all these approaches used either Markovian approximations or when including non-Markovian effects were generally rather uncontrolled. Another main aspect of quantum speed-ups in quantum searches is entanglement.

Quantum entanglement is, generally, more fragile than quantum coherence because it requires more than one particle and is, thus, far easily disturbed by environmental fluctuations. Hence, as main second step in our studies, we investigate how the slow environmental fluctuations, which favor long-lived quantum coherence, disturb quantum entanglement.

3.1. Model for two coupled chromophore pairs

We address entanglement between two chromophore pairs (two donor–acceptor pairs) under the influence of a slow bath. We consider four equal chromophores, which form two donor–acceptor pairs described by $\sigma_{x/z,i}$, coupled by an interpair dipole–dipole interaction J, where the two dipoles are provided by the two pairs. Moreover, they are coupled to a harmonic bath. The total Hamiltonian reads

$$H_2 = \sum_{i=1,2} \frac{\hbar\Delta}{2}\sigma_{x,i} + \hbar J(\sigma_{x,1}\sigma_{x,2} + \sigma_{y,1}\sigma_{y,2}) + \frac{\hbar}{2}(\sigma_{z,1} + \sigma_{z,2})\sum_{\kappa} c_{\kappa}(b_{\kappa}^{\dagger} + b_{\kappa}) + \sum_{\kappa} \hbar\omega_{\kappa} b_{\kappa}^{\dagger} b_{\kappa}, \tag{2.10}$$

which is expressed in the basis of the states $\{|d_1\rangle = |e_1 g_2\rangle, |a_1\rangle = |g_1 e_2\rangle, |d_2\rangle, |a_2\rangle = |g_3 e_4\rangle\}$, where $e_i(g_i)$ refers to the exciton i in its excited (ground) state. The interpair interaction J describes the possibility for an exciton to be transferred from donor (acceptor) of pair 1 to the acceptor (donor) of pair 2. This allows for an energy transfer of two excitons to become entangled even when originally starting from a nonentangled state. As before, the bath spectral density is assumed to be Ohmic following from a Debye dielectric model. The time-dependent reduced density matrix $\rho(t)$ is computed using an adapted QUAPI scheme. We should point out that we couple both donor–acceptor pairs to the same fluctuations by using $\sigma_{z,1} + \sigma_{z,2}$. In other words, the fluctuations at both donors (acceptors) are fully correlated. Figure 2.2 shows the time-evolution of

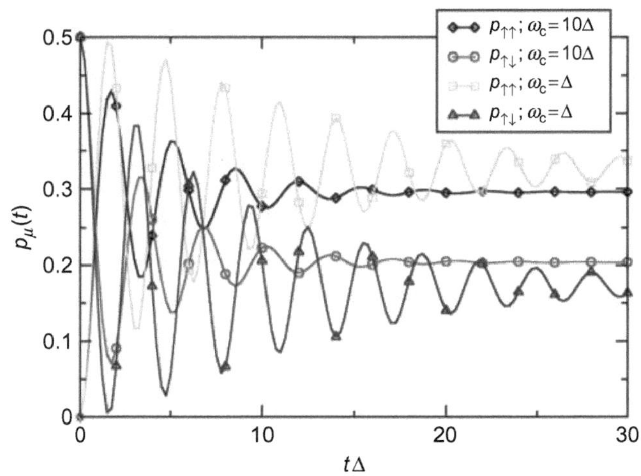

FIGURE 2.2 Time evolution of the populations $p_{\mu}(t)$ for two coupled chromophore pairs for a slow ($\omega_c = \Delta$) and a fast ($\omega_c = 10\Delta$) bath, for $k_B T = 0.1\hbar\Delta$, $\alpha = 0.1$, and $J = 0.1\Delta$.

the populations $p_{d_1d_2}(t) = p_{a_1a_2}(t)$ and $p_{d_1a_2}(t) = p_{a_1d_2}(t)$ of the four basis states for different values of ω_c for the initial preparation $|\psi_0\rangle = (|d_1a_2\rangle + |a_1d_2\rangle)/\sqrt{2}$. After a transient oscillatory behavior, the stationary equilibrium values are reached. The corresponding decay occurs on shorter times for large ω_c, i.e., fast baths, compared with the rather slow decay for small ω_c.

3.2. Entanglement of two chromophore pairs

To quantify the two-pair quantum entanglement, we study the negativity $N(t) = \max\{0, -2\zeta_{\min}(t)\}$ (Horodecki, 1996; Peres, 1996), where $\zeta_{\min}(t)$ denotes the smallest eigenvalue of the partially transposed reduced density operator, which possesses the matrix elements $\rho^{T_2}_{m\mu,n\nu} = \rho_{n\mu,m\nu}$. A separable state has $N = 0$, while for a maximally entangled state, $N = 1$.

Figure 2.3A shows $N(t)$ for two values $\omega_c = \Delta$, and $\omega_c = 50\Delta$, for the maximally entangled initial state $|\psi_0\rangle$. Starting from $N(0) = 1$, we observe a decay to zero with small oscillations superimposed. For the Markovian bath $\omega_c = 50\Delta$, the decay occurs faster than for the non-Markovian bath $\omega_c = \Delta$, indicating that entanglement survives on a longer timescale under the action of a slow bath. For a larger interpair coupling $J = \Delta$, the superimposed oscillations are more pronounced (Fig. 2.3A inset) which is because of constructive interference of the transitions within the chromophore pair. For a quantitative picture, we fit an exponential $N(t) = N_0 \exp(-\Gamma t) + N_1$ with a decay constant Γ, which contains the influence of the bath. Figure 2.3B shows the dependence of Γ on ω_c. Clearly, Γ strongly decreases for small ω_c, whereas for large ω_c, the decay rate saturates to a constant value. The dependence of Γ on ω_c is more pronounced for larger values of α. This observation indicates that entanglement could be, at least, as robust in biomolecular systems as in other macroscopic condensed-matter devices (Makhlin *et al.*, 2001), which display quantum coherent behavior. We note that this tendency is already captured by the result of a perturbative one-phonon analysis, i.e., in second-order perturbation theory. It would predict that for $\omega_c \leq \Delta$, effectively no bath modes for efficient one-phonon processes are available as they are exponentially suppressed, following $\Gamma \propto G(\Delta) \propto e^{-\Delta/\omega_c}$. A fit to the data points in the region of large ω_c is shown by the dashed line in Fig. 2.3B for $\alpha = 0.01$. Clearly, when $\omega_c \leq \Delta$, multiphonon contributions become significant. This is even more pronounced for larger α (not shown).

To study the cross-over between fast and slow baths, we show $N(t)$ for varying ω_c in Fig. 2.4 for the initial state $|\psi_1\rangle = |d_1d_2\rangle$. Figure 2.4A shows the result for $J = 0.1\Delta$. In the regime $\omega_c \gg \Delta$, no substantial entanglement exists. However, for $0.1\Delta \lesssim \omega_c \lesssim \Delta$, we find an initial buildup of entanglement and a subsequent regular oscillatory dynamics of $N(t)$. In this

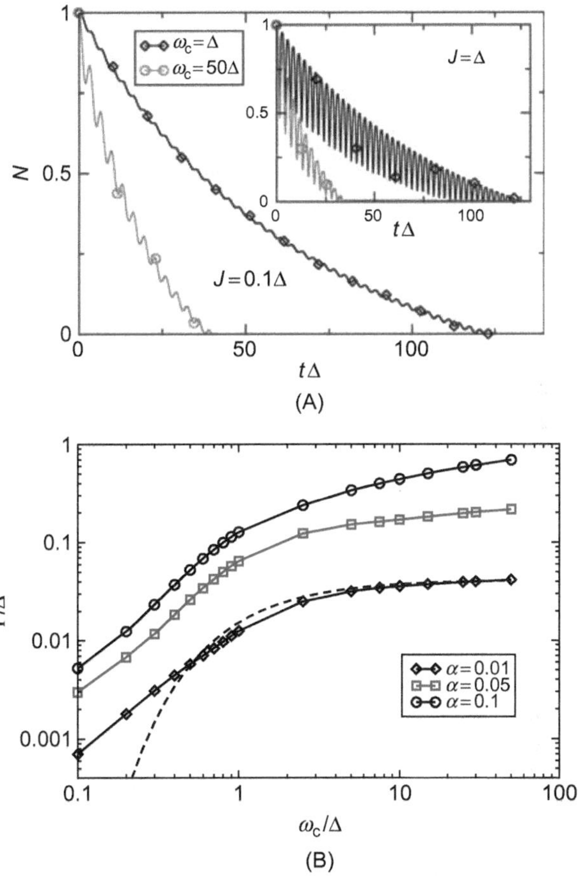

FIGURE 2.3 (A) Time evolution of the negativity $N(t)$ for the cut-off $\omega_c = \Delta$ (black) and $\omega_c = 50\Delta$ (red) for $\alpha = 0.01$ and for $J = 0.1\Delta$ (main) and $J = \Delta$ (inset). Moreover, $k_B T = 0.1\hbar\Delta$. (B) Decay constant Γ as a function of the cut-off ω_c for different values of α (symbols with solid lines) for $k_B T = 0.1\hbar\Delta, J = 0.1\Delta$. Dashed line: Corresponding one-phonon result $\Gamma = \Gamma_0 e^{-\Delta/\omega_c}$, where the proportionality constant $\Gamma_0 = 0.041\Delta$ has been obtained from a fit to the three data points $\omega_c = 25\Delta, 30\Delta, 50\Delta$. (See Plate no. 1 in the Color Plate Section.)

regime, complete entanglement disappearance and revivals alternate. The timescale of the entanglement oscillations is given by $2\pi/J$. This clearly illustrates the constructive role of a slow bath. Further illustration is shown in the inset of Fig. 2.4A, where $N(t)$ is depicted for vanishing direct interpair coupling $J = 0$. In fact, in the regime $\omega_c < \Delta$, we find that entanglement between the two pairs is generated by their common interaction with a slow bath. Most interestingly, for $\omega_c = 0.1\Delta$, $N(t)$ steadily grows even over rather long times up to $t\Delta = 500$. In view of the single-pair

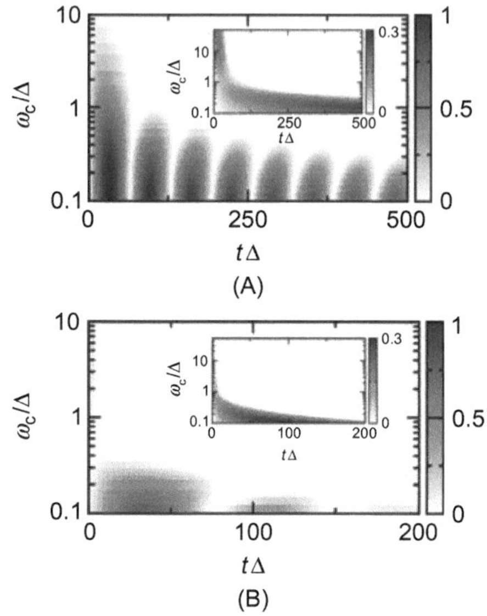

FIGURE 2.4 (A) Negativity $N(t)$ as a function of ω_c for $J = 0.1\Delta$ (main) and $J = 0$ (inset), for $\alpha = 0.01$ and $k_B T = 0.1\hbar\Delta$. (B) Same as in (A) but for the strong coupling case $\alpha = 0.1$.

results described earlier, this seems counterintuitive because for small ω_c, a reduced influence of the bath modes would be expected. However, in this regime, the bath is rather efficient in generating entanglement. This feature survives even for larger values of α, see Fig. 2.4B. The oscillatory behavior of the entanglement generation still occurs for $J = 0.1\Delta$, where $N(t)$ assumes all values between zero and one. The bath-induced destruction happens here earlier because of the large α. Entanglement is also produced when $J = 0$, see inset of Fig. 2.4B, for $0.1\Delta \lesssim \omega_c \lesssim \Delta$. Also here, $N(t)$ can even reach the maximal value at intermediate times.

The generation of entanglement can be qualitatively understood by performing a polaron-like transformation $U = \exp[i(\sigma_{z,1} + \sigma_{z,2})p/2]$ with $p = \sum_\kappa i c_\kappa (b_\kappa^\dagger - b_\kappa)$. Setting $J = 0$ and assuming that the two qubits are spatially close enough, the resulting Hamiltonian $\tilde{H}_2 = U^\dagger H_2 U$ acquires an effective direct pair coupling $\tilde{H}_{2,\mathrm{int}} = \hbar J_{\mathrm{eff}} \sigma_{z,1}\sigma_{z,2}$ with $J_{\mathrm{eff}} = -\alpha\omega_c/8 \sim E_r$. Then, the long-wave length bath modes are efficient in generating coherent coupling, and thus entanglement. Its dynamical generation occurs on a timescale $1/J_{\mathrm{eff}}$, see insets of Fig. 2.4. However, damping destroys coherence on a timescale Γ related to ω_c, see Fig. 2.3, i.e., for large ω_c, damping beats entanglement generation.

So far, we have studied not so high temperatures, similar to the experimental conditions in Refs. Engel *et al.* (2007) and Lee *et al.* (2007). However,

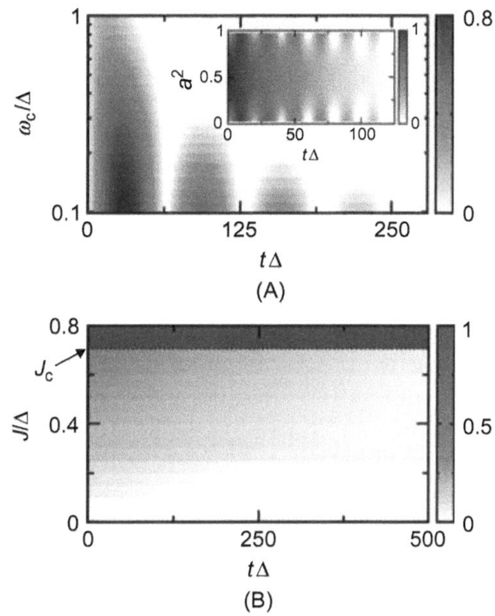

FIGURE 2.5 (A) Negativity $N(t)$ for varying ω_c; $J = 0.1\Delta, \alpha = 0.01$, and $k_BT = \hbar\Delta$ (Main). Inset: $N(t)$ for different initial preparations $|\psi_2\rangle = a|\uparrow_1\downarrow_2\rangle + b|\downarrow_1\uparrow_2\rangle$, for $J = 0.1\Delta, \alpha = 0.01, k_BT = 0.1\hbar\Delta$, and $\omega_c = \Delta$. (b) $N(t)$ for varying J; $\alpha = 0.01$, $k_BT = 0.1\hbar\Delta, \omega_c = 0.1\Delta$. $J_c = 1/\sqrt{2}$ marks the border above which the initial ground state belongs to a DFS.

in Fig. 2.5A (main), we plot $N(t)$ for varying ω_c, for $k_BT = \hbar\Delta$, for the initial state $|\psi_1\rangle$. We still find large entanglement oscillations at short to intermediate times, for $0.1\Delta \lesssim \omega_c \lesssim \Delta$ despite the rather large temperature. This is a remarkable hardware feature that could provide a useful resource for the artificial design of controlled, robust, and efficient biomolecular nanostructures for quantum information processing (Kroutvar *et al.*, 2004; Rabl *et al.*, 2006; Thorwart and Hänggi, 2002).

Furthermore, we have varied the initial preparation to the state $|\psi_2\rangle = a|d_1a_2\rangle + b|a_1d_2\rangle$ with $a^2 + b^2 = 1$. The inset of Fig. 2.5A shows $N(t)$ for varying a^2 and $J = 0.1\Delta$. $|\psi_2\rangle$ is maximally entangled for $a^2 = 1/2$, for which $N(t)$ decays monotonously with time, while away from this region, the negativity again shows collapses and revivals. For the borders $a^2 \to 0, 1$, $|\psi_2\rangle$ is a separable state, but entanglement is rather quickly generated with time before it finally dies out. Robust entanglement, thus, depends on the initial preparation and is favored by the choice of initially separable (or weakly entangled) states.

Finally, we analyze the dependence on the interpair coupling J. The negativity $N(t)$ is shown in Fig. 2.5B for varying J for the respective ground state as the initial preparation. From Eq. (2.10), it follows that a critical value $J_c = 1/\sqrt{2}$ exists such that for $J \geq J_c$, the state $|\psi_g\rangle = (|d_1 a_2\rangle - |a_1 d_2\rangle)/\sqrt{2}$ is the two-pair ground state, which, however, belongs to a decoherence-free subspace (DFS) of H_2. Hence, $N(t)$ remains constantly maximal. For $J < J_c$, the ground state has some weight outside of the DFS and hence suffers from decoherence.

3.3. Conclusions

We found that non-Markovian effects of slow environmental fluctuations allow for long-lived quantum entanglement. Interpair dipole–dipole coupling allows for the generation of entanglement out of nonentangled initial states and shows death and revivals of entanglement on timescales relevant for excitonic energy transfer. Even without interpair coupling, entanglement was generated by a slowly fluctuating environment, which is a result of spatial correlations of the environmental fluctuations at different chromophore sites. Thus, in biomolecular environments as typical for chromophores in light-harvesting complexes, entanglement is long-lived and will be generated by interpair dipole–dipole couplings and/or spatially correlated fluctuations. This strongly supports the idea that speed-ups because of quantum coherence and entanglement might be responsible for the near-unity quantum efficiency of the excitonic energy transfer in photosynthetic systems, although a more rigorous proof still has to be given. However, it also clearly shows that corresponding investigations must take the non-Markovian behavior of the slow environments fully into account, in order to be predictive.

4. ROLE OF SPATIAL CORRELATIONS

In the last section, we have seen that spatial correlations in the environmental fluctuations at different chromophoric sites influence the dynamics and entanglement for double donor–acceptor systems. Additionally, the experimental coherence beatings (Lee *et al.*, 2007), found by mixing of the bacteriopheophytin and accessory bacteriochlorophyll-excited states in the reaction center of the purple bacterium *Rhodobacter sphaeroides* could only be explained (Cheng and Fleming, 2009) including strong correlations between protein-induced fluctuations in the transition energies of neighboring chromophores. The influence of these correlations received little attention in the theoretical investigations so far. Nazir (2009) investigated the influence of correlated fluctuations on a donor–acceptor system for strong system-bath coupling and finds explicitly that correlations in a super-Ohmic bath suppress the crossover to incoherent dynamics at high temperatures. Fassioli *et al.* (2010) discussed the influence of correlations on the trapping probability in a ring of chromophores within a Lindblad master equation approach. They find that the correlations between environmental fluctuations allows to tune the trapping probability.

Generically, all environmental fluctuations are viewed as localized. When including spatial correlations, we are led to introduce a finite localization length ξ. This viewpoint is in contrast to a condensed-matter point of view, in which fluctuations are normal modes of the bulk material and, thus, are typically phonons that propagate through the material with a finite speed. Propagating modes naturally couple to all chromophores with amplitude differences determined by the phase differences resulting from finite propagation times from one chromophore site to the next. However, rattling of side chains of macromolecules in highly disordered protein environments might well exist and certainly the discrete vibration spectrum of the proteins should be viewed as a localized excitation as well.

In the following, we investigate systematically the role of spatial correlations for propagating, as well as for localized modes with finite localization lengths.

4.1. Correlated environmental fluctuations at different sites

At first, we discuss the functional form of the spectral density and how spatial correlations modify our description of the environmental fluctuations. For localized fluctuations with localization length ξ, which is taken to be independent of the mode energy ω, at each chromophoric site a spectral density

$$J_{ij}^{\mathrm{loc}}(\omega) = 2\alpha\omega \mathrm{e}^{-\omega/\omega_{\mathrm{c}}} \mathrm{e}^{-r_{ij}/\xi} \tag{2.11}$$

results, where we again assume an exponentially cut-off spectrum with cut-off frequency ω_{c} and damping strength α. The on-site spectrum for a single chromophore J_{ii} is identical to the one used earlier. New is the intersite spectrum J_{ij}, which now depends on the distance r_{ij} between chromophores i and j and the localization length. The intersite spectrum $J_{ij}^{\mathrm{loc}}(\omega)$ naturally vanishes for sites far apart $r_{ij} \gg \xi$ and the fluctuations at the donor and the acceptor sites then become uncorrelated. For close sites $r_{ij} \ll \xi$, the intersite spectrum becomes identical to the on-site spectrum. In the later case, the fluctuations at both sites are fully correlated and thus actually identical. As shown in Fig. 2.6, both excitons then *see* the same electric field, which, in turn, only modifies the total energy but not the energy difference between donor and acceptor. Accordingly, these fully correlated fluctuations cannot influence the dynamics of the donor–acceptor system.

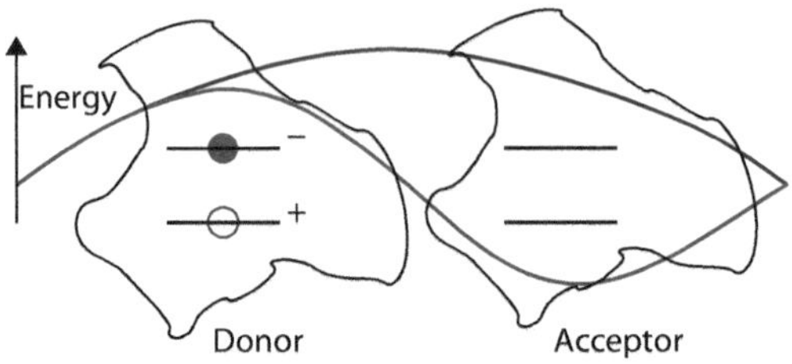

FIGURE 2.6 Donor and acceptor with two environmental field with different wave length are illustrated. The donor holds an electron in the excited state, which forms with the hole left in the ground state an exciton having a finite electric dipole moment.

In crystals, environmental fluctuations acting, e.g., on electrons or specific defect structures, are generated by vibrations of the lattice atoms and are the well-known phonons. Phonons are also present in disordered media (condensed, soft, or fluid). In the sense of propagating modes of the host material, which evolve with time through the medium, they are commonly limited to the low-energy sector or, more specifically, to energies associated to wave lengths on which the material appears homogeneous. For wave length smaller than the disorder length scale, the modes are, generally, thought of as localized vibrations. However, their localization length (or radius) is still connected to the wave length of the mode. Thus, even a *localized* mode extends, in general, over some finite spatial range. Dipolar fluctuations in solvents and vibrations of charged macromolecular side chains forming the bioenvironment of light-harvesting complexes are generically similar and the same pictures apply.

Excited chromophores have an electric dipole moment $\vec{\mu}$, which couples to the electric field $\vec{E}(\mathbf{r})$ generated by the environmental dipolar fluctuations (as shown in Fig. 2.6) at the exciton position $\mathbf{r}$. This results in the interaction energy $H_{\mathrm{SB}} = \vec{\mu} \cdot \vec{E}(\mathbf{r})$. For simplicity, we ignore the angular dependence in the following which only causes correction factors of the order of one (Nalbach, *et al.*, 2001). Within the donor–acceptor model, the dipole moment is described by $\mu = |\vec{\mu}| = \mu_0 |i\rangle\langle i|$, where we furthermore have assumed that the dipole moments at each chromophore site are the same (again neglecting factors of the order one because of angular dependence). The electric field is proportional to the amplitude of the propagating normal modes of the medium, $E(\mathbf{r}) = \mathrm{sgn}\{\vec{E}(\mathbf{r})\} \cdot |\vec{E}(\mathbf{r})| = E_0(1/\sqrt{N}) \sum_{\mathbf{k}} q_{\mathbf{k}} e^{i\mathbf{kr}}$, finally leading to the interaction Hamiltonian in Eq. (2.16) with $\nu_{\mathbf{k}}(\mathbf{r}) = (\mu_0 E_0/\sqrt{N}) e^{i\mathbf{kr}}$ where we exchange $\kappa \to \mathbf{k}$ because the sum over all environmental fluctuation modes is now described as sum over all wave vectors of propagating environmental modes. Similar ideas have been used to describe the phonon influence on double quantum dot charge qubits (Eckel *et al.*, 2006; Thorwart *et al.*, 2005) or tunneling defects (Nalbach, *et al.*, 2001).

For propagating modes in three spatial dimensions, the spectral function of intersite fluctuations between chromophores i and j becomes

$$J_{ij}(\omega) = \sum_{\mathbf{k}} \frac{\nu_{\mathbf{k}}(\mathbf{r}_i)\nu_{-\mathbf{k}}(\mathbf{r}_j)}{2\omega_{\mathbf{k}}}\delta(\omega - \omega_{\mathbf{k}}) = 2\alpha\omega e^{-\omega/\omega_c}\frac{\sin(\omega t_0)}{\omega t_0},$$
$$\text{with} \quad t_0 = \frac{r_{ij}}{v}, \tag{2.12}$$

with the sound velocity v (assuming linear dispersion $\omega_{\mathbf{k}} = vk$ and $k = |\mathbf{k}|$), the distance $r_{ij} = |\mathbf{r}_i - \mathbf{r}_j|$ between site i and j, coupling strength α and upper cut-off ω_c using an exponential form for the cut-off function again. We note that a linear dispersion for the normal modes is a strong assumption, and it is not clear if the simple Debye picture holds in biological soft matter up to energies of the electronic coupling $\Delta = 2V_{\text{da}}$. For on-site fluctuations at site i, the spectral function simplifies to

$$J_{ii}(\omega) = \sum_{\mathbf{k}} \frac{|\lambda_{\mathbf{k}}(\mathbf{r}_i)|^2}{2\omega_{\mathbf{k}}}\delta(\omega - \omega_{\mathbf{k}}) = 2\alpha\omega e^{-\omega/\omega_c}. \tag{2.13}$$

When $\Delta t_0 \gg 1$, all modes with $\omega \geq V_{\text{da}}$ will not contribute to the intersite spectral function. At least at weak coupling ($\alpha \ll 1$), mainly the modes resonant with the tunneling splitting are relevant, and thus, we expect the intersite spectrum to be irrelevant. The environment acts as two independent baths at each chromophore site separately. When the shortest wave length λ_c in the spectrum is larger than the distance between donor and acceptor, we have that $\omega_c t_0 = (r_{ij}/\lambda_c) \ll 1$. Then, the environmental fluctuations are fully correlated between the sites and, as for fully correlated localized modes, do not affect the donor–acceptor system.

In order to see, clearly, the possible drastic effects of spatial correlations, we can transform the Hamiltonian as discussed below in Eq. (A.1) in a form resembling more a spin-boson-type model. We, therefore, define a single effective spectral function (as for a spin-boson problem (Leggett *et al.*, 1987; Weiss, 2008)), resulting in

$$J_{\text{eff}}(\omega) = 4\alpha\omega e^{-\omega/\omega_c}\left(1 - \frac{\sin(\omega t_0)}{\omega t_0}\right). \tag{2.14}$$

In the limit $\omega_c t_0 \ll 1$, we get

$$J_{\text{eff}}(\omega) \simeq 4\alpha t_0^2 \omega^3 e^{-\omega/\omega_c}, \tag{2.15}$$

which is of super-Ohmic form. Super-Ohmic environmental fluctuations can neither cause overdamping (except at large temperatures) nor localization, in clear qualitative contrast to pure Ohmic fluctuations. This is a drastic qualitative effect, which spatially correlated environmental fluctuations caused on coherent exciton transfer.

Within solvation model approaches to describe environmental fluctuations (Gilmore and McKenzie, 2006), the spatial correlations are connected to the **k**-dependent dielectric function of the environment (Dogonadze, 1977; Gilmore and McKenzie, 2006). To describe the solvent in bioenvironments, water is the first choice. Its dielectric function is, however, rather complicated in the relevant wavevector regime of wave length of the order of $\sim 10\,\text{Å}$ (Bopp *et al.*, 1996; Omelyan, 1998). Experimentally, the atomic pair–pair correlation functions show nonmonotonic structures for $|\mathbf{k}| \sim 3\,\text{Å}^{-1}$, corresponding to a wavelength $\sim 2\,\text{Å}$ emphasizing that spatial correlations are likely to play a distinct role at chromophore distances between 3 and 30 Å as they occur in light-harvesting complexes like the FMO complex (Li *et al.*, 1997). Nevertheless, it is not possible to directly deduce whether the relevant bioenvironmental excitations are weakly damped and thus propagating modes or rather strongly damped and thus merely localized fluctuations with localization length ξ. Thus, it is not possible to decide in favor of propagating or localized modes, and experimentally, little is known beyond the fact that spatial correlations are highly relevant (Cheng and Fleming, 2009). We will, therefore, discuss both variants in the following.

4.2. Spatial environmental correlations in a single chromophore pair

As before, we focus in a first step on the simplest possible model of single donor–acceptor pair, given by the Hamiltonian

$$H_{\text{da}} = \frac{\Delta}{2}\{|d\rangle\langle a| + |a\rangle\langle d|\} + \sum_{j=d/a} |j\rangle\langle j| \sum_{\kappa} \nu_{\kappa}^{(j)} q_{j,\kappa} + \frac{1}{2}\sum_{j=d/a}\sum_{\kappa}\left(p_{j,\kappa}^2 + \omega_{j,\kappa}^2 q_{j,\kappa}^2\right), \tag{2.16}$$

with momenta $p_{j,\kappa}$, displacement $q_{j,\kappa}$, frequency $\omega_{j,\kappa}$, and coupling $\nu_{\kappa}^{(j)}$ for chromophore $j = d/a$ and index κ running over all fluctuation modes. We consider equal chromophores with identical site energies and an electronic coupling Δ between donor and acceptor.[2] When discussing spatial correlations of the fluctuations, we have to introduce the position of the chromophores and their spatial distance in the description leading to couplings $\nu_{\kappa}^{(j)}(\mathbf{r}_j)$, depending on the position $\mathbf{r}_j$ of chromophore j.

[2]The electronic coupling between chromophores strongly depends on the distance between them. We, however, omit this dependence in our discussion in order to focus fully on the effects due to spatial correlations in the environmental fluctuation.

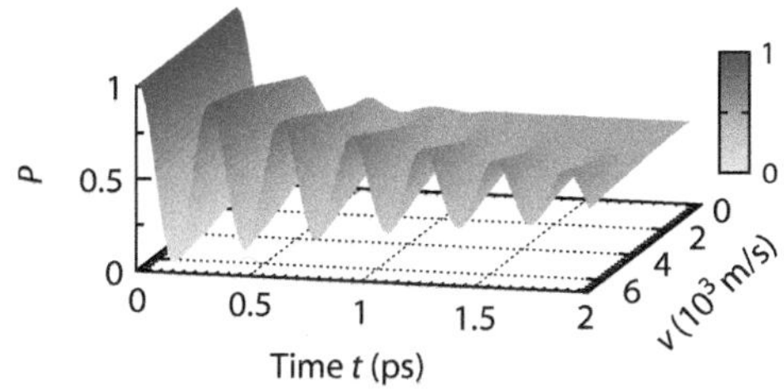

FIGURE 2.7 Occupation of donor and acceptor versus time and speed of sound for $\omega_c = \Delta = 106$/cm, $T = 152$ K, $\alpha = 0.08$, and $r_{da} = 3.8$ Å assuming propagating environmental environmental modes.

We evaluate the occupation $P(t) = \langle |d\rangle\langle d| \rangle$ between donor and acceptor. In Fig. 2.7, $P(t)$ is plotted over time versus sound velocity v with which the modes are assumed to propagate. We have chosen all parameter to match rather closely the properties of chromophores in the FMO complex (Cho *et al.*, 2005). To be specific, we have used $\Delta = 106/\mathrm{cm}$ as tunneling element, which corresponds to the largest dipole–dipole coupling in the FMO complex (Cho *et al.*, 2005) between chromophore 1 and 2, but have neglected the energy difference between the two sites. The distance between site 1 and 2 in the FMO complex of *Chlorobaculum tepidum* (Li *et al.*, 1997) is $r_{12} = 3.8$ Å which are the closest two chromophores. Site 2 and 7 are maximally apart, $r_{27} = 11.3$ Å. The bath cut-off frequency varies in the literature (Adolphs and Renger, 2006; Cho *et al.*, 2005) between $\omega_c = 32/\mathrm{cm}$ and $150/\mathrm{cm}$. To be specific, we choose $\omega_c = 106/\mathrm{cm}$ and fix temperature at $T = 152$ K$= \Delta/k_B$.

Quantum coherent oscillations occur which decay within about 1 ps for the smallest value of the sound velocity of several hundred meters per second where the environmental fluctuations are uncorrelated. For larger sound velocities, meaning increasing correlations of the fluctuations, the decay slows down considerably as expected because the wave length of the modes causing decoherence becomes larger than the distance between the chromophores and, thus, cannot harm coherence any longer. To the best of our knowledge, the precise values of sound velocities for the biological embedding materials of the FMO complexes are experimentally not known. As a guide, we might use the sound velocity of water, $v \simeq 1500$ m/s, which falls into the range of our plot. When frozen to ice, as in the low temperature experiments at 77 K or 180 K, one finds that $v \simeq 3150$ m/s and coherence lives considerably longer.

Figure 2.8 shows $P(t)$ for localized modes with localization lengths between $\xi = 0$ nm and $\xi = 2$ nm. Again as expected, for small localization lengths, the fluctuations at each site are uncorrelated, and the occupation difference decays in less than a picosecond. Assuming a distance

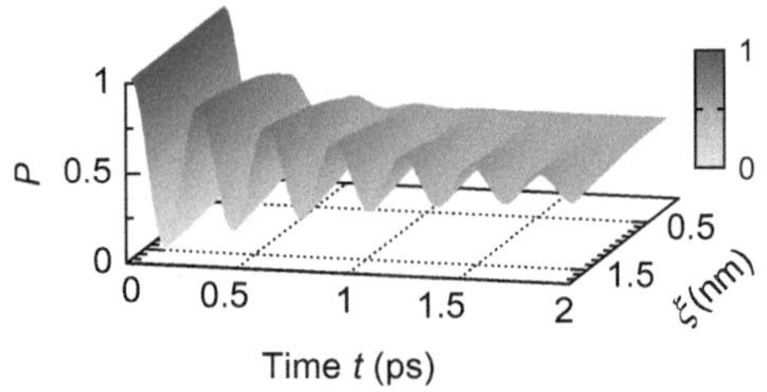

FIGURE 2.8 Occupation of donor and acceptor versus time and localization length ξ of localized environmental modes. Parameters are chosen as $\omega_c = \Delta = 106/\text{cm}$, $T = 152$ K, $\alpha = 0.08$, and $r_{da} = 3.8$ Å.

between donor and acceptor of $r_{12} = 3.8$ Å, the localization lengths plotted in Fig. 2.8 reach up to about four times the donor–acceptor distance. Then, sizable correlations are expected and coherent oscillations for more than 2 ps occur. All effects show the expected dependence on temperature and coupling/damping strength, namely that coherence becomes stronger suppressed at higher temperatures and/or stronger coupling. However, in all cases, decoherence is suppressed and coherence prevails when the fluctuations of the environmental fluctuations at the donor and acceptor site become fully correlated.

In conclusion, assuming localized or propagating modes result qualitatively in the same behavior. Strong correlations of the environmental fluctuations at the donor and acceptor sites suppress decoherence and thus strongly favor quantum coherence in excitonic energy transfer. All used parameters are taken for the case of the FMO complex, and thus, our results suggest that spatial correlations of the environmental fluctuations as a result of finite propagation time of the modes are highly relevant in light-harvesting complexes. In order to judge on the quantitative effect, a comprehensive experimental investigation of the environmental modes is needed, in particular, whether the modes are propagating or localized, and accordingly, whether the sound velocity and/or the localization length is relevant. So far, we have discussed the influence of spatially correlated environmental fluctuations on the coherence of a *single* donor–acceptor pair. These results extend to a chain of several chromophoric sites without qualitatively changing the physical picture.

4.3. Spatial environmental correlations for two chromophore pairs

The FMO complex consists of three identical subunits, each of which consists of seven chromophoric sites and acts as a conductor for the excitons. Most likely, this structure has been optimized with respect to efficiency and seems to contain also some redundancy, which might be a measure of reliability in nature. In any case, the complex structure gives rise to the question whether a crosstalk between the subunits exists, and this even in a quantum coherent manner. In turn, the question whether this serves any purpose for functionality of increased efficiency is reasonable.

In order to tackle this question on a qualitative level, simple low-dimensional effective models are useful, and we model a single subunit by one donor–acceptor pair. We discuss in the following two identical donor–acceptor pairs separated by a distance r consisting of four identical chromophores, thus all on-site energies are identical. We assume that each of the two pairs initially contains a single exciton at the respective donor site. In this section, we explicitly suppress exciton transfer from one pair to the other as we included in Section 3.2 in order to exclusively study the correlation effects coming from the *spatially* correlated environmental fluctuations. Accordingly, we start from the Hamiltonian

$$H_{\text{pda}} = \frac{\Delta}{2} \sum_{j=1}^{2} \left\{ |d_j\rangle\langle a_j| + |a_j\rangle\langle d_j| \right\} + \sum_{j=1}^{2} \sum_{i=a_j/d_j} |i\rangle\langle i| \sum_{\kappa} \nu_{\kappa}(\mathbf{r}_i) q_{\kappa}$$
$$+ \sum_{j=1}^{2} \sum_{i=a_j/d_j} \frac{1}{2} \sum_{\kappa} \left(p_{i,\kappa}^2 + \omega_{i,\kappa}^2 q_{i,\kappa}^2 \right). \quad (2.17)$$

We assume in the following that each chromophore couples separately to its own environmental fluctuations but allow each chromophore to feel also the correlations of the others. In contrast to before, here, there are two distinct distances involved. As before, each donor is separated by a distance $r_{\text{da}} = |\mathbf{r}_{a_1} - \mathbf{r}_{d_1}| = |\mathbf{r}_{a_2} - \mathbf{r}_{d_2}|$ from its acceptor. We assume this distance to be identical for both donor–acceptor pairs. The separation between both pairs is $r = |\mathbf{r}_{a_1} - \mathbf{r}_{a_2}| = |\mathbf{r}_{d_1} - \mathbf{r}_{d_2}|$.

Since propagating and localized (within a finite-localization length) modes cause similar results for the decay of coherence for a single donor–acceptor pair (see above), we restrict the following investigation to propagating modes. As before, we set the tunneling element $\Delta = 106/\text{cm}$ and the fluctuation cut-off frequency $\omega_c = 106/\text{cm}$. Figure 2.9 shows the probability $P_{d_1,d_2}(t)$ that both excitons are located at the two donor sites versus time for various values of the sound velocity for a weak coupling $\alpha = 0.04$. Our initial condition implies $P_{d_1,d_2}(t = 0) = 1$. The reorganization energy is then $\lambda \simeq 2\alpha\omega_c = 8.5/\text{cm}$, and we used a rather low temperature $T = 15.2\,\text{K}$. In Fig. 2.9A, we fix the distances $r_{\text{da}} = 3.8\,\text{Å}$ and $r = 38\,\text{Å}$, which reflects two rather distant donor–acceptor pairs. Thus, both donor–acceptor pairs are expected to be independent of each other. Accordingly, their dynamics is qualitatively identical to the case of a single pair as described in Section 4.2. Differences arise as a result of the weaker

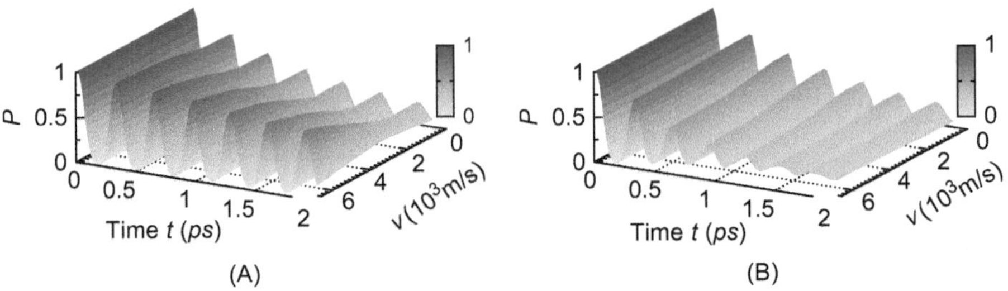

FIGURE 2.9 Probability $P_{d_1,d_2}(t)$ of both exciton being at the respective donor sites versus time and sound velocity assuming propagating environmental modes. Parameters are chosen to be $\omega_c = \Delta = 106/\text{cm}$, $T = 15.2$ K, and $\alpha = 0.04$. The distances are for (A) $r_{da} = 3.8$ Å and $r = 38$ Å , and for (B) $r_{da} = 38$ Å and $r = 3.8$ Å.

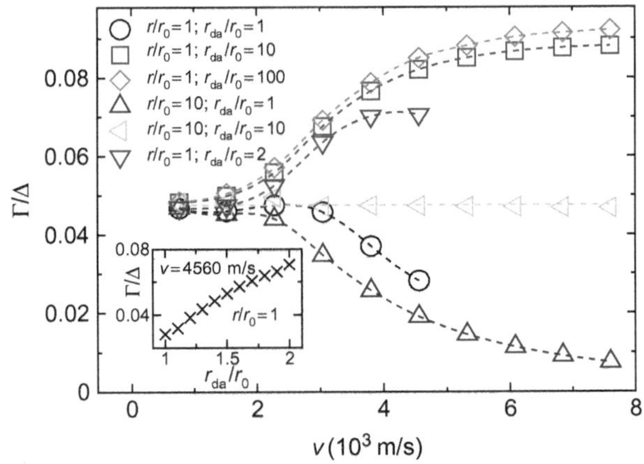

FIGURE 2.10 Decay rate Γ associated to the occupation probability $P_{d_1,d_2}(t)$ versus sound velocity v. Parameters are chosen as $\Delta = 106/\text{cm}$, $T = 15.2$ K, $\alpha = 0.04$, and $\omega_c = 106/\text{cm}$. Inset: Γ versus the ratio r_{da}/r_0 for $v = 4560$ m/s in the range $r_0 \leq r_{da} \leq 2r_0$.

coupling and lower temperature. In contrast to the former case, results for two close-by donor–acceptor pairs, $r = 3.8$ Å, but with large donor–acceptor, distance $r_{da} = 38$ Å, are plotted in Fig. 2.9B.[3] Here, the effect of decoherence increases with increasing sound velocity, in clear contrast to the earlier discussion in Section 4.2. Hence, increasing spatial correlations between the two donor–acceptor pairs destroy quantum coherence.

For a quantitative investigation of this observation, we determine the associated decoherence rate Γ. For this, we fit an exponentially damped cosine to the data for $P_{d_1,d_2}(t)$ (shown in Fig. 2.9) and plot in Fig. 2.10,

[3] Here we actually neglected any variation in the donor-acceptor coupling 1 due to the change in distance in order to fully focus on the effects due to spatial correlations in the environmental fluctuations.

the decay rate versus the sound velocity for several ratios of the two distances.

As fundamental distance scale, we use $r_0 = 3.8$ Å, the distance of the chromophores 1 and 2 in the FMO complex of *Chlorobaculum tepidum* (Li *et al.*, 1997). At the sound velocity $v = 7600$ m/s, a mode can travel this distance within the time of $\Delta^{-1} = 50$ fs.

When both donor–acceptor pairs are far apart, $r = 10\,r_0$, and the distance between donor and acceptor is $r_{da} = r_0$ (shown by the up-triangle in Fig. 2.10), we recover the result of the previous Section 4.2. The decay rate decreases with increasing sound velocity. The same behavior is found, when both pairs are close to each other, and the donor and acceptor sites themselves are also close. Again, the decoherence rate Γ decreases with increasing sound velocity (circles in Fig. 2.10). When all distances are large, i.e., the donor–acceptor distance is large, $r_{da} = 10\,r_0$, and donor–acceptor pairs are far apart from each other, $r = 10\,r_0$, there is no dependence of Γ on v for the investigated range of sound velocities (left triangles in Fig. 2.10). The spatial correlations of the fluctuations simply do not extend from the donor to the acceptor site and, thus, the fluctuations are uncorrelated. A totally different case is reached when donor and acceptor sites are well separated, $r_{da} = 10\,r_0$ and $r_{da} = 100\,r_0$ (squares and diamonds in Fig. 2.10), but the two pairs are close, $r = r_0$. With increasing sound velocity, the decoherence rate increases and approximately doubles. The effect is slightly larger with larger distance between donor and acceptor.

With increasing sound velocity, the wave lengths of the propagating modes increase and, thus, spatial correlations extend further. When the fluctuations at both donors and both acceptors are fully correlated, which is approximately the case for sound velocities of $v \approx 7600$ m/s for $r = r_0$, then each donor–acceptor pair basically feels twice as many fluctuations. Thus, the influence of the fluctuations effectively doubles, which is reflected in doubling the decay rate. For smaller donor–acceptor distance r_{da}, they as well become more correlated with increasing sound velocity, which, as discussed in the Section 4.2, results in decreasing decay rates. Thus, both effects are competing with each other. This also explains why for $r_{da} = 10\,r_0$ (squares in Fig. 2.10) the increase of the rate Γ is weaker than for $r_{da} = 100\,r_0$ (diamonds in Fig. 2.10). At equal distances, $r_{da} = r = r_0$ (circles), the suppression of decoherence as a result of spatial correlations between donor and acceptor sites is the dominant effect, but it is weakened in comparison to the case of $r_{da} = r_0$ and $r_{da} = 10\,r_0$ (up triangles). Accordingly, there are two distinct regimes in which either one of the two effects dominates. How sharp the crossover between the two regimes is, becomes visible when looking at the data for $r_{da} = 2\,r_0$ and $r = r_0$. Additionally, the inset of Fig. 2.10 shows the change of the decay rate Γ when changing the donor–acceptor distance r_{da} from r_0 to $2\,r_0$ for a fixed sound velocity $v = 4560$ m/s, where the change is linear in r_{da}.

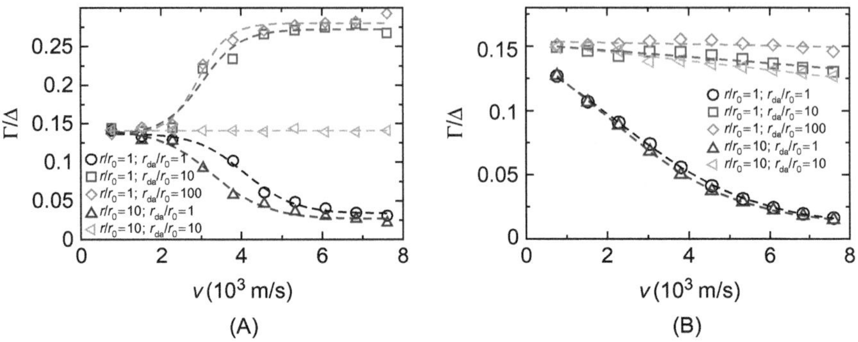

FIGURE 2.11 Decay rate Γ associated to the occupation probability $P_{d_1,d_2}(t)$ versus sound velocity v. Parameters are $\Delta = 106/\text{cm}$, $\alpha = 0.04$, and in (A) $T = 15.2$ K, $\omega_c = 1060/\text{cm}$, and in (B) $T = 152$ K, $\omega_c = 106/\text{cm}$.

Similar behavior (not shown) is also found for a smaller fluctuation cut-off frequency $\omega_c = 53/\text{cm}$ and otherwise identical parameters. Qualitatively similar behavior is encountered for very large fluctuation cut-off frequencies $\omega_c = 1060/\text{cm}$ (as shown in Fig. 2.11A for otherwise identical parameters). Note that in this regime, non-Markovian effects are suppressed. The increase (decrease) of Γ for correlated donor–acceptor pairs (for correlated fluctuations at donor and acceptor site) becomes sharper.

At higher temperature, $T = 152$ K, shown in Fig. 2.11B for otherwise identical parameters, we find that for small donor–acceptor distance, $r_{da} = r_0$, the decoherence rate decreases with increasing sound velocity. However, the picture changes for large donor–acceptor distance, $r_{da} = 10r_0$. Then, the effect of decoherence is almost independent of the sound velocity, irrespective of the distance r between the donor–acceptor pairs.

4.4. Discussion and conclusions

To summarize this part, we have investigated the effect of spatially correlated environmental fluctuations on the quantum coherent transfer dynamics. When the spatial correlations extend from the donor to the acceptor site, their decohering influence is strongly reduced because then the energies at both sites are identically modified. The energy difference between donor and acceptor is not changed but only the global reference energy fluctuates, which does not influence dynamics. Spatial correlations of propagating modes are characterized by their wave length which itself is determined by the sound velocity assuming linear dispersion.

In contrast, the spatial correlations of localized modes are determined by their localization length. Although these two cases are physically different, the qualitative effect on quantum coherence is the same and depends only on the ratio of the distance between donor and acceptor and the correlation length given either by the localization length or by the wave length of resonant modes.

At low temperatures, two close donor–acceptor systems show an increase in the decoherence rate in dependence on their spatial distance. When the donor and acceptor sites are far apart and their fluctuations are only weakly correlated, correlations of close-by donor–acceptor pairs become relevant, when the distance between the two donor–acceptor systems becomes small enough such that their environmental fluctuations are correlated. Then, each donor–acceptor pair is also influenced by the fluctuations at the site of the other one, and thus, the decoherence rate is effectively doubled. For intermediate spatial distances, both effects are competing with each other. At higher temperature up to physiological temperatures relevant for excitonic energy transfer, the effect of an increased decoherence rate, however, is suppressed.

As a main result, we conclude that quantum coherence in the excitation transfer crucially depends on spatial correlations in the environmental fluctuations as soon as correlations lengths are of the order of the spatial distances of the chromophores. For realistic material parameters for light-harvesting systems (in particular, sound velocities), noticeable influence of the finite propagation times of environmental modes should occur. In fact, correlated fluctuations can reduce the decohering effect of the chromophore environment, when the correlation range extends over typical transfer distances within a chromophore chain. This effect even survives (even though diminished) up to room temperature and, thus, might be relevant for exciton transfer in real biological systems. These findings are in line with the recent experimental findings reported in Refs. Cheng and Fleming (2009) and Lee *et al.* (2007).

5. CONCLUSIONS

In total, our studies provide a systematic argument on how quantum coherence in the excitonic energy transfer can live for up to several hundred femtoseconds despite the strong coupling to high-temperature environmental fluctuations. Studying a simple donor–acceptor pair shows that typical environmental fluctuations in light-harvesting complexes are *slower* than the electronic transfer dynamics and, thus, systematically support quantum coherence substantially which allows the coherence to live on timescales comparable with the total transfer time. Thus, long-lived quantum coherence is a result of the constructive fluctuations spectra which the chromophores experience. These spectra are shaped by the protein host in which the chromophores are embedded, and it is conceivable that evolution trimmed the spectra in order to allow for quantum coherence in order to promote transfer efficiency.

Additionally, we have shown that non-Markovian effects of such slow environmental fluctuations support and even generate long-lived quantum entanglement. Interpair dipole–dipole coupling allows for the generation of entanglement out of separable initial states and shows death and revivals of entanglement on timescales relevant for excitonic energy transfer. Even without interpair coupling, entanglement is generated by a slowly fluctuating environment, which is a result of spatial correlations of the environmental fluctuations over different chromophore sites. This allows to conclude that in biomolecular environments as typical for chromophores in light-harvesting complexes, entanglement can be long-lived and will be generated by interpair couplings and/or spatially correlated fluctuations. This strongly supports the ideas that speed-ups resulting from quantum coherence and entanglement might be responsible for the near-unity quantum efficiency of the excitonic energy transfer in photosynthetic systems. At the same time, however, it also clearly shows that corresponding investigations must take the non-Markovian behavior of the slow environments fully into account in order to be reliable and predictive.

Focussing in our last part on the relevance of spatial correlations between different chromophore sites, we found that quantum coherence in the excitation transfer crucially depends on spatial correlations as soon as correlations lengths are of the order of the spatial distances of the chromophores. Rough estimates point in the direction that indeed this case is realized in light-harvesting systems in line with the experimental findings (Cheng and Fleming, 2009; Lee *et al.*, 2007). Unfortunately, few experimental results exist that directly investigate these spatial correlations.

We should point out, once more, that we studied simplified model systems, which allowed us to determine two major physical processes, namely slow and spatially correlated environmental fluctuations, but which can indeed explain the long-lived quantum coherence experimentally observed in light-harvesting systems (Collini and Scholes, 2009; Engel *et al.*, 2007; Lee *et al.*, 2007; Scholes, 2010) on a qualitative level. Beyond establishing the relevance of these two physical processes, our model systems need more refinement in order to fully describe the observed dynamical behavior on a quantitative level.

This work was supported by the Excellence Initiative of the German Federal and State Governments.

APPENDICES

A. Comparison of the donor–acceptor model with the spin-boson model

The donor–acceptor Hamiltonian, Eq. (2.6), can easily be transformed into a Hamiltonian, which is reminiscent to the widely studied spin-boson model (Leggett *et al.*, 1987; Weiss, 2008) with $\Delta = 2V_{\text{da}}$

$$H_{\text{da}} = \Delta \frac{\sigma_x}{2} + \frac{\sigma_z}{2} \sum_{\kappa} \left\{ \nu_{\kappa}^{a} - \nu_{\kappa}^{d} \right\} q_{\kappa} + \frac{\mathbb{1}}{2} \sum_{\kappa} \left\{ \nu_{\kappa}^{a} + \nu_{\kappa}^{d} \right\} q_{\kappa}$$
$$+ \frac{1}{2} \sum_{\kappa} \left(p_{\kappa}^{2} + \omega_{\kappa}^{2} q_{\kappa}^{2} \right) \qquad \text{(A.1)}$$

by introducing the Pauli matrices $\{\mathbb{1}, \sigma_x, \sigma_y, \sigma_z\}$ with $\sigma_x = |d\rangle\langle a| + |a\rangle\langle d|$ and $\sigma_z = |d\rangle\langle d| - |a\rangle\langle a|$.

One difference is given by the term proportional to $\nu_{\kappa}^{a} + \nu_{\kappa}^{d}$, which couples to the identity operator $\mathbb{1}$ of the donor–acceptor pair, thus causing only fluctuations of the reference energy, which are irrelevant for the dynamics. The term solely shifts the zero-point energies of the bath modes and thus changes their thermal equilibrium state. In the spirit of dissipative quantum dynamics, the treatment of system-bath problems, typically, relies on the assumption that the bath is weakly influenced by the coupling to the system itself, and thus, the mentioned effects should not affect the dissipative dynamics of the donor–acceptor system. At strong coupling or for a slow bath with cut-off frequency $\omega_c \lesssim \Delta$, however, the validity of these assumptions is questionable (Lucke *et al.*, 1997), and we have to consider three aspects in which the dynamics generated by our donor–acceptor Hamiltonian in Eq. (2.6) might differ from the standard spin-boson model. First, the thermal equilibrium state to which the total system is driven is different and, second, the factorized initial conditions for both cases reflect two different initial conditions. Most importantly, however, from experience of open quantum dynamics (Weiss, 2008), it is known that these two differences will not influence the decoherence rates when the dynamics can be interpreted by damped coherent oscillations. Third, in the spin-boson model, a single bath is coupled to the system, whereas in the donor–acceptor Hamiltonian, two baths are coupled to the respective system states, separately. Thus, even when both baths are mutually uncorrelated, the resulting rates for the donor–acceptor system are twice as large compared with the spin-boson model (assuming that all baths are coupled with equal strength). This has to be taken into account when comparing results from both approaches.

B. Details of the used method

In the context of excitonic energy transfer, it has recently been shown (Ishizaki and Fleming, 2009a,b,c; Ishizaki *et al.*, 2010; Nalbach and Thorwart, 2010; Thorwart *et al.*, 2009) that under realistic conditions in biomolecular complexes, time-local master equations become increasingly unreliable. In addition to the violation of the Markovian assumption as a result of the slow environmental fluctuations, the coupling between chromophores and environment cannot be considered as weak enough to allow for a lowest order perturbative treatment (Gilmore and McKenzie, 2005, 2006, 2008). It was recently shown that the latter condition renders any weak coupling approach questionable (Nalbach and Thorwart, 2010). Non-Markovian approaches have been used beyond a lowest-order treatment (Ishizaki and Fleming, 2009a,b,c; Ishizaki *et al.*, 2010). Slow fluctuations have also been treated (Palmieri *et al.*, 2010) by different variants of cumulant expansion techniques and by statistical averaging approaches over static disorder in sum-over-eigenstates approaches. Recently, the standard Redfield equations, which are valid in the weak-coupling regime, have been extended by generalizing the Redfield relaxation tensor on the basis of the Lindblad quantum master equation (Palmieri *et al.*, 2009). This technique goes beyond the secular approximation and, thus, can include effects of stronger coupling. However, the approach is still memoryless and leads to time-local evolution equations.

As an efficient alternative, we use the numerically exact quasi-adiabatic propagator path-integral (QUAPI) (Makri and Makarov, 1995a,b; Makri *et al.*, 1996; Nalbach and Thorwart, 2009; Thorwart *et al.*, 2000, 1998) in order to treat the real-time dynamics of quantum coherent energy transfer under realistic conditions (Eckel *et al.*, 2009; Nalbach, *et al.*, 2010; Nalbach and Thorwart, 2010; Thorwart *et al.*, 2009).

We are, in general, interested in the quantum mechanical population dynamics of the donor and acceptor influenced by the environmental fluctuations but not on the actual environmental dynamics itself. The full dynamics is determined by the von Neumann equation

$$\partial_t W(t) = -\frac{i}{\hbar}\left[H_{\mathrm{da}}, W(t)\right] \tag{B.1}$$

for the statistical operator $W(t)$ of the total system. Its solution permits the definition of a time evolution operator $\mathcal{U}(t, t_0)$ with $W(t) = \mathcal{U}(t, t_0)W(t_0)$. Thus, the dynamics of the donor–acceptor system is characterized by the time evolution of the reduced density matrix $\rho(t)$, which is obtained after tracing out the environmental (or bath) degrees of freedom, i.e.,

$$\rho(t) = \mathrm{Tr}\left\{U(t,0)W(0)U^{-1}(t,0)\right\}_B \tag{B.2}$$

and

$$U(t,0) = \mathcal{T}\exp\left\{-\frac{i}{\hbar}\int_0^t \mathrm{d}sH_{\mathrm{da}}\right\}. \tag{B.3}$$

Here, $U(t,0)$ denotes the propagator of the full system plus bath and $\mathcal{T}$ denotes the time-ordering operator. $W(0)$ is the total density operator at initial time set at $t = 0$ for which we assume standard factorizing initial conditions (Weiss, 2008), i.e., $W(0) \propto \rho(0)\exp(-H_{\mathrm{B}}/T)$, where the bath with the Hamiltonian $H_{\mathrm{B}} = \frac{1}{2}\sum_k (p_k^2 + \omega_k^2 q_k^2)$ is at thermal equilibrium at temperature T, and the system is prepared according to $\rho(0)$.

In brief, the QUAPI algorithm is based on a symmetric Trotter splitting of the short-time propagator $\mathcal{K}(t_{k+1}, t_k)$ for the full Hamiltonian into a part depending on the system Hamiltonian and a part involving the bath and the coupling term. The short-time propagator describes time evolution over a Trotter time slice δt. The Trotter slicing is by construction exact in the limit $\delta t \to 0$ but introduces a finite Trotter error for a finite time increment. By choosing δt small enough, such that convergence is achieved, the Trotter error is systematically eliminated. On the other side, the bath degrees of freedom generate correlations being nonlocal in time. For any finite temperature, these correlations decay exponentially fast at asymptotic times, thereby setting the associated memory timescale. QUAPI now defines an object called the reduced density tensor, which lives on this finite memory time window and establishes an iteration scheme in order to extract the time evolution of this object. All correlations are included exactly over the memory time $\tau_{\mathrm{mem}} = K\delta t$ and can safely be neglected for times beyond τ_{mem}. Then, the memory parameter K has to be increased, until convergence is found. Both strategies to achieve convergence are working against each other because reducing the Trotter time increment also decreases the considered memory time. Thus, when reducing δt, K must be increased just to keep the considered memory time equal. Nevertheless, convergent results can be obtained in a wide range of parameters.

For including several environments, which are possibly correlated, we have to extend the standard formulation of QUAPI, which only includes the coupling to one bath. The entire influence of a single bath coupled through the operator $\hat{s}$ to the donor–acceptor system is described in terms of the real-time, path-integral formulation by the influence functional

$$I\left(\{s_i^+, s_i^-\}; \delta t\right) = \exp\left\{-\frac{1}{\hbar}\sum_{i=0}^{N}\sum_{i'=0}^{i}\left[s_i^+ - s_i^-\right]\left[\eta_{ii'}s_{i'}^+ - \eta_{ii'}^* s_{i'}^-\right]\right\}, \qquad \text{(B.4)}$$

where the path segments $s_i^\pm$ associated to a Trotter time slice i given as interval $\left[\left(i-\frac{1}{2}\right)\delta t, (i+\frac{1}{2})\delta t\right]$ (with total time $t = N\delta t$) are assumed to have constant values over a single time increment. The number of path segments associated to a single Trotter time slice is given by the dimension of the Hilbert space in which the system-bath coupling operator lives. The superscript $\pm$ denotes the propagation direction forward or backward in time because we have to work with density operators. The full integration over all paths $s^\pm(t')$ has to be performed as the discrete sum over all configurations $\{s_i^+, s_i^-\}$ of paths segments between initial and final time. The time-discrete bath correlators $\eta_{ii'}$ are defined in Refs. Makri and Makarov (1995a,b) and the superscript * denotes the complex conjugate.

Multiple independent baths, $H_{B\alpha}$, which couple to system operators $\hat{s}_\alpha$ will cause a product of influence functionals because each bath acts separately as described earlier. Thus, the total influence functional assumes the form

$$I(\{s_{i,\alpha}^+, s_{i,\alpha}^-\}; \delta t) = \exp\left\{-\frac{1}{\hbar}\sum_{\alpha}\sum_{i=0}^{N}\sum_{i'=0}^{i}[s_{i,\alpha}^+ - s_{i,\alpha}^-]\left[\eta_{ii'}^{(\alpha\alpha)}s_{i',\alpha}^+ - \eta_{ii'}^{*(\alpha\alpha)}s_{i',\alpha}^-\right]\right\}, \qquad \text{(B.5)}$$

where we denoted the (discretized) bath correlators $\eta_{ii'}^{(\alpha\alpha)}$ with additional superscripts in order to allow for differing baths where the correlators will differ.

The question whether the environmental fluctuations act *locally* or in a correlated manner can be tackled by the following extension. Local fluctuations couple to the donor and to the acceptor separately and independently. This implies that Eq. (B.5) describes *all* effects resulting from environmental fluctuations. In case that the fluctuations are caused by extended waves, like phonon modes or that the fluctuations rattling the donor extend at least partially to the acceptor site, then the fluctuations at the various sites are no longer independent and spatial correlations have to be taken into account. Hence, Eq. (B.5) has to be generalized to

$$I(\{s_{i,\alpha}^+, s_{i,\beta}^-\}; \delta t) = \exp\left\{-\frac{1}{\hbar}\sum_{\alpha,\beta}\sum_{i=0}^{N}\sum_{i'=0}^{i}[s_{i,\alpha}^+ - s_{i,\alpha}^-]\left[\eta_{ii'}^{(\alpha\beta)}s_{i',\beta}^+ - \eta_{ii'}^{*(\alpha\beta)}s_{i',\beta}^-\right]\right\}, \qquad \text{(B.6)}$$

where $\eta_{ii'}^{(\alpha\beta)}$ are the mixed bath correlators expressing the correlations of the fluctuations acting at operator $\hat{s}_\alpha$ and $\hat{s}_\beta$. The detailed numerical evaluation of the influence functional in the extended QUAPI scheme becomes more involved, but the general procedure is not affected by this extension.

REFERENCES

Adolphs, J., and Renger, T. (2006). *Biophys. J.* **91**, 2778.

Beljonne, D., Curutchet, C., Scholes, G. D., and Silbey, R. J. (2009). *J. Phys. Chem. B* **113**, 6583.

Blankenship, R. E. (2002). "Molecular Mechanisms of Photosynthesis." Blackwell Science Ltd., Oxford.

Bopp, P. A., Kornyshev, A. A., and Sutmann, G. (1996). *Phys. Rev. Lett.* **76**, 1280.

Brixner, T., Stenger, J., Vaswani, H., Cho, M., Blankenship, R. E., and Fleming, G. R. (2005). *Nature* **434**, 625.

Bulla, R., Lee, H.-J., Tong, N.-H., and Vojta, M. (2005). *Phys. Rev. B* **71**, 045122.

Cao, J. S., and Silbey, R. J. (2009). *J. Phys. Chem. A* **113**, 13825.

Caruso, F., Chin, A. W., Datta, A., Huelga, S. F., and Plenio, M. B. (2009). *J. Chem. Phys.* **131**, 105106.

Caruso, F., Chin, A. W., Datta, A., Huelga, S. F., and Plenio, M. B. (2010). *Phys. Rev. A* **81**, 062346.

Cheng, Y. C., and Fleming, G. R. (2009). *Annu. Rev. Phys. Chem.* **60**, 241.

Chin, A. W., Datta, A., Caruso, F., Huelga, S. F., and Plenio, M. B. (2010). *New J. Phys.* **12**, 065002

Cho, M., Vaswani, H. M., Brixner, T., Stenger, J., and Fleming, G. R. (2005). *J. Phys. Chem. B* **109**, 10542.

Collini, E., and Scholes, G. D. (2009). *Science* **323**, 369.

Collini, E., Wong, C. Y., Wilk, K. E., Curmi, P. M. G., Brumer, P., and Scholes, G. D. (2010). *Nature* **463**, 644.

Dogonadze, R. R., Kuznetsov, A. M., and Ulstrup, J. (1977). *J. Theor. Biol.* **69**, 239.

Eckel, J., Reina, J. H., and Thorwart, M. (2009). *New J. Phys.* **11**, 085001.

Eckel, J., Weiss, S., and Thorwart, M. (2006). *Eur. Phys. J. B* **53**, 91.

Egger, R., and Mak, C. H. (1994). *Phys. Rev. B* **50**, 15210.

Engel, G. S., Calhoun, T. R., Read, E. L., Ahn, T. K., Mancal, T., Cheng, Y. C., Blankenship, R. E., and Fleming, G. R. (2007). *Nature* **446**, 782.

Fassioli, F., Olaya-Castro, A., Scheuring, S., Sturgis, J., and Johnson, N. F. (2009). *Biophys. J.* **97**, 2464.

Fassioli, F., Nazir, A., and Olaya-Castro, A. (2010). *J. Phys. Chem. Lett.* **1**, 2139–2143.

Fenna, R. E., and Matthews, B. W. (1975). *Nature* **258**, 573.

Förster, T. (1948). *Ann. Phys.* **2**, 55.

Forster, T. (1965). in "Modern Quantum Chemistry Part III," ed. by O. Sinanoglu. Academic Press, New York, pp. 93–137.

Gilmore, J. B., and McKenzie, R. H. (2005). *J. Phys.: Condens. Matter* **17**, 1735.

Gilmore, J., and McKenzie, R. (2006). *Chem. Phys. Lett.* **421**, 266.

Gilmore, J., and McKenzie, R. (2008). *J. Phys. Chem. A* **112**, 2162.

Herek, J. L., Wohlleben, W., Cogdell, R. J., Zeidler, D., and Motzkus, M. (2002). *Nature* **417**, 533.

Horodecki, M., Horodecki, P., and Horodecki, R. (1996). *Phys. Lett. A* **223**, 1.

Ishizaki, A., and Fleming, G. R. (2009a). *Proc. Natl. Acad. Sci. USA* **106**, 17255.

Ishizaki, A., and Fleming, G. R. (2009b). *J. Chem. Phys.* **130**, 234110.

Ishizaki, A., and Fleming, G. R. (2009c). *J. Chem. Phys.* **130**, 234111.

Ishizaki, A., Calhoun, T. R., Schlau-Cohen, G. S., and Fleming, G. R. (2010). *Phys. Chem. Chem. Phys.* **12**, 7319.
Knox, R. S., and Gülen, D. (1993). *Photochem. Photobiol.* **57**, 40.
Kroutvar, M., Ducommun, Y., Heiss, D., Bichler, M., Schuh, D., Abstreiter, G., and Finley, J. (2004). *Nature* **432**, 81.
Lee, H., Cheng, Y.-C., and Fleming, G. R. (2007). *Science* **316**, 1462.
Leggett, A. J., Chakravarty, S., Dorsey, A. T., Fisher, M. P. A., Garg, A., and Zwerger, W. (1987). *Rev. Mod. Phys.* **59**, 1.
Li, Y.-F., Zhou, W., Blankenship, R. E., and Allen, J. P. (1997). *J. Mol. Biol.* **271**, 456.
Lucke, A., Mak, C. H., Egger, R., Ankerhold, J., Stockburger, J., and Grabert, H. (1997). *J. Chem. Phys.* **107**, 8397.
Makhlin, Y., Schön, G., and Shnirman, A. (2001). *Rev. Mod. Phys.* **73**, 357.
Makri, N., and Makarov, D. E. (1995a). *J. Chem. Phys.* **102**, 4600.
Makri, N., and Makarov, D. E. (1995b). *J. Chem. Phys.* **102**, 4611.
Makri, N., Sim, E., Makarov, D., and Topaler, M. (1996). *Proc. Natl. Acad. Sci. USA* **93**, 3926.
May, V., and Kühn, O. (2004). "Charge and Energy Transfer Dynamics in Molecular Systems." Wiley-VCH, Weinheim.
Mercer, I. P., El-Taha, Y. C., Kajumba, N., Marangos, J. P., Tisch, J. W. G., Gabrielsen, M., Cogdell, R. J., Springate, E., and Turcu, E. (2009). *Phys. Rev. Lett.* **102**, 057402.
Milder, M. T. W., Brüggemann, B., van Grondelle, R., and Herek, J. L. (2010). *Photosynth. Res.* **104**, 257.
Mohseni, M., Rebentrost, P., Lloyd, S., and Aspuru-Guzik, A. (2008). *J. Chem. Phys.* **129**, 174106.
Mühlbacher, L., and Egger, R. (2003). *J. Chem. Phys.* **118**, 179.
Nalbach, P., Eckel, J., and Thorwart, M. (2010). *New J. Phys.* **12**, 065043.
Nalbach, P., Terzidis, O., Topp, K. A., and Würger, A. (2001). *J. Phys.: Condens. Matter* **13**, 1467.
Nalbach, P., and Thorwart, M. (2009). *Phys. Rev. Lett.* **103**, 220401.
Nalbach, P., and Thorwart, M. (2010). *J. Chem. Phys.* **132**, 194111.
Nazir, A. (2009). *Phys. Rev. Lett.* **103**, 146404.
Olaya-Castro, A., Lee, C. F., Fassioli Olsen, F., and Johnson, N. F. (2008). *Phys. Rev. B* **78**, 085115.
Omelyan, I. P. (1998). *Mol. Phys.* **93**, 123.
Palmieri, B., Abramavicius, D., and Mukamel, S. (2009). *J. Chem. Phys.* **130**, 204512.
Palmieri, B., Abramavicius, D., and Mukamel, S. (2010). *Phys. Chem. Chem. Phys.* **12**, 108.
Panitchayangkoon, G., Hayes, D., Fransted, K. A., Caram, J. R., Harel, E., Wen, J., Blankenship, R. E., and Engel, G. S. (2010). *Proc. Natl. Acad. Sci.* **107**, 12766.
Peres, A. (1996). *Phys. Rev. Lett.* **77**, 1413.
Plenio, M. B., and Huelga, S. F. (2008). *New J. Phys.* **10**, 113019.
Rabl, P., DeMille, D., Doyle, J., Lukin, M., Schoelkopf, R., and Zoller, P. (2006). *Phys. Rev. Lett.* **97**, 033003.
Read, E. L., Schlau-Cohen, G. S., Engel, G. S., Wen, J., Blankenship, R. E., and Fleming, G. R. (2008). *Biophys. J.* **95**, 847.
Rebentrost, P., Chakraborty, R., and Aspuru-Guzik, A. (2009a). *J. Chem. Phys.* **131**, 184102.
Rebentrost, P., Mohseni, M., and Aspuru-Guzik, A. (2009b). *J. Phys. Chem. B* **113**, 9942.
Rebentrost, P., Mohseni, M., Kassal, I., Lloyd, S., and Aspuru-Guzik, A. (2009c). *New J. Phys.* **11**, 033003.
Reineker, P., Kenkre, V.M., (1982). in "Exciton Dynamics in Molecular Crystals and Aggregates." Springer Tracts in Modern Physics, vol. 94. Springer, Heidelberg.
Rivas, A., Huelga, S. F., and Plenio, M. B. (2010). *Phys. Rev. Lett.* **105**, 050403.
Savolainen, J., Fanciulli, R., Dijkhuizen, N., Moore, A. L., Hauer, J., Buckup, T., Motzkus, M., and Herek, J. L. (2008). *Proc. Natl. Acad. Sci.* **105**, 7641.
Scholak, T., de Melo, F., Wellens, T., Mintert, F., and Buchleitner, A. (2009). preprint arXiv:0912.3560.

Scholes, G. D. (2010). *J. Phys. Chem. Lett.* **1**, 2.
Thorwart, M., Eckel, J., and Mucciolo, E. R. (2005). *Phys. Rev. B* **72**, 235320.
Thorwart, M., Eckel, J., Reina, J. H., Nalbach, P., and Weiss, S. (2009). *Chem. Phys. Lett.* **478**, 234.
Thorwart, M., and Hänggi, P. (2002). *Phys. Rev. A* **65**, 012309.
Thorwart, M., Reimann, P., and Hänggi, P. (2000). *Phys. Rev. E* **62**, 5808.
Thorwart, M., Reimann, P., Jung, P., and Fox, R. F. (1998). *Chem. Phys.* **235**, 61.
Urboniene, V., Vrublevskaja, O., Trinkunas, G., Gall, A., Robert, B., and Valkunas, L. (2007). *Biophys. J.* **93**, 2188.
van Amerongen, H., Valkunas, L., and van Grondelle, R. (2000). "Photosynthetic Excitons." World Scientific, Singapore.
van Groendelle, R., and Novoderezhkin, V. (2006). *Phys. Chem. Chem. Phys.* **8**, 793.
Weiss, U. (2008). "Quantum Dissipative Systems," 3rd edn. World Scientific, Singapore.
Wohlleben, W., Buckup, T., Herek, J. L., and Motzkus, M. (2005). *Chem. Phys. Chem.* **6**, 850.
Zhang, W. M., Meier, T., Chernyak, V., and Mukamel, S. (1998). *J. Chem. Phys.* **108**, 7763.
Zigmantas, D., Read, E. L., Mančal, T., Brixner, T., Gardiner, A. T., Cogdell, R. J., and Fleming, G. R. (2006). *Proc. Natl. Acad. Sci. USA* **103**, 12672.

CHAPTER 3

Sunlight, Purple Bacteria, and Quantum Mechanics: How Purple Bacteria Harness Quantum Mechanics for Efficient Light Harvesting

Richard J. Cogdell and **Jürgen Köhler**

Contents

1. INTRODUCTION

The essential feature of photosynthesis is the conversion of light energy into chemical (redox) energy that can be used as the driving force for subsequent metabolic reactions. A specialized pigment–protein complex, the photochemical reaction center (RC), acts as the key transducer (Fig. 3.1). This complex contains a dimer of (bacterio)chlorophyll ((B)Chl) molecules, called the special pair, which is the primary electron donor for the electron transfer chain. On electronic excitation of the special pair, an electron is

Semiconductors and Semimetals, Volume 83
ISSN 0080-8784, DOI: 10.1016/B978-0-12-375042-6.00003-1

© 2010 Elsevier Inc.
All rights reserved.

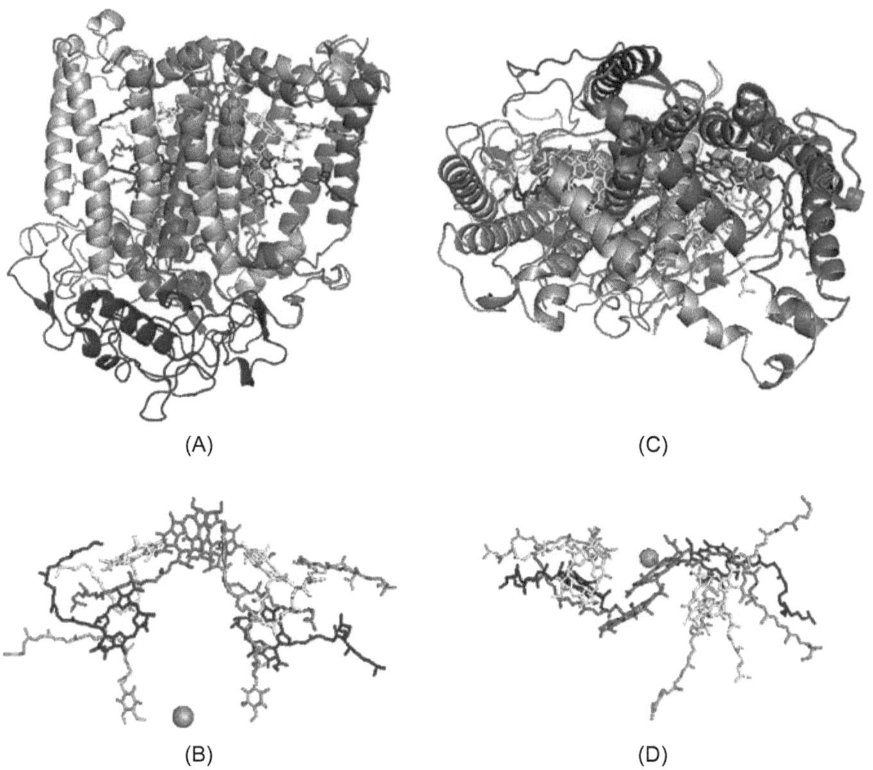

FIGURE 3.1 RC *sphaeroides*; side (A, B) and top (C, D) views with (A, C) and without (B, D) protein backbone. Red: special pair; yellow: accessory bacteriochlorophylls; blue: bacteriopheophytins; green: quinones; and dot: iron. (See Plate no. 2 in the Color Plate Section.)

rapidly transferred ($\sim 2.5\,\text{ps}$) to a nearby electron acceptor (Blankenship, 2002; Zinth and Wachtveitl, 2005). The charge-separated state is further stabilized by a cascade of ultrafast secondary reactions that prevent energy wasteful back reactions. Eventually, other, slower processes lead to the production of high-energy molecules that can be used to fuel the cellular metabolism.

On a clear day, the light intensity from the sun incident on the Earth corresponds to about $1\,\text{kW/m}^2$. If we imagine, for the moment, that all the photons have the same wavelength of 400 nm, this intensity corresponds to a flux of $2 \cdot 10^{21}$ photons/m^2s. Given that the absorption cross section of a Chl molecule is about $10^{-20}\,\text{m}^2$ (i.e., $1\,\text{Å}^2$), this corresponds to an absorption of only 20 photons/s. In reality, this number will be further reduced by orders of magnitude because the intensity of the sunlight will be reduced by clouds, scattering and absorption in the atmosphere, and by other obstacles. Furthermore, the incident photons are distributed over a large spectral range and only part of the spectrum can be absorbed by Chl. Hence, if we compare the time interval between two absorptions by a single Chl, we can safely state that under realistic illumination conditions, the absorption of a photon (from the sun) by such an individual Chl molecule is a rare event! This simple estimation demonstrates that exploitation of sunlight as a source for energy requires an efficient light-harvesting apparatus for collecting as many photons as possible. In photosynthesis, this light-concentration step is accomplished by a network of pigment–protein complexes that serve as antennas, i.e., specialized proteins that capture photons and transfer the excitation energy with high efficiency to the RC. Thereby, the number of Chl molecules organized in antennas and serving a light-harvesting function usually exceeds a few hundred per RC.

In relatively simple photosynthetic organisms, such as the well-studied photosynthetic purple bacteria, the light reactions are carried out by only a few different types of proteins, whereas in green plants more than 50 types of proteins are involved in two different light reactions (Green *et al.*, 2003). This large number of proteins reflects the complexity of oxygenic photosynthetic organisms and is needed for efficient photosynthesis under a wide variety of different environmental conditions. Yet, in all these organisms, the light reactions of photosynthesis follow the same basic pattern: (1) absorption of (sun)light by a pigment, (2) ultrafast transfer of the excitation energy to a "photoactive" pigment, (3) oxidation of this excited photoactive pigment, and (4) stabilization of the charge-separated state by secondary electron-transfer reactions. The pigment–protein complexes involved in the first two processes are the antenna or light-harvesting (LH) complexes. Interestingly, the spatial organization of the BChl molecules in the purple bacterial antenna proteins is such that the excitation energy of the pigments increases as a function of the distance from the RC, forming an efficient funnel that directs the excitation energy toward the RC. The primary electron transfer steps (3) and (4) then occur in the RC. The total energy conversion process, starting with the absorption of a photon and ending with a stable charge-separated state, occurs within less than 100 ps and has an overall quantum yield of more than 90% (Blankenship, 2002).

Remarkably, while the architectures of the RCs found in the types of photosynthetic organisms show rather little variation, their antenna complexes are structurally very diverse. This reflects the strict conditions that have to be fulfilled to comply with the demands of the physics of electron transfer, which has led to the conservation of the structure of the RCs in the course of evolution. The physics of energy transfer is much more tolerant, and this leaves considerable degrees of freedom that are reflected in the wide range of architectures seen in the different types of antenna systems.

Here, we will provide an overview of the basic (quantum mechanical) features of the light-harvesting apparatus found in purple bacteria. There are several advantages of focussing on this group of photosynthetic organisms. First, their antenna (energy-transfer components) and reaction center (charge-transfer components) pigment proteins can be separated biochemically. This is in contrast to the photosynthetic machinery in higher organisms like plants where often these components are bound to the same polypeptides. Second, the different pigment groups in these complexes are spectrally well separated, which makes functional studies much easier to interpret compared with Chl-containing photosynthetic organisms. Finally, high-quality structural information is available for both the RC and a some of antenna complexes from purple bacteria, which greatly facilitates the detailed study of structure–function relationships.

2. THE LIGHT-HARVESTING APPARATUS OF PURPLE BACTERIA

Purple photosynthetic bacteria have evolved an elegant system of modular units that make up the light-harvesting apparatus. These modules consist of pairs of hydrophobic, low-molecular weight polypeptides, called α and β (usually 50–60 amino acids long) that noncovalently bind a small number of bacteriochlorophyll (Bchl a) and carotenoid (Car) molecules. The modules then oligomerize to produce the native circular, elliptical, or horseshoe complexes (Cogdell *et al.*, 2004). Most purple bacteria have two main types of complexes: the core complex (RC-LH1) and the peripheral complex (LH2). In the near infrared, LH2 has two strong absorption bands around 800 nm and 850 nm, respectively, whereas the RC-LH1 complex has a single strong absorption band around 880 nm, Fig. 3.2.

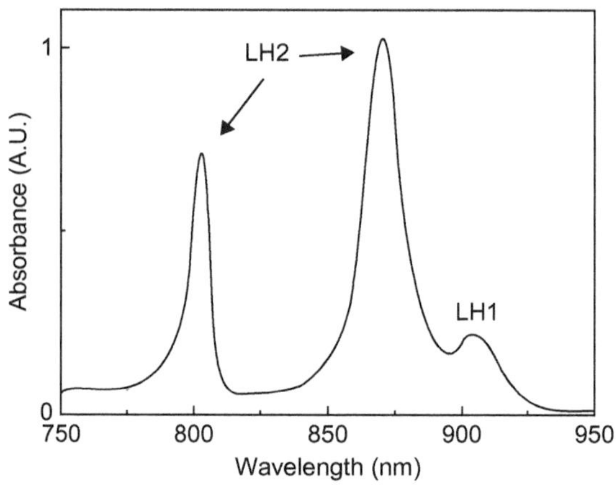

FIGURE 3.2 Absorption spectrum of a solution of membrane fragments from *Rhodopseudomonas acidophila*. The spectrum was recorded at 10 K.

The basic building block of LH2 is a protein heterodimer ($\alpha\beta$), which accommodates three BChl a pigments and one carotenoid molecule (Fig. 3.3A and B). Depending on the bacterial species, the LH2 complex usually consists either of eight or nine copies of these heterodimers, which are arranged in a ring-like structure (Koepke *et al.*, 1996; McDermott *et al.*, 1995; Papiz *et al.*, 2003; Walz *et al.*, 1998).

The BChl a molecules are arranged in two pigment pools labelled B800 and B850, according to their room-temperature absorption maxima in the near infrared. In the case of LH2 from *Rps. acidophila*, the B800 assembly comprises nine well-separated BChl a molecules, which have the planes of their bacteriochlorin rings aligned nearly perpendicular to the symmetry

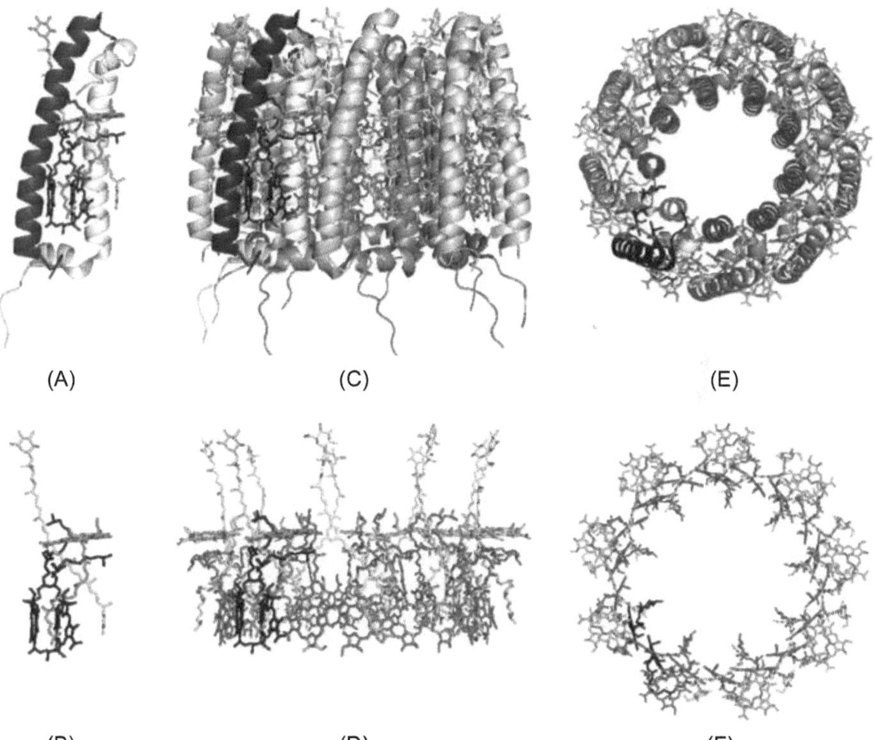

FIGURE 3.3 X-ray structure of LH2 from *Rps. acidophila*. For this species, the LH2 complex consists of nine $\alpha\beta$-subunits and features a diameter of about 6.5 nm. The top row shows the full protein structure, in the lower row the protein backbone is omitted. (A, B) Monomer unit. (C, D) Side view. (E, F) Top view. The colors refer to the α-helixes (gray), β-helixes (blue), B800 (yellow), B850 (red), and carotenoids (cyan). In (C–F) one monomer subunit is highlighted for illustration. (See Plate no. 3 in the Color Plate Section.)

axis, whereas the B850 assembly comprises 18 BChl a molecules in close contact oriented with the plane of their bacteriochlorin rings parallel to the symmetry axis (see Fig. 3.3). In contrast to LH2, where highly resolved X-ray structures are available, the discussion in the literature about the structural properties of RC-LH1 complexes, where there is currently no high-resolution structural information, is much more controversial.

The LH1 complexes surround the reaction center (RC) to form the so-called core complex. The current view is that there are at least two distinct classes of RC-LH1 complexes. One class is monomeric, i.e., consists of one RC surrounded by one LH1 complex. An example of this class is the RC-LH1 complex from *Rps. palustris* (Fig. 3.4A), for which the first X-ray structure has been recently determined (Roszak *et al.*, 2003). In this complex, the RC is enclosed by an overall elliptically shaped LH1 consisting of 15 $\alpha\beta$-apoproteins each accommodating two, light-harvesting BChl a molecules. Interestingly, the LH1 structure features an interruption. Instead of a 16th $\alpha\beta$-apoprotein, another small protein, termed W, has been found that effectively opens the LH1 ring and results in a gap in the arrangement of the BChl a molecules. The second class are dimeric, i.e., consist of two RC-LH1 units. An example of this class is the RC-LH1 complex *Rb. sphaeroides*, Fig. 3.4B (Qian *et al.*, 2005).

In the photosynthetic membrane, the RC-LH1 complexes are surrounded by the LH2 complexes. Light energy absorbed by LH2 is transferred through LH1 to the RC. Energy transfer within the LH2 complex occurs from B800 to the B850 in less than 1 ps. Once the energy arrives in B850, it equilibrates within the B850 manifold an order of magnitude faster (Jimenez *et al.*, 1996; Kennis *et al.*, 1996). The transfer of energy from LH2 to LH1 and subsequently to the reaction center occurs in vivo on a timescale

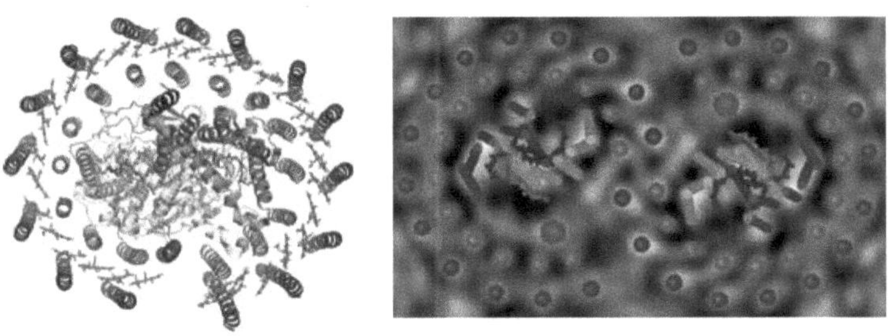

(A) (B)

FIGURE 3.4 (A) X-ray structure of RC-LH1 from *Rps. palustris* (Roszak *et al.*, 2003). This monomeric RC-LH1 consists of 15 $\alpha\beta$-subunits. The outer dimension of the ellipse is about 11 nm. (B) Electron micrograph from RC-LH1 from *Rhodobacter sphaeroides* (Qian *et al.*, 2005). This dimeric RC-LH1 complex consists of 28 $\alpha\beta$-subunits. The elongation of the structure is about 20 nm.

of 5–50 ps, i.e., very fast compared with the decay of the B850-excited singlet state within an isolated LH2, which process has a lifetime of 1.1 ns. In the RC, the energy is used to drive a series of electron transfer reactions that result in the reduction of ubiquinone (UQ) (Feher *et al.*, 1989). In the photosynthetic membrane, when the secondary UQ in the RC has been fully reduced to UQH_2, the quinol must leave the RC in order to transfer its reducing equivalents to the cytochrome b/c1 complex, as part to a rather simple cyclic electron transport pathway (Petty *et al.*, 1979), Fig. 3.5.

It appears that in vivo, the whole structure is highly optimized for capturing light energy and funnelling it to the RC. The supramolecular architecture of these complexes in intact photosynthetic membranes has been beautifully imaged using atomic force microscopy (AFM; Fig. 3.6A) (Bahatyrova *et al.*, 2004). A schematic drawing of the arrangement of the photosynthetic apparatus of the species *Rb. sphaeroides*, which is based on the available structural information in combination with theoretical modelling, is shown in Fig. 3.6B (Chandler *et al.*, 2008).

It is now well established that the spatial arrangement of the pigments determines, to a large extent, the spectroscopic features of the complexes

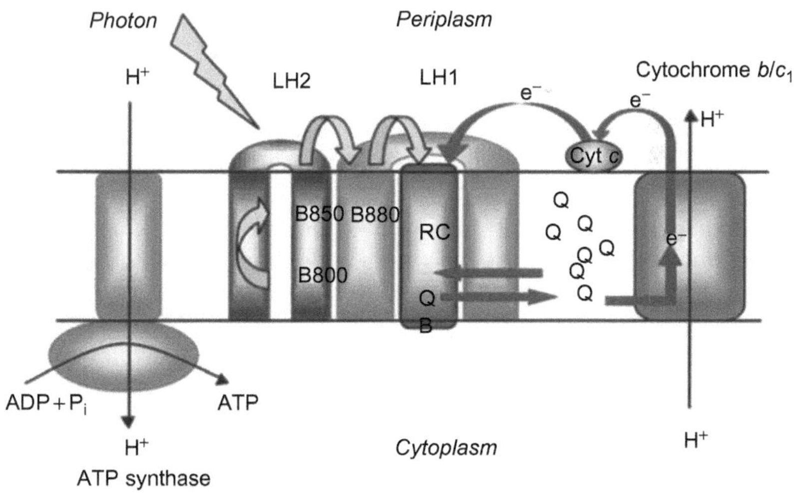

FIGURE 3.5 Schematic sketch of the photosynthetic membrane of a typical purple bacterium. The light gray arrows indicate energy transfer and the dark gray arrows the redox reactions involved their simple cyclic electron transport pathway. The reaction center (RC) reduces the secondary electron acceptor (ubiquinone, Q_B), which has to pass through the LH1 complex in order to deliver its reducing equivalents to cyclic electron pathway. Electron transport pumps protons across the membrane and the resultant transmembrane proton motive force is used by the ATP-synthase to generate ATP. Adapted from Cogdell *et al.* (2006).

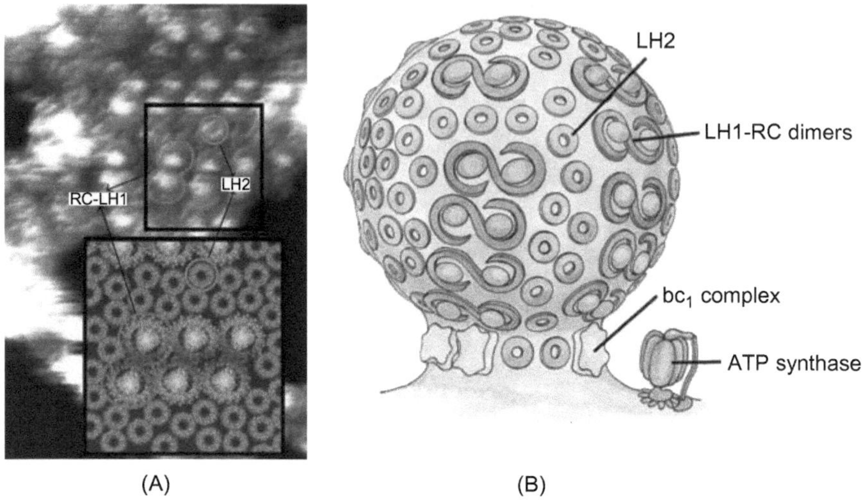

FIGURE 3.6 (A) AFM image of native photosynthetic membranes from *Rb. sphaeroides* together with a model for the mutual arrangement of the LH2 (small open structures, green line) and the RC-LH1 complexes (large filled structures, red line) within the membrane (Figure 1C, Bahatyrova *et al.* Nature 430 (2004) 1058). (B) Schematic drawing of the vesicular photosynthetic chromatophore for *Rb. sphaeroides*. The RC-LH1 complexes and LH2 complexes are packed as observed by AFM. The bc_1 complex and ATP have been tentatively placed by the authors of Chandler *et al.* (2008) near the neck of the chromatophore. Adapted from Chandler *et al.* (2008). (See Plate no. 4 in the Color Plate Section.)

and that, in these systems, collective effects (especially in the case of the B850 BChls) have to be considered in order to appropriately describe their electronically excited states (Jang and Silbey, 2003; Mostovoy and Knoester, 2000; Sauer *et al.*, 1996; van Amerongen *et al.*, 2000; Wu *et al.*, 1997). This leads to so-called Frenkel excitons, which arise from the interactions of the transition-dipole moments of the individual pigments, and which correspond to delocalized electronically excited states.

3. FRENKEL EXCITONS

A natural starting point for the description of the electronically excited states of a molecular aggregate of interacting molecules is provided by the model of molecular excitons developed by Frenkel and Davydov (Davydov, 1971; Frenkel, 1931a,b; Knox, 1963), which leads to the Hamiltonian

$$H = \sum_{n=1}^{N} E_0 \left|\mathrm{n}\right\rangle \left\langle\mathrm{n}\right| + \frac{1}{2} \sum_{n=1}^{N} \sum_{n \neq m} V_{\mathrm{nm}}^{(0)} \left|\mathrm{n}\right\rangle \left\langle\mathrm{m}\right| . \tag{3.1}$$

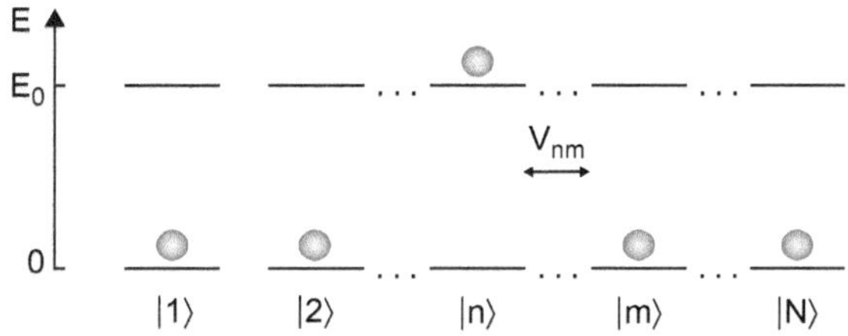

FIGURE 3.7 Schematic sketch of an assembly of N identical interacting molecules. The molecules are represented as two-level systems with an electronic ground state at energy zero and an electronically excited state at energy E_0.

Here, a state $|n\rangle$ represents molecule n in the electronically excited state and all other molecules $1, 2, \ldots, n-1, n+1, \ldots, N$ in the ground state (Fig. 3.7). Each molecule is described as a two-level system consisting of a ground state and a single electronically excited state separated by an excitation energy E_0 and $V_{\mathrm{nm}}^{(0)}$ denotes the interaction between molecules "n" and "m." The states $|1\rangle$ to $|N\rangle$ feature the same excitation energy E_0, which is localized on an individual molecule.

Because of the interaction term in the Hamiltonian, it is clear that the localized states $|n\rangle$ are not the eigenfunctions of the system. For periodic boundary conditions, the proper eigenstates are given by the Bloch states

$$|\mathrm{k}\rangle = \frac{1}{\sqrt{N}} \sum_{n=1}^{N} \mathrm{e}^{\mathrm{i}2\pi k \frac{n}{N}} |\mathrm{n}\rangle \quad k = 0, \ldots, N-1. \tag{3.2}$$

The states $|k\rangle$ are denoted as Frenkel excitons and represent linear combinations of the localized excited states $|n\rangle$. The initial degeneracy of the excited states, as depicted in Fig. 3.7, is lifted by interactions and a manifold of energy levels results – the exciton band – which is given by

$$E(k) = \frac{1}{2} \sum_{n=1}^{N} \sum_{n \neq m} V_{\mathrm{nm}}^{(0)} \mathrm{e}^{\mathrm{i}2\pi k \frac{(n-m)}{N}} \tag{3.3}$$

For this ideal system, where all molecules are equivalent, the exciton wavefunctions $|k\rangle$ have equal amplitudes on each pigment and the excitation is fully delocalized over all N pigments. The transition dipole moments that connect the exciton states with the electronic ground state $|g\rangle$ follow from

$$\vec{\mathrm{M}}(k) = \langle g | \vec{\mathrm{D}} | k \rangle = \frac{1}{\sqrt{N}} \sum_{n=1}^{N} \mathrm{e}^{\mathrm{i}2\pi k \frac{n}{N}} \langle g | \vec{\mathrm{D}} | n \rangle = \frac{1}{\sqrt{N}} \sum_{n=1}^{N} \mathrm{e}^{\mathrm{i}2\pi k \frac{n}{N}} \vec{\mathrm{m}}(n) \tag{3.4}$$

where $\vec{D}$ is the electric dipole moment operator and $\vec{m}(n) = \langle g | \vec{D} | n \rangle$ is the transition-dipole moment of molecule n. From Eq. (3.4), it becomes clear that the transition-dipole moment of an exciton state $|k\rangle$ corresponds to the sum of the individual transition dipole moments multiplied with a phase factor. A macroscopic transition-dipole moment $\vec{M}(k)$ results only if the phase factors interfere constructively.

Everything that disturbs this ideal situation of fully equivalent molecules leads to a scattering among the $|k\rangle$ states and finally thermalizes the exciton band. Such disturbances are, for example, variations in the site energies of the individual molecules that result from local heterogeneities or even isotopic substitution (Köhler and Schmid, 1996). This requires replacement of E_0 in the Hamiltonian, Eq. (3.1), by $E_n = (E_0 + \Delta E_n)$, where ΔE_n denotes the deviation of the site energy of molecule "n" from the average value E_0 (diagonal disorder). Similarly, the interaction strength between the molecules can vary, for example, caused by vibrations of the atomic nuclei (phonons). This can be incorporated into the Hamiltonian by the modification $V_{\mathrm{nm}} = V_{\mathrm{nm}}^{(0)} + \Delta V_{\mathrm{nm}}$, where ΔV_{nm} refers to the spread in the respective interaction strengths (off-diagonal disorder). Then the states associated with the excitons are represented by wave-packets of Bloch states

$$|k_{\mathrm{exciton}}\rangle = \int g(k - k_0)\, |\mathrm{k}\rangle\, \mathrm{d}k \tag{3.5}$$

where $g(k - k_0)$ is a weighting function. If the temperature is sufficiently low, which means that the interaction of excitons and phonons is still weak, the wave-function of the exciton, $|k_{\mathrm{exciton}}\rangle$, is centered around a mean value k_0 with a width Δk, which is small compared with π/a, where a is the nearest neighbor distance between the molecules. This is equivalent to the statement that the average time between two scattering events is long compared with $\mathrm{h}/V_{\mathrm{nm}}$, where h is Planck's constant. In this case, the exciton is called coherent, and the energy transfer among the molecules is wavelike. This implies that the distribution of k states of the wave-packet does not change significantly during the migration of the exciton. Raising temperature leads to a growing scattering rate among the exciton states resulting in a change of the average value k_0 and the width Δk of the wave-packet. According to the uncertainty relation $\Delta x \Delta k \geq 2\pi$, the width of the wave-packet Δk is associated with the region of localization Δx of the excitation, which decreases with increasing width of the wave-packet. When Δx approaches the order of the nearest neighbor distance, a, between two molecules, the excitation becomes localized, and its motion can be visualized as a random walk from molecule to molecule (hopping). This is referred to, in the literature, as an incoherent exciton. Whether the energy transfer in a specific system is coherent or incoherent depends on the competition between the excitation transfer and the scattering processes that determine the timescale for the loss of the coherence of the wave-packet (Scholes and Rumbles, 2006).

4. LINEAR VERSUS CYCLIC AGGREGATE: A COMPARISON

In order to illustrate how the intrinsic properties of the exciton states and the mutual arrangement of the molecules within the aggregate determine the macroscopic photophysical properties of the entire aggregate, it is instructive to compare a linear chain of equidistant molecules with parallel transition dipole moments and an aggregate of molecules equidistantly arranged around a circle in the x, y plane (Fig. 3.8). For the linear aggregate, the orientation of the individual transition-dipole moments in Eq. (3.4) is the same for all molecules in the chain.

A constructive interference of the phase factors results only for $k = 0$, which yields $\vec{\mathrm{M}}(k = 0) = \sqrt{N}\vec{\mathrm{m}}(n)$. Hence, optical transitions are allowed only between the electronic ground state and the exciton state $|k = 0\rangle$ (Knoester and Agranovich, 2003). The transition probability is enhanced by a factor of N, with respect to the transition probability of an individual molecule, and the polarisation of the transition is parallel to the orientation of the transition-dipole moments $\vec{\mathrm{m}}(n)$ of the individual molecules. For the cyclic aggregate, the directions of the individual transition-dipole moments $\vec{\mathrm{m}}(n)$ vary around the structure according to

$$\vec{\mathrm{m}}(n) = \begin{pmatrix} m_{||}\cos\left(2\pi\frac{n}{N}\right) \\ m_{||}\sin\left(2\pi\frac{n}{N}\right) \\ m_{\perp} \end{pmatrix}. \tag{3.6}$$

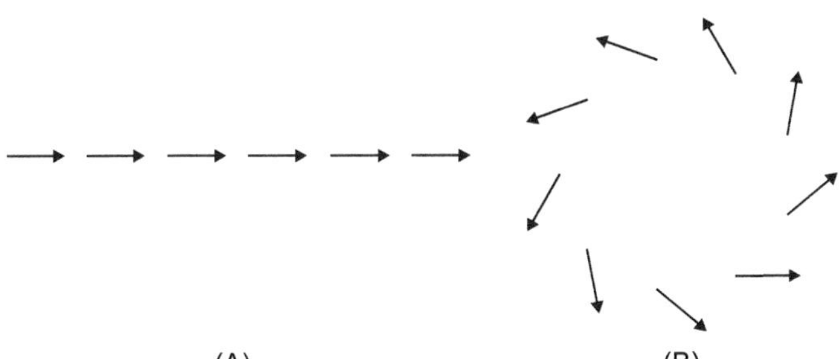

FIGURE 3.8 Sketch of an array of transition-dipole moments. (A) Linear chain. (B) Cyclic structure.

Here, we have split the individual transition-dipole moments into an in-plane component $m_{||}$ (in the x, y plane) and an out-of plane component $m_{\perp}$ (along the z-direction). This yields for the transition-dipole moment of the exciton states

$$\vec{M}(k) = \frac{1}{\sqrt{N}} \sum_{n=1}^{N} e^{i2\pi k \frac{n}{N}} \begin{pmatrix} m_{||} \cos\left(2\pi \frac{n}{N}\right) \\ m_{||} \sin\left(2\pi \frac{n}{N}\right) \\ m_{\perp} \end{pmatrix}$$

$$= \frac{1}{\sqrt{N}} \begin{pmatrix} \frac{1}{2} m_{||} \sum_{n=1}^{N} \left(e^{i\frac{2\pi}{N}(n(k+1))} + e^{i\frac{2\pi}{N}(n(k-1))} \right) \\ \frac{1}{2i} m_{||} \sum_{n=1}^{N} \left(e^{i\frac{2\pi}{N}(n(k+1))} - e^{i\frac{2\pi}{N}(n(k-1))} \right) \\ \sum_{n=1}^{N} e^{i2\pi k \frac{n}{N}} m_{\perp} \end{pmatrix} \tag{3.7}$$

Again, a nonvanishing macroscopic transition-dipole moment results only if the phase factors interfere constructively, which is only the case for $k = 0, 1, N-1$. Because $e^{i\frac{2\pi}{N}(N-1)} = e^{-i\frac{2\pi}{N}}$, we find the correspondence $|k = N-1\rangle = |k = -1\rangle, |k = N-2\rangle = |k = -2\rangle$, and so on and the more familiar selection rules $k = 0, \pm 1$, for a nonvanishing macroscopic transition-dipole moment of a cyclic aggregate (Hu *et al.*, 2002; Mostovoy and Knoester, 2000; Sauer *et al.*, 1996; Wu *et al.*, 1997). For the $k = 0$ state, we obtain

$$\vec{M}(k = 0) = \sqrt{N} \begin{pmatrix} 0 \\ 0 \\ m_{\perp} \end{pmatrix}. \tag{3.8}$$

This situation is reminiscent of the linear chain. This transition can be excited with a probability $Nm_{\perp}^2$ with light that is polarized perpendicular to the plane of the ring. For $k = \pm 1$, we find

$$\vec{M}(k = \pm 1) = \frac{\sqrt{N}}{2} m_{||} \begin{pmatrix} 1 \\ \pm i \\ 0 \end{pmatrix} \tag{3.9}$$

and a transition probability $\frac{N}{2} m_{||}^2$. In order to illustrate this result in more detail, we have to consider that the transition-dipole moments oscillate with a frequency ω, which has been skipped, as yet, for clarity. Taking the oscillation into account by replacing $\vec{m}$ by $\vec{m} \cdot e^{i\omega t}$ yields

$$\vec{M}(k = \pm 1) \cdot e^{i\omega t} = \frac{\sqrt{N}}{2} m_{||} \begin{pmatrix} 1 \\ \pm i \\ 0 \end{pmatrix} \cdot e^{i\omega t} = \frac{\sqrt{N}}{2} m_{||} \begin{pmatrix} e^{i\omega t} \\ e^{i(\omega t \pm \frac{\pi}{2})} \\ 0 \end{pmatrix} \quad (3.10)$$

which reveals that the transition-dipole moments that are associated with the $|k = \pm 1\rangle$ states are counter-rotating in the plane of the assembly. These states can be excited with circular polarized light. Because the states $|k = \pm 1\rangle$ are degenerate, any linear combination as, for example, $|k_x\rangle = \frac{1}{\sqrt{2}}\left(|k = 1\rangle - |k = -1\rangle\right)$ and $|k_y\rangle = \frac{1}{\sqrt{2}}\left(|k = 1\rangle + |k = -1\rangle\right)$ are also eigenstates of the exciton Hamiltonian. These states can be excited with mutually orthogonal linear polarized light.

5. THE B850 ASSEMBLY OF LH2 AS A QUANTUM AGGREGATE OF MOLECULES

So what properties do we expect in the case of a good antenna? First, for efficient light harvesting, it should have a high-absorption cross section; second, the whole antenna apparatus should have a good spectral coverage; and third, energy transfer within the antenna system and to the RC should be favored over wasteful fluorescence and other loss mechanisms. The B850 assembly of LH2 is an elegant example of the clever exploitation of quantum mechanics to produce an efficient light-harvesting system (Beljonne *et al.*, 2009; Cogdell *et al.*, 2006; Jang *et al.*, 2007; Scholes, 2010; Sumi, 2001). Figure 3.9 shows a part of the fluorescence-excitation spectrum from an individual LH2 complex for two mutually orthogonal polarizations of the incident radiation.

Apparently, the transition-dipole moments of these two transitions are perpendicular with respect to each other, which is in line with the $k = \pm 1$ selection rule for a cyclic aggregate. It should be noted that the single-molecule experiment reflects the situation when the exciton is "born." The coherence of the exciton states is rapidly destroyed by fast dephasing processes such as electron–phonon coupling.

This leads to an ultrafast relaxation (≈ 100 fs) of the exciton states and a localization of the excitation energy on a smaller part of the aggregate (Fig. 3.10), a process that has been studied with a variety of time-resolved methods (Sundström *et al.*, 1999; Zigmantas *et al.*, 2006). However,

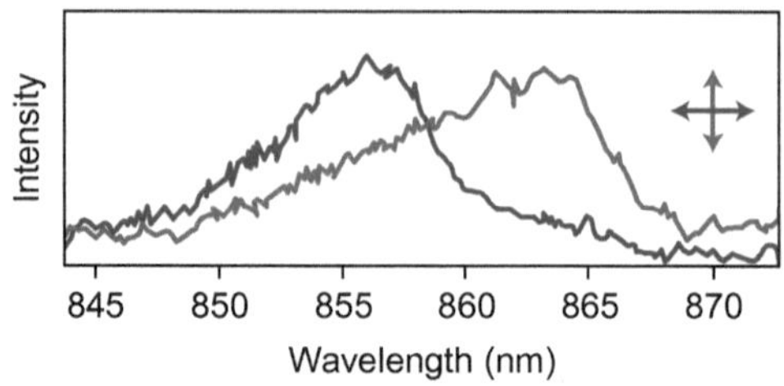

FIGURE 3.9 Fluorescence-excitation spectrum of the long-wavelength part of the B850 band from an individual LH2 complex of *Rps. acidophila* at 1.4 K. The blue and red spectra have been recorded for mutually orthogonal polarization of the excitation light. Adapted from Hofmann *et al.* (2004). (See Plate no. 5 in the Color Plate Section.)

there is increasing evidence that for antenna systems found in several photosynthetic organisms, the coherences between the exciton states are not fully destroyed, and that even at room temperature, the excitation energy is still partly delocalized (Scholes, 2010).

The relatively strong interactions between the B850 pigments with a large in-plane component of the individual transition-dipole moments enforces, by reason of symmetry, that the transition probability for each state of the lowest degenerate pair ($k = \pm 1$) increases at the expense of all other exciton states by a factor $N/2$, where N is the number of molecules in the ring. These states can be excited with light of any polarization within the plane of the aggregate. After excitation of one of these states, the energy relaxes to the lowest exciton state, which features a relatively small transition probability to the ground state. In other words, the excitation energy is trapped for a time that is sufficiently long to favor energy transfer over wasteful fluorescence. The advantages of a circular array for light-harvesting and energy transfer become clear by comparison with a linear arrangement of the chromophores. For such a geometry, the lowest exciton state gains oscillator strength by a factor of N, which leads also to an enhancement of the radioactive decay rate by this factor. Moreover, the aggregate can be excited exclusively with light that is polarized along the direction of the transition-dipole moments of the individual molecules. This means that even under ideal conditions, i.e., when the propagation direction of the incident light is perpendicular to the transition-dipole moments of the chromophores, half of the light intensity cannot be absorbed by the aggregate.

Furthermore, the ladder of the B850 exciton states is spread over $\sim 1200\,\text{cm}^{-1}$ in energy. These higher exciton states are not "useless" because they do not carry a net transition-dipole moment; they can act as accepting states for energy transfer from the B800 molecules (Jang *et al.*, 2007; Mukai *et al.*, 1999; Sumi, 1999) and so contribute to a better spectral coverage by the whole antenna system.

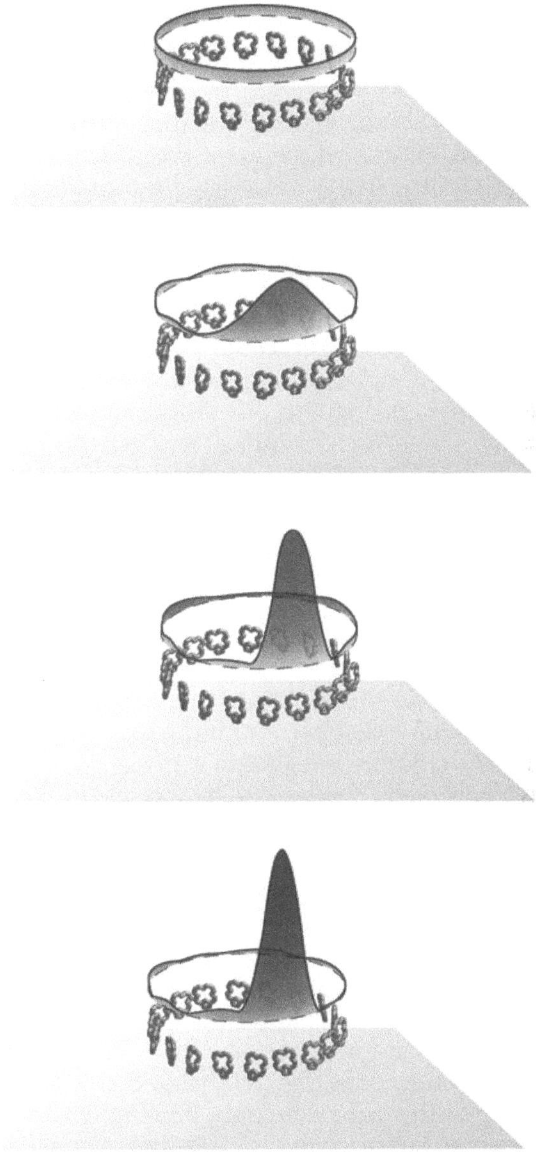

FIGURE 3.10 For a perfectly symmetric B850 ring, initially the excitation energy is fully delocalized over all 18 BChl a molecules. Any deviation from this situation tends to localize the excitation energy on a few BChl a molecules and the wavefunction of the excited state is given by a wave-packet. The figure shows from top to bottom the probability density to find the excitation energy at the position of a distinct BChl a molecule for a pure exciton state, and for wave-packets that result from the superposition of the lowest 5, 7, and 15 exciton states, respectively. In the native system, the localization of the excitation energy as sketched here from top to bottom takes place on an ultrafast timescale of some hundred femtoseconds.

6. CAN WE LEARN FROM NATURE HOW TO SYNTHESISE ARTIFICIAL LIGHT-HARVESTING MOLECULES?

There are now high-resolution crystal structures of several antenna complexes. Moreover, for most of these, we have a detailed understanding of how they work. Is it possible to use this information to help design artificial systems capable for functioning as efficient light harvesters? The natural system (photosynthesis) shows that light-harvesting complexes are structurally very diverse, both in terms of their proteins and the organization of their light-absorbing pigments. It appears, therefore, that there are many possible solutions to the problem of constructing light-harvesting complexes. In spite of this, are there any general principles that can be identified? Taking the purple bacterial antenna system as one of the easier ones to understand, a few general principles can be seen. First, the different types of light-harvesting complexes are spectrally different with LH2 absorbing at shorter wavelengths than LH1. This introduces an energy gradient that effectively funnels the energy from LH2 downhill to LH1, where LH1 closest to the RC, i.e., to the trap. This allows quite large light-harvesting systems to be used without the absorbed light energy failing to reach the trap. Within a given light-harvesting complex, the antenna pigment groups are well aligned for optimal interpigment energy transfer. Even though different types of light-harvesting complexes have strikingly different pigment arrangements, these are not random and within a given class of complexes are usually strongly conserved from species to species. In the photosynthetic membrane, the supramolecular arrangement of the light-harvesting complexes is not one showing high order or regularity. However, the individual light-harvesting "rings" allow for fast, efficient interring energy transfer so long as the ring-to-ring distance is sufficiently small, and this condition does not require a highly ordered arrangement. This is a special feature of the purple bacterial system and reflects the exact properties of their type of light-harvesting complexes. Building long-range order into artificial light-harvesting systems is a major synthetic challenge, perhaps if the individual light-harvesting modules synthesized could mimic the purple bacterial system, then this problem could be readily overcome. Each LH complex has carotenoids associated with it that acts as photoprotectors. Finally, the absorption spectrum of the light-absorbing pigments, Bchl and carotenoids, absorb solar radiation in that part of the spectrum that is available to the purple bacteria in the ecological niches in which they grow. Any artificial antenna system must use pigments with appropriate absorption characteristics.

ACKNOWLEDGMENTS

RJC thanks the BBSRC, EPSRC, and the DOE for financial support. JK acknowledges financial support from the Volkswagen Foundation and the DFG.

REFERENCES

Bahatyrova, S., Frese, R. N., Siebert, C. A., Olsen, J. D., van der Werf, K. O., van Grondelle, R., Niederman, R. A., Bullough, P. A., Otto, C., and Hunter, C. N. (2004). *Nature* **430**, 1058–1062.

Beljonne, D., Curutchet, C., Scholes, G. D., and Silbey, R. J. (2009). *J. Phys. Chem. B* **113**, 6583–6599.

Blankenship, R. E. (2002). "Molecular Mechanisms of Photosynthesis." Blackwell Science, Oxford.

Chandler, D. E., Hsin, J., Harrison, C. B., Gumbart, J., and Schulten, K. (2008). *Biophys. J.* **95**, 2822–2836.

Cogdell, R. J., Gardiner, A. T., Roszak, A. W., Law, C. J., Southall, J., and Isaacs, N. W. (2004). *Photosynth. Res.* **81**, 207–214.

Cogdell, R. J., Gall, A., and Köhler, J. (2006). *Quart. Rev. Biophys.* **39**, 227–324.

Davydov, A. S. (1971). "Theory of Molecular Excitons." Plenum Press, New York.

Feher, G., Allen, J. P., Okamura, M. Y., and Rees, D. C. (1989). *Nature* **339**, 111–116.

Frenkel, J. (1931a). *Phys. Rev.* **37**, 17–44.

Frenkel, J. (1931b). *Phys. Rev.* **37**, 1276–1294.

Green, Beverly, R. and Parson William, W. (2003). "Light Harvesting Antennas in Photosynthesis." Kluwer Academic Publishers, Dordrecht, The Netherlands.

Hofmann, C., Aartsma, T. J., and Köhler, J. (2004). *Chem. Phys. Lett.* **395**, 373–378.

Hu, X., Ritz, T., Damjanovic, A., Autenrieth, F., and Schulten, K. (2002). *Quart. Rev. Biophys.* **35**, 1–62.

Jang, S., Newton, M. D., and Silbey, R. J. (2007). *J. Phys. Chem. B* **111**, 6807–6814.

Jang, S., and Silbey, R. J. (2003). *J. Chem. Phys.* **118**, 9324–9336.

Jimenez, R., Dikshit, S. N., Bradford, S. E., and Fleming, G. R. (1996). *J. Phys. Chem.* **100**, 6825–6834.

Kennis, J. T. M., Streltsov, A. M., Aartsma, T. J., Nozawa, T., and Amesz, J. (1996). *J. Phys. Chem.* **100**, 2438–2442.

Knoester, J., and Agranovich, V. M. (2003). "Frenkel and charge-transfer excitions in organic solids." In *Thin Films and Nanostructures*, Vol. 31, pp. 1–96. Elsevier, Amsterdam, Amsterdam.

Knox, R. S. (1963). "The Electronic Structure." In *Theory of Excitons*, ed. H. Ehrenreich, F. Seitz and D. Turnbull, pp. 7–37. Academic Press.

Koepke, J., Hu, X., Muenke, C., Schulten, K., and Michel, H. (1996). *Structure* **4**, 581–597.

Köhler, J., and Schmid, D. (1996). *J. Phys. Condens. Matt.* **8**, 115–141.

McDermott, G., Prince, S. M., Freer, A. A., Hawthornthwaite-Lawless, A. M., Papiz, M. Z., Cogdell, R. J., and Isaacs, N. W. (1995). *Nature* **374**, 517–521.

Mostovoy, M. V. and Knoester, J. (2000). *J. Phys. Chem. B* **104**, 12355–12364.

Mukai, K., Abe, S., and Sumi, H. (1999). *J. Phys. Chem. B* **103**, 6096–6102.

Papiz, M. Z., Prince, S. M., Howard, T., Cogdell, R. J., and Isaacs, N. W. (2003). *J. Mol. Biol.* **326**, 1523–1538.

Petty, K., Jackson, J. B., and Dutton, P. L. (1979). *Biochim. et Biophys. Acta* **546**, 17–42.

Qian, P., Neil Hunter, C., and Bullough, P. A. (2005). *J. Mol. Biol.* **349**, 948–960.

Roszak, A. W., Howard, T. D., Southall, J., Gardiner, A. T., Law, C. J., Isaacs, N. W., and Cogdell, R. J. (2003). *Science* **302**, 1969–1971.

Sauer, K., Cogdell, R. J., Prince, S. M., Freer, A. A., Isaacs, N. W., and Scheer, H. (1996). *Photochem. Photobiol.* **64**, 564–576.

Scholes, G. D., and Rumbles, G. (2006). *Nature Materials* **5**, 683–696.

Scholes, G. D. (2010). *J. Phys. Chem. Lett.* **1**, 2–8.

Sumi, H. (1999). *J. Phys. Chem. B* **103**, 252–260.

Sumi, H. (2001). *Chem. Rec.* **1**, 480–493.

Sundström, V., Pullerits, T., and van Grondelle, R. (1999). *J. Phys. Chem. B* **103**, 2327–2346.

van Amerongen, H., Valkunas, L., and van Grondelle, R. (2000). "Photosynthetic Excitons." World Scientific, Singapore.

Walz, T., Jamieson, S. J., Bowers, C. M., Bullough, P. A., and Hunter, C. N. (1998). *J. Mol. Biol.* **282**, 833–845.

Wu, H.-M., Ratsep, M., Lee, I.-J., Cogdell, R. J. and Small, G. J. (1997). *J. Phys. Chem. B* **101**, 7654–7663.

Zigmantas, D., Read, E. L., Mancal, T., Brixner, T., Gardiner, A. T., Cogdell, R. J., and Fleming, G. R. (2006). *Proc. Natl. Acad. Sci.* **103**, 12672–12677.

Zinth, W., and Wachtveitl, J. (2005). *Chem. Phys. Chem* **6**, 871–880.

INDEX

Q

R

S

T

U

V

W

CONTENTS OF VOLUMES IN THIS SERIES

Volume 7 **Application and Devices**

Part A

Part B

Volume 8 **Transport and Optical Phenomena**

Volume 9 **Modulation Techniques**

Volume 10 **Transport Phenomena**

Volume 11 **Solar Cells**

Volume 12 **Infrared Detectors (II)**

Volume 13 **Cadmium Telluride**

Volume 14 **Lasers, Junctions, Transport**

Volume 15 **Contacts, Junctions, Emitters**

Volume 16 **Defects, (HgCd)Se, (HgCd)Te**

Volume 21 **Hydrogenated Amorphous Silicon**

Part A

Part B

Part C

Part D

Volume 22 **Lightwave Communications Technology**

Part A

Part B

H. Morkoç and H. Unlu, Factors Affecting the Performance of (Al,Ga)As/GaAs and (Al,Ga)As/InGaAs Modulation-Doped Field-Effect Transistors: Microwave and Digital Applications

N. T. Linh, Two-Dimensional Electron Gas FETs: Microwave Applications

M. Abe et al., Ultra-High-Speed HEMT Integrated Circuits

D. S. Chemla, D. A. B. Miller and P. W. Smith, Nonlinear Optical Properties of Multiple Quantum Well Structures for Optical Signal Processing

F. Capasso, Graded-Gap and Superlattice Devices by Band-Gap Engineering

W. T. Tsang, Quantum Confinement Heterostructure Semiconductor Lasers

G. C. Osbourn et al., Principles and Applications of Semiconductor Strained-Layer Superlattices

Volume 25 **Diluted Magnetic Semiconductors**

W. Giriat and J. K. Furdyna, Crystal Structure, Composition, and Materials Preparation of Diluted Magnetic Semiconductors

W. M. Becker, Band Structure and Optical Properties of Wide-Gap $A^{II}_{1-x}Mn_x B_{IV}$ Alloys at Zero Magnetic Field

S. Oseroff and P. H. Keesom, Magnetic Properties: Macroscopic Studies

T. Giebultowicz and T. M. Holden, Neutron Scattering Studies of the Magnetic Structure and Dynamics of Diluted Magnetic Semiconductors

J. Kossut, Band Structure and Quantum Transport Phenomena in Narrow-Gap Diluted Magnetic Semiconductors

C. Riquaux, Magnetooptical Properties of Large-Gap Diluted Magnetic Semiconductors

J. A. Gaj, Magnetooptical Properties of Large-Gap Diluted Magnetic Semiconductors

J. Mycielski, Shallow Acceptors in Diluted Magnetic Semiconductors: Splitting, Boil-off, Giant Negative Magnetoresistance

A. K. Ramadas and R. Rodriquez, Raman Scattering in Diluted Magnetic Semiconductors

P. A. Wolff, Theory of Bound Magnetic Polarons in Semimagnetic Semiconductors

Volume 26 **III–V Compound Semiconductors and Semiconductor Properties of Superionic Materials**

Z. Yuanxi, III–V Compounds

H. V. Winston, A. T. Hunter, H. Kimura, and R. E. Lee, InAs-Alloyed GaAs Substrates for Direct Implantation

P. K. Bhattacharya and S. Dhar, Deep Levels in III–V Compound Semiconductors Grown by MBE

Y. Ya. Gurevich and A. K. Ivanov-Shits, Semiconductor Properties of Supersonic Materials

Volume 27 **High Conducting Quasi-One-Dimensional Organic Crystals**

E. M. Conwell, Introduction to Highly Conducting Quasi-One-Dimensional Organic Crystals

I. A. Howard, A Reference Guide to the Conducting Quasi-One-Dimensional Organic Molecular Crystals

Volume 32 **Strained-Layer Superlattices: Physics**

Volume 33 **Strained-Layer Superlattices: Material Science and Technology**

Volume 34 **Hydrogen in Semiconductors**

Volume 35 **Nanostructured Systems**

Volume 36 **The Spectroscopy of Semiconductors**

Volume 37 **The Mechanical Properties of Semiconductors**

Volume 38 **Imperfections in III/V Materials**

U. Scherz and M. Scheffler, Density-Functional Theory of sp-Bonded Defects in III/V Semiconductors
M. Kaminska and E. R. Weber, E12 Defect in GaAs
D. C. Look, Defects Relevant for Compensation in Semi-Insulating GaAs
R. C. Newman, Local Vibrational Mode Spectroscopy of Defects in III/V Compounds
A. M. Hennel, Transition Metals in III/V Compounds
K. J. Malloy and K. Khachaturyan, DX and Related Defects in Semiconductors
V. Swaminathan and A. S. Jordan, Dislocations in III/V Compounds
K. W. Nauka, Deep Level Defects in the Epitaxial III/V Materials

Volume 39 **Minority Carriers in III–V Semiconductors: Physics and Applications**

N. K. Dutta, Radiative Transition in GaAs and Other III–V Compounds
R. K. Ahrenkiel, Minority-Carrier Lifetime in III–V Semiconductors
T. Furuta, High Field Minority Electron Transport in p-GaAs
M. S. Lundstrom, Minority-Carrier Transport in III–V Semiconductors
R. A. Abram, Effects of Heavy Doping and High Excitation on the Band Structure of GaAs
D. Yevick and W. Bardyszewski, An Introduction to Non-Equilibrium Many-Body Analyses of Optical Processes in III–V Semiconductors

Volume 40 **Epitaxial Microstructures**

E. F. Schubert, Delta-Doping of Semiconductors: Electronic, Optical and Structural Properties of Materials and Devices
A. Gossard, M. Sundaram, and P. Hopkins, Wide Graded Potential Wells
P. Petroff, Direct Growth of Nanometer-Size Quantum Wire Superlattices
E. Kapon, Lateral Patterning of Quantum Well Heterostructures by Growth of Nonplanar Substrates
H. Temkin, D. Gershoni, and M. Panish, Optical Properties of Ga_{1-x} In_x As/InP Quantum Wells

Volume 41 **High Speed Heterostructure Devices**

F. Capasso, F. Beltram, S. Sen, A. Pahlevi, and A. Y. Cho, Quantum Electron Devices: Physics and Applications
P. Solomon, D. J. Frank, S. L. Wright and F. Canora, GaAs-Gate Semiconductor-Insulator-Semiconductor FET
M. H. Hashemi and U. K. Mishra, Unipolar InP-Based Transistors
R. Kiehl, Complementary Heterostructure FET Integrated Circuits
T. Ishibashi, GaAs-Based and InP-Based Heterostructure Bipolar-Transistors
H. C. Liu and T. C. L. G. Sollner, High-Frequency-Tunneling Devices
H. Ohnishi, T. More, M. Takatsu, K. Imamura, and N. Yokoyama, Resonant-Tunneling Hot-Electron Transistors and Circuits

Volume 42 **Oxygen in Silicon**

F. Shimura, Introduction to Oxygen in Silicon
W. Lin, The Incorporation of Oxygen into Silicon Crystals
T. J. Schaffner and D. K. Schroder, Characterization Techniques for Oxygen in Silicon
W. M. Bullis, Oxygen Concentration Measurement
S. M. Hu, Intrinsic Point Defects in Silicon
B. Pajot, Some Atomic Configuration of Oxygen
J. Michel and L. C. Kimerling, Electrical Properties of Oxygen in Silicon
R. C. Newman and R. Jones, Diffusion of Oxygen in Silicon
T. Y. Tan and W. J. Taylor, Mechanisms of Oxygen Precipitation: Some Quantitative Aspects
M. Schrems, Simulation of Oxygen Precipitation
K. Simino and I. Yonenaga, Oxygen Effect on Mechanical Properties
W. Bergholz, Grown-in and Process-Induced Effects
F. Shimura, Intrinsic/Internal Gettering
H. Tsuya, Oxygen Effect on Electronic Device Performance

Volume 43 **Semiconductors for Room Temperature Nuclear Detector Applications**

R. B. James and T. E. Schlesinger, Introduction and Overview
L. S. Darken and C. E. Cox, High-Purity Germanium Detectors
A. Burger, D. Nason, L. Van den Berg, and M. Schieber, Growth of Mercuric Iodide
X. J. Bao, T. E. Schlesinger, and R. B. James, Electrical Properties of Mercuric Iodide
X. J. Bao, R. B. James, and T. E. Schlesinger, Optical Properties of Red Mercuric Iodide
M. Hage-Ali and P. Siffert, Growth Methods of CdTe Nuclear Detector Materials
M. Hage-Ali and P. Siffert, Characterization of CdTe Nuclear Detector Materials
M. Hage-Ali and P. Siffert, CdTe Nuclear Detectors and Applications
R. B. James, T. E. Schlesinger, J. Lund, and M. Schieber, Cd_{1-x} Zn_x Te Spectrometers for Gamma and X-Ray Applications
D. S. McGregor, J. E. Kammeraad, Gallium Arsenide Radiation Detectors and Spectrometers
J. C. Lund, F. Olschner, and A. Burger, Lead Iodide
M. R. Squillante and K. S. Shah, Other Materials: Status and Prospects
V. M. Gerrish, Characterization and Quantification of Detector Performance
J. S. Iwanczyk and B. E. Patt, Electronics for X-ray and Gamma Ray Spectrometers
M. Schieber, R. B. James and T. E. Schlesinger, Summary and Remaining Issues for Room Temperature Radiation Spectrometers

Volume 44 **II–IV Blue/Green Light Emitters: Device Physics and Epitaxial Growth**

J. Han and R. L. Gunshor, MBE Growth and Electrical Properties of Wide Bandgap ZnSe-based II–VI Semiconductors
S. Fujita and S. Fujita, Growth and Characterization of ZnSe-based II–VI Semiconductors by MOVPE

E. Ho and L. A. Kolodziejski, Gaseous Source UHV Epitaxy Technologies for Wide Bandgap II–VI Semiconductors

C. G. Van de Walle, Doping of Wide-Band-Gap II–VI Compounds – Theory

R. Cingolani, Optical Properties of Excitons in ZnSe-Based Quantum Well Heterostructures

A. Ishibashi and A. V. Nurmikko, II–VI Diode Lasers: A Current View of Device Performance and Issues

S. Guha and J. Petruzello, Defects and Degradation in Wide-Gap II–VI-based Structure and Light Emitting Devices

Volume 45 **Effect of Disorder and Defects in Ion-Implanted Semiconductors: Electrical and Physiochemical Characterization**

H. Ryssel, Ion Implantation into Semiconductors: Historical Perspectives

You-Nian Wang and Teng-Cai Ma, Electronic Stopping Power for Energetic Ions in Solids

S. T. Nakagawa, Solid Effect on the Electronic Stopping of Crystalline Target and Application to Range Estimation

G. Miller, S. Kalbitzer, and G. N. Greaves, Ion Beams in Amorphous Semiconductor Research

J. Boussey-Said, Sheet and Spreading Resistance Analysis of Ion Implanted and Annealed Semiconductors

M. L. Polignano and G. Queirolo, Studies of the Stripping Hall Effect in Ion-Implanted Silicon

J. Sroemenos, Transmission Electron Microscopy Analyses

R. Nipoti and M. Servidori, Rutherford Backscattering Studies of Ion Implanted Semiconductors

P. Zaumseil, X-ray Diffraction Techniques

Volume 46 **Effect of Disorder and Defects in Ion-Implanted Semiconductors: Optical and Photothermal Characterization**

M. Fried, T. Lohner, and J. Gyulai, Ellipsometric Analysis

A. Seas and C. Christofides, Transmission and Reflection Spectroscopy on Ion Implanted Semiconductors

A. Othonos and C. Christofides, Photoluminescence and Raman Scattering of Ion Implanted Semiconductors. Influence of Annealing

C. Christofides, Photomodulated Thermoreflectance Investigation of Implanted Wafers. Annealing Kinetics of Defects

U. Zammit, Photothermal Deflection Spectroscopy Characterization of Ion-Implanted and Annealed Silicon Films

A. Mandelis, A. Budiman, and M. Vargas, Photothermal Deep-Level Transient Spectroscopy of Impurities and Defects in Semiconductors

R. Kalish and S. Charbonneau, Ion Implantation into Quantum-Well Structures

A. M. Myasnikov and N. N. Gerasimenko, Ion Implantation and Thermal Annealing of III–V Compound Semiconducting Systems: Some Problems of III–V Narrow Gap Semiconductors

W. A. Bryden and T. J. Kistenmacher, Growth of Group III–A Nitrides by Reactive Sputtering
N. Newman, Thermochemistry of III–N Semiconductors
S. J. Pearton and R. J. Shul, Etching of III Nitrides
S. M. Bedair, Indium-based Nitride Compounds
A. Trampert, O. Brandt, and K. H. Ploog, Crystal Structure of Group III Nitrides
H. Morkoç, F. Hamdani, and A. Salvador, Electronic and Optical Properties of III–V Nitride based Quantum Wells and Superlattices
K. Doverspike and J. I. Pankove, Doping in the III-Nitrides
T. Suski and P. Perlin, High Pressure Studies of Defects and Impurities in Gallium Nitride
B. Monemar, Optical Properties of GaN
W. R. L. Lambrecht, Band Structure of the Group III Nitrides
N. E. Christensen and P. Perlin, Phonons and Phase Transitions in GaN
S. Nakamura, Applications of LEDs and LDs
I. Akasaki and H. Amano, Lasers
J. A. Cooper, Jr., Nonvolatile Random Access Memories in Wide Bandgap Semiconductors

Volume 51A **Identification of Defects in Semiconductors**

G. D. Watkins, EPR and ENDOR Studies of Defects in Semiconductors
J.-M. Spaeth, Magneto-Optical and Electrical Detection of Paramagnetic Resonance in Semiconductors
T. A. Kennedy and E. R. Claser, Magnetic Resonance of Epitaxial Layers Detected by Photoluminescence
K. H. Chow, B. Hitti, and R. F. Kiefl, μSR on Muonium in Semiconductors and Its Relation to Hydrogen
K. Saarinen, P. Hautojärvi, and C. Corbel, Positron Annihilation Spectroscopy of Defects in Semiconductors
R. Jones and P. R. Briddon, The *Ab Initio* Cluster Method and the Dynamics of Defects in Semiconductors

Volume 51B **Identification Defects in Semiconductors**

G. Davies, Optical Measurements of Point Defects
P. M. Mooney, Defect Identification Using Capacitance Spectroscopy
M. Stavola, Vibrational Spectroscopy of Light Element Impurities in Semiconductors
P. Schwander, W. D. Rau, C. Kisielowski, M. Gribelyuk, and A. Ourmazd, Defect Processes in Semiconductors Studied at the Atomic Level by Transmission Electron Microscopy
N. D. Jager and E. R. Weber, Scanning Tunneling Microscopy of Defects in Semiconductors

Volume 52 **SiC Materials and Devices**

K. Järrendahl and R. F. Davis, Materials Properties and Characterization of SiC
V. A. Dmitiriev and M. G. Spencer, SiC Fabrication Technology: Growth and Doping
V. Saxena and A. J. Steckl, Building Blocks for SiC Devices: Ohmic Contacts, Schottky Contacts, and p-n Junctions

Volume 53 **Cumulative Subjects and Author Index Including Tables of Contents for Volumes 1–50**

Volume 54 **High Pressure in Semiconductor Physics I**

Volume 55 **High Pressure in Semiconductor Physics II**

Volume 56 **Germanium Silicon: Physics and Materials**

Volume 57 **Gallium Nitride (GaN) II**

Volume 58 **Nonlinear Optics in Semiconductors I**

Volume 59 **Nonlinear Optics in Semiconductors II**

Volume 60 **Self-Assembled InGaAs/GaAs Quantum Dots**

Volume 61 **Hydrogen in Semiconductors II**

Volume 62 **Intersubband Transitions in Quantum Wells: Physics and Device Applications I**

Volume 63 **Chemical Mechanical Polishing in Si Processing**

Volume 64 **Electroluminescence I**

Volume 65 **Electroluminescence II**

Volume 66 **Intersubband Transitions in Quantum Wells: Physics and Device Applications II**

Volume 67 **Ultrafast Physical Processes in Semiconductors**

Volume 72 **Silicon Epitaxy**

S. Acerboni, ST Microelectronics, CFM-AGI Department, Agrate Brianza, Italy
V.-M. Airaksinen, Okmetic Oyj R&D Department, Vantaa, Finland
G. Beretta, ST Microelectronics, DSG Epitaxy Catania Department, Catania, Italy
C. Cavallotti, Dipartimento di Chimica Fisica Applicata, Politecnico di Milano, Milano, Italy
D. Crippa, MEMC Electronic Materials, Epitaxial and CVD Department, Operations Technology Division, Novara, Italy
D. Dutartre, ST Microelectronics, Central R&D, Crolles, France
Srikanth Kommu, MEMC Electronic Materials inc., EPI Technology Group, St. Peters, Missouri
M. Masi, Dipartimento di Chimica Fisica Applicata, Politecnico di Milano, Milano, Italy
D. J. Meyer, ASM Epitaxy, Phoenix, Arizona
J. Murota, Research Institute of Electrical Communication, Laboratory for Electronic Intelligent Systems, Tohoku University, Sendai, Japan
V. Pozzetti, LPE Epitaxial Technologies, Bollate, Italy
A. M. Rinaldi, MEMC Electronic Materials, Epitaxial and CVD Department, Operations Technology Division, Novara, Italy
Y. Shiraki, Research Center for Advanced Science and Technology (RCAST), University of Tokyo, Tokyo, Japan

Volume 73 **Processing and Properties of Compound Semiconductors**

S. J. Pearton, Introduction
Eric Donkor, Gallium Arsenide Heterostructures
Annamraju Kasi Viswanatli, Growth and Optical Properties of GaN
D. Y. C. Lie and K. L. Wang, SiGe/Si Processing
S. Kim and M. Razeghi, Advances in Quantum Dot Structures
Walter P. Gomes, Wet Etching of III–V Semiconductors

Volume 74 **Silicon-Germanium Strained Layers and Heterostructures**

S. C. Jain and M. Willander, Introduction; Strain, Stability, Reliability and Growth; Mechanism of Strain Relaxation; Strain, Growth, and TED in SiGeC Layers; Bandstructure and Related Properties; Heterostructure Bipolar Transistors; FETs and Other Devices

Volume 75 **Laser Crystallization of Silicon**

Norbert H. Nickel, Introduction to Laser Crystallization of Silicon
Costas P. Grigoropoidos, Seung-Jae Moon and Ming-Hong Lee, Heat Transfer and Phase Transformations in Laser Melting and Recrystallization of Amorphous Thin Si Films
Robert Černý and Petr Přikryl, Modeling Laser-Induced Phase-Change Processes: Theory and Computation
Paulo V. Santos, Laser Interference Crystallization of Amorphous Films
Philipp Lengsfeld and Norbert H. Nickel, Structural and Electronic Properties of Laser-Crystallized Poly-Si

Volume 76 **Thin-Film Diamond I**

Volume 77 **Thin-Film Diamond II**

Volume 78 **Semiconducting Chalcogenide Glass I**

Volume 79 **Semiconducting Chalcogenide Glass II**

Volume 80 **Semiconducting Chalcogenide Glass III**

Volume 81 **Conducting Organic Materials and Devices**

Volume 82 **Semiconductors and Semimetals**

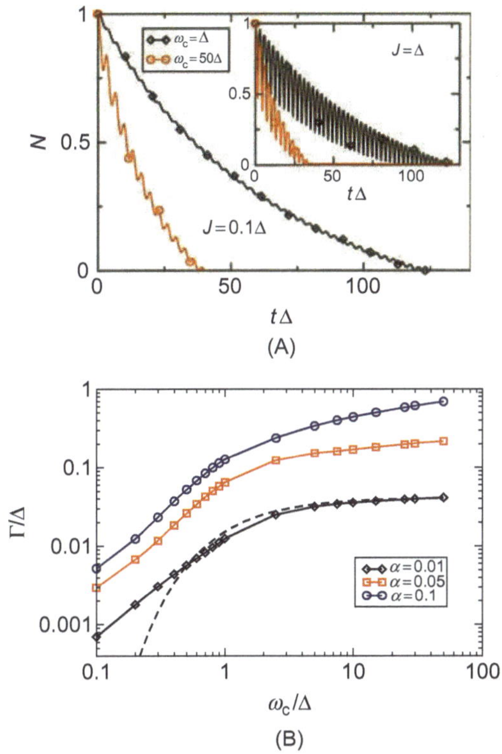

FIGURE 2.3 (A) Time evolution of the negativity $N(t)$ for the cut-off $\omega_c = \Delta$ (black) and $\omega_c = 50\Delta$ (red) for $\alpha = 0.01$ and for $J = 0.1\Delta$ (main) and $J = \Delta$ (inset). Moreover, $k_B T = 0.1\hbar\Delta$. (B) Decay constant Γ as a function of the cut-off ω_c for different values of α (symbols with solid lines) for $k_B T = 0.1\hbar\Delta, J = 0.1\Delta$. Dashed line: Corresponding one-phonon result $\Gamma = \Gamma_0 e^{-\Delta/\omega_c}$, where the proportionality constant $\Gamma_0 = 0.041\Delta$ has been obtained from a fit to the three data points $\omega_c = 25\Delta, 30\Delta, 50\Delta$. Plate 1 (Figure 2.3 on page 53 of this volume)

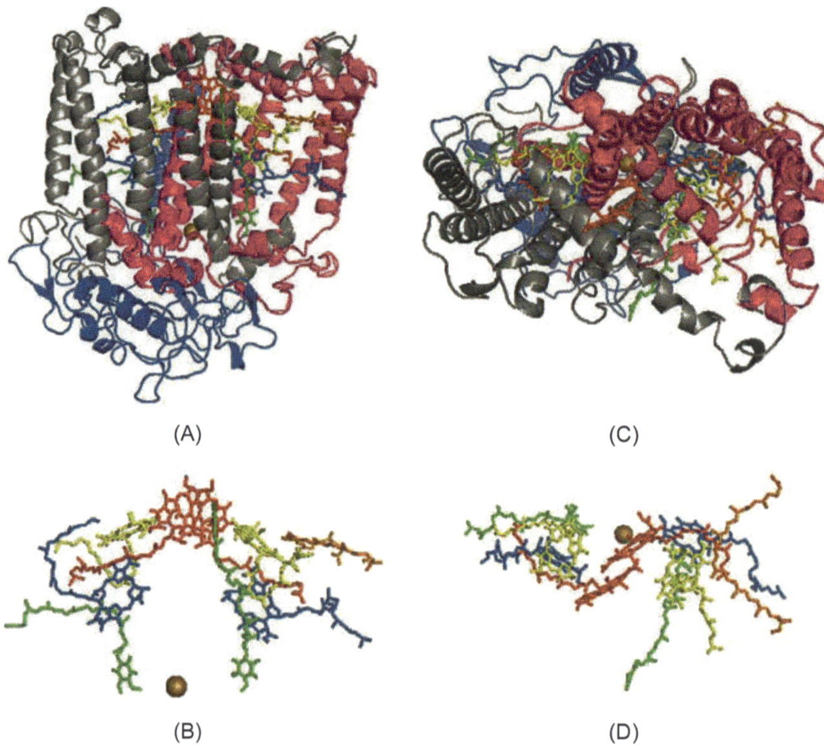

FIGURE 3.1 RC *sphaeroides*; side (A, B) and top (C, D) views with (A, C) and without (B, D) protein backbone. Red: special pair; yellow: accessory bacteriochlorophylls; blue: bacteriopheophytins; green: quinones; and dot: iron. Plate 2 (Figure 3.1 on page 78 of this volume)

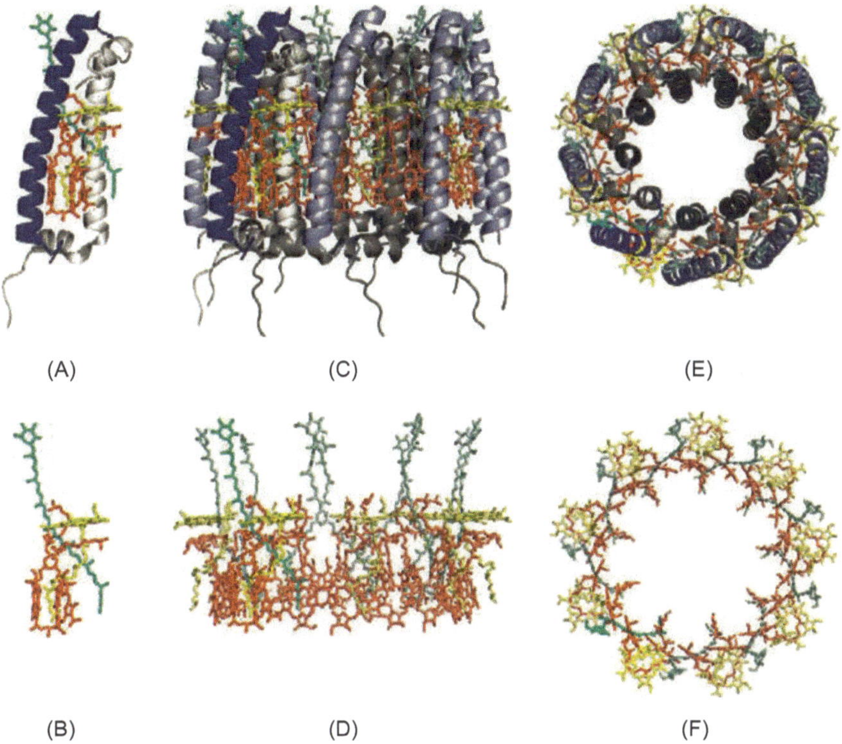

FIGURE 3.3 X-ray structure of LH2 from *Rps. acidophila*. For this species, the LH2 complex consists of nine $\alpha\beta$-subunits and features a diameter of about 6.5 nm. The top row shows the full protein structure, in the lower row the protein backbone is omitted. (A, B) Monomer unit. (C, D) Side view. (E, F) Top view. The colors refer to the α-helixes (gray), β-helixes (blue), B800 (yellow), B850 (red), and carotenoids (cyan). In (C–F) one monomer subunit is highlighted for illustration. Plate 3 (Figure 3.3 on page 81 of this volume)

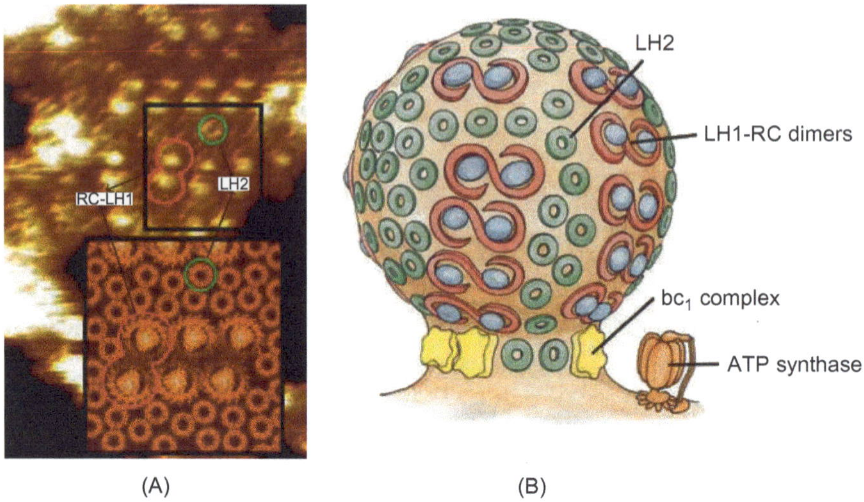

FIGURE 3.6 (A) AFM image of native photosynthetic membranes from *Rb. sphaeroides* together with a model for the mutual arrangement of the LH2 (small open structures, green line) and the RC-LH1 complexes (large filled structures, red line) within the membrane (Figure 1C, Bahatyrova *et al.* Nature 430 (2004) 1058). (B) Schematic drawing of the vesicular photosynthetic chromatophore for *Rb. sphaeroides*. The RC-LH1 complexes and LH2 complexes are packed as observed by AFM. The bc_1 complex and ATP have been tentatively placed by the authors of Chandler *et al.* (2008) near the neck of the chromatophore. Adapted from Chandler *et al.* (2008). Plate 4 (Figure 3.6 on page 84 of this volume)

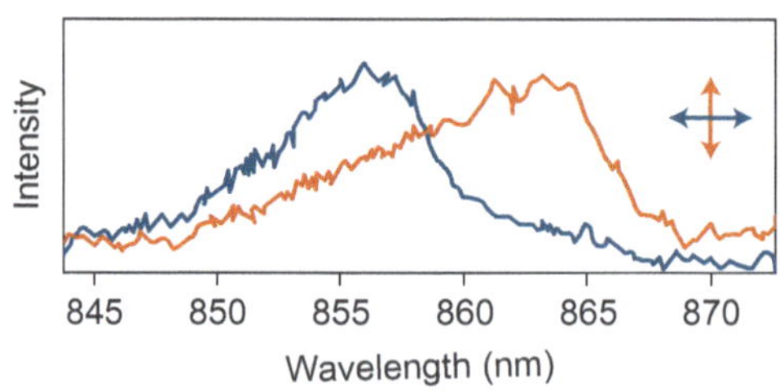

FIGURE 3.9 Fluorescence-excitation spectrum of the long-wavelength part of the B850 band from an individual LH2 complex of *Rps. acidophila* at 1.4 K. The blue and red spectra have been recorded for mutually orthogonal polarization of the excitation light. Adapted from Hofmann *et al.* (2004). Plate 5 (Figure 3.9 on page 90 of this volume)

FSC
www.fsc.org
MIX
Papier | Fördert
gute Waldnutzung
FSC® C083411

Kolibri 360 GmbH
Ferdinand-Jühlke-Straße 7
99095 Erfurt, Deutschland
produktsicherheit@kolibri360.de